GREATER GOOD

GREATER GOOD

How Good Marketing
Makes for Better Democracy

John A. Quelch
Katherine E. Jocz

Harvard Business Press
Boston, Massachusetts

Library of Congress Cataloging-in-Publication Data

Quelch, John A.
  Greater good : how good marketing makes for better democracy / John Quelch, Katherine Jocz.
    p.   cm.
  ISBN-13: 978-1-4221-1735-4
  1. Marketing. 2. Democracy. I. Jocz, Katherine E. II. Title.
  HF5415.Q38 2007
  658.8—dc22

                                                    2007029812

Contents

Preface

The idea for this book stemmed from our reflections on a century of marketing practice and scholarship. Critiques of marketing practices abound in the general literature, but we could find little work that had systematically and explicitly addressed marketing's social value in democratic societies. In parallel with this appraisal, we were also exploring the use (and abuse) of marketing in political campaigns. It was the cross-fertilization between these two areas of inquiry that led us to the insight that the benefits that good marketing provides to consumers mirror the benefits that democracy provides to citizens.

We believe that the framework developed in this book can guide future thinking around what constitutes socially good (and socially bad) marketing and can also illuminate the strengths and weaknesses of modern representative democracies. We hope that the work will be thought provoking not only to those in the marketing profession worldwide but also to political opinion leaders, social commentators, media executives, and, not least, consumers and citizens in general.

This book has been a bridge-building effort, connecting familiar territory with research into new domains in an effort to draw parallels that are fresh and provocative. Our work rests on the foundation of previous intellectual inquiry, and we relished the opportunity to spend time reacquainting ourselves with the writings of our predecessors in the marketing field as well as with such scholars as Daniel Boorstin, Robert Dahl, Peter Drucker, Mark Granovetter, and Joseph Schumpeter, among others.

A number of colleagues and friends kindly agreed to read and comment on the manuscript at various stages of development. We are particularly grateful to Herman Leonard, Alvin Silk, and Richard Tedlow for their sound advice at crucial points. We also thank Jeremy Bullmore, Frank Cespedes, John Deighton, and David Moss for their help.

At Harvard Business School Publishing, our editor Kirsten Sandberg proved a steadfast supporter. We are also grateful to Betsy Hardinger for copyediting the manuscript and Marcy Barnes-Henrie for seeing it through production.

Funding for the research underpinning this work was provided by the Harvard Business School Division of Research. We thank deans Kim Clark and Jay Light for their continuing support of the project.

Marketing and Democracy

ANYONE ATTUNED to the words *democracy*, *democratic*, or *democratization* will find daily mentions in the mainstream media in a broad range of contexts. Predictably, many of the references concern domestic politics, foreign policy, and the state of democratic institutions around the world.[1] Perhaps less expected is the rising number of casual references to democracy appearing in the nonpolitical contexts of popular culture, consumption, and art criticism.[2] Take, for example, *The Gates, Central Park, New York, 1979–2005*, created by artists Christo and Jeanne-Claude. This temporary public installation was praised as a reclamation of the spirit of park designer Frederick Law Olmsted, who envisioned it "as a place of dignity for the masses, a great locus of democratic ideals."[3]

As applied to everyday life and culture, *democracy* often implies a non-elitist appeal to popular tastes, or a mix of choices to suit a diversity of tastes. It often connotes freedom of choice, freedom of speech, access to information, and participation open to everyone. More often than not, democracy is couched in terms of individuals' enjoyment of rights to lead their lives as they choose. It seldom expresses the notion of individual responsibilities or the idea of a greater good.

The word *democracy* comes from the Greek *demos*, or "people," and *kratein*, "to rule," and means "rule by the people." The term *democratic* is thus an apt descriptor of the consumer marketplace in the United States and other developed countries. Empowered consumers have great latitude in what they can buy and when and where they can buy it. Marketers cater to their desires, court them with offers of new and improved products, customized options, price-off sales, easy credit, and promises of enhanced personal efficacy and happiness. Typical Westerners may be forgiven for feeling that they have more power as consumers than as citizens to improve the quality of their lives.

For at least the past fifty years, the marketing field has advocated that companies should embrace the marketing concept of putting customers' interests first. It is a philosophy now expressed in many corporate mission statements. For instance, Johnson & Johnson's credo, formulated in 1943, outlines the company's responsibilities—in descending order of priority—to customers, employees, the community, and shareholders: "We believe our first responsibility is to the doctors, nurses and patients, to mothers and fathers and all others who use our products and services."[4] This credo guided the company's actions during the Tylenol tampering crisis of 1982, when CEO James E. Burke quickly withdrew all Tylenol capsules from stores at a cost of $100 million. By assuming a moral obligation to protect consumers, recalling the product, and then later relaunching it in tamperproof bottles, the company restored consumer confidence—and thereby its market share.[5]

But if Johnson & Johnson represents the gold standard, what about the rest of the field? Clearly some marketers fail to put consumers' interests ahead of other considerations; the defensive, stonewalling actions of tobacco companies are a glaring example.

A book about marketing usually takes one of two routes. Either it tells managers how to use better marketing techniques to boost sales and profits, or it tells consumers what is wrong with the marketing system and how marketers are exploiting them. This book sets a different course. We explore the fundamental characteristics of the marketing system and its role in society. The thesis is twofold: first, marketing performs an essential societal function and does so democratically; and second, people would benefit if the political and public realms were guided by the best of marketing, and vice versa.

We aim to speak to citizen consumers about what the public, individually and collectively, receives from and contributes to both the marketing system and the political system. Our portrayal of marketing is nuanced; it acknowledges a dark side along with the positive contributions. However, the message to citizen consumers is that they have influence over marketers and politicians and can use this power to press for greater benefits for individuals and society.

Roles of Marketing

If one were to ask a few people picked at random what they think marketing is, chances are the answers would include "selling products" or "advertising" or "persuading people to buy things." But consult instead the trade organization for marketing professionals and the answer is, "the process of planning and executing the conception, pricing, promotion, and distribution of ideas, goods, and services to create exchanges that satisfy individual and organizational objectives."[6] The two definitions hardly sound like the same thing.

In truth, marketing encompasses a wide range of business activities, of which consumers see only a fraction. Like any complex phenomenon, marketing can be looked at on a number of levels. Here we consider three overlapping perspectives: marketing as an economic function, marketing as a business practice, and marketing as a societal force.

Marketing as an Economic Function

To look at marketing as an economic function is to focus on the role marketing plays in the general economy and specifically on the distribution and sale of goods—that is, getting goods and services from producers to consumers, and market exchanges between buyers and sellers. In other words, marketing is the interface between supply and demand. Participants include brokers and distributors, wholesalers, retailers, the marketing departments of manufacturing companies, advertising agencies, and online intermediaries like eBay, among others. At least 17 million people in the United States are employed in the marketing sector, with nearly 14 million of them in sales.[7]

Marketing, in this sense, dates back to ancient traders, merchants, and shopkeepers, markets and bazaars, and the truly global networks of trading, markets, and merchants established by the fifteenth century.[8] Participants in these marketing systems transported goods and stored them safe from theft or damage. In doing so, they assumed substantial risks and also the risk that they might misjudge market demand for their wares.

Historically, distribution capabilities were an important accelerator of economic growth, especially following the Industrial Revolution. In the words of Converse and Huegy, marketing "makes goods and services more valuable by getting them where they are wanted, when they are wanted, and transferred to the people who want them."[9] Consider the United States, with its large and scattered population. During the late nineteenth century, retailers such as Montgomery Ward and Sears, Roebuck & Co. leveraged the new railroad service to rural communities and free delivery of mail to farms, developing a huge national retail business in general merchandise sold through mail-order catalogs. Consumers anywhere could order nearly anything—even houses—by mail.

More recently, Dell introduced efficient distribution practices—selling computers via direct mail, then via telephone sales, then via the Internet—and the practice of assembling computers to order, to lower prices of home computers and give consumers new flexibility in choosing options. Wal-Mart's skill in driving down procurement and warehousing costs via large-scale buying allows the company to offer consumers a wide assortment of goods at "everyday low prices."

Note that this economic function perspective does not restrict marketing to a particular type of economy. For example, one author concluded that the marketing structure of the Soviet Union in the centrally planned economy of the 1950s was similar to that of the United States. Goods moved through the same distribution channels. The difference was that the Soviet government owned every stage of the channel along the way to the consumer.[10]

Marketing as a Business Practice

To approach marketing from the business practice perspective is to focus on how a firm manages demand and shapes consumer behavior to achieve its objectives. This is closer to the typical consumer view of marketing as an effort to persuade consumers to buy products. Put simply, for a business, marketing is mainly about how to put the right product in front of the right customer at the right time and place at the right price in order to reap profits.

Marketing's prominence as a business practice is closely tied to the emergence of modern corporations and the opening of mass markets. Although the groundwork was being laid, until the late nineteenth century there were few major changes in the way industry was organized. The vertically or horizontally integrated firm of later years was virtually unknown. Advertising and branding had grown in importance, but manufacturers as well as distributors were specialized and small; they exerted little control over other channel members or over consumers. In the United States, with its vast territory, there were few national marketers. Tedlow calls this phase of marketing in the United States the "era of market fragmentation" and characterizes the dominant business strategy as making profits by charging high prices on relatively low sales volumes.[11]

In the 1880s, though, the distinctive U.S. environment—distinctive in laissez-faire policies, rate of growth, and sheer size—gave rise both to the large, vertically integrated corporation and to the mass consumer market. This was a time when corporations achieved significant efficiencies through economies of scale in supply, production, and distribution, and also through vertical integration and national selling, advertising, and branding. In contrast to the high-price, low-volume strategy of businesses operating in fragmented markets, the strategy of aggressive businesses operating in mass markets was to charge low prices but make high profits through high sales volume of a standard product.[12] A testimony to the power of this approach is the host of company and brand names originating in the 1880s that are still well known, including Johnson & Johnson, Kodak, H.J. Heinz, Ivory soap, and Coca-Cola.

As the mass market grew, consumer choice increased, and increased choice stimulated consumption. High levels of consumption generated profits that marketers plowed back into R&D to sustain a flow of superior new products. Manufacturers aiming at a mass market had at least two pressing needs. First, if marketers wanted to persuade masses of consumers to buy their product and not a closely competing product carried by the same or a nearby store, they needed to give consumers convincing evidence of product superiority.

Second, to accelerate adoption of new and unfamiliar products on a large scale, they could not afford to rely on slow, informal word of mouth to communicate product benefits. Rather, they needed to educate consumers and retailers directly. The answer to these needs was to employ mass advertising and personal communications by salespeople on a much greater scale than ever before.

Mass marketers also faced the problem of sustaining a large volume of sales over time. For businesses that depended on the efficiencies of mass production, creating a profitable and stable—or, better yet, growing—customer base was a key marketing objective. Finding new customers at home or abroad would help but would not be sufficient. Marketers had to learn more about how to keep existing customers satisfied and motivated to repeat their purchases, how to supply the products and services they wanted, and how to price for value. Although meeting distribution requirements (i.e., having products in stock) was still a prerequisite to making a sale, paying greater attention to the drivers of consumer demand separated the more successful from the less successful marketer. Information for consumers and insight about them, based on market research, became the defining characteristics of modern marketing.

A further shift in marketing occurred in the latter part of the twentieth century, when mass markets increasingly splintered into segmented markets. Marketers sought to optimize profits by serving different niches of consumers with different value propositions. Given the extent of available choices, marketers today usually do not expect all consumers to buy their products. They select and target only those who are most likely to need and want particular benefits, and they produce differentiated products and services for those segments. Southwest Airlines, for example, targets a segment of cost-conscious customers, so it strips out those features that are not important to its customers and that would increase costs beyond what they are willing to pay.

The consumer marketplace is dynamic. As consumers gain product experience and talk to each other, their purchase behavior and expectations change. Competitors always try to offer superior benefits. This means that whatever meets a consumer's expectations today may not meet them next time. So marketing can't stand still.

At the least, marketers constantly must reinforce—and live up to—the promises they make regarding their products' functional and emotional benefits. To live up to the claim of being the "ultimate driving machine," BMW must engineer automobiles at the leading edge of high performance and must create an aura around the brand comparable to that of belonging to an exciting and exclusive club.

If marketers can change the basis of competition and delight consumers (i.e., exceed their expectations), they can do well. Starbucks transformed a place to get a cup of coffee into an experience defined by aroma, music, special flavors, ambience, and comfortable seating. For this, consumers were willing to pay a price premium. Moreover, Starbucks needed very little advertising to attract new customers; satisfied customers spread the word, and the stores, located in high-traffic sites, served as brand billboards.

Given that marketing is a business practice instrumental in driving corporate growth, its proponents began, in the 1950s, to claim a much greater role for marketing in the management of firms. Following Peter Drucker's lead, the *marketing concept* asserted that, above all, firms must create value for customers and must see the business from the customer's point of view.[13] This customer orientation vied with alternatives such as a manufacturing orientation, an R&D orientation, a sales orientation, and a finance orientation.

Proponents tended to view the acceptance and implementation of the marketing concept as the final and highest stage in a firm's evolution.[14] Although the concept was seldom fully adopted, it received a great deal of attention; at the least, the marketing concept elevated the topic of customers' interests within management thinking. Among firm managers, marketing experts remain the strongest advocates for consumer interests. To use an analogy from democratic politics, within a corporation one important role of marketers is to advocate for consumers in the same way politicians are supposed to advocate for the citizens they represent.[15]

From the business practice perspective, customers are the means to an end. But beyond that lies the supposition of two equally important and inextricably linked objectives for marketing—on the one hand, consumer satisfaction and, on the other hand, profit (or other organizational objectives). To maximize long-term profits, marketers must be guided by the best interests of consumers.[16] (Of course, not everyone is convinced that consumers' interests neatly coincide with those of businesses.)

Marketing as a Social Force

To adopt the societal force perspective is to examine these and other cumulative impacts of marketing on society. Breyer wrote in 1934 that "marketing is not primarily a means for garnering profits for individuals. It is, in the larger, more vital sense, an economic instrument used to accomplish indispensable social ends."[17]

What is the indispensable social end served by marketing? The consensus is that it is society's consumption needs. Marketing leads to a better standard of living, an efficient flow of goods to consumers, perhaps a socially beneficial distribution of goods—or even transmission of culture. The societal perspective of marketing thus emphasizes consumer welfare. Marketing is the beneficial process of exchange that allows consumers to satisfy their needs and promote their greater well-being.

Beyond this function, marketing has been credited with contributing to improved standards of living and national economic development. Proponents argue that it has provided consumers with more choices, created economic efficiencies, and spurred the spread of radical innovations. Trade along the ancient Silk Route connecting the Far East and the West enabled a European to buy silk fabric from China, which held the secret to its production; eventually the technology spread to the West; now a European can purchase Chinese-made clothing at a fraction of the price a domestic manufacturer would charge.

From the societal perspective, business profits are secondary. There is no suggestion that firms should not earn profits, but profits are a means to the end. This perspective also holds that businesses operate in a society that is entitled to constrain their actions, most often through laws and government policies. Governments can regulate product standards, decide which products can be exported or imported or sold to consumers, prevent companies from colluding on prices, establish rules for competition, and so on.

Like the economic perspective of marketing, the societal perspective can be applied to a broad range of societies. Consider the Moscow consumer of the 1960s who bought a costly Georgian orange from a state-owned store, supplied by state-owned distributors, and grown in a state-owned citrus grove as directed by a central government plan. This flow of goods can be analyzed in terms of, and possibly benefit from, work on such concepts and principles as distribution efficiency, exchange, and socially beneficial consumption.

Contemporary Marketing

For the remainder of this book, we employ these varied perspectives in examining marketing as it exists in the twenty-first century in advanced industrialized countries with market economies. Crucially, in this context consumers have considerable power: the worldwide overcapacity of production in many industries and the free flow of goods enabled by trade agreements and low shipping costs favors consumers compared with producers. Thus, when marketing, as a business practice, seeks to create value for businesses, it does so by competing to create superior value for consumers. This sought-after advantage invariably stems from gaining insights into explicit and latent customer needs; from launching products and services that leverage these insights; from branding, communicating, and distributing these products to customers; or from managing customer relationships.

As an economic function, the total marketing system is a mechanism for delivering supply that matches consumers' demands, needs, and wants. It is safe to say that the vast majority of business marketing does not aim at creating value for society. Marketing's positive impact on society is the cumulative impact of multiple marketing programs, which, through being well thought out and well executed, create value for consumers.

So far, the point has been made that marketing covers a wide range of economically and socially important activities. However, it certainly does not include all economic activities or business functions—for instance, manufacturing or finance or R&D—although it often intersects with them. And even though the word *marketing* derives from *market*, not all markets fall under the domain of marketing. Transactions within, for example, two economically important markets—labor markets and capital markets—typically are not considered to be part of the marketing system though they share many of the same elements. The primary domain of marketing is markets for products and services—those bought by businesses and those bought by individuals or households. The consumer marketplace, rather than the business-to-business marketplace, is the principal focus of this book.

Recently the domain of marketing has broadened to include the marketing of ideas or the marketing of celebrities, politicians, and nations using concepts and techniques borrowed from the marketing of goods and services. Application of marketing to the not-for-profit and public sectors is also growing.

Problems with Marketing

Throughout history, recurring criticisms have been leveled at marketing.[18] Accusations of dishonest trade practices, unfair profiteering by middlemen, incitement of consumer desires for unnecessary goods, displacement of locally produced goods by imported versions made by cheaper labor, and the unwelcome spread of foreign values and culture—all these go back to ancient times. For example, the charge that retail trade is not productive, or that intermediaries do not deserve to profit from exchange, was leveled by Aristotle.[19] A century ago, people worried about information overload, overexploitation of natural resources, and the rise of materialism.

There are some marketers who deliberately deceive and cheat consumers particularly if they have information about their products that consumers cannot access. In some cases marketers knowingly sell harmful products or ignore or conceal evidence indicating that products previously thought to be beneficial turn out to have detrimental effects. After information about the danger of tobacco made the U.S. market less attractive, manufacturers hastened to market cigarettes to developing countries. Marketers of subprime mortgages promised home ownership to people who could not qualify for conventional loans, but overaggressive lending practices resulted in many borrowers defaulting on their loans and losing their houses.

However, it is now generally accepted that most intermediaries perform useful facilitation functions, and the overwhelming majority of marketing transactions are fair. Marketers value their good reputation and profit from repeat business; it is not in their long-term interest to treat consumers badly. Informed consumers, ethical competitors, and the media rein in some misbehaviors. Laws and government regulations prevent and correct others. Realistically there will always be bad actors trying to compete unfairly and trying to take advantage of consumers. For this there is no excuse, but neither is it a problem peculiar to marketing.

Many current complaints about marketing concern "too much" marketing and marketers that are "too big." Large chain stores and national brands seem to dominate the marketplace. In industrialized nations, the retail landscape in one town or city appears nearly identical to its counterparts across the country or across national borders. Views differ as to whether this consolidation is a natural outcome of healthy competition or a result of predatory behavior. Views also differ as to whether consumers benefit (e.g., in having access to the same goods as everyone else) or lose (e.g., when fast-food outlets displace local alternatives).

Concerns that marketing can alter society have a basis in reality. Undoubtedly, marketing directed at satisfying personal needs, wants, and preferences reinforces a trend toward greater materialism and individualism. The more efficient and effective marketing becomes, the more incentive there is for businesses to allocate more resources to it, as well as for people—at least those with disposable income—to consume things they may not strictly need. Marketers and consumers tend to look at the small picture—a consumer's personal consumption or a marketer's advertising campaign. They tend to overlook the cumulative effects of all the advertising and all the individual consumption decisions on a country's culture and resources.

To all this, one reply is that consumers and marketers share responsibility. In most cases, consumers willingly buy from marketers because they perceive that they are getting something of value. If competing businesses fail to understand consumers' needs and to provide equivalent value, then consumers will not patronize them. To be sure, as a recipe for decreasing any unwanted impact of marketing, that is an oversimplification, because individuals are unlikely to have the capacity or information needed to make exhaustive comparisons among marketers or comprehensive assessments of the long-term effects of purchase decisions. Small businesses may not have access to marketing skills that would allow them to attract and satisfy customers more effectively. When products deemed to be more socially responsible, such as organic produce, cost more, not all consumers can afford the higher prices.

But consumers, particularly when they act together, have the power to alter the marketplace. In the United Kingdom, for example, substantial public debate has convinced many consumers to shift purchases to fair trade and locally produced food items; the largest supermarket chains are starting to post the carbon ratings of foods.[20]

Marketing offers a set of skills, frameworks, and approaches that can be misapplied if the marketplace is not vigilant. Yet it is hard to imagine that consumers in countries with poor marketing distribution systems and limited choices would not embrace the access to goods and services that a stronger, more efficient marketing system can provide. The issue, then, is how to harness marketing to minimize abuses and maximize benefits by means of countervailing institutions that safeguard consumers' and society's interests.

The Principles of Democracy

To recap some key features of democracy—and to lay the groundwork for highlighting commonalities between democracy and marketing—note that, although the scope and meaning of the term *democracy* have changed over time, the core idea of rule by the people persists.[21] Strictly speaking, the United States and other modern democracies are republics, governed by elected representatives rather than direct democratic rule by the people, but citizens remain the ultimate authority and the government is *for* them.

The vast literature on democracy offers many perspectives on how to define and measure it. However, one basic criterion for judging a government to be a democracy is that it operates by the consent of the governed, given in free and fair competitive elections. Prominent political theorist Robert Dahl says that in an ideal democracy five conditions must be met: effective participation by citizens, equality in opportunity to vote and votes that count equally, enlightened understanding on the part of citizens, the opportunity for citizens to control and choose items placed on the agenda, and inclusion of all adults.[22]

To fulfill these ideal conditions, six political institutions are required in modern representative democracies: decisions are made by representatives elected by citizens; elections are free, fair, and frequent; citizens are free to express themselves on political issues; citizens have access to diverse and independent sources of information; citizens are free to form political parties and other groups; and all adult permanent residents have the right to vote and run for office.[23]

Theories of the social contract—tracing back to Aristotle, Thomas Hobbes, John Locke, and Jean-Jacques Rousseau—offer another criterion for modern representative democracies. According to social contract theory, people create, or consent to, governments to achieve common ends and to provide for collective needs. In modern democracies, representatives are empowered to coordinate and resolve conflicts among individuals and groups, including, according to a number of theorists, balancing production and consumption activities.[24]

In addition to referring to both ideal and actual forms of government, democracy has come to mean a set of values and principles.[25] Prominent among these are the values stated in the motto of the French Republic: "Liberty, equality, fraternity." These values are often expressed as basic rights and freedoms, including freedom of expression, freedom of association, freedom of religion, the right to equal protection under the law, the right to take part in government, and the right to choose employment.

To liberty, equality, and fraternity, many thinkers add a fourth value: human development. This might be expressed as an obligation of democracies to ensure adequate standards of living and health, provide education, preserve public spaces, and more.[26] Put another way, democracy also means that individuals have the right to engage in the "pursuit of happiness," in the words of the U.S. Declaration of Independence.

Thus, in addition to political rights, modern democratic states guarantee citizens basic human rights, civil liberties, and equal rights and due process before the law.[27] Majority rule is tempered by minority rights. Also, modern democracies, to varying degrees, seek to ensure sufficient levels of economic and social well-being for all their citizens.

Democracy and the Market Economy

From a pragmatic perspective, market economies or mixed-market economies (where public ownership or central planning exist alongside a market economy) are good for democracies. Dahl notes that modern representative democracies exist only in countries that have market or mixed-market economies and that basic features of this type of economy make it favorable for democracy.

In contrast, democracies have never endured in centrally planned economies. Dunn casts the story of modern democracies as the triumph of the "order of egoism," which emphasizes individualism and the market economy, over the "order of egalitarianism," which emphasizes the collective good and the removal of social and economic distinctions. At the same time, market economies have undemocratic aspects: they result in economic inequalities and concentrate power in the hands of a few, something that fosters political inequalities.[28]

Political theorists are well aware that considerable tensions exist among and within the core democratic values of liberty, equality, fraternity, and human development. One person's rights constrain another person's freedoms. An individual's liberty to pursue his or her self-interest can conflict with the interests of larger social units. For instance, John Rawls's political theory grapples with the principles underpinning a just society, including the distribution of social and economic goods and the ways it affects the least-advantaged members of society, as well as the establishment of rights of each person to basic liberties compatible with similar rights for others.[29]

In the real world, people are unequally endowed in the circumstances of their birth and the natural abilities they possess. Should democracies provide equality of opportunity, or equality of condition? Achieving equality of condition would override individual liberty. The most extreme egalitarianism exists in "democracies" (in name only) such as North Korea or China during the Cultural Revolution.[30] But defining equality solely as equality of opportunity permits great inequalities in individual welfare.[31]

Democracies that embrace economic and political liberalism, as in the United States, give primacy to liberty and, in terms of equality, favor equality of opportunity over equality of condition. Though conceding that there is a role for government in regulating markets and in supplying some public goods, such systems presume that the market is the most efficient mechanism for achieving material welfare.

Social democracies, as in Scandinavia, place relatively more emphasis on fraternity and equality, including equality of condition. In addition to a market economy, these states employ a system of public ownership and central planning of resource usage for the purpose of maximizing public welfare.[32] A recent ranking of the degree to which countries are democratic placed Sweden, the other Nordic countries, and the Netherlands at the top of the list; the United States and the United Kingdom were seventeenth and twenty-third, respectively.[33]

At the beginning of the twenty-first century, all but a few nation-states in all regions of the world profess to have a democratic form of government. Even so, democracy is not very well entrenched. During the second half of the twentieth century, the number of nations adopting a democratic form of government accelerated, but new democracies proved to be fragile. By the end of the century, about half of the world's population lived in countries considered to be somewhat democratic, but only about one-tenth lived in countries considered to be fully democratic.[34]

There is little dispute that even the most securely democratic countries fall short of some of the conditions required of an ideal democracy. In the United States, for example, it's often noted that political participation is on the wane. Moreover, not all votes have equal weight and not all votes are counted equally. It is argued that the public is ill informed, in part because political information is more about personalities and missteps than about facts and issues. Voters have little real choice or control over their representatives or over policy. Although universal suffrage is nominally the rule, some segments of adults are still excluded or face high hurdles.

In an influential work, Joseph Schumpeter argued that the classical view of democracy, which he characterizes as institutional arrangements for achieving the common good by having the people elect representatives who will reflect and carry out the popular will, is unrealistic.[35] For one thing, it is highly unlikely that different groups and different people within society will agree on the common good. In fact, they may profoundly disagree.[36]

Furthermore, an ordinary citizen's distance from many national issues and a lack of specific volitions contribute to ignorance and poor judgment in matters of domestic and foreign policy. This situation allows politicians to manipulate voters and set the agenda.

Instead, to Schumpeter (who was primarily an economist), democracy is a political marketplace for selecting leaders. It is a competition among political parties and politicians to garner the votes of citizens—political consumers—and to govern for a specified period until the next election (or transaction).[37] The role of voters is to produce a government, and not to decide political issues. Whether or not we agree with his conclusions, Schumpeter's critique of the classical view and substitution of the narrower, marketplace view of democracy offers a provocative framework for analyzing the current state of politics.

Marketing as Democracy and Marketing for Democracy

In industrialized democracies, the consumer marketplace and the political marketplace have something important in common: in both cases the consumer is the ultimate authority. Moreover, the consumer marketplace evolved within the context of democratic societies. Thus, in the consumer marketplace we see close parallels to the conditions that define democracy.

The consumer marketplace offers consumers benefits that are equivalent to those of a democracy: free and fair transactions (which we call *exchange*), control and choice over offerings (*choice*), active participation in shaping the marketplace (*engagement*), informed understanding (*information*), nearly universal inclusion (*inclusion*), and the ability to satisfy basic needs and other wants and preferences (*consumption*). These six benefits combine to make marketing—as it should be practiced—highly democratic.

Marketing's six benefits

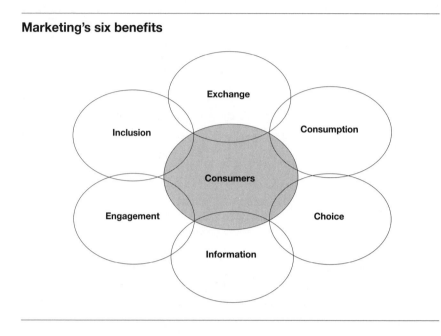

And like democracy, marketing can be evaluated in terms of its adherence to the same four higher principles of liberty, equality, fraternity, and human development.

The remainder of this book is divided into two parts: part one, "Marketing as Democracy," and part two, "Marketing for Democracy." The chapters in part one, which are organized around the six core benefits of marketing, contend that marketing is democratic and that the commercial practice of marketing develops and reinforces capabilities among consumers that they can put to good use as citizens in the political marketplace.

Exchange

In modern societies, consumers obtain virtually all their goods and most services through voluntary transactions. A buyer and a seller enter into an exchange because it creates value for both. Both parties hope to be better off, and both value the freedom of consent.

This is analogous to the value individuals prize in political democracies, where voluntary consent provides the basis for legitimate governments. In marketing exchanges, consumers obtain products and services, as well as functional and emotional benefits, in return for both monetary and non-monetary compensation.

What consumers give up and what they acquire extend beyond narrow economic considerations. For instance, consumers spend time viewing ads (which may be enjoyable) in return for free or subsidized entertainment. They acquire goods to gain the symbolic value of the brand as well as the functional benefits delivered by the product. A wider view of marketing exchange considers it as part of a complex system of exchange among the public, government, businesses, and other social institutions. From this perspective, marketers have an implied obligation to provide value to consumers and to society.

Compared with the consumer marketplace, exchanges between citizens and the government are more prescribed and less individualized. In nearly all democracies, these exchanges are grounded in a constitutional framework that guarantees all citizens a comprehensive set of rights. But in the Schumpeterian political marketplace, exchanges between a citizen and instruments of the government occur infrequently, at specified times, in a prescribed manner, and involve citizens selecting a representative to act on their behalf rather than obtaining a direct benefit. With public services, exchanges between citizens and providers typically aim to provide goods and services uniformly to achieve some greater public good as opposed to maximizing individual satisfaction.

Consumption

Democracies aim to satisfy the fundamental needs for life and to foster human development. For most of history, most societies have struggled with underconsumption of goods and services needed to sustain healthy, productive populations. Democracies view consumption as a public good. They promote citizens' consumption of adequate levels of beneficial goods and services through a variety of means, including central planning, state ownership, public–private partnerships, public services, and the consumer marketplace.

Marketing has democratized consumption and raised standards of living. In a number of societies, the privileged classes have or had exclusive access to certain goods, but now there is a presumption that consumption is democratic: all have an equal-opportunity right to consume (even if they lack the same means to exercise that right).

Marketers compete vigorously to sell more things to more people. They have incentives to introduce new products and to make products initially affordable only to the elite available to a broader segment of the population in the way that the Ford Model T brought access to the automobile to the broader public. Consumption has been a strong driver of economic growth as well as a contributor to individual well-being.

However, individual consumption above a modest level is not necessarily correlated with happiness. In societies wholly dedicated to consumption, there is a need to examine possibly detrimental effects of overconsumption on individuals, household debt levels, the social fabric, natural resources, and the environment. At the same time, underconsumption of necessary goods and services continues to be a problem in many developing nations and in impoverished segments of developed societies.

Choice

Democracies allow people to make choices. When people have marketplace choices, what they buy and consume expresses whom they are and whom they want to be. Choice allows people to satisfy a full range of physical and psychological needs.

The proliferation of products, retail channels, and media adds up to a huge increase in the number of consumption alternatives. Marketers are providing increased choices and customization to satisfy individual needs across a diverse consumer population. At the same time, having too many choices can burden and confuse consumers, so marketing provides mechanisms to help consumers manage choice. Choice liberates consumers, but they may grow more dependent on expert agents to help make decisions.

In the political marketplace, choice is comparatively limited. Democracies allow individuals to make choices through elections. However, the number of options, particularly in nations or states dominated by two or three political parties, is relatively small. And outcomes of elections are determined collectively and apply to everyone regardless of individual preferences.

Information

To align outcomes with people's needs, markets, like democracies, require informed consumers and informed citizens. Freedom of information in democracies allows citizens to make intelligent choices and hold government accountable. Open, accurate, and timely information from marketers allows consumers to make intelligent choices. Information about consumers enables marketers to target them with appropriate offers. Information also keeps the market in check; expert opinion and word-of-mouth comments that spread from consumer to consumer often trump corporate advertising.

Both the consumer marketplace and the political marketplace depend on the art of persuasion.[38] Marketers and politicians communicate by using a mix of information and persuasion; they use advertisements that appeal to the emotions as well as to the intellect. From the beginnings of mass advertising, a long-standing debate has posed the question of whether consumers can hold their own against advertising or whether marketers succeed in manipulating consumers against their will. (Interestingly, many more consumers believe that advertising can deceive than acknowledge having been deceived.)[39]

With information comes power. Democracies attempt to mitigate the potential power of the government over individuals by guaranteeing the right to privacy. Now that technology affords marketers access to vast amounts of personal information about consumers, recent debates pit the privacy concerns of consumers against the benefits that marketers can provide by using consumers' personal information.

Engagement

Consumers are engaged and involved with marketing and the consumer marketplace. They relish expressing their identity, being part of a community, and exercising their creativity—not through every purchase decision they make but through those in which they have chosen to be more involved. In contrast, in many political democracies, it appears that citizens are becoming less engaged. Yet grassroots participation still plays a large role in the political marketplace.

Marketers are arriving at a threefold realization: letting consumers participate is a way to better understand their wishes; some consumers want deeper relationships with marketers and brands and are willing to pay for customized service; turning over marketing tasks and functions to consumers can simultaneously reduce costs and increase consumers' sense of empowerment. Just as political democracies are more robust and more representative of the public when there exists strong social capital, or willingness of citizens to engage in public affairs, marketers increasingly take the view that consumer engagement will bolster, and not weaken, marketing.

Interactive communication technologies allow marketers to invite direct participation from consumers as part of determining market demand and efficiently managing the supply chain. Many consumers display a willingness, even an eagerness, to promote their favorite brands. Consumers participate in designing and producing customized products for their own use (for which marketers may charge a higher price). Alone or as part of a network, some consumers take the lead in designing products. In the digital world, consumers are creating content and forming communities around consumption. On the other hand, even though self-service participation may reward consumers with lower prices and liberation from long lines, it may also shift more of the work and time costs to consumers, as occurred with the invention of the supermarket.

Inclusion

Democracies have grown progressively more inclusive with respect to equal rights and liberties for all their citizens as well as more accepting of diversity. In the modern era, inclusion embraces the idea that every person has the right to live in a democracy and every adult has the right to be a part of the political process. However, political marketplaces often are elitist; the rich and well connected control the political parties and the public agenda.

Consumer marketplaces are naturally inclusive, because they benefit from expanding the number of consumers and linking producers and consumers worldwide. Democratic nations, like other countries, are exclusive rather than inclusive with regard to guarding national borders and national identity, but marketing's horizon is global. Consumer marketplaces are not elitist; they serve the vast majority of the population, and the rich pay a price premium if they want unique, specialized, or luxury items.

But the right to self-determination tempers the right to inclusion. Marketing needs to respect and adapt to economic and cultural contexts. Global marketing and branding, and the shared consumer experience they have created, have in some ways brought the world closer together. But to deploy Western-style advertisements without adaptation can be offensive in some cultures. Marketers selling goods to desperately poor populations at the bottom of the economic pyramid walk a tightrope between exploiting consumers and liberating them. Marketing in the developing world calls for creativity and flexibility, as well as a reexamination of Western assumptions about the functions and methods of marketing.

Part two, "Marketing for Democracy," turns to the interrelationships between marketing and democratic societies. It covers arenas in which marketing and democracy intersect or where marketing can help democracies better serve citizens and the public interest. Our aim is to provide an overview and sampling of such topics, each of which deserves a book of its own, as well as to spark further discussion and debate.

Politics

Injecting marketing into a democratic political process is problematic. Especially in the United States, political parties have seized on sophisticated marketing techniques to promote candidates and sway public opinion. The trouble is that politics becomes less democratic when well-funded candidates, political parties, and interest groups can overwhelm opponents with costly advertising and marketing. Just as marketers are likely to be more responsive to a large, long-standing customer rather than a small, occasional customer, so are elected politicians likely to favor the views of large campaign contributors or vocal special-interest groups.

In the consumer marketplace, one can accept that not all customers have equal weight. In the political marketplace, it is less easy to accept that not all voters are created equal. Citizen participation in a number of established democracies is on the wane. In some cases, barriers systemic to particular types of political systems or regimes inhibit citizens from exercising political power. In other cases, there are procedural barriers. We propose a number of marketing-based recommendations, many of which echo solutions proposed by political scientists, to make democratic regimes more democratic.

Media

The interrelationship between marketing and the media is a complex one. On the one hand, by subsidizing the media through advertising, marketers contribute to a diverse and independent media landscape. This media diversity allows both marketers and journalists to reach either mass audiences or specialized niche audiences through many channels.

On the other hand, media owners may slant their content so as not to offend advertising sponsors. To remain viable, media businesses must also attract consumers. Thinking like marketers, that is, tailoring their offerings to what most consumers prefer, they may therefore cut back their news operations.

Marketers have helped make the new interactive media widely available, and ordinary citizens are starting to use these media to engage in political discourse and air alternative views. However, such activities are not a substitute for professional journalism. Democracy requires a free, independent, and diverse array of news media, which need to be safeguarded from undue marketplace and political forces.

Programs

Governments, not-for-profit organizations, and nongovernmental organizations all operate programs that deliver products and services to the public. Creative and appropriate application of marketing tools and techniques can improve the quality of these programs, producing better outcomes for citizens.

For example, marketing can publicize government-administered services to target citizens and promote adoption of new attitudes and behaviors, as in campaigns to improve diets or seat-belt use. Measuring program results using relevant marketing metrics can increase accountability and guide the design of improved programs. However, in the United States, public distrust of government and politicians is expressed in limits placed on government agencies' ability to market specific programs to citizens, as well as in measures guarding individuals' privacy. And a government's use of persuasive communication techniques can slip into propaganda. There is an important distinction between governments using marketing to improve the quality and availability of services and governments using marketing to promote a partisan political agenda.

Nations

Countries use marketing to promote their national interests. For example, in "public diplomacy" initiatives, nations promote foreign policy objectives; in combat operations, the armed forces use propaganda to achieve military objectives. Democracies need to ensure that they walk the talk—that such claims are consistent with their own adherence to democratic values. If efforts like the U.S. government's public diplomacy campaign to promote democracy in the Middle East do a poor job of marketing, they can not only backfire with their intended audience but also create negative spillover to other audiences.

Nations are turning to marketing to improve economic development. For example, to attract foreign investment they use marketing to create a favorable image and differentiate themselves from competing nations. To the extent that this type of marketing spurs nations to back up a desired national image with genuine democratic reforms, marketing aids democracy.

One of the great questions in political economics is whether economic development promotes democratic governments or vice versa. The same question can be asked about marketing and democracy. Clearly, marketing cannot deliver its full range of benefits to consumers in the absence of democratic institutions, or in places that do not enforce personal security or property rights. But the introduction of an effective marketing system, one based on democratic principles, can help create a stronger civil society and, in effect, lay the groundwork among citizens for political democracy in nations where it does not yet exist.

Underlying the discussions in these chapters is the conviction that marketing is not a superficial irrelevance but is of fundamental importance to society. In particular, good marketing reinforces democracy. By assessing marketing's accomplishments, its shortcomings, and its achievements, we aim to shed light on ways marketing can continue to enrich individuals' lives as well as support strong, vibrant, democratic societies and contribute to the greater good.

PART ONE

MARKETING AS DEMOCRACY

CHAPTER 1

Exchange

A Promise Is a Promise

E ACH PERSON IN A SOCIETY engages in multiple exchanges with others. Virtually every form of social institution, from the family to the state, from commerce to religion, can be framed in terms of exchange. Anthropologists such as Bronislaw Malinowski and Claude Levi-Strauss consider exchange to be a fundamental aspect of society and organizations.

Exchange seems to be a straightforward act, but in reality it is fraught with complications. How we view an exchange depends on the nature of the parties, what is exchanged, and how and why the exchange occurs. Virtually any exchange raises questions about power relationships, including the degree of coercion, the dependence of one party on the other, and the existence of alternatives. The object of the exchange may be a good or a service or something ephemeral; its value may be mutually agreed upon or exist only in the eye of the beholder.

The terms of exchange range from a gift to an even exchange to a taking, as in the expression "being taken." Payment may be made by barter or cash, handed over immediately or promised for later delivery. The reasons for exchange may be utilitarian—to obtain things useful in themselves—or symbolic, to obtain things that carry psychological or sociological meaning. These motives may be implicit or explicit, understood equally by both parties or comprehended quite differently. Society judges an exchange in terms of value received, fairness, reciprocity, and accordance with accepted social practices.

Marketing as Exchange

The propensity to truck, barter and exchange one thing for another . . .
is common to all men, and to be found in no other race of animals.

—Adam Smith[1]

If marketing is the process through which buyers and sellers exchange goods and services, then marketing dates to ancient times. For much of human history, people have negotiated with overlords, neighbors, artisans, merchants, and itinerant traders to obtain goods for barter or cash.

For millennia, buyers and sellers have been meeting in designated markets, such as the *agora* in Athens, where vendors and customers compare competing offers. In medieval England, transactions in marketplaces supplemented the allocation of goods and services by lords to serfs.[2] In the former Soviet Union, gaps in the centrally planned economy were filled by a market-based "shadow" economy, including farmers selling surplus food from private plots.[3] Sellers have always marketed their products in the sense of using persuasive techniques—say, proffering a cup of tea or extending a discount—to convince people to buy.

However, to put marketing into context, it's important to note that people's living standards worldwide remained stagnant until the Industrial Revolution, except for isolated pockets for brief periods (such as the wealthy elites in civilizations of Greece, Rome, China, India, and Mexico). In both past and contemporary agrarian societies, personal income stayed at slightly above subsistence level, or the equivalent of about $400 to $800 per capita per year in current dollars.[4] Overall, most of the world's population had little exposure to marketing. With the exception of traveling peddlers carrying wares to remote villages (still evident in rural India and Indonesia) and merchants participating in periodic market days, marketing was largely confined to the minority of the population that lived in towns and cities.[5]

One group of scholars maintains that there was no such thing as a market economy, or even an independent market, in the ancient world. Rather, "primitive" economies were characterized by reciprocal exchange (in which people try to balance what they receive and what they give in accordance with social obligations and traditions) and redistribution (in which a central authority, whether in a unit as small as a household or as large as a state, collects goods or taxes from unit members and redistributes goods and services).[6]

However, other scholars have countered with evidence that markets and financial institutions existed in ancient Mesopotamia, Egypt, Greece, and Rome and that the economy of the early Roman empire was primarily a market economy.[7]

Standard economic theory holds that in free-market exchanges, both parties gain. If people enter into a trade, it's because they expect to be better off. It's assumed that the parties are on an equal footing; the actors are autonomous and independent, rational, and informed; and the relationship is entered into freely.

Marketers' View of Exchange

In many respects, marketing's view of the buying–selling exchange follows that of economists. Most marketers would reject the assertion that marketing can force consumers to buy against their will or best interests (and certainly not to buy again if they are dissatisfied) or that consumers buy marketers' products and services only because they are misinformed or duped.

Although marketers accept basic economic premises, they tend to view marketing exchanges in a more nuanced and pragmatic fashion than do economists. Bagozzi postulates a more realistic "marketing man" who is a variation of a more theoretical "economic man" (see "'Economic Man' and 'Marketing Man'").[8]

Furthermore, marketers acknowledge that the legacy of past market exchanges, as well as the expectation of future exchanges, affects marketing man's purchase decisions. Economists, in contrast, tend to treat market transactions as discrete events.

Buyers' motives for entering into market exchanges, and the benefits they derive, are multifaceted. The most practical of purchases—say, a beverage to quench a thirst—may be loaded with cultural and social meanings; a coffee drinker may feel out of place among a group of tea drinkers, and vice versa. At the very least, marketers hope to understand these meanings. The more aspiring among them aim to create layers of meaning that will motivate consumers to enter into an exchange.

For guidance, the field has turned to insights on human behaviors and motivations derived from anthropology, psychology, and sociology. For instance, anthropologists gain a fuller understanding of gifts when they examine them in the context of the history of the giver and the receiver and explore the role of gifts in modifying or extending people's social relationships.[9] The market

"Economic Man" and "Marketing Man"

Economic Man	Marketing Man
Man is rational in his behavior.	Man is sometimes rational, sometimes irrational.
	He is motivated by tangible as well as intangible rewards, by internal as well as external forces.
He attempts to maximize his satisfaction in exchanges.	He engages in utilitarian as well as symbolic exchanges involving psychological and social aspects.
	Although occasionally striving to maximize his profits, marketing man often settles for less than optimum gains in his exchanges.
He has complete information on alternatives available to him in exchanges.	Although faced with incomplete information, he proceeds the best he can and makes at least rudimentary and sometimes unconscious calculations of the costs and benefits associated with social and economic exchanges.
These exchanges are relatively free from external influence.	Exchanges do not occur in isolation but are subject to a host of individual and social constraints: legal, ethical, normative, coercive, and the like.

Source: Richard P. Bagozzi, "Marketing as Exchange," *Journal of Marketing* 39 (October 1975): 38–39. Used with permission of American Marketing Association.

research functions in firms such as Procter & Gamble and Unilever have borrowed freely from the social science disciplines in attempting to understand the symbolic and social aspects of consumer behavior.

The complexities of the exchange with marketing man lead marketers to a conflicted view of its nature. On the one hand, marketers use war metaphors.[10] Their rhetoric includes phrases like "capture customer segments," "captive audience," "target markets," and "rifle versus shotgun marketing." The customer is someone to be competed for and conquered.

On the other hand, marketers frequently use relationship metaphors to characterize the buyer–seller exchange.[11] They employ phrases like "customer for life," "relationship marketing," "loyal customers," and "customer satisfaction." The customer is someone to be romanced over a long time through multiple exchanges and not just a single transaction.

When the relationship falters, marketers may want to "divorce" unprofitable customers or customers who behave badly, but usually they can only discourage such customers and not bar them from doing business. Marketers see themselves as servants to cynical, fickle customers. They worry about exchanges that formerly satisfied consumers but no longer do so, loyalty that can no longer be taken for granted.[12]

The view of the marketer as increasingly subservient and as having to reenlist customers every day appears to be widespread.[13] Even Coca-Cola, which owns the world's most valuable brand, has seen home-market declines in sales of its flagship brand.[14] Far from feeling in control of the market exchange, able to foist excess inventories of unwanted products on consumers, companies in increasingly competitive global markets are apt to see themselves in a constant struggle for continued consumer acceptance.

In contrast, companies with market power can exert considerable control over the buyer–seller exchange. Monopolists or near monopolists, such as the giant oil companies and railroads of the late nineteenth and early twentieth centuries, succeeded in controlling distribution and production and fixing prices to end customers—initially, setting artificially low prices to drive out competitors, followed by high prices to reap profits.[15]

Thanks to antitrust legislation, John D. Rockefeller's Standard Oil Company may be an extreme case of monopoly power that will not be seen again, but powerful sellers still exist. Microsoft's success in building innovative operating systems for business and personal computers attracted large numbers of buyers. Eventually the company was able to push successive product upgrades on trusting, but sometimes reluctant, customers who would otherwise be left with obsolete systems. Patent rights on genetically modified corn gave Monsanto market exclusivity and the ability to sell the corn to farmers under contracts that prevented them from collecting seed corn for future plantings. Wal-Mart dominates the U.S. retail market by virtue of superior operating efficiencies and hard-nosed bargaining with suppliers. It uses its power to dictate the magazine, video, and music content that can be sold in its stores; vendors modify original versions to conform to Wal-Mart's "family friendly" policies.[16] But as powerful as these companies may be, if history is any guide their long-term success will depend on continually giving customers superior perceived value over competitors. If complacency lulls them into failing to refresh their marketing offerings or programs, competitors will find an opening wedge.

The Marketing Orientation

But what constitutes value—or even what it is that is being exchanged—is not always self-evident. Companies with a manufacturing or production orientation see themselves as making things. The objects of exchange are tangible objects or clearly defined services. In the developed countries, however, unadorned products and services are a dime a dozen. They don't stand out in the marketplace.

Enterprises with a selling orientation see themselves as skilled at locating and selling to customers. They realize that part of what they are providing is a product that fits the buyer's particular need: a carpenter needs certain kinds of tools for certain tasks.

Businesses with a marketing orientation, in contrast, perceive that they are supplying not products but solutions, not functions but benefits. Theodore Levitt told his Harvard Business School students, "People don't want a quarter-inch drill—they want a quarter-inch hole."[17] The company is selling a tool, but beyond that it is providing the buyer the ability to construct things. Part of the value of the item being exchanged is an intangible property: fitness for use or conformance to customers' needs. By exceeding expectations, the exchange may deliver value that actually delights the customer.

In companies with a marketing orientation, brands and reputations are paramount. Branded consumer products provide buyers a promise of consistency and quality. Similarly, in the business-to-business marketplace, products may be near commodities, but a seller's reputation for benefits—

such as fast and reliable delivery, convenient quantity breakpoints, and responsive after-sales service—differentiate it from competitors. Now, part of the value of what is being exchanged is neither a tangible nor an intangible property of the product, but rather assurance about the product. In exchange, buyers are willing to pay a price premium.

But many brands now offer more than a promise of quality. Brand advertising sells images, ideals, aspirations, and lifestyles. A brand may promise cutting-edge innovation or trend-setting style. When branding is done well, customers reward the company with loyalty, word-of-mouth recommendations, and a willingness to pay higher prices. Often, part of the value of what is being exchanged is the promise of transformation: the buyer will become a more capable homemaker, a better-looking person, a smarter, healthier, wealthier, or more popular individual.

As global manufacturing capabilities have improved and competition has increased, it has generally become harder, except in cases of genuine discontinuous innovation, for firms to differentiate their product or its benefits from others in the market. Sustaining that differentiation is even trickier. Japanese and now Chinese manufacturers have perfected the art of quickly reverse-engineering innovative products and launching close imitations. With increased outsourcing of manufacturing, different companies with different brands—for example, Nike and adidas—may be selling almost identical products made in the same Chinese factory.

So brand building has spread. But when the object of marketing exchange is ephemeral, it's harder to figure out what to do when things go wrong. Was Snapple's steep decline in sales following its 1994 acquisition by Quaker a result of a decision to drop feisty brand spokesperson Wendy (a real Snapple employee)? Or was it a switch from a trendy image emphasizing natural, individualistic, playful, and irreverent qualities to a more mainstream image emphasizing healthy, crowd-pleasing qualities? Or was it a change in distribution from small vendors to supermarkets?

Marketers themselves cannot always pinpoint what it is they are selling to customers. Gap sells a line of basic, casual clothing. In the early 1990s, when sales skyrocketed, it was also selling "cool." But as sales dropped steadily over the past several years, critics said, "They've lost their cool and don't stand for anything anymore."[18] Despite expert marketing counsel and repeated attempts to duplicate its earlier success, Gap is having trouble figuring out what cool is. Customers, in turn, may be able to tell marketers what physical product they are purchasing, but not all customers can articulate the emotional benefits they are acquiring along with it.

Consumer Power in an Exchange: Pawn or Free Agent?

"Caveat emptor." "The customer is king."

Theoretically, a marketing exchange takes place only if both buyer and seller expect to be better off. Historically, though, "Buyer beware" has taken precedence over "The customer is king." Obviously, buyers are most vulnerable to opportunistic or deceitful sellers when they need essential goods and supply is scarce. Wartime profiteering is a case in point. So too is exploitation of consumers during famines.

But buyers are also vulnerable in less extreme circumstances. In some exchanges, the quality of goods cannot readily be determined at the time of purchase. A shady seller can take advantage of this lack of transparency, or asymmetry of information, to charge normal prices for shoddy goods, particularly if the transaction between buyer and seller is expected to be a one-time event. Some buyers are simply less capable, less experienced, or less astute than others and are more apt to be misled or deceived. Elderly home owners, for instance, frequently fall victim to fraudulent construction businesses selling expensive, unneeded items financed at exorbitant interest rates using the home as collateral. A normally astute buyer may be less vigilant than usual in extreme circumstances—for example, choosing to believe the promises of a vendor of quack medicine when a family member is seriously ill.

Traditionally, the presumption is that buyers must watch out for their own best interests. Consumers have been expected to determine the quality and suitability of a product, to search out and negotiate with vendors, and to obtain the best prices. The more skilled consumers are, the more apt they are to achieve a satisfactory outcome in a specific exchange. Buyer be wary.

During the twentieth century, consumers organized politically to press for consumer protection regulations that required marketers to act in consumers' interests. Still, the complexity of products such as financial services and loyalty programs requires vigilance. For example, some bank account plans tend to mislead consumers with respect to their available balance, because the "true" balance is aggregated with balance protection amounts that incur substantial fees and interest. Other banks offer free checking combined with high overdraft charges. Mileage reward programs carry fine-print restrictions that make it hard to redeem points. Health club contracts and cell phone contracts lock consumers into multiyear commitments. Car rental agencies offer costly insurance plans that may duplicate coverage provided by the renter's credit-card company or personal auto insurance policy.

For modern consumers, negotiating—including negotiating with sellers, bidding against other consumers, and making deals through agents—is the most challenging type of purchase.[19] For one thing, the average consumer has little experience with head-to-head commercial negotiations, the buying situations where consumers need to negotiate, such as purchasing a house, car, home improvements, insurance, or financial services. In addition, quite often involve significant financial outlays. The decisions involved often are complex, including choosing add-ons to the core product, structuring payments over time, or selecting delivery terms and service packages. Salespeople and agents are more expert than buyers and use their persuasive powers to encourage buyers to veer from the rational model.

The Power of Consumers

Although it behooves buyers to take care, a number of factors aid them, especially over repeated exchanges. The vendor's concern for its good reputation, its desire to exchange with the buyer in the future, its rivalry with other sellers, and the power of information shared among consumers—facilitated by the Internet—all curb any inclination to cheat. And even though a buyer's power may be small compared with the seller's, the collective power of all customers may be great. In sum, there are powerful long-term incentives for sellers to engage in fair exchanges.

These forces play a role in all marketplaces. However, the sophistication of modern advertising and promotion techniques prompts observers to question whether the current match between marketer and consumer is an even one. The concern is twofold: first, that consumers are being persuaded to buy items they don't really need or that aren't good for them, and second, that consumers are adopting materialistic values that enslave them to the marketplace at the expense of other social institutions.

Consider the cosmetics industry. No other industry has done more to arouse fantasies and desires for products that cost pennies apiece to make but dollars apiece to buy. Charles Revson famously said that Revlon didn't sell cosmetics; it sold hope. For a hundred years, cosmetics have occupied prominent shelf space in drugstores, department stores, and mass merchandisers, and slick advertising campaigns have dominated women's magazines. Large corporations have profited hugely by convincing women to buy expensive branded goods, including some of dubious efficacy.

But a fuller version of the story is not so one-sided. Rather, it is a story of businesses emerging to satisfy Victorian women's culturally conditioned aspirations and desires for beauty.[20] The industry originated with thousands of women entrepreneurs who owned hair-care parlors or operated franchises for cosmetics and makeup. After World War I, national corporations started to take over the industry and began advertising intensively. But young women didn't have to be convinced to apply makeup. Rather, they saw it as fun, liberating, and somewhat of a challenge to authority.[21] Consumers may have been influenced by marketers, but their desire for independence and personal expression was real.

The evolution of the cosmetics industry demonstrates a recurring interplay between the emergence of consumers' wants and of marketers' offerings to satisfy them. Product markets, it seems, are often developed by consumers as well as producers. In the U.S. minivan market, a study finds that "product markets are neither imposed nor orchestrated by producers or consumers but evolve from producer-consumer interaction feedback effects . . . [From] the cacophony of uses, claims, and product standards that characterize emerging product markets—product markets become coherent as a result of consumers and producers making sense of each other's behaviors."[22]

The Power of Marketers

But does advertising—the most frequent target of critics' concerns—give marketers undue power? In the United States, annual advertising spending exceeds $263 billion, or $895 for every man, woman, and child, compared with $34 billion, or $570 per person, in the United Kingdom.[23] Presumably, advertising must have marketplace power, because otherwise companies would not waste money on it. At the least, marketers believe that by reminding consumers of the brand, advertising combats possible gradual erosions in market share and sales. And if consumption levels are any indication, advertising has succeeded in selling products. Without doubt, Americans consume and possess in excess of what other populations consider sufficient for a comfortable lifestyle, perhaps sometimes to the detriment of their well-being.[24]

Marketers argue that most individuals are adept at threading their way through the modern marketplace. Furthermore, they say a generation of consumers that has been raised in a commercially saturated media environment is experienced at decoding the meaning and intent of commercials. Consumers are skeptical of advertising promises and use technology aids, such as remote-control buttons and TiVo, as well as selective attention, to avoid commercials. They know when they are paying for symbolic value, and they choose brands according to how they fit into a preferred lifestyle. The Internet gives consumers access to more marketplace information than ever before, information they use to research competing offers.[25] In this environment, a seller must offer good value.

If it is true that consumers are ignoring advertising, then in one respect they are coming out ahead in the market exchange. That's because marketers have been providing free or subsidized entertainment to all consumers in return for the time spent by target customers in viewing ads. Furthermore, if information "pull" from consumers using the Internet comes to dominate commercial "push" from traditional advertising media, then consumers will assume even greater power in the marketplace.

Finally, it can be argued, at least for the developed world, that marketers are more dependent on consumers for survival than consumers are on marketers. If people generally have more stuff than they need, then individuals can cut back on consumption with no degradation of their quality of life. When producers have miscalculated the extent of demand, they frequently cut prices, thereby benefiting consumers who remain in the market (although cutting prices may also promote additional—and some would argue, needless—consumption).

Companies also are under tremendous pressure from financial markets to generate ever-increasing revenues and profits; sustained declines severely threaten long-term viability. The intense competition to survive forces marketers to offer high-quality, innovative products at the lowest possible prices, explaining the emergence of powerful value brands such as Vanguard and Costco ("Our mission: To continually provide our members with quality goods and services at the lowest possible prices").[26]

Fair and Equitable Outcomes

*According to the law of nature it is only fair that no one should become
richer through damages and injuries suffered by another.*

—Marcus Tullius Cicero[27]

When the rule of law prevails, marketplaces are remarkably civilized places.
Despite sporadic misunderstandings or disputes, the vast majority of transactions proceed harmoniously. An exchange of greetings and pleasantries
typically accompanies the exchange of products and money. Buyers walk
away with goods or services they value. Sellers deposit payments for these
goods into the till. Occasionally, the buyer or the seller will experience the
satisfaction of getting a good deal. Occasionally, one or the other will suffer
the misery of being cheated. But more often than not, both parties are satisfied with the transaction, or at least have no cause to be dissatisfied.

Societies apply principles of equity and fairness to the commercial marketplace. There is agreement that, at a minimum, buyers and sellers both
deserve to benefit from an exchange in a competitive marketplace. Beyond
that, there is a sense that outcomes should be equitable—that what a buyer
gains and gives up in the exchange is proportional to what the seller gains
and gives up. Additionally, market exchanges appear to be governed by the
"dual entitlement" principle—that sellers are entitled to a profit and that
consumers are entitled to prices and other treatment that are acceptable in
terms of reference standards set by the community.[28]

What Is a Fair Price?

What is considered a fair price, or a fair outcome, differs by society, place,
and time. In Soviet Russia, for example, a low price for bread was considered fair because bread was a necessity, even if the selling price didn't cover
the cost of production. Banking and credit services greatly facilitate exchange, but the literature and history of Judaism, Christianity, and Islam
contain specific prohibitions against usury, or profiting from lending money,
and prohibitions remain in force in Islam. There is widespread prejudice
against middlemen (intermediaries) in the marketing system, because they
are thought to take more than their fair share. But there is little consensus
on what a fair share is. Like value received, fairness is in the eye of the beholder and is also socially conditioned.

People most often characterize exchange outcomes in terms of the price paid: "My repair shop overcharged me," "I got a great deal on cookies—two for the price of one," "At that price I should be able to find a salesperson to talk to," "It's worth every penny I paid for it," and so on. In part, this is because price is standardized, visible, and easily communicated. It's also because, during an exchange, buyers and sellers use price to adjust the equity of outcomes.[29] Although price is but one aspect of an exchange outcome, it's a convenient surrogate or summary measure.

Exchanges that take place in traditional markets and bazaars, among villagers, or along trade routes frequently are associated with hard bargaining over price. Because many of the goods sold in these transactions are hand-produced and vary in quality, the market "reference" point for a product covers a wide range of prices. Ultimately, a merchant who is selling a higher-quality product and is a good negotiator should obtain a higher price compared with competitors. But uneven supply and uneven demand—and small numbers of buyers and sellers—also create price fluctuations. Strong relationships and social ties may also matter. In the end, negotiation establishes what a product is worth to a particular buyer and seller at a particular point in time. A fair price today may not be a fair price tomorrow.

In contrast, modern consumer marketplaces display less latitude in what buyers and sellers consider a fair price. In particular, a fair price is a marketwide price that is transparent and available equally to all buyers. What accounts for the difference? Clearly, many goods are standardized, mass-produced, branded products for which quality doesn't and shouldn't vary from one unit to another. Merchants selling large numbers of goods to large numbers of customers would find negotiating every price impossibly time-consuming and inefficient. Likewise for customers buying more than a few items during a day. However, supply and demand, though relatively stable, do vary: both tradition and economic theory suggest that producers should maximize their profits by raising and lowering prices as demand varies.

Posted prices, market prices, prevailing profit margins, and the history of previous transactions between buyer and seller all serve as reference transactions for what's considered fair.[30] The public scorns profiteering or exploiting of shortages. It is easier to set a high retail price, discount it when demand is low, and remove promotions and revert to list price when demand is high.

Consumers are sometimes willing to pay more for a product under certain circumstances—for example, for food or drink at airports or ballparks. They have accepted the logic behind differential prices for airline seats: the early booker gets a discount, and the last-minute booker pays full fare (as much as triple the discount fare). Interestingly, social norms dictate that strangers sitting next to each other don't usually compare prices, thus insulating the marketer from perceptions of unfair pricing.

But firms often hesitate to raise prices in response to unexpectedly high demand; classic examples are the hardware store owner who could raise the price of snow shovels after a heavy snowstorm and the theater or stadium that could raise prices on the remaining tickets of an event that is selling out.[31] Doing so would violate accepted standards of fairness. Consumers rejected as exploitative and unfair an experiment by Coca-Cola wherein prices at vending machines would automatically increase when the weather got hotter.

Consumers largely agree that it's fair for a firm to pass on increases in its costs; a gasoline station whose supplier has raised prices by 10 cents a gallon can fairly charge 10 cents more per gallon at the pump, although 20 cents would be unfair. When prices fluctuate in response to cost changes, they tend to increase faster going up than fall going down. That is not necessarily a situation marketers like. Gasoline stations display the most easily compared prices in the United States. The steep week-by-week (if not day-by-day) rises in pump prices during 2005 and 2006 inevitably led to charges of price gouging and calls for penalties. Consumers also think it's unfair for a station to raise prices immediately upon news of higher world oil prices or bottlenecks in supply—while it is still selling off lower-cost inventory— or to be slow to drop prices after the threat of lower supply has passed. To minimize such criticism, the major oil companies try to absorb day-to-day volatility and keep prices as stable as possible.

A fair price isn't necessarily the lowest price in the market. Because not all consumers thrive on bargain hunting, some companies will minimize price variations to increase consumers' confidence that they are getting a fair price (and to simplify operations, as in the Southwest Airlines model). Some retailers employ an everyday low pricing strategy wherein, say, a bottle of ketchup sells for about the same price all year. Other retailers employ a high-low pricing strategy, wherein the same bottle of ketchup is priced higher most of the time, but is heavily discounted during promotional periods. Both types of stores continue to compete successfully by selling to different segments of consumers.[32]

Mutual Fairness

According to the traditional view held by classical economists, the reasons buyers and sellers engage in "fair" marketplace behavior boil down to self-interest. Thus, the appearance of concern for fairness or social conscience can ultimately be explained by clever strategic behavior. In contrast, social scientists and a smaller number of economists have entertained the idea that consumers and firms are motivated by fairness and may even apply fairness "rules" that are not in their best interest.[33] For instance, consumers think it's fair for a firm to maintain its normal price levels in the event that the firm's costs decrease as a result of having learned to operate more efficiently. Or consumers may pay a higher price elsewhere to avoid doing business with a merchant that they perceive has treated other people unfairly.

This presumption of fairness isn't to say that consumers think firms always act fairly, or vice versa. Rather, it's a presumption that fairness is a norm to which buyers and sellers can and should be held accountable. Firms in the entertainment industry believe that consumers are acting unfairly, indeed criminally, in using peer-to-peer file-sharing services to download music and movies for free rather than pay for them.[34] Best Buy, a consumer electronics chain, has taken action to thwart consumers who unfairly "buy products, apply for rebates, return the purchases, then buy them back at returned-merchandise discounts" or "load up on 'loss leaders,' severely discounted merchandise designed to boost store traffic, then flip the goods at profit on eBay."[35] If consumers are inclined to accept or applaud such attempts to beat the system, they might reflect on the fact that merchants raise prices to cover these kinds of costs.

In one recent study involving U.S. consumers, participants believed that prices are unfair. But they also greatly underestimated firms' costs and overestimated firms' profits; for instance, they guessed that grocery store profits were about 27 percent, although the actual average figure is about 1 to 2 percent. This erroneous belief aggravated perceptions of unfairness.[36]

In judging fair price, these consumers may be folding in nonprice aspects of their treatment by firms, such as how well they are treated by store employees, the convenience of the transaction, or the quality of the product assortment. Perceptions of unfair price may also capture consumers' sense of inequity in being held captive to a seller; witness the complaints about price increases in the quasi-monopolistic cable television industry, the lowest-scoring industry in the American Customer Satisfaction Index.[37] Consumers' perceptions of fair price may also be colored by the seller's or industry's general reputation. For instance, the corporate scandals of World-Com, Enron, and Marsh & McLennan may increase perceptions that prices in the telecommunications, energy, and insurance industries are unfair.

Trust and the Social and Political Context of Marketing Exchange

*Trust men, and they will be true to you; treat them greatly,
and they will show themselves great, though they make
an exception in your favor to all their rules of trade.*

—Ralph Waldo Emerson[38]

Many people, remembering their first e-commerce transaction on the Internet, can recall vividly the fear that the order would never be sent, that the goods wouldn't arrive in the condition advertised, or that their financial information would be stolen. For assurance in dealing with an unseen seller, a buyer may take extra precautions, such as asking friends or using search engines, the news media, or *Consumer Reports* to search for information from impartial third parties.

Sellers, too, must place their faith in unknown consumers, hoping that payments will be made on time, checks won't bounce, or customers won't try to return used goods as new. Hence, vendors pay for access to electronically available credit rating information on prospective customers. However, such precautions play a minor marketplace role compared with trust.

Trust is the invisible bond underpinning nearly every exchange between buyers and sellers. Without trust, both parties would want to seek extra information about every exchange to reduce perceived risk. Transaction costs would be greater. All but the simplest transactions would create a lawyer's paradise, for provisions specifying the obligations of each party to the exchange would need to be spelled out. With trust comes confidence that the other party will serve our interests and will make things right if they should happen to go wrong.

Trust is earned on the basis of past transactions, but it also comes from promises and pledges. During the infancy of the retail catalog business, the money-back guarantees of Montgomery Ward and Sears are credited with bolstering consumers' willingness to place orders with distant merchants.[39] In the global village, it is a challenge to create trust; eBay builds trust by posting evaluations of sellers by buyers, and of buyers by sellers.

Brands, too, are a source of trust, because they convey an implicit promise that the product or service will meet a certain standard. One bottle of Coca-Cola will deliver the same satisfaction as every other bottle; every cleaning product carrying the Tide brand will perform equally well. For consumers, trust in brands simplifies exchanges, and for this convenience and assurance they are willing to pay a premium.

Trust also can be supplied by third parties. Montgomery Ward allied with the Grange, a national farmers' organization, to build trust in its offerings among rural communities.[40] Internet buyers and sellers who do not know each other use PayPal (an eBay subsidiary) to increase their sense of security in financial transactions. Trade associations establish codes of conduct to protect the reputation of the industry as a whole.

Accreditation

Exchanges become more efficient when the larger marketing and social systems work together to create trust. Early examples of such systems were the medieval craft guilds, which regulated the training of workers and the quality of their output; these groups also assumed some responsibility for maintaining standards of morality and conduct. Guilds were closely connected with political institutions: in many cases, the monarch or other state authority granted a guild's members supply exclusivity in certain markets.[41] A similar medieval institution—the merchant guild—regulated merchants' activities in trading centers, centralized record keeping, punished violations, and enforced contracts with local political authorities.[42]

In contemporary societies, professional accreditation promotes public trust in the competence, integrity, and public-mindedness of doctors, lawyers, accountants, and others. (Professionalism is no guarantee against questionable or shady practices, however, as witness the accountants who aided and abetted or willfully overlooked problems at Enron, WorldCom, Tyco,

Fannie Mae, and others.) In return, the professions control who can enter the field; governmental bodies allow them considerable autonomy in setting standards and self-regulations.

Marketing is not a profession. There is no exam or license to become a marketer, as there is to become a public-school teacher or a hairdresser.[43] Low barriers to entry probably contribute to instances of marketing malfeasance, but they also foster entrepreneurship and creativity. Society relies on consumers and competitors to promote good behavior by marketers. It also relies on a legal and regulatory system.

Laws and Regulations

Enforcement of property rights and the rule of law are essential for a well-developed system of marketing exchange. In failed states, where such rights are not enforced, where plunder and corruption by public officials and private individuals are the norm, marketers face huge risks in securing and transferring ownership of goods.[44] Furthermore, the *free* in free-market economies is a misnomer. Virtually every aspect of market exchange is potentially subject to formal government regulation. Civil justice systems exist mainly to hear disputes over contracts and to punish infractions. Knowing that government and the courts may step in gives marketers—and consumers—incentives to deal fairly.

Of course, democracies also allow marketer and consumer interest groups to lobby for rules and legislation that maximize their own benefit. Businesses press for the freedom to compete as they wish but also lobby for protection from "unfair" monopolies and tariffs on foreign goods. In the United States, successive waves of sustained consumer pressure have achieved food and drug regulation, antitrust legislation, the right to obtain objective information, product safety regulation, and restrictions on advertising to children, among others. In twentieth-century Britain the idea that consumers had the right to a fair price for milk led to demands for consumer representation in economic decision making by the state and worked to undermine unquestioning belief in the virtues of free trade and capitalism.[45]

Social Norms

Less visible than laws and regulations, but perhaps more powerful, are social norms. Every market exchange takes place in the context of local cultural norms concerning proper conduct. Sometimes these norms condone exchanges that would be considered reprehensible in different places or situations—for example, tourist traps that deliberately provide poor quality at high prices, or companies that pay government officials "fees" to expedite services—but in others, they serve the interests of society.

Although it is notoriously difficult to formulate universal norms for ethical behavior, scholars of marketing have developed frameworks for ethical marketing exchange. Smith and Quelch review a wide range of ethical issues potentially facing marketing actors, including those having to do with trust, honesty, respect, and fairness in customer relationships, issues of consumer exclusion and inclusion, and gray areas of specific marketing practices.[46]

One set of ethical frameworks builds on John Locke's political theories. Locke argued that the legitimacy of state authority rests in the consent of citizens and that in the resulting social contract, citizens and the state have reciprocal obligations. As stated by Dunfee et al., "The particular relevance of social contract theory for marketing ethics lies in part in its shared focus on exchange. Essentially, . . . the firm offers advantages to society—its customers and employees—in exchange for the right to exist and even prosper."[47]

As applied to firms, social contract theory suggests that marketers need to behave in ways to which a relevant group of consumers would consent. Because firms benefit society, consumers have reciprocal obligations. Consideration of reciprocal obligations and balanced interests could usefully inform debates such as those over pharmaceutical companies' right to market prescription drugs that benefit some consumers but carry side effects that may harm others. Such considerations also raise questions about the ethical and social obligations of consumers who harshly criticize Wal-Mart for economic exploitation of its workers but cannot resist its low prices.[48]

Under the Foreign Corrupt Practices Act, the United States has set uniform global standards for doing business that go against the "When in Rome, do as the Romans do" philosophy. However, Dunfee et al. posit a role for local ethical norms by defining local economic communities and "microsocial" contracts as the relevant sphere for ethical judgments.

At the same time, however, the actions of global corporations anywhere in the world affect their brand reputation in the rest of the world. No marketer can afford to have its reputation sullied by questionable practices in developing countries. Notably, allegations that Nike's independent subcontractors exploit workers still affect the willingness of some consumers to buy Nike products.

Social Obligations

Although "Do no harm" is always a good rule, considerable debate exists about the proper role of marketers in ameliorating poverty and disease in countries where they may or may not be doing business. Some political economists contend that the only proper role of corporations is to turn a profit—that businesses should stay away from "do-goodism."[49] On the other hand, increasing numbers of corporate leaders embrace the view that business leaders should leverage their corporate assets and knowledge to tackle problems of poverty and equitable globalization.[50]

At the very least, policy makers and others need to ask whether the people of the third world want to have the opportunity to engage in exchange with global corporations. From the perspective of the marketing function, corporate social responsibility matters: increasing numbers of consumers calibrate their willingness to buy a manufacturer's products according to whether the company is meeting broader social responsibilities in addition to delivering products with good functional performance.

Political Exchange

The true forms of government, therefore, are those in which the one,
or the few, or the many, govern with a view to the common interest;
but governments which rule with a view to the private interest,
whether of the one or of the few, or of the many, are perversions.

—Aristotle[51]

Western-style marketing systems and democratic political systems have enjoyed widespread support for the same reason: they improve people's welfare. Both kinds of systems put individual rights and interests front and center. Of course, the reason people enter into marketing exchanges is to achieve their own self-interest, and the reason people enter into democratic political exchanges—voting, campaigning, attending town meetings, or running for office—is to have a say in public matters affecting everyone. Yet in each system, exchanges have consequences for both individuals and society as a whole. That poses the problem of how to balance individual interests and collective interests.

In the modern consumer marketplace, you enter into exchanges for particular goods and services more or less when and where you want to. From an assortment of options in the marketplace, you pick the ones that come closest to meeting your needs and ability to pay. Typically, most exchanges are intended to maximize your welfare or the welfare of your family. But social welfare is achieved in the aggregate when you and everyone else participate in exchanges that are satisfactory.

Quite evidently, there are flaws in this model. For one thing, the maximization of individual satisfaction ignores the collective costs of consuming, say, unsustainable amounts of timber or energy. For another, the exchanges available to the rich vastly surpass the exchanges available to the poor.

In politics you are less apt to get exactly what you want from an exchange; an opposing political party wins, or your taxes pay for programs that don't benefit you, or the representative you elect doesn't perform as promised. You cannot readily place a value on the exchange as you do with prices in the commercial marketplace. That it is more difficult for people to see the value in political exchange than in marketing exchange may be one reason citizens opt out of political exchanges.

The political exchange is intrinsically collective. The representatives who win elections make decisions on your behalf whether or not you voted for them or agree with them. And elected representatives are apt to make compromises needed to pass legislation and run a government, causing some supporters to experience buyer's regret. On a practical level, exchanges in the political marketplace, for example, caucuses or elections—occur infrequently, often at specified times, in a prescribed manner, and offer few choices. Government agencies typically deliver public goods and services to citizens in a uniform manner.

Thus there is a natural tension between individual and collective benefits in the realm of politics and government. The tension is less acute in marketing, in part because marketing is extremely effective at serving diverse individual needs, and in part because public costs (for example, environmental damage) frequently are hidden or evident only with the passage of time. On the other hand, democratic forms of government contain constitutional frameworks, laws, regulations, and enforcement bodies that serve to protect individual rights and freedoms and address the problem of reconciling diverse interests and needs.

In truth, in modern Western societies, marketplace exchanges and political exchanges, pursuit of self-interest and pursuit of the common good, are inextricably, if not always visibly, linked. To reinvigorate democracy, a number of social activists are trying to draw people's attention to the connections between their lives as consumers and their lives as citizens.[52] People can use political exchanges—for example, supporting politicians who favor antitrust enforcement—to address problems they experience in marketing exchanges. They can use marketing exchanges—for example, boycotting producers or subscribing to left-leaning or right-leaning publications—to achieve social or political goals.

CHAPTER 2

Consumption

The Happiness of Pursuit

C ONSUMPTION—eating, drinking, switching on a light, talking on the telephone, attending an artistic or sporting event—is the stuff of everyday life. Each instance of consumption is an individual, private act, mostly routine and not much deliberated on. Yet it has far-reaching consequences. Consumption ripples beyond a household to the larger economy. It affects the national wealth and international trade.

Taken together, all the small, everyday, individual decisions we make about whether and what to consume influence what's available in the marketplace; marketers make decisions on their product and service offerings largely in response to past consumption patterns. In turn, marketers' efforts to provide satisfactory consumption experiences stimulate further consumption.

Closer to home, each single act of consumption affects the well-being of a household. Clearly, consumption decisions affect financial health. People balance daily consumption against their budget constraints. They explicitly or implicitly sense that long-term goals may or may not be met depending on current consumption patterns. Consumption also influences how people feel emotionally and physically. Unfortunately, in an imperfect world, consumption that gives immediate pleasure may prove deleterious to lasting well-being.

For societies, both underconsumption and overconsumption present problems. When some citizens don't have basic necessities or when a slowdown in consumer spending depresses the economy, the problems of underconsumption are obvious. Overconsumption can produce financial or physical distress for individuals, or overuse or damage of natural resources and the environment. Overconsumption may also be said to occur when society considers a particular form of consumption morally repugnant or socially undesirable. Although modern democracies relegate most consumption decisions to individuals and the market, these types of concerns become matters of political debate.

The Engine of the Economy

Here's a great way you can help us. Come here,
go to a restaurant, a play. Spend some money.

—Rudolph Giuliani[1]

Consumption by ordinary people is the bulwark of national economies. Although few people give much thought to the effect of their spending on the national economic well-being, Americans were made aware of it following the terrorist acts of September 11, 2001. Amid fear and uncertainty and an ongoing economic downturn, President George W. Bush and New York City Mayor Rudolph Giuliani told citizens how they could do their part for the country: go out and spend money. This advice contrasted with traditional notions of personal sacrifice in times of national peril.

In the United States, consumer spending on durable goods, nondurable goods, and services represents about two-thirds of the national economy, as measured by GDP, or gross domestic product. During 2004, some 291 million residents spent about $8.2 trillion. To put these numbers into perspective, the average household spent almost $43,400, about two-thirds of which was for housing, transportation, and food.[2] Associated with this spending, taxes on consumption represent significant revenue for local and state governments.

Accordingly, closely watched indicators of the economy's health include housing starts, new-home sales, new orders for durable goods, and retail and food service sales. In addition to adjusting consumption according to their current income, prices for goods, and finance rates, consumers also base their spending on what they think prices, the job market, general economic conditions, and so on will be like in the future. Consequently, consumer confidence levels are another vital economic indicator, one that Bush and Giuliani were likely trying to boost.

The Dynamics of Consumer Demand

Consumption is part of an economic and marketing system that extends from extraction of raw materials to manufacture, maintenance, and disposal of household goods and that increasingly involves global transfers of materials and goods. Facilitated by world trade, sourcing from lowest-cost suppliers, and inexpensive transportation, the supplies of goods are more plentiful and affordable than ever. Consider a simple packet of Demerara sugar on a U.S. breakfast table. It traveled from Mauritius, where sugar cane grown on plantations was processed and refined, to Liverpool, where the sugar was packed and branded. Then it went to a wholesaler in the United States, to a local grocer, and thence to the household.[3] The economic value created in each step ultimately depends on consumer demand.

With the exception of the Great Depression and World War II, consumer demand in the United States steadily expanded during the twentieth century. Consumption did not slow down after a basic stock of goods was acquired; the average U.S. household continued to consume new things and upgrade existing consumption.[4] Few present-day households would be satisfied with earlier levels of consumption: numbered among daily necessities are goods, such as televisions and refrigerators, that were unknown a hundred years ago and are still rare in many parts of the world. The size of an average new home has doubled from one built fifty years ago, even though during the same period average family size in the United States has declined.[5] With few exceptions, no matter how wealthy U.S. households are, they continue to acquire additional goods and services.[6]

In terms of risk psychology and attitudes toward consumption, the number of U.S. adults who lived through the Great Depression is dwindling. In the twentieth century, Americans, unlike Europeans, never experienced the upheavals of war on home soil. This stability has contributed to Americans' traditional optimism about the future and their own prospects of upward mobility.

Still, large questions remain. Will consumers in the United States and other industrialized nations continue to consume at the current rate? One possibility is that Western consumers will maintain the same overall rate of spending but shift their consumption from things to experiences. At some point even Americans may show less appetite to buy more and bigger vehicles, more things in general, and bigger houses to accommodate all their stuff.[7] They will decrease consumption of things that require maintenance and upkeep. They won't own more things, but they'll trade them in more often to get the latest luxury versions. They'll increase consumption of experiences: entertainment, travel, spa treatments, and the like.[8]

For various reasons, consumers in other industrialized nations may be less eager than Americans to spend readily. National political climate, employment levels, wage rates, and the availability of credit temper consumption, as do beliefs about the advisability of spending instead of saving.

For example, faced with downward pressure on wages and rising costs of the welfare system, for the past five years cautious Germans have kept consumption stagnant, preferring saving to spending. But U.S. consumers, in similar conditions, seemed willing to keep consuming, buoyed by a higher sense of optimism and by faith in the investment value of homes. (In 2005, Germany's rate of home ownership was 43 percent, compared with 82 percent in Spain and 68 percent in the United States.)[9]

Now, according to a Pew Research Center study, about two-thirds of Americans agree that their standard of living is better than that of their parents when they were at the same age. More than half expect their own children to enjoy a better standard of living than they have. However, people are less optimistic about this than they were five years ago. And half of adults say that children in general will grow up to be worse off than people are today.[10] If the more pessimistic trend continues, Americans may feel more need to save for a less rosy future.

Japan, the world's second-largest economy, experienced a long period of stagnant growth from which it is only now emerging. Consumers grew used to frugality and saving, a mind-set ingrained in a generation of twenty- and thirty-year-olds. Rather than exhibit a huge pent-up demand for consumption, Japanese consumers remained reluctant to make large purchases, thus holding back the pace of economic recovery.[11] Japanese ownership of durable goods is also limited by smaller living spaces.

A potentially significant factor is the aging of the population in developed countries. Given the low rate of household savings in the United States, combined with the uncertainties of the Social Security and pension systems and rapid inflation of health-care costs, some elderly Americans will be forced to spend less than they anticipate on goods and services. In any case, the elderly will more likely shed possessions than acquire them and will spend more on medical and other services than on furnishings and cars.

Consumption in Developing Countries

Can or will developing or underdeveloped countries replicate the Western experience in building their economies through personal consumption? Some economists predict that workers in developing Asian economies—those producing inexpensive goods for the world market—will sooner rather than later insist on fulfilling their own pent-up consumer demand.[12] When that happens, China will become the world's largest economy.

Current patterns of consumption in China suggest that Chinese consumers aspire to replicate as quickly as possible the Western lifestyle, with its emphasis on material comforts and badge brands as status symbols. Encouraged by multinational auto companies manufacturing in China as well as state construction of a huge modern highway network, Chinese consumers have rapidly embraced the automobile. From 6 million cars in 2000, there are now about 20 million. Every day a thousand new cars are sold in Beijing alone.

An American reporter described car owners' pleasure in taking weekend drives as reminiscent of the United States in the 1930s and 1940s and quoted a Chinese consumer as saying, "Driving is our right." Another commented, "Once China opened up and Chinese people could see the other side of the world and know how people lived there, you could no longer limit the right to buy cars."[13]

Marketing and the Multiplication of Desire

One set of messages of the society we live in is: Consume.
Grow. Do what you want. Amuse yourselves.

—Susan Sontag[14]

Much of the marketing consumers see is intended to increase consumption (as opposed to switching brands). Consider soup. At the point of purchase in the grocery store, the aim is to encourage consumers to stock up on soup. Marketers offer bonus packs and two-for-one promotions, price discounts on regular-size cans, and a lower price per ounce for the larger, "economy" size. Switching to a larger package increases consumption at home, and introducing a smaller package increases consumption at work.

Introducing a new flavor appeals to consumers' desire for variety, and introducing a freeze-dried version opens up alternative usage occasions.[15]

To put the product in front of consumers, marketers seek to maximize shelf-space coverage in as many outlets as possible. Distribution of individual serving sizes through vending machines also stimulates impulse consumption.

Consumption-oriented advertising can be as straightforward as a Pavlovian stimulus-response scenario. Showing a mom serving soup to her kids reminds consumers to take the product out of the cupboard and heat a serving. Advertising beer during sports events motivates fans to go to the fridge, and that means maintaining a replenished supply. Advertising may also educate consumers on new uses; not only is Arm & Hammer baking soda a cooking ingredient, but it is also a deodorizer and cleanser.

Intangible products and services cannot be stored in inventory, but a bank can blanket a city with ATMs, and an airline can try to dominate gate space. Service marketers also turn to loyalty reward programs and premier relationship levels to boost consumption. Airlines, hotels, and casinos reward high-consumption customers with extra privileges and discounts. Banks offer lower fees and additional services to customers who do more business with them, and credit-card issuers offer cards that confer extra benefits and extra status.

Intensifying and prolonging the emotional benefits derived from consumption are powerful ways for marketers to stimulate sales. Marketers kindle dreams and imagination, which promote consumption; they awaken consumers' latent desires. Advertising frames how consumers perceive a product and consumption experience, as, say, exciting, fun, doing the best for your family, taking good care of yourself, fitting in with your friends. Advertising also encourages the tendency to attach meaning to possessions. Retailers create shopping environments to match the mood of the product and target consumers. Good product design increases satisfaction with ownership and use.

Of course, it is not only marketers who promote emotionally rewarding "affirmative" consumption. Harley-Davidson clubs deepen their members' affiliation by promoting consumption of additional gear. The many Christian churches that urged parishioners to see the film *The Passion of the Christ* were treating this consumption as a badge of faith. What the Girl Scouts are selling in their annual cookie drives is primarily the feeling of helping (or avoiding the guilt of not buying) and only secondarily the cookies. The connection between consumption and emotion harks back to the primordial mother who exhorts her child, "Eat, eat. If you're not eating my food, it's because you don't love me."

Despite all this, most marketers find it difficult to influence decisions on when, where, what, and how much to consume. And with the many factors affecting competitive activity and consumers' decisions, it is difficult to isolate the effects of any one marketing element. However, introducing new products into a category can lead to permanent increases in demand for that category. That was the finding of research that looked at 560 consumer product categories in the major Dutch supermarkets during a four-year period. In contrast, coupons and other price promotions had essentially no long-term effect on category demand.[16]

Dekimpe and Hanssens identify four scenarios found in markets. In two of them, marketing spending fails to produce long-term gains in either total category consumption or brand market share, although it may help maintain the status quo.

Things are different in the "evolving business practice" scenario, where sustained marketing spending reinforces broader strategies to grow the market. For example, in the 1970s and 1980s, Japanese automobile makers simultaneously improved quality, expanded distribution channels, built brand image, and priced aggressively to increase demand.

In the fourth scenario, a particularly effective short-term marketing push —for instance, Super Bowl advertising by Monster.com—can produce long-lasting changes in brand share or category consumption.[17] All in all, these sorts of results suggest that there are limits on the extent to which marketers can stimulate greater consumption of a brand or product category in the absence of new benefits to consumers.

Democratization of Consumption

None shall wear in his apparel: Cloth of gold, silver, tinseled satin, silk, or cloth mixed or embroidered with any gold or silver: except all degrees above viscounts, and viscounts, barons, and other persons of like degree, in doublets, jerkins, linings of cloaks, gowns, and hose.

—Elizabeth I[18]

In modern societies people take for granted equality of consumption rights: if the Smiths have the means, they can buy and consume whatever the Joneses consume. It isn't that there are no restrictions on consumption. Laws and regulations prohibit or limit time, place, and quantity of consumption of substances like alcohol. Minors cannot buy cigarettes. Certain drugs must be prescribed by doctors. Highly hazardous materials are available only to licensed operators. Some country-club memberships are available only to approved nominees. But equality of consumption rights means that any restrictions that apply to Smith apply equally to Jones.

Equality of consumption has not always been the norm. Possessions and consumption are visible indicators of social rank and wealth, and historically it seemed natural and right for the privileged to have exclusive rights to some goods—such as the imperial purple—and equally abhorrent for the lower classes to mimic their betters. A sumptuary law in colonial Massachusetts stated its "utter detestation and dislike that men and women of mean condition should take upon them the garb of gentlemen by wearing gold or silver lace . . . which, though allowable to persons of greater estates or more liberal education, we cannot but judge it intolerable."[19]

The democratization of consumption has taken firm hold in industrialized countries. In the context of the Great Depression, Franklin Roosevelt declared, "If the average citizen is guaranteed equal opportunity in the polling place, he must have equal opportunity in the market place."[20]

In addition to the right, consumers have the ability to consume, constrained mainly by their means or credit limits. Low costs of goods—including groceries, household items from discount stores, electronics or appliances with their declining prices, and cheap auto imports from Asia—along with the availability of consumer credit mean that most consumers can acquire most types of goods and services.[21] Middle-income buyers can move up from "adequate" goods to higher-quality goods and even luxuries. Vehicle ownership in the United States has risen to 85 percent of households.[22] Some 48 percent of families owned stock in publicly traded companies in 2004, up from about 40 percent a decade earlier.[23]

Consumption choices remain a badge of social class and status, but standards of taste come from all parts of society. Scores of knockoffs imitate luxury goods like Rolex watches. But other fads and fashions originate with teenagers in the East Village, the Bronx, or South Los Angeles and spread to the mainstream. "Coolhunters" working for marketers accelerate the process by tracking what "cool" kids consume.[24]

Marketers of luxury goods also do their part to democratize consumption. At the risk of diluting the cachet derived from exclusivity and costliness, as well as quality, some makers offer lower-priced versions of their traditional luxury products. Mercedes-Benz, for instance, brought out an A class of smaller vehicles. Burberry offers accessories that are more affordable to middle-income consumers than its iconic trench coat. Isaac Mizrahi sells outfits at Target.[25]

In the 1970s, when hi-fi components were considered a technically complex purchase sold through specialized audio dealers at high prices, Bernie Mitchell, CEO of U.S. Pioneer Electronics Corp., set out to bring good-quality sound to the mass market. He cut prices, offered decent basic equipment, distributed Pioneer products widely, and advertised broadly to the general public.[26] In the 1990s, sales of personal computers followed a similar path.

Marketers also create finer versions of mass-market products. Even if consumers cannot afford a luxury brand, premium versions of relatively small-ticket items like ice cream or coffee are within the reach of nearly everyone.

Technology-Enabled Consumption

Technology, too, democratizes consumption. Online retailing allows consumers in remote areas to gain access to nearly every product at competitive prices; they are no longer hostage to the prices charged by one or two local distributors. Small suppliers of specialized products can serve narrow niches worldwide. eBay has created a massive global marketplace where consumers can find products discoverable locally only by chance—such as a vintage tablecloth—and can purchase items other consumers are finished with. In a further democratization, eBay allows any consumer to finance consumption by reversing roles and acting as a seller as well as a buyer.

In short, the retail space is democratic in that it is the individual consumer who decides what and how much to consume. Marketers don't dictate consumption. They broker consumers' consumption needs and what's available. The match is not perfect, but technology lets marketers track people's consumption in close-to-real time and make quick adjustments of stock levels and pricing in response.

For example, a combination of manufacturing and information technology helps innovative marketers refashion the clothing business. Benetton, an Italian company, fabricates all its sweaters in gray and only in the final stage does it dye the finished garments depending on what colors are selling. Zara, a Spanish company, has cut fashion cycles from a matter of months to weeks or days; it monitors daily sales trends in each of its two thousand stores, quickly sews up small batches, and delivers assortments of merchandise customized to the demand and replenishment needs of each store.[27]

Consumers gain in several ways: they see merchandise assortments with popular products, encounter fewer instances of out-of-stock items and sizes, and pay lower prices when they hold out for marked-down prices on slow-moving items. During crucial selling times like the Christmas season, when retailers are eager to boost sales, the resulting savings can lighten the burden on consumers' pocketbooks. Driven by computer algorithms that consider the percentage of seats sold and number of days or hours to flight time, airlines reward consumers who book far in advance, travel at off-peak times, or fill vacant seats at the last minute.

Technology can also let people engage with other consumers in shaping consumption. A popular feature of Apple's online iTunes music store is iMix. This online space lets customers upload personal mixes of favorite songs, or playlists, they have created as well as browse and rate others' playlists. In less than a year after launch, customers contributed more than 150,000 playlists. Going beyond the usual circle of family, friends, and coworkers, iTunes customers can democratically share their consumption experience with any other customer who goes online.[28]

Consumption Communities

Daniel Boorstin coined the term *consumption communities* to describe the social affiliations created by consumption in the nineteenth- and twentieth-century United States, and he contrasted the unifying effect of using similar or similarly branded objects in "invisible" consumption communities with the dissipating ties of physical communities in a highly mobile society: "Never before had so many men been united by so many things."[29] He also noted their adaptability and availability: "These consumption communities were quick; they were nonideological; they were democratic; they were public, and vague, and rapidly shifting."[30]

Boorstin's consumption communities aren't very different from online communities, such as the one centered on the iPod. They're also similar to marketers' lifestyle segments, which group people by what they consume and want. Lifestyle groupings may correspond with demographics, such as where people live, their age group, their income level, their profession, or their religious affiliation, but don't necessarily have to. Global segments cross national boundaries, grouping consumers in London, Singapore, or Mumbai who share similar aspiration and consumption patterns. These groupings are fluid and mutable, responsive to shifts in the marketplace.

From everyday life to the afterlife, consumption is closely related to people's self-image and self-identity. Driving the household minivan might reinforce a suburban parent's image of self as family chauffeur and errand-runner, whereas driving the sedan might accentuate the wage-earner aspect. The link between possessions and sense of self vividly emerges in the case of loss or damage. The monetary and time loss is magnified by the accompanying sense of personal injury.[31] For some, attachment of objects to self extends past death. From royal burial sites in ancient Egypt and China to modern times, possessions have accompanied people to their final resting places.

Consumption and possession of objects are "a major contributor and reflection of our identities," concludes Russell Belk.[32] Possessions can extend the self literally—a new tool allows you to accomplish a task you otherwise could not—or symbolically: a framed diploma reinforces a sense of competence. A platinum American Express card conveys a sense of status and enhances self-esteem. The freedom of consumption in open economies goes hand in hand with the freedom to develop and express a unique personal identity.

Happiness and Consumption

Can one desire too much of a good thing?

—William Shakespeare[33]

The United States has been labeled a materialistic society for good reason. Encouraged by advertisers, retailers, the media, and credit companies, Americans are devoted to spending and acquiring. Self-help books and motivational speakers advise people that anything is possible and within reach. In the mall culture, shopping is a prime-time leisure activity. Seventeenth-century

Puritans equated wealth with fulfilling one's God-appointed calling to pursue a suitable occupation.[34] Now some televangelists preach the "prosperity gospel" and point to their opulent lifestyles as proof of faith.[35]

Moreover, Americans adopt materialistic attitudes at a young age. A survey of youths in fifteen countries revealed that the Americans were more apt to want to be rich and famous, and to believe that brands define their social status.[36] Schor reports that 63 percent of ten- to thirteen-year-old Americans said their overriding goal is to become rich, and she concludes that children "are the household members with the most passionate consumer desires, and are most closely tethered to products, brands, and the latest trends."[37] Through family examples and television at home, through peer pressure and Channel One advertising at school, children learn to equate happiness with consumption. In a media-saturated culture, children covet the wealth and lifestyles of sports heroes and entertainers.

In expanding, mobile societies, people can escape their origins. A mobile population calibrates status by what people have, and the brands they use, more than by their family backgrounds. As tens of millions of Chinese enter the middle class and move from rural to urban areas, their rate of consumption is steadily increasing, and global brands help shape their tastes. Although Chinese consumers remain price conscious, they, like their Western counterparts, embrace products and brands that project an aura of success.[38]

But materialistic adults and children—those who covet income and possessions—are less happy than their unmaterialistic counterparts. Researchers say they have lower self-esteem, more anxiety, and poorer social relationships.[39]

Can Wealth Buy Happiness?

Economists, psychologists, and sociologists have all addressed the age-old question of whether actual wealth can buy happiness.[40] Setting aside the problems involved in measuring happiness, surveys consistently find, as one would expect, that people in rich countries like the United States or Switzerland are happier than people in poor countries like Bangladesh. But surprisingly, once a country's level of per capita income reaches a moderate threshold—about US$10,000—there are small, if any, increases in its citizens' sense of well-being.[41]

For instance, in the United States, Japan, and other countries, average life satisfaction has stayed flat since the end of World War II, even though the GDP per capita has climbed steadily. In the United States, income tripled during this period, but life satisfaction scores remained constant.[42] In part, that is because there is always a gap between what people have and what they want; increases in national income levels are accompanied by increases in material aspirations. An economist would say that these aspirations are essential because they motivate economic growth. But national well-being also depends on social capital and political capital—people in stable, democratic societies are happier—as well as on economic capital.[43]

Still, these conclusions are based on averaging scores across entire populations. How do individuals within a country compare with each other? The good news is that most people are happy, if *happy* is defined as "feeling slightly positive most of the time."[44] Also, as one would expect, people with more money are indeed happier. But in the wealthier countries, happiness levels off at a certain income level. Beyond that point, more money produces only very small gains in happiness.[45]

What about an individual whose income level changes over time? Does starting poor and striking it rich lead to happiness? The evidence is mixed. Winning the lottery can increase happiness, but big fluctuations in income from year to year can decrease happiness. Also, if your income rises over time but so does everyone else's around you, then your happiness doesn't change very much.[46]

Lawrence and Nohria postulate that one of four fundamental human drives is to acquire objects and experiences that improve our status relative to others.[47] Does the display of superior status lead to happiness? Thorstein Veblen introduced the term *conspicuous consumption* to describe the phenomenon of people choosing to buy certain goods in order to advertise their social standing and not because of the intrinsic enjoyment they get from consuming the good.[48]

Clearly, wealthier people can flaunt their social status by buying a Lexus instead of a Toyota or staying at the Four Seasons rather than the Marriott. The question is whether they get more intrinsic enjoyment from the Lexus than the Toyota. Veblen's theory finds support from a study showing that wealthier households spend a greater share of their income on luxury goods visible to others.[49]

Perhaps the ultimate luxury consumption in the United States occurs through philanthropy. If donors choose, recognition for big gifts can be highly visible and long lasting, with their names literally engraved on museum walls or university portals.

But, says economist Robert Frank, there is considerable evidence that buying a larger house or a more expensive car when your income rises doesn't lead to greater happiness. Instead, the ability to afford "*inconspicuous* goods—such as freedom from a long commute or a stressful job" and the ability to devote more time "to families and friends, to exercise, sleep, travel, and other restorative activities" result in "healthier, longer—and happier lives."[50]

This advice echoes that of commentators who argue that the European lifestyle, which places more weight on free time, the family, and the community, is superior to the U.S. model.[51] Although it's a gross generalization, there is some truth to the saying that Americans live to work, and Europeans work to live. U.S. workers, whose benefits include fewer vacation days on average than workers in other industrialized countries, don't even use all the days allocated to them.[52]

The Social Side of Consumption

So materialistic attitudes and ever-higher salaries don't necessarily lead to happiness. Instead, economists, sociologists, and psychologists find that strong social relationships are a hugely important component of individual happiness and national well-being.[53] But this observation actually helps explain the lure of consumption. Building social relationships is one reason—though, of course, not the only reason—that people keep consuming.

U.S. consumers spend $6 billion annually on gear for the 4 million babies born each year.[54] The cribs, strollers, and high chairs of fifty years ago have been joined by a stream of inventions designed to make babies safe, happy, and smart.[55] From a utilitarian perspective, it's baffling that parents buy such products; babies apparently are no safer, happier, or smarter today than before. In part, parents may be keeping up with their peers or avoiding the guilt of not buying if there is a chance the product makes a difference. But from the perspective of social ties this consumption makes sense: most parents hope to take the best possible care of their children and gladly consume products that promise to help them do so and, perhaps more important, make them feel they are doing so. Despite the spiraling costs of higher education, many parents highly value it as a launch pad for their offspring (and a brand-name education can furnish bragging rights as well). And some parents may hope that well-off children will, in turn, look after them in their old age.

On the other hand, parents don't necessarily enjoy taking care of their children as much as they enjoy certain consumption activities. A recent study kept track of how nine hundred women felt during the day as they engaged in activities such as working, commuting, socializing, shopping, housework, and child care. Watching television and shopping ranked fairly high on the list—higher than taking care of children, which rated lower than preparing food or talking on the phone.[56] And in line with Frank's suggestions on areas where investments in improving happiness could pay off, commuting and work proved to be the least enjoyable activities.

Perhaps people are blocking out or forgetting simpler sources of satisfaction—booking a costly cruise instead of sitting in their own backyard, or playing the latest video game instead of hanging out with friends. For driven achievers, leisure seems to mutate into work and consumption. You hire a coach to help perfect your tennis game, consult a landscaper and invest in expensive plants and equipment so that your garden looks like a magazine photo, buy the latest-model high-end mountain bike to shave minutes off competition time. To be sure, plenty of people relax in front of a television set, but TV programming and ads further promulgate the consumption lifestyle.

Whether or not materialistic attitudes and consumption produce lasting happiness, there's no doubt that consumption experiences—dining out, movie-going, occupying a new home, or driving a new car—can bring at least transient satisfaction. Shopping—the search itself as well as the things acquired—can be pleasurable. For some consumers, bingeing on consumption temporarily alleviates unhappiness. Many societies condone and formalize binge consumption during feast days, holidays, weddings, and other ceremonies.

Prudent and Imprudent Consumption

Bankruptcy is perhaps the greatest and most humiliating calamity which can befall an innocent man.

—Adam Smith[57]

Common wisdom about prudent consumption used to be simple: pay as you go, put aside something for a rainy day, save up a nest egg for your old age. But in modern economies, consumers have wider latitude. Easy access to mortgages and credit, along with expectations of steady income, means that pay as you go isn't the only option. Pensions and Social Security supplement nest eggs. At the same time, much of the practical wisdom still applies: spending on necessities comes before spending on discretionary items. Current income must cover payments on debts. Savings are needed to buffer unexpected contingencies, such as loss of a job.

Nobel laureate economist Franco Modigliani theorized that rational and far-sighted consumers will plan their consumption over their entire lifetime.[58] In this life-cycle view of consumption, consumers recognize that their earnings will most likely rise during their working years and that they need to accumulate savings and other assets for retirement. Typically, consumers want a consumption plan that maximizes quality of life throughout their lifetimes and are concerned with maintaining a reasonable standard of living during retirement.

One implication of this goal, in combination with uneven earnings, is that people will consume more than they earn during their early working years. They accomplish this by accumulating debt. Later, as income rises, earnings exceed consumption, and consumers begin paying off debt. Once debts are paid, consumers will begin to accumulate wealth, which will reach a peak at retirement. During retirement, when income ceases or drops sharply, consumers will draw down their accumulated wealth to finance consumption.[59] If all works well, consumers won't face an impoverished old age.

Although the general idea of a life cycle of consumption is still accepted, economists have modified it to account for real-world behavior. In general, people are less forward-looking than the original model presumes. Younger people seem to "underconsume" in terms of the theory; they borrow less against future earnings, perhaps because they estimate future income conservatively or don't qualify for loans. In the middle stage, many people at the peak of their earning power "overconsume"; they don't save enough for retirement. In the late stage, the elderly don't spend down their assets, particularly their home equity, as much as would be predicted, possibly because they want to leave an inheritance.[60]

For the most part, however, households prudently manage their consumption in line with their finances. They don't necessarily map out a consumption strategy over their lifetime and run all the numbers on spreadsheets, but they approximate economists' models of a rational strategy.[61] With the help of public and private pensions, relatively few retirees in Europe and the United States face significant hardship. Retirees significantly cut down on consumption, but on average their happiness or welfare doesn't appear to drop significantly.[62] There is evidence that the leisure time gained by retirees allows them to participate in activities—for example, cooking or do-it-yourself home repairs—that substitute for purchasing products.[63] Thrifty shoppers who collect coupons and compare prices can cut spending but maintain consumption. Some prefer to consume less by disposing of possessions and downsizing their households.

Concerns About Savings Rates

On the other hand, concerns are voiced about the extremely low savings rate of U.S. households.[64] One estimate of 2002 rates put the euro area countries at 9.6 percent, Japan at 5.2 percent, and the United States at a mere 2.4 percent.[65] More recent U.S. savings rates are lower still—a negative 1.2 percent in December 2006.[66] These differences may reflect differences in the extent of public services provided to households in different regions, the way households are taxed, or computational differences in the treatment of Social Security versus private pensions. Yet after adjusting for these variations, the gap between euro area and U.S. saving rates actually increases.[67]

Another explanation is that households view purchases of durable goods such as cars, furniture, and major appliances as assets or investments rather than as consumption.[68] (Governments count them as consumption.) Americans own more vehicles per capita than people in any other country, and the median value of these vehicles rose more than 14 percent from 1998 to 2001.[69] In addition, the active market for secondhand cars means that they can readily be converted into cash.

The situation with housing is similar. Consumers count home equity as savings, although governments don't. A high proportion—about 68 percent—of U.S. families own their own home. The $14 trillion in real estate assets owned by U.S. households is almost double the amount they possess in mutual funds and stocks.[70] The U.S. government reinforces the personal drive toward home ownership by allowing tax deductions of mortgage interest and providing low-interest loans to eligible first-time buyers.

U.S. household savings rates are low and declining, but net worth is rising. From the 1990s to the early 2000s, the overall median value of homes and median home equity rose significantly.[71] In a year when families see the market values of their homes or financial holdings increase, they feel less need to set aside other savings.[72] This behavior may not be prudent in the long run—it leaves families susceptible to bubbles in the housing and financial markets—but neither is it irrational to count capital gains, with an appropriate risk discount, as a form of savings. And households appear to differentiate between liquid and illiquid assets. It's estimated that spending goes up by 19 cents for every dollar of capital gain on corporate equities. But when homes appreciate, spending increases by much less.[73]

Concerns About Debt Ratios

Worries about imprudent consumption don't end with savings rates. U.S. indebtedness rates are equally a matter of concern. Over the past two decades, the share of household income committed to paying the interest and principal on debt—the debt service ratio—rose, to about 13 percent in 2004. A more general measure of recurring financial obligations, which includes items such as property taxes, home owners' insurance, rents, and auto leases, has risen to more than 18 percent.[74] Any such increases mean that households have less money available to consume goods and services and a smaller cushion against adversities.

To the extent that a household's assets rise in concert with its debt ratio, it's buffered against financial distress. This has been the case for home owners, but not for renters. Their debt service ratios went up sharply during the 1990s, and they don't have home equity to fall back on. Some of these renters are younger workers who are paying student and car loans and can expect to improve their financial picture later. But others are at risk.[75]

Bankruptcy is the ultimate expression of financial distress. In 2003, there were more than 1.6 million personal bankruptcy filings in the United States, an historic high.[76] Canada, too, saw a rising trend in bankruptcy over the past twenty-five years, although at a lower rate per capita—about 2.7 filings per thousand in 2003 versus about 8 per thousand for the United States.[77] Many reasons have been given for the high U.S. rates, including an out-of-control consumer culture and mass mailings of credit cards to households, which push people to consume; the rising costs of basic necessities like housing and utilities; job losses and stagnant or falling wages; medical bills; poverty; divorce; and opportunistic abuse of the bankruptcy system.

There's evidence to support all these contentions, but one observation is striking: "More than 90 percent of the families in bankruptcy qualify as middle class . . . [they] are co-workers, neighbors and families woven throughout the fabric of American society."[78] About two-thirds of filers in 1981 had suffered an interruption in income that caused them to sharply increase their debt load to the point where they couldn't pay it back even after they went back to work: the average family in bankruptcy owed two times its annual income in nonmortgage debt.[79]

Other analyses detect a greater inclination over the years for people to file for bankruptcy due to a lessening social stigma.[80] Historically, consumers owed debt to family and acquaintances, local merchants, or banks; bankruptcy meant a violation of trust in a personal relationship. Now, financial relationships are conducted with faceless institutions; bankruptcy is less apt to be seen as causing personal harm. And it is relatively easy for debtors to escape social ostracism by relocating to a new community.

In 2005 Congress passed legislation that requires a greater number of bankruptcy filers to set up five-year debt repayment plans instead of writing off most of their unsecured debts. Even so, the law is predicated on giving consumers a fresh start, in contrast to many European countries, where until recently there were no bankruptcy provisions and consumers had lifelong liability for debt obligations.[81]

Credit Access

Overall, the democratization of finance—the ready availability of mortgage debt, car loans, and unsecured debt such as consumer credit cards—gives prudent consumers the financial freedom to consume things that otherwise would be out of reach.[82] In many developing countries, financial institutions' willingness or ability to extend credit to emerging consumers lags households' ability to pay. Alternatively, in developing, as well as developed, countries, consumers may be able to obtain direct credit from marketers. Local shopkeepers often run tabs. Manufacturers of high-ticket goods may offer lease-purchase or extended-payment plans. In Turkey, Arçelik, the country's dominant manufacturer of major household appliances, maintains extensive distribution networks for its brands. Local agents know the neighborhoods, can assess the creditworthiness of prospective buyers, and can offer appropriate extended-payment plans.

In the long run, greater democratization of credit offered by financial institutions will be critical to increased consumption and economic growth in developing economies. For example, most Mexican consumers have for years lacked easy access to banking and credit. Major purchases had to be paid for in cash, so consumption of durable goods was low. Houses were built room by room over time, paid for from savings. Since 2000, however, consumer credit has tripled. Now, more middle-class families can buy homes, cars, and major appliances on credit. As a result, sales of high-ticket items have gone up, and volatility in consumer spending has decreased.[83]

Societal Problems of Too Much or Too Little Consumption

Our houses are such unwieldy property that we are often imprisoned rather than housed in them.

—Henry David Thoreau[84]

In affluent societies, consumption possibilities abound. To all appearances, there is so much inventory of goods held in supply chains and in households that the world could stop manufacturing for a year and there would be no shortages.

That isn't to say that underconsumption and inequalities don't exist in affluent societies. Underconsumption of medical services is a serious problem for the many Americans who are uninsured. Not everyone can afford higher education, even public higher education. Poorer families struggle to afford winter heating bills. Children go hungry. Some consumers make poor consumption trade-offs, failing to spend on things like needed home repairs to maintain the value of their housing investment and instead spending on things that bring immediate gratification.

Ironically, though, overconsumption is a problem for the poor as well as those who are better off. Overconsumption of food, combined with a lack of balance in diet, results in obesity and related health problems. Overconsumption of tobacco and alcohol is a leading cause of disease. A sedentary lifestyle, aggravated by heavy consumption of television and an automobile culture, also induces poor health. Parents who try to make children happy by buying them things may substitute consumption for parental guidance and engagement.

Observers also worry that excessive private consumption of goods and services may degrade democracy. Civic associations, religious institutions, and other community groups—the associations Tocqueville saw as the building blocks of U.S. democracy—compete with consumption for people's time, attention, and money. Consumption encourages people to focus more on themselves than on society or the public good; on what they can get, rather than what they can give; on benefits rather than responsibilities. College students with a consumption mentality, for example, expect to receive a good grade for a course in exchange for paying for the product. If people have only a finite level of loyalty that they can distribute among loved ones and friends, their community, their church, their political party, and brands, then loyalty toward brands and consumption—the goal of media advertising—subtracts from other public and private loyalties.

Spurred by concerns about overconsumption, individuals and societies occasionally try to cut back. Millions embark on diets in usually futile attempts to lose weight. In the spirit of Thoreau or Gandhi, some consumers embrace voluntary simplicity and shed possessions and consumption to achieve a more harmonious and purposeful life.[85] Others get fed up with having too much clutter and opt to consume services or experiences rather than buy new things.

Political and moral beliefs drive some consumers to limit consumption. Animal-rights activists don't consume products like furs or animal-tested cosmetics, and they mount protests to dissuade other consumers from doing so. In the 1960s, a long-running consumer boycott of California grapes reinforced the labor movement led by Cesar Chavez to improve the welfare of migrant farm workers. The slow-food movement based in Europe rejects American-style fast food and eating-on-the-run habits in order to preserve locally produced foods and the custom of preparing the evening meal as a family social event.[86]

Paradoxically, these kinds of voluntary cutbacks can give rise to other consumption opportunities. The Body Shop, for instance, created a market niche for cosmetics produced without animal testing. The appeal of the slow-food movement has increased tourism to the member cities of the International Network of Slow Cities.[87] Disposing of unwanted items on eBay extends consumption of stuff that otherwise would go to the landfill. Charitable contributions from wealthier people cutting down on their personal consumption helps increase recipients' consumption of necessities.

National governments at times intervene to limit consumption, often without much success. Major emergencies are needed to galvanize consumers into compliance. During and after World War II, for example, citizens in the United States and Britain patriotically submitted to government-imposed rationing, for the most part willingly.[88] Prewar Germany alternated between trying to stimulate mass consumption for the good of the economy and discouraging consumption of particular goods for ideological and armament reasons; citizens were much more receptive to the former messages.[89] Consumers may endorse limiting the consumption of foreign goods—a common goal of nationalistic governments—in the abstract, but few are prepared to observe it at the checkout counter.

Social opposition to certain forms of consumption leads governments —even those most committed to free markets—to ban or restrict consumption of things like tobacco, alcohol, narcotics, indecent material, and gambling. But consumers find ways around restrictions, and criminal enterprises exploit prohibitions to serve markets that are off limits to legitimate marketers.

More successful are affirmative disclosure regulations designed to protect consumers from unsafe consumption of food, pharmaceutical drugs, automobiles, and financial services. Painful as it may be for pharmaceutical companies like Merck to withdraw profitable drugs like Vioxx when unintended side effects come to light, it's part of the bargain society has made: in return for limited governmental oversight, companies are free to produce and market, and consumers are free to consume, as long as consumer health and safety are not endangered.

Rather than impose bans and regulations, governments can indirectly influence consumption through tax policies. Taxes may reflect judgments on the social desirability of certain forms of consumption or offset their societal costs. In Massachusetts, for example, the general state sales tax does not apply to grocery-store food purchases because they are considered a necessity. California's high taxes on gasoline purchases help fund highway construction and maintenance but may also discourage consumption.

Heavy consumption of natural resources like water, energy, and tropical forests by some nations can have far-reaching environmental consequences for other nations. For example, global warming affects all countries, whether or not their consumption contributes to the problem. Inequities in resource use or competition for limited resources can aggravate economic, political, and military disputes. Even among developed countries, the United States consumes a disproportionate share of energy: approximately twenty-five barrels of oil annually per capita, versus twelve for Germany, and sixteen for Japan.[90] What will happen as developing nations—China, India, or others—try to obtain a greater share?

Nevertheless, underconsumption is typically a greater concern for governments, and perhaps especially for democracies, than is overconsumption or "bad" consumption. Everywhere, vastly more government energies are directed toward ensuring that affordable goods and services are available than toward cutting consumption. Only with great prodding do states enter into pacts that could shift or diminish consumption, particularly of goods required for basic well-being.

Marketers certainly share the goal of increasing consumption. At the same time, far-sighted marketers may exercise restraint in choosing the kinds of consumption they promote. In response to increasing concerns about childhood obesity, for example, Kraft Foods, Inc., announced it would shift advertising of sugar-laden Oreos and Kool-Aid away from children between the ages of six and eleven.[91] The soft drink industry recently reached a voluntary agreement to restrict the marketing of high-calorie carbonated beverages in school vending machines. No doubt the long-term goal is to retain consumers' good faith in the companies marketing these products. So, too, far-sighted marketers should be sensitive to social and cultural concerns about consumption practices and the public interest as they spread the doctrine of consumption around the world.

Globally, marketers will likely see continuing and increasing pressure to cut down on consumption, or forms of consumption, that affect the environment and the availability of natural resources. The Kyoto agreement to help avert global warming by reducing the emission of greenhouse gases may be faltering, but the issue will not go away. Neither will concerns about the use of pesticides, chemical fertilizers, and genetically altered seeds in farming. In the democracy of the marketplace, consumers may increasingly choose to consume those products and services they consider to be healthy and environmentally sound or otherwise socially valuable.

CHAPTER 3

Choice

UBU (You Be You)

FROM CHOOSING among two hundred varieties of cereal, to deciding which town to live in and what occupation to pursue, to electing a political representative, choice is an integral part of life. Most people in Western societies hold a deep-seated belief that choice is essential to individuals' well-being, to democracy, and to transactions in the marketplace. Images of Soviet citizens standing in hours-long lines to buy bread or waiting years for a household appliance symbolized for many the differences in the quality of life when choice is limited.

Individual choice as a fundamental principle is expressed in two key texts: the U.S. Declaration of Independence, which ushered in modern representative democracies, and Adam Smith's *Wealth of Nations*, which in the same year formulated the theory of free-market economies. The Declaration asserted that a just government is one that is freely chosen and that personal liberty means not only freedom from restraint and compulsion but the freedom of each individual to choose how to pursue a fulfilling life.

Smith's theory of the market economy stated that an optimal economy results when firms are permitted to produce any goods or services they choose, to offer them for sale, to brand and advertise them, and to price them. Correspondingly, consumers need to be free to choose the items that best suit their needs and pocketbooks. Under these conditions, the market mechanism—Smith's "invisible hand"—rewards the firms that supply what people choose and punishes those that offer things consumers do not value.

Competition to meet consumers' emerging demands is a source of dynamism in the economy. Free choice—of consumers and producers—to engage in exchange drives competition, efficiency, quality, and innovation.

But in practice, things are not so simple as theory suggests. The dynamism of market economies has worked so well that consumers must choose among a relentlessly expanding number of options. Marketers introduce endless product variations little different from the competition's. Consumers so far have displayed a virtually limitless appetite for more choice, but some people question whether an overload point has been reached.[1] Consumers can't process all these choices in a considered way. Marketers try to please consumers but may fail to anticipate or satisfy their precise preferences.

In contrast, the political marketplace offers a relatively limited range of options, and citizens may or may not obtain outcomes that accord with their preferences. Nevertheless, choice is essential to representative democracies.

Choice and Desire

Choice is deliberate desire.

—Aristotle[2]

Choice springs from desire—that is, choice is necessary to reconcile multiple desires and multiple ways of satisfying them. Drawing on the thinking of scientists and humanists—from evolutionary biologists, psychologists, anthropologists, and economists, to neuroscientists, neurologists, archeologists, paleontologists, historians, philosophers, and linguists—Lawrence and Nohria posit four primary innate drives that are hardwired in our brains and shape the choices we make. These are the drives to acquire things that improve our status, to bond with others, to make sense of the world, and to defend what matters to us.[3] The multiple reasons to acquire are apparent in our appetite to consume a variety of goods and experiences.

Desire is deep seated and emotional. At the extreme, it leads to addictive behavior, where the desire to consume outweighs the desire to stop. But classical economics posits that choice is rational: level-headed, well-informed individuals coolly weigh the pros and cons of various options against the benefits they expect to receive or the goals they wish to satisfy.

How then are choice and desire reconciled? Current thinking holds that, in most instances, choices are based on both reason and emotion. (Or on similar dichotomies, such as rationality and intuition, cognition and emotion, deliberation and reaction, the conscious and the unconscious.) A man buys a Polo shirt because he's attached to the brand but also because it's made well; the latter is sometimes used as a rationalization for the former.

How do people make choices when they are simultaneously driven to bond with others and to acquire for themselves? Abraham Maslow's influential theory of the hierarchy of needs says that humans are motivated to fulfill needs in a particular order, from lower-level needs to higher-order needs; generally we must meet lower-level needs before moving on to the next higher level. In Maslow's terminology, people's most basic needs are physiological, followed by safety, love, esteem, cognitive, aesthetic, self-actualization, and self-transcendence needs.[4] A hierarchy intuitively makes sense. Individuals must first be able to subsist before they can seek the approval of others.

Other psychologists have proposed different hierarchies. William James, for example, hypothesized three categories of human needs: material (physiological, safety); social (belongingness, esteem); and spiritual. Social belonging and bonding with others is a component of most theories.[5]

Often, marketers' approaches to building brands parallel the psychological categories of human needs. They begin by laying a foundation of functional superiority. They proceed to show who uses the brand and how it can be used. They then communicate how the brand's core values harmonize with people's higher-order needs. This last step is intended to build an enduring emotional bond with consumers, to the exclusion of competing brands.

Not only does marketing influence brand choice, but it also acts to create or make consumers aware of an underlying need or want that the product can fulfill. A recurrent criticism is that marketing stimulates desire for needs and wants that are not "necessary," "true," or "natural." Hegel, however, proposed that a distinctively human characteristic, and one prevalent in culturally refined societies, is the ability to want products of the imagination and, indeed, to perceive them as needs. The marketplace's ability to create needs, and not merely satisfy existing needs, is a source of dynamism. On the other hand, says Hegel, problems arise when individuals' consumption choices are overly influenced by fashions of the marketplace rather than being grounded in a strong conception of what one's life should be.[6]

According to psychologists, people inherently like having choices. It provides a feeling of control and increases our intrinsic motivation and sense of satisfaction; conversely, lack of choice and control leads to ill effects in health, life satisfaction, and intrinsic motivation.[7] For some consumers, the process of confronting choice and then choosing is enjoyable; shopping is a pleasure. eBay appeals to the thrill of choosing and winning, perhaps more than the actual possession of the object. Still, choice does not always lead to happiness or even satisfaction. Choosing one option means forgoing the possible pleasures of another. Choosing too many options can lead to credit-card debt. Making a choice that doesn't turn out well can bring feelings of inadequacy, regret, and blame.

Choice means taking responsibility for actions. Choice means constructing the self.

Choice and Identity

Sir, a man may be so much of everything,
that he is nothing of anything.

—Samuel Johnson[8]

Choice allows individuals to construct their own personal identities. At the same time, choice expresses social standing and group affiliation. Buying a Mercedes or a Cadillac signifies that the owner has achieved a comfortable level of wealth. Choosing a Cadillac over a Mercedes may signal a strong patriotic attitude or the owner's desire to fit in with a community where the norm is to drive U.S. cars. Consumers' preferences are influenced by the general culture and by the attitudes and opinions of the groups they belong to or wish to belong to.

North American and Western European cultures emphasize a concept of the self as independent and autonomous. It follows that choice is an opportunity to assert our individuality and uniqueness. Western philosophers, politicians, economists, and psychologists have assumed that choice is not only desirable but also critical to autonomy and the sense of freedom.

Asian cultures emphasize a concept of the self as interdependent with others. Individuals strive for interconnectedness, harmony, and belonging with social in-groups. In a collectivist culture, choice is an opportunity for individuals to conform with the group. Choice may be less critical to sense of self and may even be threatening if the result could mark an individual as being different from the group. In traditional Japanese schools having and making choices are not part of students' normal routines. Daily rituals encourage students to conform to the social group.[9]

Weber and Hsee caution that national differences can be either culturally based or a result of more transient circumstances.[10] And results may be surprising. For example, these authors found that in making financial decisions, Americans are significantly more averse to risk than are Chinese consumers. It appears that members of collectivist cultures can take greater financial risks because their social networks cushion them against adverse consequences. At the same time, they need to be much more cautious about taking social risks. Germans, who are closer to Americans in political system, heritage, and socioeconomic conditions but closer to Chinese in degree of collectivism, also appear more willing to take financial risks.[11] Americans frequently cushion risk through the legal system and insurance.

But despite such differences, it's closer to the truth to say that all choice is inherently social. It expresses personal identity and group identity. The teenager who must have the latest adidas sneaker "because that's the only kind anyone wears" but insists on buying a pair of sunglasses "because nobody else has them" embodies the complex way group norms and individual tastes affect choice. And this teenager could be American, French, or Japanese.

Individualistic and collectivist cultures differ mainly in the relative emphasis they place on the value of fashioning a unique identity versus a common identity. In societies that offer a range of choices, both values are present. In collectivist China, consumers quickly embraced a wide variety of new clothing styles as soon as restrictions were lifted.

Group Identity

Every high school student expresses identity by affiliating with a small or a sizable subculture, which may range in size from a few members to a dominant group. Those who don't choose a subgroup will be placed in one anyway by their peers. Consumer choices are integral to subculture identity. An ethnographic study of teenagers in nine places—Argentina, Australia, Czechoslovakia, France, Germany, Mexico, Puerto Rico, the United Kingdom, and the United States—concluded that choice of music and clothing, along with attitudes toward "the establishment" and preferences for free-time activities, were the key defining features of subcultures. These subcultures are not unique to a school, city, region, or country. Rather, teenagers have created global templates for subcultures—such as "rappers," "rockers," and "mainstream"—linked by a common awareness gained from broadcast media and the Internet.[12]

Choice based on group affinity is not just a matter of style or fashion trends. It can be integral to self-identity. Many adults, for example, choose to live in communities where inhabitants have interests and lifestyles similar to their own. French sociologist Pierre Bourdieu and others emphasize the manifestation of social distinctions and social class in consumption choices, as well as consumption's role in creating personal social "capital."[13] Choices may also contain an element of competition to improve one's status. Among sports fans are those who compete to obtain the best seats at the stadium or the largest-screen TV.

Consumers' choices are framed by the products that are available and socially desirable in their groups. But consumer choices themselves can create a sense of group identity. Recent car buyers routinely check out other drivers who've bought the same model to see who's part of the "club." Brand choice can even attain cultlike status, as with Harley-Davidson motorcycles. Devotees of Macintosh computers see themselves as a community of creative, nonconforming individualists set apart from the lemming-like masses of Windows users depicted in Apple Computer's famous "1984" television commercial.

In modern societies, any one person is a member of a network of overlapping groups defined by family, ethnicity, neighborhood, work, religion, sports, hobbies, politics, volunteer associations, and so on. Alexis de Tocqueville famously noted the importance of civic institutions to U.S. society and democracy.[14] Crass as it may seem, in a materialistic society, brand choice can give consumers the same sense of participation—what critic Naomi Klein calls a "kind of pseudo-spirituality"—formerly filled by other affiliations.[15] Starbucks, according to its chairman, Howard Schultz, aspires to be a "neighborhood porch," the "third place" in your life after your home and your place of work. Disney's planned community in Florida, called Celebration, celebrates a semimythical America patterned after Norman Rockwell's idealized vision of a socially cohesive New England village.

Choice in the Global Market

Paradoxically, at the global level greater freedom of consumer choice brings less diversity and greater homogenization. Individual choice is freer and more diverse, but much of the world is gravitating toward a single universe of goods, services, and media. Consumers in Shanghai eat at McDonald's, snack at TCBY, wear Western-style fashions, shop at Carrefour and Wal-Mart, furnish their homes at IKEA, and drive Hondas and Fords.[16] Crowds are exposed to huge billboards cajoling them to drink Pepsi or Coke. Chinese authorities have resisted democratic politics more effectively than they have the seductions of consumer choice. Advertising and entertainment across the world shape the notion that the freedom to be part of global brand communities is the true meaning of the pursuit of happiness.

To be fair, the global market is receptive to influences from a variety of cultures. Eventually China, along with India, will have a large voice. There will be global brands that are Chinese and Indian, just as there are now global Japanese and Korean brands. And, as with Japanese brands—which forty years ago were regarded as cheap quality but now dominate the electronics and, increasingly, the automotive markets—consumers everywhere will willingly express their identity by choosing these new Chinese and Indian brands.

The Provision of Choice

Taking sorting as a central concept . . . leads directly to a fundamental explanation of the contribution of marketing to the overall economy of human effort in producing and distributing goods.

—Wroe Alderson[17]

In economies of scarcity, producers or intermediaries hold the balance of power over consumers. Consumers must accept the goods that are available, however shoddy, and are grateful they have the means to pay for them. In economies of abundance and oversupply, consumers gain power. To be successful, producers must cater to consumers' needs and desires and turn to marketing to influence choice.

In well-supplied marketplaces, the role played by marketing depends on the industry type and the firm's strategy. If success is based on dependably providing commodity-type products like wheat or oil at competitive prices, then marketing may appear to play a lesser role. (Even here, however, the quality of the exchange, including service terms and delivery, may lead customers to choose one supplier over another.) If success depends on identifying distinct customer needs, providing differentiated products and services, and creating brand loyalty, then marketing comes to the forefront. That's true of most businesses selling to individual consumers, and it's also true of many businesses selling to other businesses.

Retail salespeople, advertising, and other forms of marketing communications are the visible face of marketing. Market segmentation and targeting are the nuts and bolts. Segmentation describes the marketplace; the assumption is that not all consumers are alike. So marketers sort customers into groups, or segments, with particular needs, preferences, and priorities. Targeting selects the segments to serve; the assumption is that the firm can't serve all of them equally well. Marketers look for segments where the firm has a competitive advantage. Good marketers also know which segments not to target.

It may be argued that targeting is undemocratic, in the sense that it is exclusionary. To be sure, there are market failures, where populations are underserved or have no choice at all, because it is not profitable to serve them. But these problems usually stem not from segmentation and targeting but rather from factors such as geographical remoteness, small market size (e.g., patients with rare diseases), poverty, or high crime rates. And targeting is democratic in the sense of respecting each consumer's wants and needs rather than forcing a consumer to choose a product designed for the statistically "average" consumer.

When segmentation and targeting are done capably, marketers have a good idea of what their chosen consumers want. They then offer an assortment of relevant and desirable products as long as any extra customization costs can be more than covered by the profit gained from increased volume or higher prices.

Challenges to Targeted Marketing

Marketers compete with one another to create innovations that improve the standard of living, solve problems, and generally make life easier. Targeted marketing results in fewer wasted advertising impressions and less likelihood of offending uninterested consumers. Differentiation can mean new products. It can also mean opening new channels for buying and for obtaining marketplace information—for instance, mall outlets as an alternative to department stores; mail-order catalogs or Internet shopping as an alternative to stores. All this is admirable and straightforward.

But life for marketers isn't always simple, in part because consumers aren't simple. Marketers need to expend a great deal of effort analyzing consumers' choices. They track purchase behavior through sales data. They try to understand consumers' underlying preferences and motivations. They try to understand how consumers make decisions and thereby determine when and how to influence them. They try to predict the next new toy or the next new fashion. They employ cultural anthropologists and consumer psychologists to observe people and figure out their unspoken needs and unconscious mental codes, and even hook them up to brain scans.[18] But identifying unarticulated consumer needs remains a hit-or-miss proposition.

One difficulty is that consumers don't fit into neat buckets. The same person may be completely loyal to Tide but switch between Colgate and Crest, buying the one on sale. A person may like self-service options at banks but avoid self-service checkout at grocery stores. Marketers can use data on demographics and lifestyle as well as media viewing habits to construct overall patterns, but in the end consumer choice is individualistic.

It can be argued that marketers themselves have contributed to the difficulty of understanding consumer choice. Instead of functional attributes and benefits, which are easily imitable, marketers have encouraged consumers to choose according to the emotions they connect with certain brands. Consumers themselves may not even know—let alone be able to explain to marketers—their reasons for buying.

Some scholars argue that companies have taken differentiation far beyond what customers want or care about. Barwise and Meehan write, "Customers don't want the bells and whistles and don't care about trivial differences between brands. What they really want are quality products, reliable services, and fair value for money."[19]

Segmentation and targeting have their limits as well. After all, the beauty of a mass market is its size and the ease and economy of reaching consumers through the mass media. A microsegment or niche strategy accompanied by narrowly directed communications doesn't have the usual benefits of scale. It's less likely to lead to large market growth and, unless there are special production efficiencies or high margins, is less likely to be profitable. In other words, microsegmentation is more profitable for a higher-margin brand like the Ritz-Carlton hotels than for a budget brand like Travelodge.

Challenges of the Mass Market

But mass marketing has its own vulnerabilities. Consumers may not want all the bells and whistles, but they respond to innovations that give them better quality, service, or perceived performance for the price. Large companies can ossify and fail to innovate in response to market shifts.[20] Wal-Mart capitalized on operational weaknesses among competitors, created a lower cost structure, and positioned itself as lower priced compared with local merchandisers. But to remain the number 1 retailer in the United States, Wal-Mart must continue to innovate operationally and remember that its price-conscious customers are apt to switch if they perceive a better deal elsewhere.

Mass customization strategies represent an attempt by marketers of mass-produced products to introduce greater choice through personalized solutions. Typically, the marketer offers an extensive menu of options and lets the consumer mix and match. Although not a new concept—after all, it is the idea behind à la carte ordering in restaurants, and options have long been available on automobiles—mass customization relies on flexible manufacturing techniques, information technology that expedites interactions between buyers and sellers, and sophisticated algorithms that ensure buyers don't choose incompatible options.

The result is delivery of a one-of-a-kind version of a product at about the same cost as a standard version. Having chosen a custom set of options, the potential buyer who experiments online with designs for the BMW MINI Cooper is more likely to buy one. Mass-customized Levi's jeans offer consumers the promise of a perfect fit.

Still, mass customization is not a panacea. When consumers start picking features, prices tend to go up. Not enough consumers may perceive additional value from customization, and manufacturers may not make sufficient additional profits to cover costs. Often the product's fit with the customers' desires is imperfect. For one thing, even with the aid of technology the average consumer is not as knowledgeable as expert designers about which features work optimally with one another. And expert salespeople are good at eliciting the product benefits consumers truly want as opposed to what they might think they want.

Choice and Rationality

Both the reasoning must be true and the desire right,
if the choice is to be good.

—Aristotle[21]

In most societies historically, and still in many parts of the world, wise purchasing has consisted of stretching limited resources to acquire a few essential goods from among a limited number of alternatives. Homemakers aspire to make the best choices for their families and to be respected in the community for their purchasing skill. At the marketplace, the produce stand, or the textiles stall, they carefully inspect each item to see that they get the best quality, the best value for the money. They learn which merchants can be trusted and expect shopkeepers to remember and anticipate their particular household needs. Parents teach their children these same skills.

Similarly, farmers, craftspeople, and other workers know the best tool and materials for a job, or if they don't, they seek recommendations. Younger workers acquire this same purchasing knowledge through on-the-job training and perhaps formal instruction.

In marketplaces containing numerous alternatives, however, consumers can no longer deliberate on each choice. The average number of items in a U.S. supermarket is about forty thousand. As a result, consumers may give very little consideration to any one choice. Observations of supermarket shoppers revealed that the average time spent selecting an item in a product category—say, a package of cold cereal—was about twelve seconds.[22] Even the number of cars considered seriously before purchase is low: one study of French car buyers found 22 percent considered only one brand.[23]

Luckily, many purchases don't require much deliberation. In the developed countries, the overall quality of goods is high. Brands are available to simplify choice, especially for repeat purchases. It is highly unlikely that a product will pose a risk to health or safety. And the rare defective items can easily be returned.

Common Shortcuts

Unplanned and spontaneous shopping is commonplace. Americans, for instance, often do not shop from a list: some 60 percent of grocery store purchases are unplanned, a figure that has held true for the past three decades.[24] That gives marketers and retailers the chance to influence purchase decisions in the store by offering price promotions, demonstrating the product or handing out samples, or by drawing attention to a brand via eye-catching packaging or displays. Many consumers are willing to try new, untested items, especially if they involve little money or they carry a trusted brand.

The rational man of economic theory knows his self-interest and has perfect knowledge about choice options. But rationality as envisioned by economists has practical limits. When there are numerous choices to be made and numerous adequate options, a couple of things become evident. One is that consumers sensibly resort to shortcuts in decision making. Malcolm Gladwell documents a wide range of circumstances when snap judgments are better than those made after lengthy analysis.[25] Second, the context of the choice, in combination with inherent human biases, affects the outcome.

Impulse purchasing can be viewed as a way to shortcut elaborate decision processes. So, too, resorting to routines and rules saves time-pressed consumers from choice overload. For standardized, quality-controlled products like packaged grocery items or commodities like gasoline, experience is the most useful guide to a rational buyer. The consumer knows that only one brand of, say, tuna, but whichever paper towel is on sale, is acceptable. Or a consumer may have learned from past satisfactory experiences that anything bought from a certain retailer is likely to be reliable.

Consumers also adopt routine trade-offs: items will be more expensive, but the quality will be higher or the process less time-consuming, when buying from a nearby convenience store. Such rules become habits whose origins are lost to consumers themselves. That doesn't mean they are not rational; some are, some aren't. The rules survive until they are broken, challenged, or worn out.[26]

The more options that are available, the more a consumer must become what economist Herbert Simon calls a "satisficer"—someone who settles for a choice that is good enough and doesn't worry too much about unexplored alternatives—instead of a "maximizer," or someone who seeks the absolutely best alternative.[27] Often, it isn't possible to investigate all alternatives. For most people, it's impossible to choose a single best vacation destination; a satisficer picks Italy and doesn't agonize that France might have been better (in part because France will still be there next year); a maximizer may end up making no choice at all. Schwartz recommends that people cope by satisficing more and maximizing less.[28]

Individuals can choose to be maximizers in some domains—to spend a great deal of effort on researching cars, computers, lawn care products, or whatever they care deeply about. They can grow to be experts to whom friends and families turn for recommendations. In fact, going by a trusted friend's advice is a common rule for simplifying choice. The considered opinion of one well-informed consumer can thus have widespread influence in the marketplace.

So, too, do sources like *Consumer Reports* that evaluate and recommend products. The catch is that the novice may have to accept the expert's judgment on which features are important and relevant, along with the relative weighting given to each. It is also easy for consumers to obtain and share product information, including likes, dislikes, and prices paid, over the Internet. Sites such as Epinions.com cover a range of products. Specialized sites like coffeegeek.com contain detailed information in one category.

Decision Biases

Can any choice be fully rational in the sense of maximizing self-interest? The more economists and psychologists decompose the choice process, the more this supposition fails to hold. First, decision making involves identifying what you think you need or want. Often this isn't difficult; the past is a good guide. But this may be the first time you've bought a house or invested in a mutual fund. You may think you want a house with a large lawn, but you discover later you don't like the upkeep. You may think it's a good idea to have high-risk/high-potential-return investments in your portfolio, but learn later, after a market correction, that you're more comfortable with moderate-risk/moderate-return investments.

In addition, information from previous experience may be biased. People unconsciously put more weight on the most recent part of an experience. A person will be less inclined to go back to a restaurant that had service problems toward the end of the meal compared with having problems at the beginning.[29] Particularly in contexts involving uncertainty and risk, there is a well-documented pattern of decision biases that causes choices to deviate from what would be considered optimal by a "rational" model.[30]

The second task in decision making calls for consumers to find out the options available. They also must figure out the bases, or dimensions, on which they will compare product choices. They must decide which dimensions are important to them and which are irrelevant and where they can make trade-offs. These tasks add up. For example, a partial list of dimensions on which a consumer can compare a simple product like eggs includes size, color, freshness, price, number to a package, brand name, and free-range versus factory raised.

In practice, it's unlikely that a consumer carries out every, or even most, steps in such an evaluation—certainly not for repeat purchases unless new product options have appeared. Instead, one way consumers process these choices faster is to reduce the number of points of comparison. Based on experience or marketing communications, people focus on one or two discriminating attributes that seem important. They pay most attention to price and brand name, perhaps because name serves as a "chunk" that summarizes other pieces of information.[31]

A common strategy is to buy brands that are well known; this rule minimizes downside risk even if you don't get the best value. Consumers are not alone in using this rule. For years, business buyers have known that "you can't go wrong by buying IBM," because if anything goes wrong you won't be blamed for choosing a low-quality vendor. Relying on well-known brands also reduces search time and information time per decision. And these brands are likely to be widely distributed and available.

Varying the options affects how people make choices. For instance, changing the number of items, or the mix of items, influences what consumers pick even if they have a clear preference for a particular item.[32] In one well-documented phenomenon, called the *compromise* effect, consumers are more apt to choose a product when it is positioned as a middle choice between two other products, compared with being positioned as the top-of the-line or bottom-of the-line. That is, a $12 bottle of wine sells better when it is surrounded by both a $20 bottle and an $8 bottle than when paired with either one of these. Consequently, retailers manage their shelves carefully. A sample strategy is to carry a low-price, low-quality item virtually no one will buy, because it makes a higher-priced item seem like a good buy.[33] Successful British supermarket chain Tesco uses a simple product-line approach that aims to offer three options in every category: good, better, and best.

The Burdens of Choice

The difficulty in life is the choice.

—George Moore[34]

Choice is generally a good thing. With more choices, people are more satisfied.[35] With a variety of product offerings, marketers can appeal to every taste. Decision routines and rules, habits and heuristics, allow people to process choices efficiently. But at some point does choice become too much of a good thing—for consumers and for marketers?

On balance, additional choice should be good for consumers if it doesn't significantly increase the complexity of the decision process, or if consumers can quickly learn how to process choices. Consider the number of options offered at Starbucks and other coffee emporiums. For the novice customer, faced with selecting among the various sizes of espressos, cappuccinos, lattes, and macchiatos, the number of shots, and the types of milk, the choice can be bewildering and lengthy—perhaps so intimidating that the consumer never comes in or places an order. But for experienced customers, the variety of choice ensures they get exactly what they want, adds pleasure to the experience, and encourages experimentation. They learn to shortcut the decision process by ordering their favorite latte, perhaps switching to a macchiato now and then for variety. And after ordering from Starbucks a few times, perhaps advised by a barista, the novice, too, becomes adept at processing information and making a choice.

In some situations, consumers may prefer having fewer choices. At some point, having to compare lots of options is stressful and can lead consumers to defer a purchase or decrease their confidence that they've made the right decision.[36] Regret at giving up an option not chosen may be stronger when the number of options is greater.[37] A large choice set is not necessarily perceived as a benefit when consumers are buying for, or on behalf of, someone else. Then they may prefer a restricted set of options. If it's a gift occasion, some people resort to hedging their bets by buying the best-known brand or a higher-priced alternative or by buying several gifts instead of the one best gift.

Some significant choices are beyond the average person's capacity to decide wisely. During the 1990s, employers offering 401(k) plans tended to present numerous investment options. Some employees were so overwhelmed with choices they left funds in the low-return default option of money market accounts. Others invested in highly risky portfolios. Now many employers offer a more limited array of options, including some bundled funds, and some employers make these or well-diversified balance funds the default option.[38]

Lately, it's been the fashion for marketers to propose "empowering" customers. However, empowerment may be a mixed blessing, leading to a worse consumer experience and a less satisfactory outcome, because it often entails giving consumers more choices and requiring them to do more work. Empowered consumers may feel unhappy with themselves if their choice doesn't work out.

In some cases, the cognitive effort required to make choices is within the grasp but simply beyond the endurance of the average customer. Cell phone plans, for example, are notorious for the complexity of their service options, which bundle various types of phones with complicated calling plans subject to frequent change. Many frustrated consumers stop the choice process midstream and pick what they hope will be an adequate plan. The marketer acquires a customer who is likely to remain suspicious and unlikely to be loyal or satisfied.

Marketers stand to lose if people defer decisions, make bad decisions, have a bad experience, or grudgingly enter into a service agreement predisposed to find fault with the provider. They may also lose if a special or unique product is lost in the clutter. For example, specialty movies have more opportunities than ever to get on the air somewhere, but channel-flipping viewers may skip them or never be aware of them in the first place.

Ways Marketers Simplify Choice

But when too much choice is detrimental, consumers and marketers can take action. One obvious response for a company is to reduce the number of items in its product assortment. In part to help retailers manage its brands better, Unilever pared down its brand portfolio from sixteen hundred brands to about four hundred brands.[39]

For many years, the trend in supermarkets was to increase the number of item-variety-size combinations, or stockkeeping units (SKUs), they carried. Although some SKUs move off the shelves slowly and it's inefficient to handle so many items, managers generally are reluctant to risk losing customers by eliminating products they're used to buying. Rare is the product manager who is promoted for saving a company money by eliminating unprofitable SKUs instead of taking the more usual course of launching a new one.

As it turns out, in some real-world experiments, retailers were able to drop about half the low-selling SKUs in a range of product categories without damaging sales levels; in some cases, sales dramatically increased. Consumers appreciated the reduction in clutter. As long as cuts in brands and flavors were not too deep, product variety was deemed sufficient. And even though many consumers who lost their favorite brands stopped purchasing in the category, many others switched to alternative brands.[40]

Marketers can also simplify choice by reducing the number of features on their products. Or they can provide a basic model and let consumers choose the additional features they want. That is essentially what Dell does for its personal computer line. Dell's Web site allows a high degree of customized choice but offers convenient default options of preconfigured components.[41]

Marketers can also organize choice in an easily understandable manner. Dell gears its presentation of information according to type of user (home, small-business owner, or other) as well as intended use (basic computing, media entertainment, or gaming) and level of detail desired. In a simple and effective approach, Loctite color-codes bottles of the various formulas in its range of instant adhesives. Hardware stores cluster the tools, parts, and supplies suitable for a particular job. A furniture salesperson can help customers choose one sofa out of 150,000 possible combinations of style and fabric by leading them through the decision step-by-step, sequentially narrowing choices by back shape, then cushion, and then fabric.[42]

Marketers can learn repeat customers' preferences over time and offer a reduced set of tailored choices. Learning modules embedded in some customer relationship management systems, such as those used by upscale hotels in the Ritz-Carlton family, enable marketers to delight consumers by anticipating their wishes.

In the complex world of mutual funds, where mistakes can have substantial financial consequences, Vanguard originated the convenient and straightforward index fund. On its Web site, Vanguard teaches consumers how to evaluate and compare funds. Equally important, it teaches them how to evaluate their own preferences and needs—for example, the degree of risk they're prepared to take or the appropriate time horizon for investments—and recommends products based on these criteria.

Online retailers increasingly offer choices in menu form. A few simple devices can increase the convenience of the buying decision and consumers' satisfaction: structuring choices to mirror decision-making processes; allowing consumers to reverse a decision and giving them flexibility in defining choices (a consumer may want to see all the color options but only one size); indicating where a consumer is in the process (equivalent to the moving bar on software downloads) to reduce the likelihood that the consumer will quit before completing a purchase.

Mirroring these developments, consumers manage ballooning choice by turning to technology or delegating choice to agents. To take advantage of—and control—the increase in programming on satellite, broadcast, or cable channels, consumers can store a program on TiVo to watch when they have time and follow TiVo's recommendations on other shows they might like. They can instruct Web site home pages to display chosen news categories or display local weather or stock quotes.

Advice based on the experiences of other consumers can aid choice in an empowered situation; for example, the independent bidding4travel.com site helps consumers navigate Priceline.[43] Google eases the search process so that consumers can avoid missing better options. Google's search results are democratically ranked on the frequency of user clicks, and not on advertisers' listings; the layout of results pages clearly delimits paid advertising.

Amazon.com's success is due in large part to its provision of "official" reviews and customer reviews for nearly every item it carries as well as its system of recommending choices based on the likes of customers with similar buying patterns. Parents are showing interest in screening agents for telecommunications media that will eliminate choices unsuitable for children.

Delegating to Agents

Delegating choice to agents and advisers is nothing new. Individual consumers and businesses have long relied on the services of insurance agents and stockbrokers. In the realm of taste, consumers turned to department stores in their heyday, not only because they carried a wide array of goods but also because they carefully selected and organized them and screened out products that would be unappealing to their customer base. Women's magazines continue to give their readers advice on products they're interested in buying. The wealthy employ fashion consultants, interior decorators, and landscape designers to choose for them. Home decorating shows on cable television serve as equivalent experts for the middle classes. The demand for advisers and agents will undoubtedly grow in response to the continued expansion of choice options.

However, what economists call the *principal-agent problem* arises when you delegate choice. Agents can take advantage of their clients when the information problems are complex and require specialized knowledge. Clients may not know for years or may never know that they are being taken. Thus such relationships depend heavily on trust. Merrill Lynch lost trust during the market meltdown of 2001, when some of its stock pickers privately denigrated stocks they were recommending to the public; the company has so far not recovered its credibility.

Even such "rational," well-informed customers as big corporations were allegedly duped by Marsh & McLennan, an insurance broker, according to a suit filed in 2004 by the New York attorney general. Accusations of rigging bids, price-fixing, and kickbacks led to the resignation of Marsh's CEO and expectations that the firm would eventually pay more than $1 billion in fines and restitution. Similar problems exist in the securities industry, where ten firms paid $1.4 billion in 2003 to settle charges, and in the mutual funds industry, where firms agreed to pay $1.9 billion.[44]

The consumer marketplace incorporates protections against unscrupulous agents. Information availability is one. In some cases, such as real estate, the specialized knowledge is not so extensive that consumers cannot acquire it, and a great deal of information is available on the Internet. For example, the listings of most houses are online, and market conditions are available from Zillow.com, which combines property assessment and other information from public records with aerial photographs that map nearly all of the United States. Anyone can go to its Web site, search on an address, and view an image of the property and an estimate of its worth.

In real estate and other fields, professional trade associations set standards for good behavior and discipline offenders. Further protection is provided through the regulatory and investigative authority of federal and state agencies. Finally, the "benevolent hand" of the marketplace itself polices dishonest behavior; in the long run, the totality of consumers' choices rewards honest behavior.

Opting for Choice

If choice does impose some burdens on consumers and marketers, the fact remains that the proliferation of choice options has occurred democratically, as a response to what people want. Consumers desire choice and variety, and they have developed the capacity to process a tremendous number of choices efficiently. In the marketing context, this capacity is increasing, thanks to the development of information and communication technologies that allow consumers to acquire and sort a wealth of information about choice alternatives. Businesses' search to serve profitable new segments causes them to explore and deliver additional choices in product categories. If markets are approaching an overload zone of too much choice, then consumers' resulting displeasure or lack of interest in marketers' offerings is bound to trigger a reassessment of how much choice is optimal or, more likely, a search for techniques to simplify the choice process rather than reduce the number of choices.

Democratic Choice

Because the majority ought to prevail over the minority, must the majority
have all the votes, the minority none? Is it necessary that the minority
should not even be heard? Nothing but habit and old association
can reconcile any reasonable being to the needless injustice.

—John Stuart Mill[45]

In the consumer marketplace, people select and consume alternatives that come closest to meeting their preferences. The situation for citizens in representative democracies has similarities but also fundamental differences. In the political marketplace, opposing philosophies, policies, and programs may be viewed as the ultimate outcomes. But citizens don't directly choose those outcomes. As in some cases in the consumer marketplace, citizens select agents, or representatives, to act on their behalf to produce those outcomes. That brings up the same issues—of trust, information asymmetries between voters and candidates, and the difficulty of evaluating performance, as well as the problem of agents with divided loyalties—that occur in the consumer marketplace.

And compared with consumer marketplaces, people generally have few options when they select political representatives. Choice is constrained by constitutional structures and electoral rules. For instance, voters' choices are governed by where they live and whether the election is at large (where each voters can select multiple candidates) or for a single representative per district.

In practice, where governments are chosen according to "one representative per district" and "winner takes all" rules (prevalent in the United States and the United Kingdom), competition tends to dwindle to two or three viable political parties, which differ from each other but usually only to a limited extent. Smaller parties, which may offer more distinct points of view, face significant barriers in competing against the major parties, which have the power to influence redistricting and electoral rules as well as the ability to attract extensive campaign funding and a full slate of candidates.

If you live in a district where your preferences don't coincide with those of most voters and if your representative doesn't belong to the majority party, chances are the ultimate outcomes will not coincide with your preferences. This situation is quite different from the consumer marketplace.

Democracies operate on the principle that collective choice will produce reasonably good outcomes.[46] Moreover, the value democrats attach to choice transcends outcomes. Aristotle and other political philosophers have pointed out that democracies are not necessarily better than benevolent and wise government by an autocrat or a plutocracy in terms of making good decisions on behalf of citizens. Yet given a choice between an enlightened autocracy with outcomes one likes and a representative democracy where outcomes are at odds with one's preferences, true democrats will pick the latter. Przeworski concludes that although democrats care about particular outcomes, they value the "mere possibility of being counted" and, even if they cannot affect outcomes, the ability to assert themselves: "The value of choice is that I cause my views to enter the public realm."[47]

CHAPTER 4

Information

Knowledge Is Power

JUST AS THE FREE FLOW of information is essential to well-functioning democracies, it is essential to well-functioning consumer marketplaces. Consumers need accurate, complete, and timely information to learn about alternatives and make good choices. Marketers need information about consumers to learn what they want (when and where and how much) and how much they value alternatives. Such information equips firms to offer the right product at the right place at the right time and at the right price.

Democracies and the consumer marketplace operate by persuasion and not coercion. Marketers and politicians need to make their cases through information and rhetoric. Typically they appeal to the emotions as well as to the intellect. But marketers (and politicians) are engaged in an advertising arms race, and the marketplace overflows with commercial messages, many of them irrelevant and irritating. A question is whether all this signifies marketer power or consumer power.

Marketers' use of information about consumers must be balanced against consumers' privacy. Traditionally, the marketing research profession has agreed on codes of ethics to protect consumer information, such as walling off research from sales and ensuring respondent anonymity. However, now that digital technologies enable marketers to gather, store, and connect multiple pieces of behavioral data about individuals and tailor products accordingly, consumer privacy increasingly is traded for the benefits that marketers can provide by using such information. Reputable marketers need to ensure that files containing sensitive personal information are adequately protected and that individuals' privacy and security are not put at risk.

Information issues are central to debates over marketers' rights versus consumers' rights, and governments are instrumental in mediating these clashes. Democratic governments permit marketers substantial freedom but intervene in response to sustained pressure from one side or the other, particularly when arguments convince policy makers that existing practices fail to conform to the ideal of a competitive, open, and well-informed marketing system.

Not everyone has equal access to information or equal ability to process it—for example, the poor of the world, the illiterate, and those living in remote areas. According to "new growth" economic theory, rapid sharing of new ideas and accurate information are integral to economic expansion.[1] For long-term market growth, it may be in marketers' best interest to contribute to investments that bridge the digital divide, possibly through public–private partnerships, grants, and incentives or by developing new ways to give consumers access to information.

Information, Persuasion, and Advertising

The real foundation of [the disposition to barter] is that principle to persuade which so much prevails in human nature. When any arguments are offered to persuade, it is always expected they should have their proper effect.

—Adam Smith[2]

In the consumer marketplace, much of the information about products and services comes directly from marketers, supplemented by personal experience and word of mouth. (By contrast, in the political marketplace, much of the information comes from the media.) Interactions with salespeople, assuming that they are knowledgeable and well trained, are information rich for buyers and sellers alike. Whether a consumer is shopping for a new computer or looking for the proper nut-and-bolt combination to complete a do-it-yourself project, expert assistance can help match the right product or service to the circumstance.

Salespeople, in turn, learn what consumers are looking for and which alternative solutions they are considering. Feedback from good salespeople can help marketers shape their product assortment or guide new-product development. The vaunted interactivity of new-generation Web sites is a pale approximation of the interactivity of the best person-to-person exchanges.

Marketers' merchandising activities, including packaging, pricing, and product display, as well as product samples—from a test drive to a sample taste—are another source of information. But in large, dispersed, and fast-changing marketplaces, no buyer can learn about available products based solely on experience, sales interactions, or merchandising. These sources are supplemented or substituted by commercial messages in various media.

In the developed world, commercial information is ubiquitous. It includes advertisements in newspapers, magazines, radio, television, and the Internet; street flyers, shop signs, and billboards; direct mail and e-mail; posters on buses and trains; and logos and signage at sporting events. And that's only the advertising that the average person can clearly identify as being paid messages. Public relations events, corporate press releases that form the basis for news stories, half-hour television "advertorials" presented as objective journalism, product placements in movies or television, corporate sponsorships of not-for-profit arts organizations—these are less visible, more subtle versions of promotion.

In the name of acculturation to adulthood, even schools are not exempt from the commercialization of modern life: soft-drink vending machines line hallways, and commercials are broadcast over audiovisual systems paid for by private enterprise.[3] Churches may be next.

Only a few places in the world are free from rampant advertising, and, if history is a guide, they may not be ad-free for long. Before the fall of Communism, advertising was uncommon in the shortage economies of Eastern Europe; it was used primarily to move excess inventories of poor-quality goods. In Czechoslovakia, "hidden seduction" in advertising was banned. But as these countries transitioned to free-market economies, advertising quickly became more Western in style and scale.[4]

The Evolution of Advertising

Modern consumer marketplaces exhibit a wide range of advertisements that differ in their information content and persuasive approach. Advertising has evolved from purely factual toward imagery-laden, emotional content.[5] Early ads simply informed potential purchasers about product availability.

A typical mid-eighteenth-century merchant would place a long newspaper advertisement itemizing the goods in stock following a ship's arrival.[6] Much current newspaper advertising still consists of factual information about product availability and price. Ads also introduce vocabulary or terms that educate consumers about product differences. Consumers learn to distinguish high-quality goods and to make ever finer distinctions among types —say, a two-megapixel versus a five-megapixel digital camera.

At the beginning of mass marketing, ads tended to extol the functional superiority of a product or a brand, sometimes incorporating a good dose of puffery. (This type of advertising is used in emerging economies, where advertisers need to educate consumers about basic product performance.) Marketers talked about things like maximum cleaning strength and presumed that consumers would choose the product on this basis. Marketers also sought to influence choice by framing the basis for comparison, teaching consumers which attribute was more important or what constituted product superiority versus a competitor.

In Rosser Reeves's famous "unique selling proposition" approach to advertising, all ads for a product had to demonstrate a single unique benefit: "Each advertisement must say to each reader: 'Buy this product and you will get this specific benefit.'"[7] Reeves didn't assume that consumers always knew they needed a particular feature or could see how products differed; it was advertising's job to point out consumers' latent needs.

Apart from functional benefits, marketers hoped to influence consumer choice by creating strong awareness of their product and transferring liking for an ad to liking for the product. Adman Leo Burnett forged emotional connections through association with invented characters like the Pillsbury Doughboy. The masculine symbol of the Marlboro Man made Marlboro filtered cigarettes—at the time considered a women's cigarette—more appealing to men. Creating likable ads through humor and imagery remains a mainstay of advertising.

Television advertising emphasized visual images over wordy explanations (reflecting the fact that 80 to 90 percent of the meaning in human communication is transmitted nonverbally).[8] It aimed to talk *to* rather than *at* the audience and to demonstrate rather than proclaim benefits. Increasingly, marketers promised emotional benefits, including taking good care of oneself or one's family or achieving social success by buying the right brand. Colgate toothpaste, for example, promised "the ring of confidence."

Perhaps in reaction to these developments, Vance Packard's sensationalist critique of the advertising industry in the 1950s accused advertisers of using subliminal techniques to influence consumers through their subconscious.[9] (Some advertisers may have wished they had such power, but they never did.)

In addition to acting as a stimulus for immediate sales, marketers used advertising to maintain top-of-mind awareness. For example, consumers typically purchase automobiles every three years. In the interim, mass advertising aims to keep them interested enough to consider a brand or model the next time around. Automobile advertising also increases customers' satisfaction with their choices. Recent purchasers notice advertising for their chosen brand; it reassures them that they chose well.

Advertising Information and Market Efficiency

For consumers, increasing quantities of advertising can be annoying and intrusive. For marketers, the more advertising there is, the harder it is to make it stand out. Marketers find themselves in an insidious cycle of spending more on advertising just to maintain parity. Keeping up with the times, they advertise in new media while maintaining a presence in the old media—wherever consumers can be reached.

Even with knowledge gleaned from test markets and experimentation, it is notoriously difficult to calculate returns on advertising spending. Advertising appears to be most effective in introducing consumers to new products or telling them something new.[10] But marketers also believe that some advertising is needed to remind consumers of existing products and maintain brand awareness. Although marketers may desire to cut back, they remain uncertain about where to cut back or what the effect on sales might be.[11] With Internet advertising, this situation may improve as marketers become more confident with detailed tracking measures.

An often cited, though perhaps apocryphal, figure is that the average U.S. consumer is exposed to more than two thousand messages a day. Whether the sheer amount of advertising signifies that consumers have power over advertisers or whether advertisers have power over consumers is a matter of debate. Does it indicate that marketers have found that advertising works, that speaking loudly and frequently to consumers influences choice significantly? Do consumers value the emotional connection advertising creates with brands? Or, as critics might say, can it create false desire, trick people into wanting things they don't need or excessive quantities of things they do need? This would suggest advertiser power.

Or is it a sign of desperation? Do advertisers' messages cancel each other out, suggesting that much advertising is wasted or at best defensive? Have consumers become sophisticated decoders of advertising formulas, indicating consumer power? Or, alternatively, have consumers become so inured to advertising that choice is essentially random? Despite endless debate, the jury is still out.

Furthermore, do consumers pay higher prices than they should in order to cover the costs of unnecessary advertising? Critics cite the prominent example of the pharmaceutical industry.[12] Defenders of advertising say that any extra costs are justified because ads provide valuable information.

However, the volume of advertising, together with the prevalence of non-factual messages, fuels criticisms that advertising is uninformative, intrusive, and wasteful. In any case, consumers see and hear so much advertising that it is difficult to say anything new to them. If advertising gives consumers a minimal amount of new information (except for new products and new features), that bolsters critics' accusations that it is persuasive and manipulative. Some marketers advocate responding to the marketplace clutter by trying to create more intense bonds with consumers, such as an "emotional level that can create loyalty beyond reason."[13] In trying to bypass conscious decisions perhaps they are adding fuel to the critics' fire.

Economists, too, have debated whether advertising is beneficial for markets, that is, whether it makes them more efficient and competitive. One school of thought holds that it makes markets more monopolistic by creating barriers to entry: to compete effectively, new entrants must be prepared to make large investments in advertising. Further, if advertising persuades consumers to be less sensitive to price, then monopolistic companies can raise prices over competitive levels.[14]

A second school of economists argues that advertising promotes competition. Advertising, they reason, is an efficient way for competing sellers to communicate with potential customers. It allows new products and new sellers to gain a foothold. In itself, the increased competition keeps prices lower. Further, ads containing information about prices and products reduce consumers' time and search costs.

Both schools of thought associate information with market efficiency. They differ over whether advertising stifles or promotes the flow of information. To date there is little evidence that advertising plays a significant role in creating monopolistic behavior.[15] Evidence that advertising leads to lower prices is also inconclusive.[16]

The "economics of information" reflects a third view of the role of advertising. This branch of economics considers what happens to market efficiency when a seller has much better information about product quality than a potential buyer has. This is frequently the case in modern markets, where products are complex and buyers cannot determine quality by casual inspection.

In a seminal article, George Akerlof showed that such markets do not work very well.[17] However, in his example of the used-car market, dealers whose stock is of more consistent quality offset the information problem by offering credible guarantees. They also advertise. Phillip Nelson argued that regardless of an ad's content, advertising conveys the information that sellers are committed to their product and that they are willing to back up their product and reputation by spending large amounts on advertising. Consumers rightly reason that it would make no sense for marketers to advertise and develop a brand if quality were poor or if they were fly-by-night operators.[18]

This explanation helps account for the prevalence of image-oriented "noninformational" advertising. What matters to consumers is the advertiser's pledge to its audience that it is a reputable seller offering good-quality products or services. In the emerging automobile market in China, for example, car buyers place great weight on the manufacturer's industry leadership and aura of success.[19] It is true that image advertising influences consumers through their emotions, but another part of the story is that consumers extract information from all sorts of ads. There is no strict dividing line between persuasive advertising and informative advertising.

Does advertising persuasion detrimentally affect society in a larger sense? Commercialism has become so much a part of U.S. culture that there is no longer much distinction between advertising and entertainment, or between entertainment and objective news. Democracies depend on informed, enlightened understanding. But this seems increasingly illusory. Voters' choices in the 2004 presidential election appear to have been based largely on emotions played upon in advertising—specifically, fear and likeability—more than reasoning on issues.[20] As modern persuasive techniques spill over to the political arena, the traditional paradigm of informed, rational choice seems increasingly at odds with reality.

Consumer Research

*The aim of marketing is to know and understand the customer
so well the product or service fits him and sells itself.*

—Peter Drucker[21]

To support marketing decision making, the market research industry collects and analyzes extensive information about consumers and competitors. Researchers gather data through telephone, mail, or e-mail surveys, warranty cards, focus groups, experiments, or one-on-one interviews. With or without consumers' knowledge, marketers also observe consumers' behavior either directly or by collecting transaction data.

Most survey and interview research is by necessity permission based: consumers are aware that information is being collected, and marketers cannot proceed without their consent. To preserve the goodwill on which it relies, the market research profession follows strict codes of conduct.[22] Most such codes include principles stating that the individual's identity will be kept secret, that individual data will be pooled, that researchers cannot lie to consumers to gain their cooperation or coerce them, that consumers must be informed if they will be taped or monitored, and that interviewing cannot be used as a pretext for developing sales leads. In fact, the federal government considers survey research to be an "informational" rather than a "commercial" activity.[23] Consequently, market researchers are exempt from rules that restrict telemarketing calls.

Generally, consumers receive at most a token amount for participating. Rather, their immediate reward is having their opinions taken into account. Marketers pay attention to customer satisfaction scores and use them to track brand health and quality of service; in a few cases these metrics are tied to executive compensation. A more distant reward is a marketplace offering goods and services consumers like.

Consumer research depends on a population willing to trust strangers and authorities; thus, consumer research is common in democracies and virtually inconceivable in authoritarian states. U.S. consumers' trust in market researchers is linked to a history of ethical, or at least not harmful, behavior by researchers and a history of favorable results—a flow of "new and improved" products into the marketplace. A tacit agreement between researchers and consumers defines which practices are acceptable and which are not, such as what kinds of questions can be asked. But these are not universals. In France, for example, a market research firm attracted notoriety in 2005 when it asked consumers to choose which of eleven ethnic groups they identified with. France's ethos of equality and fraternity is associated with long-standing taboos against collecting information on race, ethnicity, or religion.[24]

In the United States, marketers who cross the line between selling and research erode consumer trust in surveys. The kind of telemarketer who starts calls by asking consumers to answer a few questions and then switches to a sales pitch or a plea for donations violates industry norms and federal laws against *sugging* (selling under the guise of research) and *frugging* (fundraising under the guise of research).[25] Consumer backlash against such solicitations has also affected legitimate survey research, which has seen response rates slip.

Newer generations of marketers—as well as U.S. consumers—don't make as sharp a distinction between marketing and research as formerly.[26] In large part that is because marketers increasingly collect, analyze, and act upon personal information linked to individual consumers, as distinct from aggregate information describing groups of consumers. Some online consumers are comfortable supplying information about their habits and preferences once reserved for anonymous market research in return for such things as personalized content, improved customer service, or product discounts.[27] Still, consumers appear less willing than they were a few years ago to disclose information, in part because of the spate of e-mail offers and promotions generated by marketers.[28]

Consumer Information and Privacy

*Biographical data, even those recorded in the public registers,
are the most private things one has, and
to declare them openly is rather like
facing a psychoanalyst.*

—Italo Calvino[29]

Businesses hold a huge amount of personal information that consumers share with them. A few decades ago, consumers became accustomed to paying for purchases with personal checks displaying a home address and telephone number, supplemented by driver's license or Social Security number. Now, thanks to falling costs of data processing and storage, the amount of information collected and stored on individuals has ballooned.

The average American would find it nearly impossible to live outside the information grid: to evade all commercial gathering of personal data, the consumer would have to work under the table; pay for food, housing, transportation, and everything else in cash; never use a personal phone; avoid home and car ownership, tax, and utility bills; and never access medical care or air travel. Privacy in the sense of anonymity doesn't exist in modern societies. Privacy in the sense of access to one's personal spaces is assaulted by telemarketing calls and direct-mail solicitations promising instant credit-card approval.

In their personal lives, people daily negotiate degrees of privacy without necessarily giving it much thought. In every encounter with friends, neighbors, coworkers, or strangers, an individual decides how much to reveal through conversation and actions and how much to hold back.[30] Cultural values, too, shape norms about what is private, what should be exempted from unwanted scrutiny or surveillance.

Democratic societies value and protect privacy, particularly the privacy of citizens with respect to government surveillance and intrusion. According to political scientist Alan Westin, "The importance of that right to choose, both to the individual's self-development and to the exercise of responsible citizenship, makes the claim to privacy a fundamental part of civil liberty in a democratic society."[31]

At the same time, democracies need to balance privacy considerations with information disclosures necessary for fair business dealings and the conduct of public affairs. Issues and events such as national security and terrorist threats, passage of the Patriot Act, advances in information or genetic technologies, debates over women's reproductive rights, or the collection of government statistics to assess economic programs bring privacy issues to the forefront; they require explicit decisions or trade-offs among competing privacy values and among competing individual, organizational, and governmental interests.[32]

In commercial transactions as well, ideas about the proper balance between the privacy concerns of one party and the disclosure needs of others vary by person, context, and situation, and change over time. What one person considers a prying question from a retailer, another may appreciate as a courteous gesture. The same consumer may welcome a mail reminder that a subscription to a favorite newsmagazine is up for renewal but view a telephone reminder as an invasion of privacy. Hence, privacy demarcations often are up for negotiation among consumers, businesses, and political interests. Depending on current events—say, a highly publicized abuse of confidentiality or technological developments in information collection and analysis—accepted notions of appropriate privacy practices may shift dramatically.

Shifting notions of privacy may significantly alter business and consumer relationships. In the health-care industry, providers cannot be paid without disclosing sensitive customer information to insurers. The common practice of identifying insured consumers through Social Security numbers increases the risk that medical files can be linked to other personal data. What will happen to relationships with health-care providers as the public realizes that the changing system of medical care means that doctor–patient confidentiality is an outmoded concept?

The Cost and the Benefit

Most people would agree that businesses have legitimate needs for information about consumers. Banks and merchants need to know that the person writing a check or making a withdrawal is the same person whose name is on the account. Preventing fraud keeps prices lower for all consumers. Businesses need details on the credit histories of loan applicants. Retailers need to know a person's address if they are to deliver goods. In such instances, consumers exchange privacy—that is, access to or information about themselves in return for access to products, free or higher levels of service, customization, and fraud prevention.

Such exchanges extend to a wide range of potentially sensitive situations. Consider the Total Rewards program of Harrah's Entertainment Inc., which tracks participating customers' gambling behavior through a customer loyalty card and provides targeted rewards in return (based on calculations of a customer's lifetime value). The program has raised customer satisfaction and reduced marketing waste; "customers were not concerned about privacy issues because they perceived the rewards and mail offers to be valuable to their specific needs."[33]

But not all consumers want close relationships with marketers. Many of them have a strong desire to protect their privacy. For years, consumers objected to RadioShack's policy of asking a cash-and-carry customer for name, address, and telephone number. Consumers saw no connection to a benefit, and in similar stores anonymity was the norm. When RadioShack ultimately ended the practice, Leonard Roberts, its chairman and CEO, admitted, "Asking for names and addresses was a barrier to building superior customer relationships.[34] Yet RadioShack was trying to do exactly what marketing experts advise: collect and use customer data to add names to its mailing list to receive notification of new products and promotions and simplify processes like returns and exchanges. In short, it was trying to use database marketing to build closer and more efficient customer relationships.

On the other hand, in the past decade, consumers have willingly signed up for supermarket cards that identify them at checkout and entitle them to immediate cash discounts. Airline frequent flyer miles and hotel frequent guest programs that reward consumers with free travel are also popular, because consumers see a clear benefit.

To many consumers, the direct marketing industry represents violations of privacy. Consumers are not told when marketers sell information about them to a third party. But they have learned that one order placed with a catalog retailer triggers an avalanche of mailings; their name, address, and purchase history have been sold. Giving a marketer your e-mail address leads to an in-box filled with spam messages.

The March of Progress

If these are irritants, new developments have increased the potential for significant consumer harm. Powered by information technology, data brokers have advanced far beyond buying, renting, and selling mailing lists. Firms like Seisint, LexisNexis, and ChoicePoint compile detailed profiles on individual consumers and sell the profiles to law enforcement agencies, financial institutions, insurers, and other entities. Until serious breaches of security in 2005 brought the industry to public attention, few consumers were aware of its existence, let alone the nature of the information it develops.

The *Financial Times* reported that a consumer profile it obtained from Seisint on one individual included not only the Social Security number but also "political party affiliation, date of birth, every address at which the person had lived within the U.S., the names and birth dates of some neighbours, information about whether the individual had ever filed for bankruptcy and details of a property sale by a member of the person's family."[35] These rich profiles seem not only quantitatively but also qualitatively different from the skimpier sketches obtained under older, more primitive information collection practices. The profiles are more revealing, more private, more identifying.

Data brokers often start with public records—such as a person's name, address, and telephone number; vehicle registration and driver's license information; and court records—and scour databases for linked data. Given the ability to find and use public records for these unintended purposes, distinctions between public and private information break down. Public information becomes private: in U.S. law, the data broker, and not the individual, owns the personal data compiled from public sources. Private becomes quasi-public: brokers can buy information on magazine subscriptions, recent purchases, travel, and so on, combine it with other information, package it, and resell it to government and private organizations.

Now that extensive public and private records are posted on the Internet, a knowledgeable person using a search engine can compile similar profiles: in less than one hour a team unearthed sensitive information on about 25 million people, including "various combinations of people's names, dates of birth, Social Security numbers, and credit card information."[36] Any data on the Internet that is improperly guarded or secured is essentially publicly accessible.

Cases of identity theft and inadvertent mishandling of personal information only add to consumers' concerns. A worker for the Palm Beach County Health Department accidentally e-mailed names and addresses of 4,500 Florida AIDS patients to 800 county health workers.[37] In 2005, Lexis-Nexis reported that Social Security numbers, driver's license numbers, and addresses of 310,000 people had been stolen; ChoicePoint and Westlaw reported thefts of tens of thousands of records holding the same type of information.[38] Citigroup announced that computer tapes containing records of 3.9 million customers' names, addresses, Social Security numbers, account numbers, and loan payment histories were lost in transit. Industry observers speculated that these lapses came to light only because of a California regulation requiring organizations and government agencies to notify California customers when the data in their personal files have been compromised.[39]

Consumer Backlash

Spurred by such breaches of security, privacy concerns among the public are at a high level: a 2004 survey of North American consumers found that

97 percent of them agreed that online privacy was an important issue; a mere 6 percent agreed with the statement, "The benefits I receive from giving out my personal information outweigh my concerns"; 57 percent thought that government should regulate how companies use customer information.[40] A number of policy makers and public interest groups are pressing for greater controls on the data brokerage industry.

In general, consumers appreciate being rewarded for their patronage. But they don't want to receive uninvited, intrusive, and annoying calls from telemarketers. They want to know which personal information marketers collect about them, how it is used, and with whom it is shared. They want to require marketers to ask for permission and obtain their assent. They want to make sure that their personal data is stored securely and protected from unauthorized access. They also want to receive benefit, not harm, from use of their information.

In truth, consumers and enlightened businesses stand to benefit from a system in which fully informed consumers consent to disclose information to marketers in exchange for a benefit. Consumer participation in information gathering and market research increases the chances that marketers will supply what consumers want and need. Marketers can also learn what some consumers don't want and avoid targeting those people. Organizations forced to be open and honest about how they use information will adopt practices that build rather than erode consumer trust.[41]

Organizations pressured to demonstrate a benefit will create additional consumer value, which can only help grow business. Furthermore, organizations that adhere to strict privacy codes worldwide can more easily operate across state and national borders: when U.S. practices are unacceptable by European standards, firms must either refrain from transferring personal information or else develop costly workarounds.

Government Regulation of Information

If the average citizen is guaranteed equal opportunity in the polling place,
he must have equal opportunity in the market place.

—Franklin D. Roosevelt[42]

The legal and regulatory treatment of commercial information and information privacy in the United States echoes the nation's bias toward minimal government intervention in business. The United Kingdom and other European countries accord government a more active role in economic and social affairs, and information practices mirror this.

However, some common principles are widely shared. Gathering and communicating information are viewed as legitimate, necessary business activities. There is nearly universal agreement that advertising should not be false, deceptive, or misleading. Most countries subject advertising aimed at children to special scrutiny, although views vary on how much protection children need. Most countries single out certain products and services that could affect health—food, alcohol, tobacco, medicines—for special information oversight. Most countries agree that individuals' privacy should be protected. Most want to ensure that no citizen is disadvantaged in access to market information or is excluded by a digital divide.

Advertising Regulation

In the United States, stopping companies from issuing false and misleading information that could harm consumers is the thrust of many court rulings, government regulations, and industry self-regulation. Commercial speech—communication issued primarily to sell a product or service as distinguished from ordinary, noncommercial speech—does not fall under the free-speech protection of the First Amendment. A landmark Supreme Court case of 1941 allowed government extensive power to regulate both the content and the delivery (for example, the media employed) of commercial speech.[43] Subsequent decisions clearly upheld the power to regulate false, deceptive, or misleading advertising. Decisions since 1980 also permit regulation of *truthful* commercial speech in order to advance "substantial government interest" using means "no broader than necessary."[44]

When analyzing commercial speech cases, the Court's concerns include government's role in protecting marketers' reasonable access to media; balancing the degree of knowledge and power held by marketers and message recipients; and protecting the public against unwanted intrusion.[45] In practice, U.S. regulators allow advertisers a fair amount of leeway: for the most part, the goal is to forestall egregious abuses.

The Federal Trade Commission, the principal agency overseeing advertising, requires that to be considered unfair, an advertisement "causes or is likely to cause substantial consumer injury which is not reasonably avoidable by consumers themselves and is not outweighed by countervailing benefits to consumers or competition."[46] Typically when violations occur, agency staff negotiate a consent agreement with the advertiser, in which the advertiser admits no wrongdoing but agrees to stop the contested behavior.[47]

Privacy Regulation

With respect to privacy issues, Americans historically have been less wary about businesses' information practices and more wary about government surveillance of individuals and control of personal information: constitutional protections of individual privacy apply only to government actions. The U.S. Patriot Act is significant in that it blurs the lines. The act gives government agencies extensive powers to access personal records about consumer activities from health insurance companies, bookstores, other businesses, schools, libraries, and nonprofits, in addition to authority to monitor Internet usage, including sites visited, pages downloaded, and sent and received e-mail addresses.[48] As a result, some bookstores are significantly reducing the number of customer records they keep and the length of time they keep them.

Policy makers have favored market forces and self-regulation over regulation of business. That attitude began to change as business transitioned from the sort of personal relationships established between customers and, say, the local banker or shopkeeper retaining modest paper files for its own use to the impersonal customer relationships of modern firms collecting, storing, using, and digitally exchanging large amounts of detailed customer data. It also changed as consumer distrust of business increased.[49]

A landmark law acknowledged the sensitive nature of financial data.[50] The U.S. Fair Credit Reporting Act (FCRA), first passed in 1970 and since amended, regulates consumer reporting agencies that sell detailed credit reports about individuals to creditors, employers, insurers, and other businesses.[51] But aside from requirements giving consumers the right to review and correct information in their files, the FCRA allows the reporting agencies and their business customers virtually unlimited scope in collecting and using sensitive data. It also places much of the enforcement burden on consumers, who must take the initiative in contacting consumer reporting agencies, reviewing files, and requesting corrections. More significantly, the FCRA does not apply to data brokers outside the financial industry, which successfully lobbied the Federal Trade Commission (FTC) to let them operate under self-regulation.

Pressure from consumers irritated by the growing volume of telemarketing calls eventually led to the establishment of the Do Not Call registry by the FTC in 2003. This allows consumers to block unsolicited telephone calls from direct marketers but does not allow them to opt out of receiving calls from charitable or political marketers or from marketers with which they have an established business relationship.

Reflecting a higher priority on individuals than businesses, European privacy policies tilt toward giving governments greater oversight of information use and giving consumers greater choice with respect to the ways their personal information is used. The European Union privacy directive lays out four principles: a company must have a legitimate and clearly defined purpose for collecting information from a person; the purpose must be disclosed to the person; the person must give consent to hold and use the information for that purpose; the company cannot keep and use the data for a separate purpose.[52] Data considered particularly sensitive are subject to stronger rules, and penalties for violations can be heavy.[53] Note that marketers must ask consumers to opt in to marketing programs, compared with the less consumer-friendly U.S. approach of forcing consumers to invest time and effort to opt out.

Information Disclosure Regulation

Pro-consumer activists and pro-business advocates can agree that disclosure of truthful information about products and services is generally good for competition and helps consumers make informed decisions. This goal of the U.S. consumer movement was endorsed by President Kennedy's 1962 proclamation of the Consumer Bill of Rights.[54]

In addition to enumerating four rights—to be safe, to be informed, to choose, and to be heard—the bill assured consumers that government would strengthen regulations to protect consumer welfare and enforce laws to promote effective competition. In this spirit, the Federal Reserve truth-in-lending regulation requires uniform disclosure from issuers of credit and charge cards in a "clear, easy-to-read, and easy-to-compare manner so that consumers can shop for the credit terms that work best for them."[55]

Reluctance to Regulate

In democratic societies, consumers can press their governments to address the most glaring information problems by means of laws, regulations, and enforcement agencies. Fear of litigation forestalls some bad behaviors: public opinion, judges, and juries are harsh on marketers that knowingly hide information about potentially harmful effects of their products.

All in all, though, the federal government is not eager to take on regulatory tasks. Among the reasons are the large administrative and budgetary burden. Also, in the case of ensuring privacy, in the 1990s the federal government questioned its ability to anticipate and write into law all eventualities surrounding online information use, or its ability to enforce regulations.[56] Another difficulty is that of calculating trade-offs between benefits and costs to consumers and businesses. The spate of identity thefts in 2005 served as ammunition for privacy advocates, in part because it's possible to quantify the financial damages and the time taken to restore one's identity. Instead, government counts on marketers and industry associations to self-regulate their conduct.

Marketplace Competition and Self-Regulation

Economists have always known that the extent and accuracy of the knowledge
of the economic actor had influence, and often a decisive influence,
on his behavior and therefore on the behavior of markets.

—George J. Stigler[57]

The consumer marketplace is supposed to work like this: if consumers have good information about closely equivalent products, they will buy from the seller offering the most favorable combination of price and value. For example, if consumers are well informed about front-loaded fees on mutual funds, then other features of the funds being close to equal, they should be more apt to pick the fund with the lowest fee. Market competition will eventually impel the high-fee funds to offer a higher-value product or else go by the wayside.

In theory, competitive marketplaces contain natural mechanisms to provide good information to consumers: competing marketers inform consumers about their strengths and opponents' weaknesses. Companies adopt open and truthful information practices for ethical reasons and in the hope they will enjoy greater public esteem and stronger customer relationships. Consumers themselves, as well as advocacy groups, investigate the market and exchange word of mouth. In practice, such checks and balances serve consumers' need for information. But they are far from perfect.

The problem is that marketers usually have more information about their products than consumers do and can operate with wide latitude concerning how much information they release or withhold. An automobile manufacturer, for example, has every incentive to promote an advanced braking system and attractive styling but no incentive to release statistics on its vehicles' mediocre crash resistance. Only the lowest-fee mutual fund has an incentive to highlight its fee structure; some unscrupulous fund marketers may want to mislead consumers about the front-loading fee. And consumers may not know what a front-loading fee is, let alone be able to calculate the financial impact on fund returns.

True, the carmaker that builds in superior crash resistance will likely want to inform safety-conscious consumers of its superiority. Possibly it will compare its performance to that of an inferior rival. But for the most part, marketers believe it is more productive to tell consumers about the benefits of their products rather than the shortcomings of their rivals. (Also, marketers can be sued by competitors that believe they have been misrepresented.) And if every carmaker builds vehicles with poor crash resistance, none has an incentive to inform the public.

In some circumstances, competitive pressures may create incentives for marketers to hide important information. For instance, in the pharmaceutical industry, the lure of blockbuster profits and intense competition among painkiller drugs Vioxx, Celebrex, and Bextra—each with sales of more than $1 billion per year—constituted a powerful incentive for drugmakers to conceal from the public evidence of inefficacy or dangerous side effects.[58]

Some companies also fear that disclosing too much information from early-stage clinical tests will tip off competitors to secret scientific information or business strategy. Journal editors and scientists have criticized the companies for withholding negative data through ploys such as not registering trials, refusing to publish studies with unfavorable results, or writing up only favorable outcomes. The FDA calls for less information disclosure than do regulators in Europe, where doctors systematically collect and submit information about how patients have reacted to prescription drugs. Patients' health may take a backseat as a result.[59]

Many industries recognize these kinds of problems and form industry associations that, among other things, foster open, truthful information practices. The advertising industry, for example, formulated and promulgated the basic principles stated in the International Chamber of Commerce's self-regulatory code: "All advertising should be legal, decent, honest and truthful," "should conform to the principles of fair competition, as generally accepted in business," "should be prepared with a due sense of social responsibility," and should meet "prevailing standards of decency."[60]

For many years, the industry has subscribed to voluntary monitoring by two industry organizations.[61] High principles may or may not be a motivation, but the self-interest is clear: marketers and advertisers benefit when consumers have faith in the integrity and honesty of market information. Further, self-regulation means that infractions can often be handled discreetly or quietly forwarded to the appropriate government agency (usually, competitors tip off the FTC to problematic advertising).

From the standpoint of consumers, self-regulation by industry has several advantages. To the extent that self-regulation encourages companies to follow high standards of legality and truthfulness, including disclosure of unflattering information, problems do not reach the market. By the time federal agencies step in, consumer welfare has already been damaged. In addition, self-regulatory codes usually are designed to comply with laws and regulations; industry associations reinforce adherence. And some industry associations provide a channel for consumers to bring complaints to the oversight agency.

On the other hand, when the information interests of consumers and marketers are not aligned, industry associations constitute a wealthy, powerful opponent. In the early 1990s, the telemarketing industry instituted self-mandated do-not-call lists; however, the burden was on consumers to prove violations. Testimony during the FTC rule-making process "told a woeful tale of industry non-compliance regarding in-house do not call lists."[62] After the national registry was established, the industry mounted challenges in four federal court cases, none of which succeeded. Clearly, the stakes were high; one year after going into effect, the registry contained more than 62 million telephone numbers, and the FTC estimated that 6.85 billion calls per year would be blocked.[63]

Arguably, self-regulation by the U.S. data brokerage industry has proved inadequate to allay consumers' concerns about the privacy and security of their personal information. Industry compliance with FTC-endorsed voluntary guidelines containing five principles—notice, choice, access, security, and redress—is modest.[64] In the face of consumers' growing displeasure with highly publicized security breaches, legislation may be passed to correct some of the privacy problems despite the millions of dollars spent by the industry in lobbying against such action.[65]

No doubt, marketers will argue that it is difficult and expensive to institute information safeguards and permission mechanisms. Yet ignoring consumers' views can also impose costs: surveys showing that privacy concerns led consumers to cut back on their use of online banking and bill payment services provide evidence of real costs to business.[66] Most marketers, excluding banks, insurers, and credit-card companies, do not have a long history of collecting and storing personal data. Now that they do, those that fail to take privacy seriously stand to lose customer trust. Those that develop a sense of responsibility for consumer privacy stand to earn trust—and possibly enjoy a competitive advantage.

Information-Empowered Consumers

Knowledge is the most democratic source of power.

—Alvin Toffler[67]

All the information in the world will not improve consumer choice unless consumers comprehend and act on it. Despite mandated small-print disclosures and consumer education, the intricacies of credit-card fees remain a mystery to multitudes of indebted consumers. Despite a wealth of nutritional advice from the media, nonprofits, and governmental agencies, there's little evidence that Americans have adopted healthier diets.

Even marketers—the experts at communicating information and forging links between product attributes and consumer goals—failed to make much of a dent in the public's eating habits when they introduced and advertised "healthy" products following a loosening of FDA restrictions on the kinds of claims they could make.[68] Reduced-fat and reduced-sodium versions of foods gained in popularity, and then waned as consumers reverted to familiar tastes or embraced the next diet fad. Providing information does not necessarily mean that consumers will undertake difficult behavioral changes.

But consumers who have the motivation and ability to ferret out and act on information stand to profit. Consider complex pricing schemes. Car marketers attract consumers with low base prices while making profits from options, warranties, and financing. Retailers of major appliances pair heavily discounted appliances with expensive service contracts. Restaurant wait staff fail to mention prices in their recitation of costly, off-the-menu daily specials. Catalog retailers add hidden shipping and handling charges.

Economists Xavier Gabaix and David Laibson point out that such price *shrouding* benefits sophisticated consumers who know how to calculate and avoid the high-priced extras that in effect subsidize the inexpensive base price.[69]

Clearly, consumers cannot use information if they don't have access to it. Like universal public education or the right to vote, equal access to information provides consumers an equal opportunity to participate in the economy and society. Equal information access—regardless of education, occupation, geographic location, race, or gender—levels the playing field.

Marketers often play an egalitarian role in information access, at least for consumers in modern economies. After all, they subsidize much of the media. In addition, mass marketing has brought down the price of communication and information technologies to the point where virtually every household can afford them. But whenever a new such technology enters the market, issues of equal access move to the foreground. During the initial stages, adopters have greater access to information than do other consumers. And the gap between early adopters and late or nonadopters aggravates existing social divides: early adopters tend to be younger, better educated, wealthier, more urban; nonadopters tend to be disadvantaged and to live in rural areas.

The developing markets for computer ownership and Internet access exhibited some of these divides. In the five largest Western European countries—France, Germany, Italy, Spain, and the United Kingdom—adoption of personal computers and the Internet had spread to mainstream consumers by 2004. Overall, almost two-thirds of adults had a computer at home and about half had access to the Internet, of whom more than two-fifths had high-speed access. But younger adults were twice as likely to have home Internet access as adults aged fifty-five and older; Northern European countries outpaced Southern European countries; men spent more time online than women.[70]

Not all consumers want to adopt the new information technologies. In Europe, most adults without a home personal computer say they have no need for it and don't feel it is relevant to their lives. One-third of those without Internet access display no interest in going online. That may be one reason European countries, with their older populations, lag world leaders Korea and Hong Kong in broadband access.[71] Younger European consumers, on the other hand, want to adopt the technology but some appear to be held back by price.[72]

The question is whether such gaps in technology access create information gaps that translate into consumer disadvantages. Much of the information available online is also available offline, albeit less conveniently. Many public libraries provide Internet service. Increasingly, though, consumers with their own online access, particularly high-speed access, enjoy an information-based advantage. Consumers who research the prices of automobiles online can negotiate with dealers armed with full knowledge of the price paid by the dealer, the value of manufacturer rebates and incentives to the dealer, and the value of their trade-in. There is evidence that "the consumers who have benefited most from using the Internet when buying a car are those who used to get a raw deal in the showrooms, including women and minorities."[73]

Anyone who has access to Google's search engine can become an expert—or find one—quickly. Consumers research complex financial products like credit cards, mortgages, auto loans, home equity loans, and insurance online to find the best terms—an activity that would be almost impossible offline. To make informed health decisions, 20 to 40 percent of U.S. online consumers have researched health-related information from general health and fitness sites, their own health plan site, government or disease association sites, and drug or medical device sites.[74] Consumers who have signed up for airline e-mail lists receive notification of heavily discounted flights exclusive to the online channel. With online maps and detailed driving instructions, something as mundane as driving to an unfamiliar store is easier for the connected consumer.

The city of Philadelphia is attempting to bridge the digital divide through a public–private partnership that will supply wireless high-speed Internet access to all of its neighborhoods. This Wi-Fi network, the city hopes, will help bring minorities and poor people online, attract business to neighborhoods, and connect schools and pupils.[75] San Francisco is following suit. Other cities and towns also see broadband services as a part of municipal infrastructure. Economic development appears to be the primary motive, but at least in the case of Philadelphia, social concern for equal opportunity is also a factor.

Marketers might well ask themselves whether the Philadelphia experiment on a large scale—applied to the whole of a poor region or country—could pay off in a more vibrant society and higher-potential consumer economy. Should they join ventures that emulate Nicholas Negroponte, of the MIT Media Lab, who is creating $100 computers for African schoolchildren? In India, ITC Limited is installing solar-powered, Internet-connected computers in thirty rural villages a day. According to one report, this "e-choupal" initiative "is changing the lives of farmers on a scale no other venture has ever done . . . In many villages e-choupals have become the axis around which the local community revolves."[76]

In the information age, it's taken for granted that access to and use of information enable individuals and organizations to accomplish more. And since the beginning of widespread use of the Internet and particularly the World Wide Web in the mid-1990s, visionaries have declared that the resulting democratization of information access will transform everything from politics to society to economic inequalities. Many see possibilities for new forms of citizen engagement and empowerment that will give the people a greater voice in governments and markets.

It is not clear that greater information availability alone will galvanize formerly apathetic citizens to engage in politics or community building, but there are signs that marketing is changing. Younger consumers, especially, are becoming involved with marketing by way of the new information technologies. They are receptive to receiving information from and sharing information with marketers, contributing content and ideas as well as information about themselves. In the movement to "buy local" and support organic farmers, for example, they are investing time and energy to research social causes that directly affect consumer marketing.[77]

CHAPTER 5

Engagement

Ties That Bind

CONSUMERS SHAPE THE MARKETPLACE through the choices they make, the actions they take, and the rights they claim. In competitive markets, consumers' votes at the cash register give them a strong say about the fates of products and services. Many consumers also engage actively with marketers. They talk to market researchers, suggest service improvements, submit new product ideas. Why? It's because the marketplace is a salient part of people's lives. It provides a context for engagement and creativity. Consumers want the market to be fair, and they want it to respond to their needs.

When supplies are tight, people may want to market themselves, perhaps convince a merchant or dealer that their past loyalty or future patronage merits receiving part of a limited allocation. Potential customers line up outside trendy New York nightclubs to appeal for admittance. A family bidding on a house in a seller's market will sweeten its offer with money but may also market itself to the seller as a worthy custodian of the home.

Given the abundance of supply in contemporary Western markets, consumers, for the most part, are in the driver's seat. They seek the solutions that work best for them, at a convenient time and place, and marketers try to accommodate them. Consumers form opinions about companies and products. They experiment with product uses, and they tell one another what they know and what they like. The result, from a marketer's point of view, is reduced control over market communications and brand image.

Marketers have learned that it is the human element that molds the market. Dry economic calculations of benefits versus costs, demand versus supply, or even extensive market research and testing are not very good at explaining why products like New Coke fail, and other offerings, like Hush Puppies or Beanie Babies, unexpectedly take off. Reviewing consumer surveys or Nielsen retail sales data provides only a partial picture of consumer behavior. The best marketers want to meet consumers individually and in groups, observe them, and engage in conversation—if not in person, then through technology.

But more than accommodating or observing consumers, marketers are adopting the democratic view that consumer engagement will bolster, and not weaken, marketing. Just as political democracies are more robust and more representative when citizens engage in public affairs, companies are learning that letting consumers participate in marketing strengthens their competitive position. For one thing, it is a way to gain a better understanding of consumers' wishes. Also, some consumers value a deeper relationship with marketers and will reward the marketer with greater loyalty, higher profits, and word-of-mouth recommendations. In many cases, marketers are finding that turning over marketing tasks and functions to consumers can simultaneously shift costs and increase consumers' sense of empowerment and satisfaction.

For that matter, consumer participation in product creation and delivery can evolve to the point that consumers take over. Enabled by technology, consumers invent new networks for sharing knowledge. On their own, they create complex products and new forms of business. Peer-to-peer file sharing, open-source software production, and blogging represent a democratization of the marketplace that reduces or even circumvents the role of professional marketers.

Learning Through the Grapevine

Knowledge is of two kinds: we know a subject ourselves,
or we know where we can find information upon it.

—Samuel Johnson[1]

Consumers like to seek out and share marketplace information, a practice that harks back to survival mechanisms. Just as hunter and gatherer social groups send scouts to investigate and report on possible sources of food, so too do market scouts investigate alternative offerings and share their findings with friends, relatives, and acquaintances.

People also share information on products and brands because products and brands matter to them. Susan Fournier described fifteen types of relationships consumers have with brands, including "best friendships" (e.g., between a jogger and her trusted Reebok running shoes), "casual friends/buddies" (e.g., between one consumer and her household cleaning brands), and "enslavements" (e.g., a consumer forced to subscribe to cable television absent any other choice).[2] In strong, positive relationships, brands can make consumers "feel wanted, respected, listened to, and cared for."[3] Many consumers who feel positively about a brand recommend it to others. According to Fred Reichheld, "They behave almost as if they were adjuncts to the organization's sales force."[4] In 2003, 60 percent of Dell's customers fell into this "promoter" category.[5]

Consumer Experts

In the fluid social structure of the marketplace, highly involved consumers voluntarily take on specialized networking roles. *Opinion leaders* stand out by virtue of their deep and enduring involvement with a particular category—say, automobiles, films, or running shoes. In the course of their infatuation, they acquire extensive product knowledge and expertise. Archetypal opinion leaders enjoy telling others about the objects of their affection, and less-experienced consumers turn to them for advice. Opinion leadership in marketing resembles opinion leadership in public affairs: a few highly committed individuals can sway others. The opinion leaders gather information, and the people who are undecided seek and rely on information from them, rather than the media. In fact, consumer behavior research on the importance of interpersonal influence traces to a study of the 1940 presidential election by Paul Lazarsfeld et al.; Lazarsfeld subsequently extended his concept to food and household products, movies, and fashion.[6]

Opinion leaders tend to specialize in one or two product categories. *Market mavens* are the generalists who acquire wide-ranging product and store knowledge. They enjoy shopping and finding good deals, and they like to share their expertise.[7] Market mavens keep up with market news and help other consumers cut through information clutter. They provide customized recommendations: their information and advice varies according to what the maven knows about the recipient and what the recipient wants to know.

Early adopters hold considerable sway when it comes to new products. What better source of information is there when you're considering a new hybrid gas-electric car than the person who has just acquired one? Moreover, by buying products such as cars or cell phones, early adopters set visible examples. They constitute walking and talking advertisements, and their influence can expand quickly and far afield. Social scientists have found that a small number of people can trigger *informational cascades*, in which momentum builds for growing numbers of people to adopt a behavior in part because others have adopted it.

As a cascade develops, people who haven't yet adopted rely less on their own evaluation and more and more on the strong signal provided by people who have adopted. This pattern neatly fits the decision to buy a new product, and it is most pronounced for products that are visible to others.[8] Informational cascades can also work in reverse, when negative information triggers a steep decline in sales.[9] A CBS *60 Minutes* report alleging "unintended acceleration" problems with Audi cars caused an immediate collapse in sales that took a decade to reverse, even after Audi was cleared by national safety agencies in the United States and overseas.[10]

Word of Mouth

Influence is not limited to experts. Over time, word of mouth (or "word of mouse" via the Internet) creates a strong cumulative or snowball effect on preferences. (By some estimates, without the Internet, people who were happy with a product told, on average, five other people; if unhappy, they told ten others. With the Internet, those numbers have increased to twenty and sixty, respectively.)[11] Lucky marketers receive free advertising for their brand every time phrases like "a Kodak moment" or echoes of Nike's "Just Do It" tagline pass from consumer to consumer.

Consumer-to-consumer information exchanges are not only ubiquitous but also influential in purchase decisions, in part because people consider information received from other consumers more credible than information from marketers or most media sources. Recent surveys indicate that fewer than half of consumers trust TV or radio ads, but almost nine out of ten trust recommendations from other consumers.[12] According to one researcher, "Consumers are 50 percent more likely to be influenced by word-of-mouth recommendations from their peers than by radio/TV ads."[13]

Word of mouth is democratic. It is open to all consumers, including those who lack the means or ability to access information published in magazines and newspapers or stored in libraries and online. It does not completely level the playing field—one network of people may be much better and more quickly informed than another network—but it does serve to protect the poor or illiterate consumer. It is important in rural areas, in developed as well as emerging economies.

Similarly, word of mouth helps small companies that cannot afford to spend as much on marketing as their large competitors. Starbucks expanded from one store in 1986 to eighty-four stores in 1990 with virtually no advertising; the company relied largely on word-of-mouth endorsements from customers, as well as the signage at every new retail store, to promote the brand.[14]

The flip side of word of mouth is the spread of negative information. Sometimes that is good. If unfavorable assessments of marketers or their products help winnow out the poor performers, consumers benefit. But there is no benefit to consumers if unfounded rumors harm a reputable corporation or brand. Such rumors can be persistent. In 1980, allegations began circulating that Procter & Gamble had ties to satanism and witchcraft (the company's moon-and-stars logo was offered as supposed proof), and consumers were urged not to buy the company's products. Fifteen years later, despite prevailing in more than a dozen lawsuits against parties accused of starting or fostering the rumors, P&G was still fighting them and receiving nearly two hundred calls a day from consumers worried about satanism.[15]

If a consumer pursuing a vendetta against a business uses the Internet as a bullhorn, there is little the company can do except seek a legal injunction on the grounds of libel. In the United States, the First Amendment gives individuals rights to publish almost anything they wish. For example, patients are posting complaints on Internet sites that name names of medical providers but allow the patient to remain anonymous. Some disgruntled patients have created sites specifically to denigrate a particular physician. A more evenhanded development is the emergence of Web sites that rate doctors but require a minimum number of reviews before evaluations are posted and allow physicians to post a rebuttal.[16] Unfortunately for marketers—and for consumers seeking unbiased information—separating legitimate complaints from exaggerated grievances is next to impossible.

Buzz Marketing

Word of mouth spreads quickly on its own, but a little intervention can speed up the diffusion. *Buzz marketing* attempts to drive fashion trends, accelerate product adoption, and create a surge in demand. In buzz marketing, which is a form of informational cascade, it is not necessarily a product's functional attributes that make it a hit. Rather, interactions among people are the force that charges and aligns their collective desires. Consumer participation culminates in the explosion of demand that constitutes a hit.

One tactic is to kindle initial interest that ignites spontaneous word of mouth. Following the example of the cascade for the low-budget film *The Blair Witch Project*, New Line Cinema invested in a Web site and e-mail campaign to build advance interest in the *Lord of the Rings* trilogy; consumers downloaded 6.6 million files from the site and showed up in huge numbers on opening weekend; in turn, the opening-weekend success prompted other consumers to see the movie.[17]

Another tactic is to employ promoters posing as regular consumers. For instance, a Boston-based company called BzzAgent recruits unpaid consumers to participate in marketing campaigns in which they plug a company's products to friends, family, and colleagues.[18] Similarly, Procter & Gamble has enrolled women who possess large social networks (they speak to about twenty-five to thirty other women each day) in its Vocalpoint word-of-mouth marketing program.[19] In both cases, agents participate for free samples and the satisfaction of having influence.

These programs raise ethical issues concerning disclosure about the agent's role in initiating what recipients may take to be spontaneous and unsponsored conversations. Although BzzAgent now tells its agents to identify themselves as such, Vocalpoint leaves the disclosure decision up to the individual agent. Critics have complained to the Federal Trade Commission that not disclosing an agent's affiliation with the marketer commercializes human relations and undercuts social trust. As a practical matter, if consumers feel they've been deceived there could be a backlash against the marketer.[20]

Brand Communities

Whereas buzz marketing is a deliberate attempt to influence the public, consumers who participate in *brand communities* meet marketers more than halfway. As distinguished from market mavens or other experts, these people concentrate their energies on a particular brand. Their willingness to share opinions, and to identify themselves, is a boon for market research and advertising. For instance, Snapple invited consumers to submit ideas for new beverage mixes and names, and Snapple consumers appeared in ads with Wendy, the Snapple employee who became the brand spokesperson.

The more enduring brand communities persist because of a cliquish fascination with the brand, which frequently possesses an "outsider" appeal. Also, the brand must stay true to its essence throughout cycles of product-line revision and expansion. Harley-Davidson and Apple are among the classic examples of long-lasting brand communities, nurtured but not controlled by corporate headquarters.[21] But brand communities are not an unalloyed blessing. If a brand aspires to the mainstream, then an association with an almost cultlike following may be at odds with the desired positioning. In the worst-case scenario for marketers, a brand becomes hostage to its fiercely loyal customers.

Consumers Co-Producing with Marketers

All the world's a stage, / And all the men and women merely players. /
They have their exits and their entrances; /
And one man in his time plays many parts.

—William Shakespeare[22]

We tend to think of companies as "producers" and consumers as "receivers." In actuality, the line between the two is blurred and becoming more so. This is especially the case in service industries, which now account for more than three-quarters of GDP in the United States.[23] Delivery of *experiential* services, such as restaurant dining, where production and consumption occur at the same time, demands active participation from the customer. The quality of professional services, such as legal advice, depends on how well clients define their situation, needs, and desires.

Following Scripts

John Deighton views marketing as "an intrinsically dramatistic discipline": consumers attend performances, consumers participate in service providers' performances, consumers perform with products, and products perform for consumers.[24] The famous *Seinfeld* "Soup Nazi" episode riffs on an unstated rule of the marketplace: service results depend on how well customers play their role. In one scene, set in a soup deli, one character (Jerry) explains the strict ordering procedure to another (George), including where to stand and how to give the order clearly with no extraneous comments or questions allowed—all to keep the line moving. George violates the rules and the proprietor yells, "No soup for you!"[25]

Through personal experience, a marketer's signals, and the example of other customers, a consumer learns "scripts" that lay out an expected sequence of behaviors by the consumer and the service provider.[26] Customers must learn a wide repertoire of scripts appropriate to different buying situations. At fast-food restaurants, patrons walk to the counter to place an order; at fine restaurants, patrons wait to be seated and a server takes the order. Paradoxically, consumers most notice scripts when the script changes or they do not yet have a suitable one, such as when a customer consults an accountant for the first time and becomes aware he does not know the accountant's procedures or what financial data he needs. Otherwise, consumers play out ritualized scripts and roles automatically.[27]

How consumers behave during marketing exchanges can degrade or enhance the experience for others. Indeed, consumers' very presence in service encounters conditions how people experience the marketer's product offering. A full dining room creates a fashionable buzz; a full flight is uncomfortable; the presence of a boisterous child disrupts a quiet meal. If customers do not know how to behave or if they deviate from the script, there is the potential to disrupt the experience for other customers. A customer who does not know the ropes or has an extended argument with a store clerk slows ordering or checkout for everyone.

Furthermore, customers who don't play by the rules may indirectly harm other consumers by causing problems that add costs to marketing. Those customers who game the system—for example, by illegitimately taking advantage of "satisfaction guaranteed" offers or manipulating air miles and frequent flyer points—pressure marketers to institute restrictive rules.

Consumer-Aided Design and Marketing

When consumers participate in market research, they are essentially helping design a marketer's offering. However, participation rates have been declining, thanks to fewer people being at home, time pressures, exasperation with intrusive telemarketing calls, and the like. Or it may be that marketers have not thanked consumers properly (not so much with financial incentives as with follow-up feedback on survey results) or demonstrated that they act on consumers' input.

Lately, marketers have turned to democratic ways to involve consumers in product design and selection. For instance, consumers are invited to vote on flavors and colors of products like Life Savers and Crest toothpaste.[28] Never mind that the manufacturer probably has done preliminary research, knows the likely results, and has the new products ready for rollout.

Audiences vote for the winning amateur contestants on popular reality television shows like *British Idol, American Idol,* and *Indian Idol.* Commentators noted that more votes were cast—more than 60 million—in the spring 2006 final round of *American Idol* than in the previous U.S. presidential election. On other reality shows, such as *Survivor* and *The Apprentice,* ordinary people live together for a month or more, and their interactions, filmed by an ever-present camera crew, supply the narrative and dramatic content of the program. Does appearing on these shows represent a form of healthy self-expression, exhibitionism, or exploitation by marketers? It is difficult to tell.

Although such voting gimmicks and populist entertainment products— at least in their current form—may well turn out to be a fad, the appeal of consumer participation appears to transcend national and cultural boundaries. *Super Girl,* a Chinese program modeled after the *Idol* series, proved to be a tremendous hit, its season finale watched by more than 400 million people. Reportedly, the selection of the winner by popular election spurred a national discussion of democracy in China. Some commentators speculated that the show's success placed political pressure on Chinese leaders, while others expressed concern that it represented an erosion of Chinese culture.[29]

Engaging with marketers offers consumers creative, as well as self-promotion, possibilities. For example, consumers are creating brand advertising. Members of the public submitted more than a thousand commercials to Converse, and Firefox attracted 280 broadcast-quality ads in a recent contest.[30] Younger consumers, in particular, are conversant with the language of marketing and persuasion; they have lived their entire lives surrounded by it. In technique, visual imagery, wit, and meaning, an ad may enjoy equal standing with a television program or a magazine article. Technology provides the tools to create nearly professional quality ads and venues to display the creative effort. On the YouTube Web site, the second-place spot for Firefox received at least 23,000 viewings. A consumer-created ad for Doritos was aired during the 2007 Super Bowl.

Highly expert consumers may engage with marketers in product design. To push products to the limits of their capability, *lead users* modify equipment if necessary, even have parts custom manufactured. Eric von Hippel reports that compared with other innovation processes, companies that systematically tap in to expert lead users' prototypes and ideas for new products—3M is a prime example—can expect to introduce new products with higher market shares and greater strategic potential.[31] In particular, lead-user innovation helps overcome a problem that has long perplexed market research: how to uncover ideas for discontinuous innovations among consumers. Although the average consumer can identify problems and inconveniences that new products and services might solve, only a few can imagine complete solutions that do not yet exist.

Self-Service

More prosaically, consumers often substitute their own time and labor for tasks formerly performed by manufacturers and suppliers. They pick items from supermarket shelves and pump gas at filling stations in return for lower prices. They manage their transactions at ATMs instead of patronizing the dwindling number of bank tellers in return for faster and perhaps more reliable service. They assemble IKEA furniture and other products in return for the convenience of taking items home via the family car or receiving overnight delivery by UPS. They book airline and hotel reservations online in return for greater control over schedules and class of service.

For many consumers, this increased control translates into greater satisfaction. It eliminates dependence on a slow or reluctant service provider, a source of frustration and annoyance. Self-service consumers may spend more effort in making transactions work, but they gain a sense of empowerment.

Marketers point to the resulting cost savings they can pass on to consumers. But as some observers speculate, the notion of "outsourcing of labor to the customer" has not resulted in reduced costs, only the transfer of costs from the company to the consumer.[32] An end to such transfers appears nowhere in sight. U.S. consumers are encouraged to check themselves in at airports and out at supermarkets. Companies continue to cut down on employee help desks, and consumers are forced to seek the answer in a maze of automated telephone or online menu options.

Until consumers demand—and are willing to pay for—a higher level of service, customer participation in service delivery enabled by technology will continue to advance. If this trend continues, consumers deserve the treatment Vanguard gives them: "When an investor calls Vanguard, the rep's priority isn't to fulfill the request quickly and move on to the next call . . . The rep guides the customer through the site and teaches him how to use it."[33] At the same time, Vanguard achieves its goal: "The customer never calls again—and instead goes to the Web" at much lower cost to Vanguard.[34]

Consumer Self-Reliance and Market Democratization

I wanted to give the power of the market back to individuals.

—Pierre Omidyar[35]

Not only do consumers collaborate with marketers in designing, producing, and delivering products, but also they take on these jobs independently of marketers. Phenomena like the free or open-source software movement, blogging, and peer production of Web content are all products of consumers' collaborating and creating with each other.

In 1991, Linus Torvalds, a college student in Finland, developed a free computer operating system in the spirit of the open-source software movement, which encourages the public to download, use, modify, and distribute the software's underlying source code. Within a decade, the Linux system was embraced by technology industry giants IBM, Hewlett-Packard, Intel, and NEC Technologies; by other large companies, including DaimlerChrysler; and also by governments, particularly in developing countries.[36]

How this happened is largely attributable to the community aspect of open-source software. No one programmer, however smart, can hope to create an entire operating system. But having free and open access to code, thousands of users have added to the Linux project. Eric Raymond, a technology researcher, advised corporate users, "If you cooperate completely with the open source community, you get testing help you couldn't get anywhere else.

You multiply your company by the brain power of hundreds of thousands in the open source community out there."[37]

Collectively, consumers are knowledgeable—or like to pass themselves off as knowledgeable—on almost any subject. The democratically authored *Wikipedia* online encyclopedia contains more than a million articles in one hundred languages and is bigger than *Encyclopedia Britannica* and *Encarta* combined.[38] The original premise was complete inclusivity: anyone can contribute or edit articles. That opened the door for errors, false information, opinion, or long-winded discourse. However, the Wiki philosophy assumed that with many people reading the articles and monitoring changes, problems would be corrected quickly, and as *Wikipedia* drew more visitors, the overall accuracy would continue to improve.[39]

Social Sharing

Masses of consumers display a passion for talking and making social connections. The Internet undammed a flood of communication, through words, sounds, and images. According to an estimate for 2005, the World Wide Web contained more than 9 million blogs, with 40,000 new ones popping up each day.[40] The authors of these messages talk about anything and everything. Adding to their reach is the podcast format.[41] Within a year after its invention, some 5,000 podcasts on virtually every conceivable topic were reaching consumers.[42] People daily watch more than 100 million videos on YouTube, and users upload 65,000 videos per day, many of them created for fun as well as by comedians, musicians, videobloggers, and others hoping to reach an audience.[43] Everyone is a potential citizen publisher. As politicians and the media have discovered, news no longer is channeled through press releases, scripted public relations events, and reporters. A lone person can post words and images that within hours, if not minutes, are disseminated through networks of individuals to audiences of millions.

Sharing photos, video clips, commentary, jokes, personal news, and other content is nothing new. But the digitizing of content, and the availability of editing tools and publishing platforms, allows consumers to share their creations on an unprecedented scale and with unprecedented production and presentation quality. A New Jersey teenager uploaded a Web cam video of himself lip-synching and doing the "Numa Numa" dance to a Romanian pop song.[44] Soon the video ended up on NBC's *Tonight* show, attracted millions of Web site hits, and inspired a host of knockoff versions (including some from Japan and Jamaica), and, of course, T-shirts and accessories capitalizing on the craze. A teenager in Johannesburg could have done the same thing.

Until recently, helping people get to know people or businesses outside their immediate social circle was a labor-intensive endeavor. Matchmakers arranged marriages, and employment agencies arranged job interviews. People joined clubs and organizations as a way of meeting others with similar interests. The painstakingly compiled Yellow Pages allowed consumers to find businesses within a geographic area by specialty. But with the arrival of Internet and database technology, these services found an immediate home online, and with that came a dramatic increase in the ability to connect people with other people—lots of other people—and to update information nearly instantaneously.

Online dating services like Match.com and eHarmony.com eliminate the need for human intermediaries and provide a universe of millions of registered users and subscribers for people in search of a match.[45] Craigslist grew from an online community bulletin board serving San Francisco to forums for listing housing, jobs, personals, items for sale, community events, and so on, in more than two hundred cities around the world. For years, founder Craig Newmark has run the site bare-bones style, with little emphasis on the profit motive. Newmark's orientation is reflected in his title: "Chairman and Customer Service Representative."[46] It's also shown in his public statements: "I guess if one is building a community kind of site, whatever that means, people are really good at telling whether you're doing so through an honest intent of connecting with the community . . . or whether you're just trying to make a lot of money right away."[47]

Rapidly growing companies like MySpace.com, Friendster.com, and Facebook.com, which connect people seeking new friends, cleverly expand the customer base by leveraging consumers' social networks. Current users recruit friends, who recruit their friends, and so on. Typically, the business strategy is to build scale by trading consumer participation for service; basic levels of service are free or nearly so, with advertising and fees for higher levels of service bringing in the bulk of revenue.

Meetup Inc. uses the virtual world of the Web to help people organize interest-group meetings of all types in the "real" world. The implications of this capability for the democratic political process became apparent in the 2003–2004 presidential election primary season, when the upstart Howard Dean campaign used Meetup.com to organize grassroots efforts.

If consumer-to-consumer conversation is a source of power, then consumers are seizing more of it. Aside from posing a direct threat to the profitability of traditional publishing and media businesses, consumer-to-consumer conversation undermines any company's ability to keep tight control over its corporate and brand images. The stories, accolades, and complaints that consumers exchange are out there. Whether these accounts are false or true, no company can suppress them.

The same forces bring more transparency to internal company operations. Dissemination of a single internal memo or e-mail that happens to cast an unflattering light on company intentions, policies, or procedures can undo years of careful brand building. Information released by employees and disseminated by consumers may well join the regulatory and legal tort system as brakes on corporate behavior.

Implications for Intellectual Property

What changes might traditional businesses expect as a result of greater consumer-to-consumer sharing and engagement with the marketplace? Von Hippel discerns a trend toward greater democratization in innovation, including innovation of both physical and information products. Aided by technology, consumers are becoming self-reliant innovators. Cheap computers and Internet communication links help decentralize the means of production to groups of consumers (compared with the Industrial Revolution, which relied on large capital investments and scale economies). No longer dependent on the traditional, manufacturer-centered model, consumers can develop precisely what they want and need, whether it be high-performance windsurfers or software.[48]

Furthermore, the willingness of consumer innovators to share and freely exchange innovative ideas and products liberates other consumers and entrepreneurs from the constraints imposed by restrictive patents and copyrights. The result—a faster stream of innovation and lower costs to consumers—represents an increase in social welfare over the manufacturer-centered model, assert Lawrence Lessig, von Hippel, and other critics of the current intellectual property system.[49]

Lessig, in particular, argues forcefully that the generous terms of U.S. laws (such as the Digital Millennium Copyright Act) granting intellectual property rights to corporations take away individual freedoms, inhibit creativity, and undermine the democratic ideals on which the United States was founded. Ironically, proponents of freeing up intellectual property may be stronger believers in the free market than the capitalists who want to beef up property rights: they reason that reducing patent and other restrictions opens up competition that eventually benefits customers; competition forces firms like the big pharmaceutical or software companies to innovate faster and in more significant ways.[50]

Whether or not Lessig's fears are exaggerated, innovation in the marketplace, whatever the source, eventually erodes competitive advantages based on older technology. Defending outmoded industry niches is always a losing proposition. How then, aside from barricading themselves behind legal thickets and political lobbying, might companies respond to democratization's erosion of manufacturing- or R&D-based sources of advantage? It could be argued that successful firms have better customer insight, gained by scanning the environment to search for new trends, new consumer needs, and new solutions devised by consumers.[51] The "it's no good because it's not invented here" approach certainly will not work.

The Lessons of eBay

eBay adroitly leverages the power of consumer sharing and participation. Created in 1995 by programmer Pierre Omidyar as a Web site for his fiancée to trade Pez dispensers with other collectors, the "world's largest yard sale" quickly achieved a critical mass of users.[52] Five years later, amid the wreckage of the dot-com bust, eBay was one of a handful of profitable survivors. In 2004 it handily reached a goal of $1 billion in operating profit.[53] Participants number more than 100 million registered users worldwide, ranging from the person who buys or sells once or twice a year to the entrepreneur who is building a viable business selling through the site.

Why is eBay thriving? First, the company created a new, democratic marketplace connecting buyers and sellers around the world. Product assortment is huge: consumers can find anything from an old kitchen spoon, to a used automobile, to a piece of fine art. Participation is low cost: buyers register for free, and sellers pay a minimal listing fee and a modest sales commission on items sold. Marketplace roles are fluid: the same person is a buyer one day and a seller the next. Information is open: anyone can view product descriptions, bidding history, prices of similar items previously sold, and so on. Participants work at maintaining trust. Rules are commonsense and transparent.

Users rate each other after each transaction and monitor any suspicious behavior; this information is posted online.

Additionally, from the start Omidyar conceived of his enterprise as a democratic, self-governing community. In most cases corporate executives believe shareholders own the brand. eBay made the transition from a Web marketplace perceived as consumer driven and democratic to a more traditionally managed business by giving buyers and sellers a strong voice. That philosophy is manifest in company statements: "The eBay platform is built on trust. The millions of successful transactions that take place on the site each day are a testament to the fact that people, when left to their own devices, almost always do the right thing."[54] The user community also contributes ideas and feedback for fostering business growth, such as introducing new categories of goods and fixed-price trading, which now accounts for 30 percent of sales. An annual users' conference echoes the participatory democracy of New England towns lauded by Tocqueville.

Why Weak Ties Are Strong

Yochai Benkler suggests that "peer production" and "social sharing" deserve serious consideration as "a third mode of organizing production, alongside markets and the state" that can complement or substitute for the other modes.[55] Interestingly, Benkler's examples—which include the peer networks that produce Linux and the ad hoc system in the Washington, D.C., area that enables people to carpool safely with strangers—are not restricted to family and friends. Rather, consumers share with people they have never met and with whom they never expect to develop close ties.

In the 1970s, Mark Granovetter argued that weak social ties among individuals are actually a strong cohesive force in society.[56] At first glance this seems counterintuitive: strong ties of family, religion, ethnic group, and so on should create strong social groups and a more cohesive society. But strong ties bond only people within the group; weak ties are needed to bridge the various groups within society. Individuals who have many weak ties with others are well placed to spread information, innovations, and a broader sense of community. From this perspective, then, peer production and sharing are cohesive forces, although the mainstream software industry might be inclined to view them as corrosive forces.

The idea of business opportunities based on participation and sharing is not entirely new. Insurance and mutual funds companies, especially mutual companies owned by customers, are essentially democratic institutions that share risk; they could not thrive if a critical mass of consumers did not participate.[57] Consumers in the United Kingdom participate in an online peer-to-peer service, called Zopa, that cuts out the role of traditional, reputable banks or other credit organizations in loan arrangements. In contrast with an organization like CircleLending, which helps people arrange and manage loans with family and friends, Zopa connects strangers, who borrow or lend money to each other at mutually agreed rates of interest; lenders are attracted by better rates of return than savings accounts and more predictability than the stock market. The enterprise is based on a good dollop of trust.[58] The 6 million consumers that Zopa targets include a segment of consumers dubbed "freeformers" for their disinclination to depend on corporations or the state.[59] These individuals are part of a populist experiment in creating new kinds of social and business ties that may be far looser than anything Granovetter discussed.

Democratization of Business

The experiences of a few organizations point to possible modifications in the current undemocratic, command-and-control model of business management. eBay engages customers in running its marketplace; management operates under the assumption that its users have the enterprise's best interests in mind. The Wiki community relies on consumers to supply information content. Skype's technology platform for Internet telephone calls is nothing but the spare capacity of customers' personal computers.[60] Craigslist numbers ten million users, but the entire company staff is eighteen employees. There is no grand company strategy guiding growth; a new city is added when enough people request it.[61] By no means, though, is the business community ready to hand over the reins to consumers. After all, it is a rare corporation that empowers its owners—its shareholders—to elect corporate directors by majority vote.

To put democratization of the consumer marketplace into a broader perspective, note that since the beginning of the Industrial Revolution, consumers have ceded production of most goods and services to businesses. That is not likely to change. On average, consumers exhibit no great desire to take over from manufacturers. People want the convenience, affordability, and choice provided by manufacturers. They want things to be "simply better," to use Barwise and Meehan's term.[62] In any category, consumer innovation and production usually involve a small number of consumers who are highly engaged with the product.

It is more the exception than the rule for the average consumer to jump in, say, when companies fail to deliver key benefits. For example, people from poor African neighborhoods, tired of doing without public or private health coverage, banded together to create affordable "micro health insurance" plans.[63] Moreover, involvement is highly product specific: the engineer who participates in developing Linux-based software applications is not likely to be the same person who pushes the boundaries on 3D printers for rapid prototyping.

Free-for-All?

Man is known to be a selfish, as well as a social being.

—James Madison[64]

"Show me the money" is the typical motivator in economic production and exchange. But often, consumers participating in peer-to-peer production and social sharing are not seeking monetary rewards. It's true that some end up making money as a result of their participation. Linus Torvalds now works for an open-source software consortium. A cofounder of Flickr, a Web-based photo-sharing service, celebrated its acquisition by Yahoo! with the sentiment, "Woohoo! What does this mean? It means that we'll no longer have to draw straws to see who gets paid" while promising to "remain open wide as the all outdoors."[65]

Yet economic exchange and social sharing are different enough that blending the two systems or transitioning from a social exchange to an economic model, or vice versa, could violate people's norms about what is right. Benkler cites the example that one would never pay a friend for a dinner party but would bring flowers or wine. In some circumstances, paying people can crowd out altruistic behavior or produce poorer results, as when the British system of all-volunteer blood donation yielded higher-quality supplies in the 1970s compared with the American part-paid system.[66]

Non-Monetary Motives

If money is not the primary motivator, then why do people participate in peer production and social sharing? Altruism, difficult as it is to pin down or divorce from self-serving behavior, is one reason.[67] Evolutionary biologists observe altruistic behavior—something an individual organism does that lowers its probability of survival or reproduction but increases the reproduction or survival of others—in many species. Robert Trivers profoundly influenced a generation of sociobiologists, evolutionary psychologists, and economists by showing that *reciprocal altruism* makes sense from a Darwinian or genetic perspective.[68] In other words, organisms are endowed with a predisposition to act altruistically. Culture and upbringing reinforce sharing behaviors; rewards include the immediate satisfaction in having helped others and the eventual recognition from peers.

A sense of fairness is another possible motive. Although few customers concern themselves with things like detecting shoplifters or fraudulent coupon users—preferring to cede most enforcement to officials—consumers participate in small ways in regulating marketplace behavior. Actions such as policing customers who attempt to cut in line or posting feedback on eBay regarding fraudulent activity by sellers or buyers protect consumers' own interests. Helping fellow customers find their way around supermarket aisles or posting product ratings on Amazon.com speaks to a spirit of altruism. Forming consumerist organizations to battle perceived inequities benefits those who individually have very little market power.

Personal benefit, of course, is also a motivation. Consumers who take the time and trouble to complain to marketers invariably want the marketer to do better. They don't want to be let down in the relationship, and they want to receive better performance the next time they use the marketer.

That still does not answer the question of why people choose to volunteer time and effort in market-related activities for which other people—business employees or owners—are being paid. Inevitably, one reason is that they think they can perform services better or more reliably than the employees of a service provider. Another reason is simply that there are gaps in the marketplace that present interesting and relevant problems to solve. If consumers want access to a wide variety of music and are tired of paying for a bundle of ten tracks to get the one track they want, then someone will try to figure out an alternative. In addition to the intrinsic satisfaction gained from discovering or creating something new, there is the practical benefit of getting something useful.

Moreover, peer production allows people to share in a way that respects individual autonomy; consumers choose whether, when, and how they want to participate. They need make few, if any, fixed commitments. Consumers decide moment-to-moment how much excess computer capacity or automobile capacity or labor they want to contribute. They can participate in one project or many. Participants are not bound by strong social ties that would impose obligations. Social or economic status hardly matters. A network of weak ties is fluid. Participants can develop attachments or not. Participation is decentralized, loosely coupled, like transactions in a perfect economic market except that other motivations replace economic ones.

New Norms

Widespread access to digital information and communications technology allows consumers to share more visibly and on a larger scale than before. And when the thing being exchanged is digital information, fewer sacrifices have to be made. When friends and neighbors share a saw, only one person at a time can use it. The saw has a limited life span; with repeated use it becomes dull. In other words, sharing imposes costs on the owner. Digital information can be copied and distributed to millions at close to zero cost; the digital code does not "wear out" with use. Because there are fewer costs, the digital economy naturally engenders a more communitarian model of exchange.

Anything on the Web is free for sharing: that sentiment is, more or less, the norm among Internet users. But it is at odds with laws and customs giving ownership of content to creators and publishers. Consumers experiment with filtering, borrowing, and aggregating Web content to create personalized home pages. Blogs embed links to other blogs and run on people's passion to communicate, and not on any thought of compensation. The same spirit extends to podcasts.

It's an open question how many consumer-driven, voluntary, and participatory enterprises will survive or, failing that, manage to make the transition to a more conventional style of business. Flickr is attempting to partition free and for-profit activities; it wants to maintain its culture of sharing among participating consumers, but it needs to work on commercial use licenses to satisfy Yahoo! management.[69] *Wikipedia* has been going strong for almost five years as a free, collaborative, and open project, but it has experienced problems and controversies. According to one of the founders, persistent and obnoxious contributors have driven others away, and vandals have defaced the front page with graffiti. In addition, a large influx of newcomers has weakened a unified community ethos and sense of shared goals, and a contingent of anarchists opposes any exercise of rules and authority.[70]

Marketers are both alarmed and intrigued by consumer sharing and peer production. Microsoft is less than pleased with open-source code, but it hosts a forum for developers to share tips on enhancements to its proprietary software.[71] The R&D potential of putting lots of individuals to work on solving a problem has been turned into a business by InnoCentive Inc., which brokers client companies' needs to a network of independent scientists and pays a modest incentive to winning submitters.[72] Part of Amazon.com's success lies in its ability to fold free consumer contributions into a for-profit business: consumers' product recommendations and purchase histories influence other consumers to buy more. Clearly, the music and publishing industries see more threat than opportunity.

In the day-to-day course of events, marketers can rely on most consumers to do the right thing. The conundrum comes when a significant number of consumers simply do not share the same standards of legality and fairness held by marketers. The battle over unauthorized peer-to-peer sharing and downloading—or, from the marketer's point of view, piracy—is a prime example.

Analyzing a two-year 15 percent decline in music sales, Forrester Research proposed in 2002 that the music industry could rebound by adopting a "Music Bill of Rights" that would permit consumers "to find, copy, and pay for music on their own terms."[73] Instead, the industry preferred to solve its problems in two consumer-unfriendly ways. First, music companies sued consumers who used peer-to-peer networks to download the music for free (and who were primarily high school and college students). Second, they offered expensive subscription services hemmed in with restrictions on how consumers could use the music they paid for.

Naturally, neither strategy resonated well with the younger audience that makes up the bulk of music fans (or with their parents). Subsequently, Apple's iTunes service, which closely adhered to Forrester's specific recommendations of letting consumers download from any label, copy the files to their own media and players, and pay by the song or album—essentially a legal, paid version of file sharing—offered new hope for the industry as it chalked up sales of 500 million songs in less than two years.[74]

In comparable situations, marketers might ask themselves three questions: why don't consumers hold the same standards we do? Have we done enough to market our point of view to consumers? Can we find a solution that accommodates consumers' and our needs? The music industry, for one, appears to be more shortsighted than that, with two of the four major companies now fighting with iTunes in a battle to extract considerably higher prices from consumers.[75] However, in a democratizing marketplace, constructive engagement with consumers should be the wave of the future.

Grassroots Politics

All politics is local.

—Tip O'Neill[76]

In representative democracies, groups of citizens who are engaged in the political marketplace can frame public debate, set the political agenda, alter candidates' chances of success, and shape the policy choices of elected representatives and other government decision makers. Citizen groups pushing narrow interests have been criticized for contributing to the type of factionalism feared by James Madison. But to proponents of *associative democracy*, the existence of groups that enable all citizens to have a voice can make important contributions to democratic governance and civic consciousness.[77]

When it comes to elections, politically engaged citizens have an influence that is disproportionate to their numbers. For instance, candidates who do well in primaries are those who appeal to the most committed party members—the relatively small portion of the electorate that turns out for primaries. On the downside, if these committed voters represent atypical, extreme voices within the party, the primary winner may fail to appeal to the majority moderate or swing voters who determine outcomes in general elections.

Elections are about convincing people to cast a vote for or against a particular candidate. But politicians and parties also need to persuade supporters to contribute money, volunteer for phone banks, or go door-to-door to talk to fellow citizens. Even in the electronic age, all politics is local. At the grassroots level, supporters work throughout the campaign to convince relatives, friends, neighbors, or coworkers of the right choice. Affinity groups such as churches influence voters through opinion leadership and word of mouth. When it comes to the vital step of translating preferences into behavior, grassroots supporters register voters, see that they get to polling places on election day, and help monitor vote-counting. All this help represents the ultimate relationship between a political "product" and its engaged "buyers."

Political fund-raising is critical and relies heavily on committed individual supporters. Although each candidate received government financing for the final stage of the 2004 U.S. presidential race, George W. Bush raised $270 million and John Kerry raised $235 million to fund earlier stages.[78] Bush's network of volunteer fund-raisers included more than two hundred "Rangers," who raised at least $200,000 apiece from their circle of acquaintances, and more than three hundred "Pioneers," each of whom raised at least $100,000 (mainly in $2,000 donations).

For less-mainstream candidates, developing a core of engaged citizens is even more critical. Newer technologies such as teleconferences or Web chat rooms permit direct engagement between voters and candidates. Democratic primary challenger Howard Dean held teleconferences with house parties of supporters, enabling this unknown politician to connect quickly with potential supporters. Dean also raised more than $20 million in the primary campaign by tapping the Internet to solicit modest donations from large numbers of supporters.[79]

Technology also provides a forum for individual citizens to make their political views known apart from a connection to candidates or parties. Political bloggers in the 2004 national election fact-checked candidates' statements and campaign advertising, provided forums accessible to all Internet visitors, and influenced news coverage by the mainstream media. One analysis concluded that "political bloggers were buzz followers as much as buzz makers," but in any case they fueled word of mouth among the general public.[80]

CHAPTER 6

Inclusion

The More the Merrier

O VER THE PAST one hundred years, the granting of full political rights to virtually all adult citizens became a criterion for democracy. This was not always the case. It was long taken as normal that only men who met specified income or property ownership criteria were entitled to participate in elections or run government. These criteria excluded the female half of the population and many adult males as well. Starting with New Zealand in 1893, Western-style democracies began instituting universal suffrage, but not until 1971 could women vote in Switzerland. Even after universal suffrage was instituted in the United States, poll taxes and so-called literacy tests were intended to exclude many African Americans.

In contrast, marketing was inclusive. Marketers wooed women shoppers and extended distribution to remote areas. One person's money was as good as another's. That's not to say that all consumers had equal access to goods or that retailers and other marketers did not discriminate against ethnic, religious, or racial groups. But the exclusion was not universal, and there were economic incentives to be inclusive.

Today, the challenge for marketers is to become more inclusive worldwide. Marketing systems do not serve the world's people equally. Many rural populations in poor countries have little, if any, access to marketing systems of the type that help raise living standards by matching supply and demand, linking consumers with multiple producers, and delivering products and services that satisfy people's basic needs and individual desires.

The urban poor in less-developed countries are served by small retailers and distributors but often lack access to banking and credit. Stores in poor areas do not benefit from the efficiencies enjoyed by large, modern retailers with prosperous consumers. The transaction costs of serving consumers who live hand-to-mouth and buy in small quantities contribute to higher prices. As a result, poor consumers in a Mumbai shantytown end up paying 20 percent more for rice than do upper-class Mumbai suburbanites.[1]

In the United States, too, many residents of poor, inner-city neighborhoods lack convenient access to large supermarkets or other chain stores that offer greater product selection and lower prices than do small neighborhood merchants. When a Pathmark supermarket opened in inner-city Newark, New Jersey, its prices were 38 percent lower than in existing neighborhood markets, although higher than in similar nearby suburban stores.[2]

The global economy has become increasingly interconnected. Developing countries are attractive not only for manufacturing and extractive industries but also as sites for growing trade in goods and services. Multinational corporations are beginning to see tremendous opportunities in serving poor populations at the bottom of the pyramid. Demographic growth in developed markets is flat, so Western corporations increasingly are looking at developing countries and poorer consumer segments to achieve revenue growth. In some cases, multinational corporations are successfully adapting their developed-economy marketing programs and business models. In other cases, they are devising new ones.

Still, they run up against the absence of a supportive business environment and necessary infrastructure. Essential elements to support an effective marketing distribution system—including physical infrastructure, banking and credit, contract enforcement, and entrepreneurial skills—often are lacking. For instance, Western retailers entering the formerly planned economies of Eastern Europe had to invest in retail infrastructure: according to a 1990 assessment, "Shops have been merely places where usually scarce goods are parked for consumers to collect. Marketing, merchandising, promotion and advertising, customer service, self-service stores, computerised stock control, costing, supply and distribution networks—all the paraphernalia of modern retailing—do not exist in Eastern Europe."[3] That these constraints were remedied in a decade testifies to the lure of the market economy.

Participating in developing markets raises sensitive issues about the purity of motives and the fairness of results. The entrance of a multinational corporation into a developing market will be perceived as exploitative if it does not raise quality standards for local industries and living standards for the poor. The economic benefits of lower prices will be weighed against the losses to inefficient local producers and retailers displaced by a Wal-Mart or a Carrefour. There will be expectations for the private sector as well as governments and nongovernmental agencies to invest in human capital. Tensions exist between Western values and local values, including the treatment of women. But there are examples in which the creation of viable new marketing systems have markedly improved human welfare.

Serving Emerging and Underserved Markets

If we stop thinking of the poor as victims or as a burden and start
recognizing them as resilient and creative entrepreneurs
and value-conscious consumers, a whole new
world of opportunity will open up.

—C. K. Prahalad[4]

Nearly everywhere, upper- and middle-class consumers, their tastes shaped by foreign media or travel, have access to a wide variety of goods and services. Many are served by Western hypermarkets such as Carrefour, Wal-Mart, and Royal Ahold. In China national retail chains like Lianhua offer tough competition. India's market is less developed, but there too more affluent consumers can purchase the same items as their Western counterparts. Such consumers constitute a small fraction of global markets. Four billion people, or about two-thirds of the world's population, earn less than $2,000 a year—that is, less than $5 a day. Individually, they do not have much to spend, and most of what they spend must go for basics like food and housing. The one billion people living in extreme poverty—trying to survive on less than $1 a day—cannot afford even those basics.

Nevertheless, in the views of C. K. Prahalad and others, the poor represent an increasingly attractive market opportunity. For one, the buying power of the moderately poor is greater than may appear at first glance (in part because the barter economy does not show up in per capita GDP estimates). In Latin America, households earning annual incomes in the $1,000 to $4,000 range can afford a television, a radio, and a refrigerator.[5] The aggregate buying power of families or villages is enough to buy some goods that would appear out of reach.

For example, in India, local entrepreneurs may not have running water but they can buy cell phones, on which they rent out calls.[6] In Africa, the number of cell phone subscribers rose tenfold, to 76.8 million, between 1999 and 2004, thanks to the availability of low-cost phones, airtime sold in small, prepaid units, and services that permit the transfer of airtime to others.[7] In poorer countries, subscribers pay an average of $5 per month, compared with $50 in developed countries.[8] But with rentals and shared ownership, the individual handsets are the most used in the world.

Most marketers would like to be more inclusive in the people they serve as customers if it were not for the difficulties they face (or, in some cases, the opportunity costs of diverting resources from serving more reliably profitable mainstream consumers). Consumer poverty and low buying power —or the prejudice that these factors signal insufficient market potential— present an obstacle to the development of inclusive marketing systems. But so, too, do unstable civil societies and bad governments. Often governments and politicians seek to exploit markets; when a powerful few can intimidate the many by force, exerting control over markets is a ticket to extortion. Gray and black markets—product "diversions" and counterfeiting—drain away profits. The unpredictability of taxation and regulation creates business risk. So, too, does the politics of doing business given "opaque power and loyalty structures within complex networks of local business and political players."[9]

Global marketers require consistent product quality and availability, which depend on reliable sources of production and also on adequate distribution networks. Distributors and retailers must have the skills and resources to support the scale efficiencies and quality control on which the global business model relies. Durable goods like televisions or appliances require reliable after-sales service.

Then there are the difficulties on the consumer end. For big-ticket items, poor consumers must save up cash or obtain credit. In the absence of banking institutions, stores need to offer credit terms and layaway programs. To make informed choices, especially when it comes to altering existing buying habits, consumers need reliable information on product features and relative quality. If consumers are illiterate, marketers may have to redesign some products and use more person-to-person communication to sell products. Media reach is increasing, and consumers know about global brands, but product knowledge in emerging markets is comparatively limited.

Finding Solutions

Still, consumers and marketers are finding ways around decrepit or nonexistent infrastructure. In villages or neighborhoods without electricity, a cell phone user may pay to recharge the device on a car battery, whose owner in turn may pay to get it recharged at a filling station.[10] Generators power cellular base stations. R&D-based solutions to the lack of electricity include solar-powered devices and hand-cranked radios and computers.[11] Thanks to government policies encouraging development, less than 5 percent of China's territory is without cell phone coverage.[12] With Internet-connected computers placed in rural villages, Indian farmers can find both cheaper sources for goods and higher market prices for their crops.[13]

In rural areas, distribution systems must cope with inadequate roads and lack of refrigeration. The difficulties are not to be minimized, but marketers and others are devising a variety of solutions. In the health-care arena, pharmaceutical R&D efforts are aimed at producing vaccines that do not require refrigeration. As part of its entry into Vietnam, German retailer and wholesaler Metro Group offered expertise and a financial grant to the Ministry of Transportation to modernize the country's product distribution network, including upgrading hygiene, health, and packaging standards; the firm also invested in refrigerated transportation and warehouses so that it could safely transport fish and meats from rural areas to urban areas.[14]

As in developed markets, emerging markets call for tailor-made marketing approaches to address particular consumers' needs. Generally, poor or low-income consumers cannot buy, transport, or stockpile bulk goods or large quantities. What they need is affordable goods in small units. That makes it difficult for distributors and retailers to achieve scale or scope efficiencies. That is also why the higher prices of small shops in poor districts may not be a bad deal for consumers after all. To a consumer, the price marked on an item is only one part of the total purchase cost. Total cost might also include the cost of transportation to a store and the time spent away from child care or other work, as well as storage costs and the total cash outlay per store visit: for many emerging-market consumers, smaller quantities and shorter travel times add up to a lower total cost.

In Latin America during the 1990s, multinational and national super-market chains aggressively entered the grocery market, capturing 40 to 60 percent of retail sales for consumer packaged goods such as food, beverages, personal care, and household products. Yet small independent markets and traditional mom-and-pop stores surprised analysts by hanging on to about half the market.[15] A research study on the Latin American market concluded, "Smaller scale retailers fit the needs of emerging consumers quite well. Furthermore, small retailers manage to offset scale advantages and . . . can be surprisingly efficient."[16]

Lower-income consumers can ill afford to make a mistake in buying a product, so they care about quality and value. They expect the same high quality of fresh meats and produce as supplied by specialized vendors at street markets. For staples, they prefer familiar, branded products that have earned their trust; they are wary of ultra-low-cost products whose quality is suspect. Like higher-income consumers, they may buy branded products, such as Coke or Dove soap, because of their aspirational value, while remaining mindful of their pocketbooks.[17] In contrast to many American consumers, they value personal relationships with shopkeepers, who treat them with warmth and respect and are willing to run a short-term tab on purchases; in turn, shopkeepers can plan their assortments based on deep knowledge of what their loyal customers want.[18]

In Ecuador, retailer TIA Stores introduced a "Multiahorro barrio store" format designed to retain many of the advantages of traditional small stores while offering consumers a limited assortment of goods at the lowest possible price.[19] Brazilian retailer Magazine Luiza, operating primarily in small cities, courts lower-income customers in its furniture, consumer electronics, and household appliances business. Because lack of consumer credit is a major barrier to purchasing such high-ticket items, the family-run chain developed its own credit-score rating system; this allows it to offer customers immediate credit approval and, in partnership with a bank, affordable payment-installment plans customized to their cash flow.

Another Magazine Luiza innovation is a high-tech version of the Sears catalog showroom concept. In a "virtual showroom," employees help consumers view product images displayed on a computer screen while they inquire about customers' needs and financial constraints; offsetting the starkness of a merchandise-free environment, stores host community events ranging from computer training to cooking classes. Throughout the store's operations, the depth of the relationship between salespeople and customers is key.[20]

The Mexican cement company CEMEX developed marketing solutions to enable consumers to buy what would otherwise be unaffordable. In Mexico, as in many other parts of the world, low-income consumers buy cement to build their homes, typically one room at a time. The trouble is that the cement alone can cost the equivalent of three months' income or more, and building a single room takes approximately five years. Under its Patrimonio Hoy building program, CEMEX organizes customers into groups of three families, each of whom pays about $13 per week for seven cycles of ten weeks. After the first two weeks of each cycle, the families receive ten weeks' worth of building materials along with building advice and warehousing services. Within a year, they complete the room. Between 1999 and 2005, the program served more than 100,000 families. Beyond the benefits of a well-built home, participating families acquired a financial asset and demonstrated creditworthiness; they also experienced the satisfaction of planning and directing their lives.[21]

Rural low-income consumers have less access to markets with broad assortments than do their urban counterparts. Still, their purchases of consumer goods are growing. In India, for instance, the rural market has grown at the rate of 12 to 13 percent over the past decade.[22] One reason sales are growing is marketers' investment in distribution channels. Corporations like Hindustan Lever (a division of multinational Unilever) are building the market from the ground up, through person-to-person direct selling. Thanks to the low cost of labor, it is feasible to distribute products through bicycle vendors, street vendors or kiosks, and salespeople traveling by vans to rural areas.[23]

Marketers split the world into consumer segments, distinguished by what people want, like, need, and value and how they behave. But as long as markets in developing countries remained relatively small and difficult to reach, marketers did not have much incentive to treat "the poor" as anything other than a homogeneous bloc. Now that sales in traditionally underserved markets have expanded and market potential appears more promising because of growth in GDP per capita, marketers and market research firms are expending more effort in getting to know the unique characteristics of their customers. The head of marketing for Procter & Gamble sends new hires to Mexico for "cultural immersion."[24] Hindustan Lever assigns new managerial hires in India to live eight weeks in villages, where they work on community projects such as building roads or teaching in schools. Incumbent managers also spend time on the road reconnecting with poor customers.

Leveraging deeper insight into consumers, businesses have built marketing programs around such cultural practices as the role women play in entrepreneurial activities, household management, and product choice. Understanding the internal dynamics of communities allowed Manila Water to serve lower-income segments it had not successfully reached before by radically changing its method of delivering and billing for piped water. As an alternative to one water meter per household, the company offered an option of a bulk meter for forty to fifty households, with submeters for each; everyone using the group meter is collectively responsible for paying the total bill. It turns out that bulk installation reduced costs substantially, in part because collecting accounts receivable was largely outsourced to consumers. Impressively, peer monitoring and enforcement resulted in fully paid bills and hence no water shutoffs.[25]

Maturation of Emerging Markets

In emerging markets, multinational corporations tend to enter with a strategy of offering the affluent segment a subset of the products offered in developed markets or offering the poorer segments a narrow selection of stripped-down, basic, rugged models. This approach is consistent with historical patterns of development characterized by *market life cycles*. In newly emerging markets, consumers are offered relatively few product categories, there are few choices, and categories are basic. Growing markets have more categories, growing competition, more choices, and categories that extend beyond satisfying basic needs toward satisfying higher-order human needs for belonging, achievement, and fulfillment.

Mature markets have a great many categories appealing to a great many market segments; categories emerge from previous categories (for example, the $4 billion global market for ring tones emerged from cell phones).[26] Parallel to this development, marketing activities in the introductory phase focus on gaining distribution and communicating functional category benefits—say, the superior cleaning power of manufactured detergent—and usage instructions. As markets mature, marketing works to differentiate categories from one another—dishwashing detergent from laundry detergent—and brands within categories.

But Arnold and Quelch question the assumption that emerging markets "are at an earlier stage of the same development path followed by the advanced or developed countries, that the game is therefore one of catch-up, and that market evolution patterns seen previously in developed economies will be replicated in the EMs."[27] The major difference is the amount of pent-up demand for new products and Western brands that are known to consumers but were hitherto unavailable. Consumers in emerging markets are familiar or can quickly become familiar with the latest products and are ready to buy as soon as they have financial resources—and they are sensitive to being sold leftover inventory of obsolete models from Western markets.

There are few barriers to the global mobility of goods. Also, because there is no installed base, market development can leapfrog older products. Smart cards for banking, where customer balances are stored on the chip, may leapfrog ATM cards, where balances are stored on the network.[28] On the other hand, poor infrastructure—for example, lack of electricity in poorer economies—may mean that some cutting-edge technologies and products are less suitable than low-tech substitutes.

Degree of urbanization is another factor, both because concentration of populations in metropolitan areas permits more efficient selling, advertising, and distribution and because urban consumers have more resources. For example, in India, Vietnam, and Tanzania, "urban residents tend to enjoy better access to drinking water, sanitation, health services, jobs, and educational opportunities than their rural counterparts."[29] By 2010, more than 40 percent of the population in developing countries will live in urban areas.[30] For all these reasons, emerging economies may well show mixed patterns of market development, with some "basic needs" categories remaining below the takeoff stage and some high-tech product categories maturing more quickly than expected.

In some emerging economies, after an early infatuation with premium, imported brands, consumers become more value conscious and revert to local brands, especially if the quality of these brands has been upgraded in the interim.[31] Ironically, in part it is the initial success of global brands that makes this possible: the quality of local brands improves to compete with foreign goods, and local firms capitalize on the distribution capabilities and consumer demand developed by global marketers. In China, admittedly a special case with respect to joint ventures, the Wahaha beverage company acquired both capital and marketing skills in a joint venture with French multinational Danone Group. Now it is positioned to compete directly against Coke and Pepsi.[32] In response to this type of phenomenon, Unilever has developed a multitier product range of separately managed local brands, such as Wheel detergent, in India, which it markets alongside its global brand Surf.

Commerce and Change

If we want to preserve a wide range of human conditions because it allows
free people the best chance to make their own lives, we can't enforce
diversity by trapping people within differences they long to escape.

—Kwame Anthony Appiah[33]

Children in rural African villages dress in American-style T-shirts and baseball caps. In Saudi Arabia, women under the veil apply expensive Western cosmetics. Iowans consume burritos and tacos at a growing number of fast-food chains. Commerce and trade carry products, ideas, and bits and pieces of culture around the world. Whether intentional or not, marketing is an agent of change and cultural osmosis.

This places marketing at the center of a tension faced by all societies—and individuals—in steering their way between the traditional and the new, between preserving the past and embracing change. Global brand advertisers and U.S. entertainment marketers create vivid images of a world of abundance and of people finding happiness and fulfillment through consumption of Western products. Observers of global marketing more or less agree that, cumulatively, these messages export Western values and Western lifestyles. The question is whether including more people in marketing's sphere is, on balance, good or bad.

Western critics—and there are many—point to power imbalances and aggression. Benjamin Barber's major concern is that the power of global corporations subverts the nation-state and democratic institutions; he also worries that "McWorld's culture represents a kind of soft imperialism in which those who are colonized are said to 'choose' their commercial indenture."[34] Naomi Klein takes aim at "brand bullies," who extract premium prices from consumers and are "waging a war on public and individual space: on public institutions such as schools, on youthful identities, on the concept of nationality and on the possibilities for unmarketed space."[35]

Such criticisms are not confined to global marketing, nor are professional commentators alone in their concerns. Many Americans worry about the effects of sexualized advertising on their children; they are uncomfortable with crass consumerism and offended by the intrusion of commercial messages. But concerns about the manipulative power of marketing tend to be magnified when people with little or no previous exposure to sophisticated modern advertising and promotion are suddenly subject to its influence.

Cultures absorb readily from others, as shown in the influence of African and Caribbean music on American music and the variety of ethnic foods and restaurants. Cultural borrowing goes back to the origins of trade and the movement of people. Without exchange with others, modern cultures would not be what they are. Cowen notes, "To varying degrees, Western cultures draw their philosophical heritage from the Greeks, their religions from the Middle East, their scientific base from the Chinese and Islamic worlds, and their core populations and languages from Europe."[36] He also observes that cultural decline in the Dark Ages in Europe coincided with a dramatic contraction of trade.

In this light, market-based exchange seems healthy—a force for innovation and progress. Globalization increases people's ability to enrich themselves by consuming diverse cultures, both distant and local cultures. But something may disappear in the exchange. The new may augment or supplement the traditional—a fondness for soft drinks coexisting with the consumption of tea. But it may also displace or replace the traditional—T-shirts and other Western clothing eventually displacing traditional attire.

Cultural Changes

The ramifications of any one such product choice may be small, but what about a series of changes that adds up to a noticeable alteration in a cuisine, a musical tradition, a way of life? Does exposure to marketing intensify the divisions between the preservers of tradition and the embracers of modernity? Or does exposure to marketing fuse the modern and the traditional in an exciting way (for example, Moroccan combined with French fashion)?

To marketers, inclusion does not mean cultural homogeneity and destruction of local, folk cultures. Marketers celebrate diversity; they see adapting marketing programs to local cultures as a way of making products more relevant. Kodak sponsors folk performances to promote products in rural India and thereby helps keep these cultural traditions alive.

Many critics of globalization warn about the dangers of cultural imperialism. Fifty-three of the one hundred most valuable brands on Interbrand's annual list are American, twice what would be commensurate with the U.S. share of world GDP.[37] In one scenario, U.S. culture dominates others, resulting in a future lack of diversity across cultures; mass marketing glorifies individual choice but ends up making everyone more alike. However, this state of total homogeneity may never arrive: Western cultures still differ from one another despite one hundred years of modern marketing.

In another scenario, cultural imperialism aggravates political and economic tensions; a backlash forms in opposition to Western, democratic values, resulting in sharp conflict and attempts to limit individual liberties and choices and freedom of expression. Clearly, it behooves marketers to take account of local values and religious beliefs. The violent protests triggered by the dissemination of a Danish newspaper cartoon picturing the Prophet Muhammad (considered blasphemous by Muslims), which resulted in at least ten deaths, is a sobering reminder of just how inflammatory words and images can be. Global brands not associated with the cartoon were tarred by the same brush: Muslim consumers boycotted Danish products, including Lego toys and Bang & Olufsen electronics; Pakistani demonstrators attacked McDonald's, KFC, and Holiday Inn outlets.[38] To paraphrase poet John Donne, no corporation—or country—is an island, entire of itself.

With respect to cultural diversity, many of the people who most value diversity belong to the Western cultures that most threaten it. Many people see the value of cultural diversity as analogous to the value of ecological diversity among species. In contrast, within non-Western societies, traditionalists who reject outside influences are not so much interested in diversity across cultures as in protecting their own culture; they are taking a more self interested view. But there is also an aspect of selfishness in the desire for diversity. If it is cultural imperialism to impose values and choices on other cultures, is it not also cultural imperialism to deny other cultures access to what you have, and cultural imperialism to deny your culture access to what other cultures offer? If an African child wants to wear a T-shirt, why not? It is arrogant for patronizing Westerners to want to preserve traditional cultures mainly so that they can enjoy them on vacations or buy ethnic crafts.

Cosmopolitanism

Appiah and others applaud a different kind of diversity—a kind of pluralism or *cosmopolitanism* that lets individuals within a society choose the way they want to live.[39] Cosmopolitanism embraces change. In Appiah's view, it revitalizes cultures: "Cultures are made of continuities and changes, and the identity of a society can survive through these changes. Societies without change aren't authentic; they're just dead."[40] Cosmopolitanism is also democratic and tolerant. It leaves choices to individuals and respects their choices. If a South American villager wants to drink a Coke in order to feel part of the modern world, that is OK. If he wants to drink mate, that is OK too.

As opposed to tolerance, however, there is a nearly universal tendency to pass judgment on other people's consumption choices. Members of social groups view other people's purchase choices as a signal of identification with or alienation from the group. Moral judgments seep in. Choices may be viewed as bad for the environment or wasteful of natural resources. Western consumers who possess all sorts of material comforts offhandedly characterize a poor family's purchase of a Coke, a cell phone call, a movie ticket, or a tube of brand-name lipstick as a frivolity, notwithstanding the psychological need for everyone, once in a while, to have some small pleasure, some refuge from daily cares, some connection with the global village. Prosperous consumers criticize low-income consumers for buying shoddy goods that do not last rather than saving up for more costly, more durable goods. Educated consumers often doubt—unfairly—the ability of uneducated consumers to make wise choices. But people develop consumer skills in concert with their means and the market environment. Look at how quickly the citizens of former communist countries of the Soviet Union became selective consumers of Western brands.

The reality is that consumers in developing countries take matters into their own hands. Researchers have found that although mass media, pop culture entertainment, tourism, worker migration, and global brand advertising fuel desires for foreign products and Western lifestyles, "consumptionscapes involve neither simple emulation and spread of Western consumer culture nor simple resistance to it." Instead, "consumer cultures are becoming creolized."[41]

Consumers want to participate in the global consumer culture—a desire for television as a window on the world appears universal—but they reconfigure the functions and the meanings of consumer goods to suit local culture. For example, they may critique the family values portrayed in U.S. television programs rather than embrace them; they may find ovens useful for drying clothes.[42] They may mix and match the Western and the traditional to create new styles of clothing, food, or music. In India, consumers rejected products whose meaning was alien (e.g., McDonald's meat-based menus); accepted some products but only for certain uses (e.g., polyester cloth for modern clothing but not for saris); embraced compatible products (BBC for its objective and credible world news); and widely adopted fusion products (MTV India, which blended Indian lyrics with Western beats and visuals).[43]

Practically speaking, even though Western multinational corporations enter developing markets from a position of power, they do not necessarily expect to sell the same products and market the same way they do in home countries. Consumer needs may differ, usage contexts may differ, and marketers adapt products as a matter of course.[44] In some cases, consumers themselves—or governments acting for nationalistic reasons or under pressure from local producers—demand adaptation. In South Africa, radio stations are required to devote 20 percent of airtime to local music. When MTV, the world's dominant television music channel, came to South Africa, it committed to 30 percent local music. Note that for MTV there is the possibility of reverse diffusion—incorporating South African music into other MTV programming around the world. That would offer South African musicians a springboard to reach worldwide audiences.[45]

Profits and Social Welfare

Companies that are healthy give back.
Losing companies can't give back.

—Jack Welch[46]

There is a movement to convince multinational corporations that doing business with the bottom of the pyramid can be profitable and socially responsible. The proposition that marketing produces social value when it delivers needed goods and services to poor consumers, which they buy voluntarily and which improve their standard of living, is not very controversial. Prahalad claims that "when MNCs [multinational corporations] provide basic goods and services that reduce costs to the poor and help improve their standard of living—while generating an acceptable rate of return on investment—the results benefit everyone."[47] Giving poor consumers access to new products, more choices, and greater purchasing power expands the quality of life. It would be worse for the multinationals to ignore poor consumers than to serve them.[48]

There can also be positive externalities that benefit the social fabric. Some for-profit enterprises operating in poor areas require that community leaders and consumers be included in production and distribution. In addition to making it affordable to deliver products and services, community involvement can allow members to exercise or acquire organizing skills that are useful for economic, civic, and political action. It sets the stage for consumers to initiate new entrepreneurial activities and contributes to better morale and a sense that citizens can bring about positive changes.[49]

On the other hand, the presence of multinational corporations is not necessarily a win-win situation for everyone. One of the ways multinationals drive down costs is to eliminate distribution intermediaries.[50] Traditional neighborhood merchants and entrepreneurs also may be eliminated when scale efficiencies allow multinational corporations to undercut their prices.

Any accounting of marketing's benefits to consumers needs to record the profits reinvested in the local community versus the profits taken out. As Leonard says, "If the product or some part of it, or its distribution, or some other part of its cost structure could be designed so that it produced income within the community, its effects on poverty reduction would be much more powerful."[51] Putting cases of marketing in emerging markets to this test produces a mixed record. Hindustan Lever's employment of local residents as distributors earns it a plus. So does CEMEX Patrimonio Hoy's employment of local promoters and investment of local savings (and outside remittances from overseas relatives) in community assets in the form of better housing.

Microfinance operations have enabled income-generating entrepreneurial activities, which likely offset the profits on interest taken out of the community; the success of one entrepreneur in a village leads others to follow the same path. Metro Group purchases more than 80 percent of the products it sells in Vietnam from Vietnamese producers and 99 percent of its workforce is Vietnamese.[52] But marketers that sell low-cost consumer goods produced elsewhere that displace locally produced alternatives, and that do not expand local employment, probably do not meet the test.[53]

Fairness Versus Profit

Marketing to the poor inevitably raises questions of equitable and fair pricing. What constitutes an acceptable rate of return on investment when marketing to low-income consumers, and what constitutes price gouging? Microfinance institutions provide an indispensable service to poor entrepreneurs (most of whom are women) but charge 40 to 50 percent interest in some areas to cover the high transaction costs of processing small loans to numerous borrowers.[54] On the other hand, this is considerably less than charged by local moneylenders and businesspeople.[55] And judging from the extremely low default rate and expanding number of loans, customers do not find the terms onerous.[56] The urban poor must pay more for food than wealthier consumers, but marketers say higher pilferage rates and other factors raise their operating expenses.

Marketers need to make a profit to continue doing business. Should wealthier consumers subsidize poorer consumers? That happens naturally in markets. Often, product prices, especially for technologically innovative products, start high and drop as the market expands. On a country-by-country basis, U.S. consumers pay more for pharmaceuticals; one frequently heard explanation is that they are subsidizing R&D costs for the rest of the world. Yet richer consumers are unlikely to volunteer to subsidize poorer consumers. To the contrary, Muhammad Yunus, founder of microlender Grameen Bank, says that wealthy bank customers in Bangladesh have a tradition of defaulting on loans.[57] Presumably this raises rates for less-wealthy customers.

Multinational corporations insist on their right to make profits. In 2003, Novartis compelled Indian pharmaceutical companies to stop producing generic versions of its leukemia drug Glivec. The Indian generics were selling for $2,700 a year. Novartis then priced Glivec at $27,000 a year, offset by free treatment to a few poor patients.[58] But in some cases pharmaceutical companies do not exercise the monopoly pricing rights given them by patent laws. In 2006 Bristol-Myers Squibb licensed, without charge, a new and powerful AIDS drug to generic drugmakers in India and South Africa to make it available for patients in poor countries. The generic companies, which can make the drug inexpensively, are setting the pricing.[59]

Apart from the parties directly involved—the poor and marketers— questions about fairness and profit in the low-income sector draw in a wide constituency, including consumer advocates, government policy makers and regulators, academics, and the media. In addition, public corporations are under pressure from shareholders and customers to be socially responsible.

In the United States, H&R Block came under fire for a profitable product sold primarily to low-income consumers. Called Refund Anticipation Loan, it allowed tax filers to receive in one or two days the tax refund due them. The average fee for the loan was about $90, which on average translated into an annual percentage rate of 91 percent—far higher than bank loans or credit-card debt. Block's clients, who typically are under financial stress and many of whom do not have checking accounts, flocked to the product, but consumer advocates charge that clients were ill informed about its nature and that interest rates were unconscionable. The reputation and financial costs resulting from class-action lawsuits and proposed state regulations prompted the company to consider exiting the market, which would leave it to higher-price companies flying below the public radar screen.[60]

Resolving the Fairness Dilemma

There is no simple way to resolve the dilemma of profiting from the poor. It seems that the greater the disparity between the wealth and power of an international marketer and its customer base, the higher the standards that will be applied. Creating transparency regarding the risks and costs incurred by firms and providing a full accounting of the benefits and costs to consumers in comparison with alternatives can help mollify critics.

Some corporations serving emerging markets are doing so from a sense of corporate responsibility; they do not expect to make a profit. But that, too, has its dangers. Ventures without proof of viability and financial sustainability are subject to changing corporate priorities and may be discontinued. Unprofitable ventures may also block creative new business models that seek to be profitable at lower costs.

Part of the problem for global corporations is that most of their profit models depend on scale, and without scale they need to charge higher prices. In some circumstances, midrange companies, such as Magazine Luiza, may be better suited to be market pioneers. Smaller entrepreneurs may accept more risk. Patience, too, may be required of management and shareholders. Procter & Gamble spent $10 million on research and development for Pur, an innovative and effective water-purifying product. However, the cost, at 10 cents per packet, was high for poor consumers, and the purification process was complex. In the markets where Pur was introduced, initial interest was high, but two years later sales had not taken off.[61] P&G switched to a philanthropic model of distributing Pur at cost through a nonprofit group.

In terms of social welfare, inclusion in a global marketer's customer base may bring negative repercussions. If history repeats itself, Citibank's efforts to convert working-class Mexican families to buying on credit, efforts that are in many ways laudable, may also leave consumers with crushing debt in the event of an economic downturn.[62]

U.S. tobacco companies have not hesitated to market their products to developing countries. According to a World Health Organization (WHO) report, "As the prevalence of smoking decreases in the developed world, the planning and strategy documents of the multinational tobacco companies show their eagerness to expand profits by vigorous marketing in other parts of the world, especially where restrictions are fewer and the population less aware of the risks."[63] WHO identifies tobacco "as a major avoidable cause of illness and premature death in low-income countries."[64] Premature deaths deprive families of breadwinners. Moreover, smoking is a direct financial drain on poor families: "In countries such as Bulgaria, Egypt, Indonesia, Myanmar and Nepal, household expenditure surveys show that low income households spend 5–15% of their disposable income on tobacco."[65] According to WHO, the major tobacco companies have cynically manipulated what appear to be "socially responsible" marketing campaigns—for example, youth smoking prevention campaigns that actually increase the appeal of smoking to adolescents by portraying it as an adult activity.[66]

Few knowledgeable people, even smokers themselves, would say that the decision to consume cigarettes is wise. But in most other cases, respecting individual choice, absent harm to others, generally serves marketing and democracy well. So does maintaining a balance of power among social institutions. If consumers, citizens, and society at large conclude that marketers are not serving their best interests, they should not hesitate to set those situations right. In the case of tobacco, actions in the public interest have included funding of scientific studies, prohibition of certain forms of advertising, dissemination of facts about smoking-related diseases, court-ordered antismoking advertising, higher taxes to deter smoking, and bans on smoking in public places. International organizations, including the World Bank, the International Monetary Fund, the United Nations, and the United States Agency for International Development, have endorsed tobacco control measures and assist developing nations in implementing them.

Social Activism

In democracies, and also in some fragile authoritarian regimes, consumers acting collectively can mobilize substantial political power to counteract the clout of multinational corporations. In the late 1990s, the government of Bolivia privatized water and sewer services, awarding a forty-year contract to a subsidiary of Suez, a $53 billion French company. The expectation and promise were that the expertise and scale of the giant firm would translate into greatly expanded availability of affordable, safe, piped-in water to households in the La Paz area.

Initially, the company increased by half the number of households receiving water and sewage services, but it failed to meet revenue targets. By 2005, Bolivian consumers were protesting $450 hookup fees (equal to about eight times the average monthly wage), rate hikes of as much as 300 percent, and poor quality of service. Widespread protests by enraged consumers resulted in the cancellation of the contract and resumption of state control over water services. Similar social protest movements led to Suez's pullout from Argentina and Uruguay, which had also privatized water in the 1990s.

In the new public model for managing water and sewage services, Latin American consumers are claiming pure water as a social good and a fundamental human right rather than as something to be traded like ordinary merchandise. Citizens are seeking mechanisms to administer water resources that incorporate extensive public participation in decision making.[67]

Executives of multinational corporations cannot ignore sociopolitical issues in countries in which they wish to do business. McKinsey, a leading management consultancy, advises firms, "Companies have always had a contract with society . . . Part of it is semiformal . . . Violations of that semiformal contractual obligation can seriously harm a company's reputation as well as consumer demand for its products."[68]

Management inattentiveness to citizens' concerns is not necessarily willful or cynical. If it were, the thousands of citizens' groups around the world could expect to have little leverage. But according to McKinsey consultants, businesses often are taken by surprise when they encounter bad press and pushback from consumers. They see themselves as benefiting society by providing high-quality products at low prices and employing workers.[69] In the end, companies that market to consumers put their brands at great risk if they fail to listen to consumers on social issues as well as on personal preferences and needs.

Citizens in developing countries may have limited leeway when it comes to basing their consumption choices on sociopolitical issues—because of low purchasing power and few market choices—but Western consumers often mobilize on their behalf. The reputation of Nestlé, for example, still suffers, perhaps unfairly, from the decades-old protest in the West against the company's marketing of baby formula in Africa.

But clearly, the greatest dangers to developing countries and their traditional cultures are AIDS, other diseases, and war, and not marketing. On the contrary, marketing of products such as water purifiers and pharmaceuticals helps alleviate disease. Better distribution systems mean that produce won't rot and that children are better fed. Nearly fifty years ago, Peter Drucker spelled out broad benefits of marketing for developing countries: "a system of physical distribution; a financial system to make possible the distribution of goods; and finally, actual marketing, that is, an actual system of integrating wants, needs, and purchasing power of the consumer with capacity and resources of production."[70]

To that could be added inclusion in global information networks: a recent economic analysis suggests that "in a typical developing country, an increase of ten mobile phones per 100 people is associated with GDP growth of 0.6 percentage points."[71] Next to education and improved health care, the ability to communicate and obtain information is a route out of poverty. It enables entrepreneurial activity, and it drives democratic political activity. Spurred by enormous consumer demand, competition among marketers drives prices down and puts phones in rural African villages that lack electricity and running water. In one such Kenyan village, residents were able to track the progress of the Illinois senatorial race won by one of their kin, Barack Obama; they were able to draw aspirations from his achievement, able to imagine the possibility of better schools and a more fulfilling life.[72]

Fostering Inclusion

Democratic governments need to do their part to foster economic inclusion. Government-imposed tariffs and taxes on cell phone handsets and calling services raise costs for consumers everywhere and are especially onerous to poor consumers in Africa.[73] Corruption and fraud drive up costs for legitimate businesses and taxpayers. In the United States, according to a recent report from Transparency International, an estimated 5 to 10 percent of Medicaid and Medicare budgets go toward "overpayments." In other parts of the world, counterfeiting or diversion of drugs intended for the poor results in patients' deaths.[74] Diversion of public funds into the pockets of public officials or service providers ultimately takes away money that could be invested in basic infrastructure, education, or health services, investments that would make emerging markets more hospitable to market-based economic growth.

Although bad governance and corruption are hindrances to economic development in impoverished countries, Jeffrey Sachs, director of the United Nations Millennium Project, counters that this is an inadequate explanation of enduring problems: some well-governed countries remain poor, and some countries with high levels of corruption rapidly move out of poverty. In a number of countries, disease is the primary cause of poverty. Almost always, endemic poverty is the result of a complex mix of factors.[75]

The UN Millennium Declaration, announced in 2000, set the ambitious target of halving world poverty by 2015. The goals embody the new wave of thinking on how to support economic development: "promoting the private sector in developing countries, opening trade with them, and increasing official development assistance."[76] In this view, transformational development—investing in schools, clinics, agriculture, roads, power, clean water and sanitation, and other infrastructure—is the key to breaking out of the poverty trap.

Transformational development on a large scale requires concerted aid from world governments. According to Sachs, the U.S. government is failing to live up to its share of the commitments: it has given very little, and what it has spent has gone mainly to U.S. consultants and nongovernmental agencies.

Almost none has gone to specific programs in recipient countries.[77] But corporations, motivated either by a sense of social responsibility or by profit potential, are following the transformational development path. In scores of examples, global marketers are partnering with local suppliers or distributors, local governments, or nongovernmental organizations.

Ericsson, for example, is setting up local franchisees to own and operate telecommunications centers serving poor rural communities.[78] In partnership with a nonprofit, Unilever is marketing an iodized salt, produced in India, to African consumers to control iodine-deficiency diseases.[79] The Shell Foundation is partnering with a Ugandan bank to offer lease-lend financing to small entrepreneurs.[80] ABB and the World Wildlife Fund are collaborating on a pilot project to bring commercially viable delivery of electricity to rural Tanzanian villages.[81] Many such alliances have been formed under the auspices of the UN's Growing Sustainable Business project.

When done well, these types of programs directly benefit the poor. They also develop companies' marketing capabilities in at least two ways: they build a favorable corporate reputation, and they provide an opportunity to gain deep knowledge of local consumers and institutions. Cynics may dismiss such programs as a tool of corporate self-interest, but the results need to be considered against the alternatives of no improvement in infrastructure or people's lives.

PART TWO

MARKETING FOR DEMOCRACY

CHAPTER 7

Politics

Winner Takes All

I N THE UNITED STATES, political engagement and voting levels are low. Mistrust of politicians and the political process is high. In the political marketplace, compared with the consumer marketplace, choice is limited and information is simultaneously overwhelming and inadequate. Lobbyists and special-interest groups dominate broad-based attempts to solve complex social problems. Short of recalls, citizens have little power to rein in politicians between elections.

Although money has always played a large role in campaigns, political marketing has raised the stakes; to remain competitive, candidates need money for commercials, market research, and mass-media buys. Once safely elected, politicians benefit from having established brand names and power to attract large contributions. These give incumbents an advantage in future elections no matter how well or poorly they serve constituents.

One response is to limit the influence of marketing tactics in elections, as in Europe: strictly limit the amounts and types of advertising candidates may run. Provide free airtime. Allow campaigning only during a short time before an election. Pass campaign financing laws to control the amounts spent during campaigns and the sources of political contributions. In spite of these attempts, however, American-style election campaigns have spread to other democracies.[1] European elections increasingly feature pollsters, spin doctors, and other quasi-marketing professionals; mass media communications; an emphasis on personality over issues; and negative advertising strategies.[2]

But aside from the impressive ability of political parties and candidates to circumvent campaign regulations, to think that banishing marketing from politics would solve the most egregious problems is to ignore deeper structural elements in the political system. The unique U.S. electoral system and presidential form of government lead to such outcomes as the dominance of the two major parties, large blocs of voters whose views are not represented, and large numbers of voters who, depending on where they live, have little chance to make their votes count for change.

Borrowing more, not fewer, ideas and capabilities from marketing could be just what is needed to make American and other representative democracies more democratic. Conceivably, political parties could learn from mass marketers how, on the one hand, to accommodate diversity in constituents' interests and desires and, on the other hand, to create a common umbrella, or positioning, that unifies and motivates constituents. Election reformers could look to marketers for ways to make voting more accessible, convenient, and trustworthy, as well as for ways to motivate consumers to vote and otherwise participate in the political process.

Campaign Marketing

Principles aren't of much account anyway, except at election time.
After that you hang them up to let them season.

—Mark Twain[3]

Political marketers in the United States ply their trade in senatorial, congressional, gubernatorial, and, most conspicuously, presidential races. Their skills are so much admired that Wal-Mart hired top image and media consultants from the campaigns of former presidents Ronald Reagan and Bill Clinton, as well as from the campaigns of George W. Bush and John Kerry, to set up a rapid-response unit to repair the company's deteriorating public image among consumers.[4]

Marketing practices have long been part of the U.S. political process. Like modern campaign consultants, early-nineteenth-century politicians carefully crafted candidates' images. In 1828, Andrew Jackson's anti-elitist Democratic Party positioned him as a "man of the people" during the first U.S. presidential election in which many states allowed landless citizens to vote.

A decade later, members of the newly formed conservative Whig Party, which drew its support from the wealthy business community, turned the tables, portraying themselves as "just plain folks." Says historian Sean Wilentz, "The appeals helped the Whigs win the presidency in 1840 with their famous 'log cabin and hard cider' campaign, presenting their well-born presidential candidate, William Henry Harrison, as a plebeian hero who lived in a humble abode and drank the common frontiersman's brew."[5] Publicity was a powerful tool. The side-by-side comparisons of Illinois senatorial candidates Abraham Lincoln and Stephen Douglas in the debates of 1858 attracted newspaper coverage throughout the country and made Lincoln a national figure. In every era, politicians have reached out to voters via all the available media, from rallies, ditties, buttons, posters, pamphlets, and newspapers to T-shirts, radio, television, telephone, Web sites, e-mail, and blogs.

Campaign spending steadily escalated to the point that George W. Bush and John Kerry and their respective parties raised and spent roughly $1.26 billion in the 2004 presidential campaign, nearly double the $676 million total of the 2000 campaign.[6] Republicans and Democrats collectively spent more than $600 million on television and radio commercials, triple the amount in 2000.[7] They blanketed closely contested markets, such as Miami-Fort Lauderdale, Florida, with some five thousand ads during the last month of the campaign.[8] In the last week of the election alone, the Bush and Kerry campaigns together spent an estimated $60 million on advertising.[9] Outright vote buying is illegal, but spending $15 per vote in advertising is not.[10]

Modern Marketing of Candidates

Although political advertising is nothing new, growing public access to mass media, particularly broadcast television, and application of mass-marketing practices to politics mark a divide between what some have termed the premodern era and the modern era of campaigning in the United States.[11] The televised 1960 debates between Richard Nixon and John Kennedy inspired Daniel Boorstin to deplore "pseudo-events," "the menace of unreality" in the United States, and the collusion of journalists in packaging politicians and manufacturing news.[12] Of the debates themselves, Boorstin wrote, "The great Presidents in our history (with the possible exception of F.D.R.) would have done miserably . . . The television-watching voter was left to judge, not on issues explored by thoughtful men, but on the relative capacity of the two men to perform under television stress."[13] Those who listened to the

Kennedy–Nixon debates on radio were more likely to believe Nixon won than those who watched on TV.

Marketing a candidate through mass media results in an emphasis on personality and superficial attributes of physical attractiveness. John Kennedy may have been the first major politician to excel at projecting a compelling image on television, but Ronald Reagan had no equal in conveying "presidentiality." Substantive positions on issues reduce to sound bites, well-rehearsed talking points, and slogans that test well in focus groups. Endorsements of political statements by sports or music celebrities may sway young people's opinions.[14] (Outspoken celebrity endorsements, however, can also alienate voters.)[15] To pay for mass-media advertising, candidates must market themselves to potential donors with a steady barrage of direct-mail, telephone, and e-mail solicitations.

Voters, like consumers, reward those who communicate simply and forcefully. Similarly, voters reward those who are good at "staying on message." George W. Bush excelled in both respects and established a clear brand image. Politicians who introduce too much complexity run the risk of diluting their messages or failing to project a strong image. John Kerry's tendency to do this played into the hands of his opposition, which characterized him as a weak "flip-flopper."

Unfortunately for the public, the political marketplace provides no incentive for candidates to innovate or evolve. There is actually a disincentive for candidates to modify, and perhaps improve, a policy position during a campaign, the type of midcourse correction product marketers are freer to make. One political scientist notes that Howard Dean broke new ground in loosening control over the messages he projected: "Howard Dean did something that was smart, brave, and unprecedented—something only a candidate with little to lose would do: he created a genuinely interactive campaign Web site."[16]

Good political advertising follows the same rules as brand advertising: do not overwhelm the audience with detailed descriptions of product or policy features; build an emotional connection with the brand by demonstrating likeability, integrity, and empathy; create a clear, memorable impression by sticking to selected themes. This type of advertising should attract citizens to participate in the political process.

Often, though, poorly crafted or objectionable advertising turns voters off. Campaign rhetoric is brutal. Fear and other negative appeals are common—in contrast to consumer marketing, where they are infrequent. An analysis of television commercials aired in the 2004 presidential campaign indicates that during the eight months before the election, more than half of the ads from the Bush campaign focused on attacking Kerry, although less than 5 percent of the ads from the Kerry campaign attacked Bush.[17]

Why Do Negative Political Ads Work?

In the consumer marketplace, it is uncommon to directly criticize a competitor; in politics the opposing candidate is held to be a fair target. Ads for products may cast a competitor in an unflattering light but—for fear of reinforcing awareness of the competitor's brand—rarely name the target or make a comparison based on anything other than objective data. Pepsi Challenge advertising did not say that consumers thought Coke was bad, only that a majority thought Pepsi was better. Why then do negative political ads, such as the notorious "Swift Boat" ad used against Kerry in the 2004 election, work? There are at least four possible explanations.

First, Coke and Pepsi don't sling mud at each other, because if they did, consumer purchases would eventually shift away from both of them to alternative colas and beverages. Both brands want to enlarge the market, not reduce it. However, in politics, market share, and not market size, matters. Negative campaigning may turn off a sizable number of the electorate, but if George Bush succeeds in making John Kerry marginally less acceptable to the voters who show up on Election Day, Bush comes out ahead. And using surrogates to deliver the strongest attacks, as frequently happened in the 2004 campaign, minimizes the risk of the intensely negative approach backfiring on the attacking candidate.

Second, candidates are inherently fallible. It is easy for an opponent to seize on personal shortcomings or inconsistencies or to magnify one unpopular stance. Moreover, it is easier to standardize and improve the delivery of hamburgers at McDonald's than it is for staffers to perfect a candidate, who, as a perpetual work in progress, must respond to ever-changing and complex developments, including national and world events and unexpected attacks by opponents and hostile special-interest groups.

A third possible explanation is that most elections boil down to a voter's party identification and the twin issues of security and prosperity. (A question asked in the 2004 exit polls led to widespread explanations that moral values accounted for Bush's victory, but subsequent analysis concluded that this issue played only a "very minor part" in voters' choice.)[18] Attack messages that suggest an opponent cannot provide security and prosperity trigger fundamental human anxieties. Collecting information to resolve these fears or doubts is beyond the capacity of most voters, so the negative message prevails.

A fourth explanation is that the press has a bias toward reporting the negative. In the 1960 presidential election, three-quarters of the media coverage of the campaigns was favorable in tone; since 1980, more than half of election campaign coverage has been negative. Over these decades, reporters have given much more coverage to candidates' negative ads and attacks on their opponents than to candidates' rebuttals or positive claims about what they hope to accomplish if elected.[19] Finally, tension as the election-day deadline looms may reinforce these reasons for using mud-slinging tactics.

The Quality of Political Advertising

No experienced media planner for branded products would overload customers with the commercial schedule used for elections. Consumer marketers monitor *wearout* in ad campaigns: the point at which ad-saturated consumers tune out or turn against brands that previously caught their attention or favorably impressed them. And even though campaigning now goes on for more than a year, from the run-up to the primaries through the general election, voters have only two opportunities to make a "purchase decision": the primary and the general election. Typically, most people develop interest only after Labor Day and then many people tune out; the television audience for the October 2000 presidential debates—carried on all the major networks—represented a mere 30 percent of households.[20] Political advertisers are caught between trying to sustain the public's interest and wearing out their welcome. In Europe, on the other hand, the timing of elections is less predictable and campaigns are typically limited to a matter of weeks; interest is higher and voter participation levels greater than in the United States.

Compounding the problem is the sameness of the messages and the poor quality of the execution. Like car ads, most U.S. political ads look and sound alike; very few break through the clutter, and those that do are often the attack ads. Voters dismiss the clichéd ad featuring the candidate, surrounded by family or constituents, who makes promises not apt to be fulfilled. Most citizens surveyed during the 2000 campaign said that politicians would "say almost anything to get themselves elected."[21] Attack ads, although possibly offering novelty, contribute to citizens' perceptions that campaigns are "depressing" and not "uplifting."[22]

No one can conclusively show a direct one-to-one relationship between campaign marketing and election results; for instance, few voters would admit to basing their decision on a political ad. However, the fact that a modest number of voters change their minds preceding an election indicates an opening for advertising to persuade: during U.S. presidential elections from 1953 to 2000, 8 percent, on average, of voters changed their intentions twenty-five to thirty days before an election, and 4 percent changed their minds in the final five days.[23]

One defense of mass-media communication in politics is that it exposes large numbers of voters directly to candidates and their messages. Before radio or television, most voters' exposure to candidates was mediated through print journalism. And perhaps surprisingly, recent research has found that "political advertising is rife with both informational and emotional content and actually contributes to a more informed, more engaged, and more participatory citizenry."[24] Exposure to television commercials increased interest in an election, knowledge about the issues, familiarity with the candidates, and intention to vote. Moreover, exposure to ads were most helpful to the people who started with the smallest store of political knowledge.[25]

Voter Decision Making

Still, this does not speak to the quality of the decisions voters make. Although humans rely heavily on visual cues in virtually all aspects of daily life, it is nevertheless troublesome that a candidate's visual attractiveness "can shape how voters evaluate a candidate's personal traits, their general impression of that candidate, and their decision whether to vote for that candidate."[26] Further, when voters know little about the opposing candidates and cannot use party affiliation to distinguish them—for example, in nonpartisan local elections or in congressional primary elections in which all candidates belong to the same party—sheer name recognition is the most important factor: "In these situations, even negative coverage can benefit a campaign because it raises voter familiarity with the candidate."[27]

The paradigm of an informed, engaged citizenry choosing leaders whose policies they think will best serve the public interest is central to representative democracy. But can people choose wisely? Aristotle criticized direct democracy on the grounds that the people were easily swayed by emotion rather than persuaded by reason and were incompetent to judge the best interests of the state; hence, demagogues would thrive. Participants in the Federalist debates worried about the same problem in a representative democracy, particularly if the voting franchise extended beyond the educated. Exactly the same debate surrounds the role of information, reason, and emotion in consumer decision making.

However, choosing between a Coke and a Pepsi is an everyday transaction that entails no apparent long-term consequences. Voting for a candidate means selecting the person who will occupy an office for two to six years. Perhaps a better comparison is buying a durable product, such as a new car one expects to own for three or four years. Still, the stakes are higher in politics. Different philosophies of government are on offer (although sometimes these differences are not great), and different constituencies stand to benefit, depending on who wins. Whether conservatives or liberals are in power has a potentially greater impact on the average citizen's life than driving a Chevy instead of a Toyota. And voters are stuck with the results. If a family is unhappy with its new Chevy, it can trade it in for a different brand at any time. Except for the rare recall or impeachment, the winning candidate remains in power until the next election.

With the stakes high and the choice irrevocable, voters seemingly should be motivated to search for detailed information on candidates and to weigh alternatives carefully. There is little question that the political product is complex and multifaceted and difficult for voters to inspect. But whether choosing cola, cars, or candidates, people—however well educated—avoid information overload. That could be one reason Americans pay less attention to news about international, national, or local politics than to nonpolitical news.[28] Also, as much as people might claim they want to hear details about a candidate's positions on all the issues, media consultants find that information-laden ads are much less effective than image-driven or entertaining ads.[29]

No matter how involved they may be, most voters choose candidates in the same way they go about selecting a car: they rely on incomplete information, shortcuts, and rules of thumb. Some car shoppers are strictly loyal to the Ford brand; others care only about fuel economy; still others choose based on styling. Similarly, many voters base their decision solely on affiliation with a party brand name—Republican or Democrat.[30]

Others base it on a candidate's position on one or two issues—say, taxes or a woman's right to choose. A sizable number base it on personal likeability—a large part of the appeal of Ronald Reagan. Or if times seem bad, a disaffected citizen may vote for the "outsider" candidate regardless of political persuasion. That accounted for much of Ross Perot's appeal in 1992. Finally, roughly half of eligible U.S. voters either are not motivated to vote or can find no acceptable choice.

Disengagement

Political scientists in the 1950s characterized citizens as ill informed and apathetic; few people appeared to have a coherent political philosophy encompassing a well-organized and internally consistent set of beliefs and opinions covering a variety of issues.[31] Subsequent scholars presented little reason to believe the situation would change; higher levels of education, for example, appeared to make little difference.[32]

However, it is worth considering whether there are characteristics of the political marketplace that contribute to this lack of motivation and information. To appeal to different consumer segments, marketers can develop an extensive range of specialized products, specialized communications, or both. In government, though, policies usually apply across the board; there is one education plan and one tax policy per jurisdiction. So politicians promise policies and legislation that address the hot-button issues of various constituencies, such as supporting anti-gay-marriage amendments to assuage "family values" voters, or voting down gun-control regulations to appease the National Rifle Association. Parties and candidates present the public with policies weighted toward the "must-have" preferences of single-issue voters and campaign contributors, who may well be a minority. The preferences of the remaining voters—perhaps the mainstream majority—tend to be underrepresented. Politicians effectively trade off the votes of vocal minorities against the preferences of a quiet majority.

Tailoring the message to the audience to foster involvement is a standard marketing principle. However, politicians face constraints in saying different things about their programs in front of different groups. For one thing, politicians who are inconsistent in their communications are open to accusations of duplicity or pandering to special interests. Al Gore, normally a serious or plodding speaker, was ridiculed for addressing Iowa farmers in folksy terms like "golly."[33] The press reports it when a candidate denounces

Hollywood marketing practices before one audience and in the next week holds a fund-raising event with the help of the entertainment industry.[34] (Of course, candidates adapt to audiences by emphasizing certain themes.)

One could easily assign blame for the shortcomings of campaign politics to the influence of political marketers. The public sees a blizzard of ads, many of them attack ads. It hears sound bites rather than substantive discussion of issues. It views national conventions orchestrated to avoid dissent: invariably, any debate over contested planks of the party platform takes place behind closed doors. The televised debates between candidates are scripted and rehearsed in advance with the advice of campaign consultants. Daily tracking polls create a scorekeeping atmosphere, where candidates' advances or declines in the ratings take on more importance than what they actually say.

However, marketing is not the source of all that ails politics. An important reason for the decline in Americans' engagement in politics is that they feel their votes do not count or make a difference in deciding which candidate wins or which policies prevail. For this, election rules, the two-party system, the peculiarities of House and Senate districting, the Electoral College, and increasing geographic polarization of the population into politically lopsided districts and states bear responsibility.

The American Political Marketplace

In every election in American history both parties have their clichés.
The party that has the clichés that ring true wins.

—Newt Gingrich[35]

For truly national brands like Coke and Pepsi, a purchase by a consumer in California is as important (and profitable) as a purchase by a consumer in Florida. But in U.S. presidential campaigns, thanks to the Electoral College system, a voter's value depends on geography: the vote of a citizen living in a swing state counts more than the vote of a citizen living in a solidly partisan state. The state-by-state primary system produces similar distortions. Voters in the early-primary states have more value than those in late-primary states, when the contest is usually over. The political parties and candidates pay selective attention to the minority of voters who happen to reside in places where an election outcome is in real contention. In the 2004 presidential contest, of the billion dollars spent by the presidential candidates and national parties, more than half was on advertising targeted at 2 percent of the citizens eligible to vote.[36]

Democrats and Republicans, unlike product marketers, have little vested interest in increasing the overall level of consumption, that is, the number of votes cast; they benefit mainly from increasing their share of the votes. Many strategists in both parties appear to think it easier and less expensive to accept a situation where a low percentage of eligible citizens register and vote.

A benefit of long U.S. campaigns is the chance for obscure candidates to make themselves known (or the chance for opponents or the media to smoke out something negative in a candidate's past, especially first-time candidates). But this benefit is erased if a candidate cannot come up with the money to sustain a long campaign against a well-funded opponent. U.S. electoral rules allow for virtually unlimited spending. A candidate who can outspend an opponent can afford better market research on the issues that matter to voters, more sophisticated and better produced television commercials, and a larger volume of advertising.

The high stakes needed to compete, particularly for national or statewide office, are a barrier to entry that contributes to a lack of political choice. The advantage goes to incumbents, whose strong name recognition, access to the levers of power, and ability to influence legislation attract deep-pocketed campaign contributors (who gain a disproportionate influence on policy). Often, the exceptions to the incumbency advantage are celebrity candidates like Arnold Schwarzenegger, scions of political families like George H. W. Bush, George W. Bush, and Mitt Romney, and wealthy candidates like Michael Bloomberg or Jon Corzine.

Equivalent barriers to entry exist in the consumer marketplace, where well-known brands or well-bankrolled entrants that can afford to buy advertising and pay retailers for access to shelf space have an advantage in introducing new products. The difference is that for many consumer products consumers can make multiple choices, allowing small new entrants, like Snapple in the 1980s, greater opportunity to survive outside the mainstream.

In short, compared with the consumer marketplace, the political marketplace appears to be less democratic. It ranks lower on inclusiveness, encouragement of consumption, and choice. As will be seen, it also ranks lower on ease of exchange, thanks to such factors as preregistration requirements and access to polling stations.

The Role of Political Parties

Thus, it is not surprising that the United States has experienced a long-term decline in political engagement and voting levels. In the 1950s, about two-thirds of adults voted in presidential elections. By 2000, only half did so. To be sure, there was an uptick of participation in the 2004 presidential election. But that uptick was sparked by a polarizing president and a polarizing issue (the war in Iraq). Especially in the case of young adults, a strong dislike of a candidate was a motivator to vote.[37] It is open to question whether new younger voters or the previously apathetic older voters will continue to participate in the political process in the absence of these conditions.

Lack of choice, in particular, is linked to the two-party system. The founders did not set out to design a government dominated by two parties. On the contrary, they tried to arrange a government removed from the influence of political parties and factions. Nevertheless, parties proved essential for mobilizing the electorate and providing the cohesion and clout to propose and enact legislation; many political scientists believe that democracy can flourish only when strong parties exist.[38]

In a large, pluralistic society like the United States, a natural expectation is that a fairly large number of parties representing political philosophies or "regional brands" (as with Canada's Parti Québécois) would emerge. Many successful Western democracies have flourishing multiparty systems. But a structural aspect of the U.S. and British political systems leads to party concentration. Specifically, a single-member-district system, where the winner takes all, creates incentives for voters not to "waste" their votes on candidates representing weak parties. Inevitably, this dynamic leads political opponents to coalesce into a few parties, each of which tries to appeal to a broad base. And once entrenched, the dominant parties impose barriers to entry that make it difficult for independent candidates or small parties to place their names on the ballot or receive public funding for campaigns.[39]

The Republican and Democratic parties prevailed for the same reasons that allowed Coke, and later Pepsi, to grow into dominant national brands: a highly effective on-the-ground organization to distribute the product, economies of scale in production and communication, and a product whose taste had mass appeal. During the past century, third parties occasionally managed to win elections at the state level. The election of Reform Party candidate Jesse Ventura as governor of Minnesota is a case in point. As an expression of voter discontent with the major parties and voter concern with significant social issues, third parties offer a distinctive choice. Typically, though, third parties are short lived, limited in scope, and incapable of sustaining themselves beyond the original charismatic figurehead. The major parties have shown a consistent ability to co-opt their issues and supporters.[40]

Historically, a political system that limits choice to two parties has its virtues. To accumulate strength on a national basis, both parties must appeal to a broad swath of the electorate. Accordingly, they have embraced voters of differing socioeconomic status, religion, and race. In this sense, the two-party system has helped reinforce commonalities rather than divisions within society, as millions of Americans identify with the Coca-Cola brand as one expression of American culture. Reflecting the moderate sentiments of the majority of voters, both parties have sought common ground in doctrinal positions and ideology. Because both parties lean toward centrist positions, they can forge a governing consensus when control of the House, the Senate, or the presidency is split between them. All this has contributed to the stability of government in the United States since the 1860s.

Moreover, the system accommodates a little more diversity than is first apparent. Under the broad tents of the Republican and Democratic parties there is room for politicians with a range of views and for intense intra-party competition. In the consumer marketplace, Coke introduces brand extensions, including Diet Coke, Coke Zero, and Cherry Coke to appeal to varied tastes and retain Coke's position as the beverage of choice. At the local level in politics, nearly anyone can stand for office. At the state and national levels, the direct primary system permits all party-aligned voters, and not only party leaders, to select candidates to run in general elections. Both parties are flexible enough to embrace innovative or niche politicians who gain party nominations in the primary process.

Both the Democratic and Republican parties are successful at brand stretching, although the Democrats' embrace of civil rights in the twentieth century stretched it so far that many Southern Democrats switched allegiance. Generally speaking, the national parties allow state parties and candidates a good deal of autonomy; individual candidates develop their own brand and positioning. When it comes to governing, elected representatives at times break with the party line to promote policies that benefit their constituents. Party discipline is weak compared with parliamentary forms of government, where the prize of control over the executive branch goes to the largest legislative bloc.[41]

Problems with the Two-Party System

Nevertheless, Americans' choices reduce to a fairly narrow range of political philosophies. For example, consider a voter who is most interested in economic and moral issues. This voter has a choice between a party that promotes government intervention in the free-market economy and hands off on legislating morality versus a party that promotes hands off the free market and intervention in morality. No viable party promotes the libertarian approach of hands off both the economy and morality. No viable party combines moral intervention and free-market intervention (although Patrick Buchanan adopted this positioning in his 1996 campaign for the Republican presidential nomination).[42]

No viable party promotes a social democracy philosophy of the sort found in Europe. Limited choice means that significant segments of citizens cannot choose options that truly represent their views. In marketing, this type of situation creates a vacuum that competitors rush to fill. Or if the niche cannot be occupied profitably, the result will be a number of consumers who refrain from choosing any of the existing alternatives. That appears to be what is happening in politics.

Among the choices that exist, some segments of Americans perceive no clear differences. A Harvard University project on the vanishing voter found that, in the 1950s, nine out of ten people polled had something to say about party differences.[43] In contrast, in the 1970s, three out of ten voters drew a blank when asked what they liked and disliked about the parties. The author of the study attributes these changes to several factors, one of which is the difficulties the parties face in fashioning a clear, cohesive message from a large mix of confusing and crosscutting issues.[44] This mirrors the increasing fragmentation and diversity of society and mass markets in recent decades.

Another factor is that political issues in the era after World War II are less salient than the economic issues that galvanized working-class Americans before the New Deal (when trade union membership, with its organizing capabilities, also was higher). Citizens' belief that party choice will make a difference in their lives has been declining, particularly among lower-income Americans: in 2000, disproportionate numbers of lower-income respondents thought the outcome of the election would have very little, if any, impact on their lives; disproportionate numbers of low-income people chose not to vote.[45]

Coke and Pepsi do not just coast along on the strength of their well-known brands and broad user base. Any established consumer marketer must work to remain contemporary, to differentiate its brand from imitators and other competitors, and to retain its brand essence, all at the same time. One legacy of the polarizing presidency of George W. Bush may be an increase in citizens' perceptions of serious, meaningful differences between Republicans and Democrats. Young adults were likely to believe that the 2004 election results would substantially affect the country's future.[46]

The Republican Party and the Bush administration have shifted the party's agenda and policies away from centrist positions and toward the right of the political spectrum.[47] That is not to say that all differences between the parties will become evident to the apolitical voter overnight. The policies offered by the Republican Party—and, for that matter, the Democratic Party—have changed, but updates to the parties' brand images have not kept pace. In fact, some of the parties' political philosophies and actions run counter to their established images; lately, the noninterventionist Republicans have become the party of preemptive military action, and free-spending Democrats have become the fiscal conservatives.

Companies like General Motors and DaimlerChrysler find that it is difficult to dislodge brand images built on consumers' years of experience with a product. Given an average three-to-four-year interval between automobile purchases, it can take five to ten years to change brand perceptions. No matter what model changes GM made in an attempt to shore up sagging demand for its now-defunct Oldsmobile line or to bring in younger customers with ads proclaiming, "This is not your father's Oldsmobile," consumers persisted in believing that Oldsmobile was indeed the car your father or grandfather drove. The ads actually reminded consumers of the perception problem. Similarly, it takes many years to revise or update a brand when political philosophies or positions change. And rebranding runs the risk of alienating current buyers or voters. The Republicans, for instance, likely want to deemphasize policies that would alienate middle-of-the road voters traditionally attracted to the party. At the same time, they must pursue policies and principles that motivate their fervent conservative base.

A business's ability to introduce innovative products and services into the marketplace allows consumers to have a wide and ever-changing range of choices, and consumers and the marketplace reward those innovations that create value. Brands endure because they refresh themselves. Tide detergent formula has been improved more than forty times since the brand was launched.

Generally, the political marketplace lags the consumer marketplace in the speed with which new policies or features are introduced and implemented. In democratic government, change is glacial. Usually it takes time to form a consensus around new ideas, to fashion legislation, to roll out changes in the bureaucracy, and to withstand court challenges. Of course, having one party control the House, the Senate, and the presidency comes closer to the corporate model of consolidation of authority and ability to act unilaterally than is the more usual case in government, with its structural system of checks and balances.

In either sector, crises increase the pace of innovation. Following the 9/11 attacks, the Bush administration quickly pushed through such changes as redefining policing authority and citizen rights of privacy in the Patriot Act, reorganizing the government bureaucracy to form the Department of Homeland Security, and initiating war in Iraq. But more usually, government innovations, once enacted, tend to persist from one administration to another. True, marketers' unprofitable line extensions also linger. The difference is that in the consumer marketplace ordinary individuals have a clear say in accepting or rejecting innovations; in politics they have little opportunity to direct changes in a policy.

Structural Determinants

Structural features of the U.S. electoral system have a powerful influence on who gets elected and voters' degree of say in government. So do geography, wealth, and economic clout. The House of Representatives—which was designed to be the more democratic of the two legislative chambers— exemplifies how these factors can produce imperfectly democratic results. Specifically, the single-member constituency and winner-take-all rules by which members of the House are elected mean that the views of many voters are underrepresented. Essentially, citizens must "consume" the winning candidate and party.

There is no parallel in consumer marketing other than forced consumption due to scarcity or the allocation decisions made by Soviet-style bureaucracies. In a tight three-way race, the winner could represent as little as 33 percent of the people living in the district. In a four-way race, it could be as little as 25 percent. The possibility of rule by a small minority is mitigated only by the tendency of single-member constituency systems to coalesce around two or three major parties.

Inequities in representation exist based on where a voter happens to live. Since 1911, the number of congressional seats in the United States has been fixed at 435, apportioned equally across the states by population—modified by the rules that each state is guaranteed at least one seat and states cannot have fractional numbers of seats. Seats are reapportioned among the states every ten years, after the decennial census. But it is up to the individual states to establish the borders of congressional districts. Some states have gone decades without redistricting despite population shifts, resulting in districts of wildly uneven size. Often, the voice of people living in urban areas counts less in Congress than the voice of people living in rural areas. And of course, the apportionment of U.S. Senate seats was designed to give greater weight to the voices of people living in sparsely populated states.

Even when the sizes of districts are equal, a combination of demographics and partisan politics tilts the playing field by creating safe districts, often with rigged boundaries that do not track with naturally cohesive communities. As a result, voters on the minority side have little chance of gaining representation. Districts are sufficiently safe that the Center for Voting and Democracy states, "In most House races, we can project not only who will win but by what margin without knowing anything about the identity of the challenger, about the voting record or any other characteristic of the incumbent, about campaign spending in past or current elections, or about polling data and organizational endorsements. All we need to know are the results from recent federal elections in the district and the incumbent's party and seniority."[48]

If the one-third of U.S. voters who are Republicans, the one-third who are Democrats, and the one-third who are independent were evenly distributed, such stark patterns would not hold. Many geographically mobile Americans can choose where to live. Many prefer to live in like-minded neighborhoods and communities. The middle class moves to suburbs and gated communities stratified by socioeconomic class. Senior citizens choose age-restricted over-55 retirement communities. Fewer Americans rub shoulders with people from other walks of life.

Describing the growth of the new family-centered "exurbs" ringing American cities, a reporter quoted a Wisconsin woman's choice of a desirable location for home and employment: "Austin she rejected as being too liberal.

Houston seemed too hot . . . 'And I kept coming back to Frisco [Texas], which I'd never heard of before . . . I got twice the house for the same price . . . And politically, I feel a lot more at home here.'"[49] Perhaps the country is experiencing—despite low voter turnout—the beginning of increasing political segregation and a self-reinforcing tipping point phenomenon, where, once a critical threshold is reached, members of a political minority abandon the territory to the majority and move elsewhere, where they in turn are the majority.

Different Rules, Different Games

The problem to be solved is, not what form of government is perfect, but which of the forms is least imperfect.

—James Madison[50]

The vast majority of Americans—all of them except immigrants—have grown up knowing only one form of democratic government. With the possible exception of the debate over abolishing the Electoral College, most Americans have not questioned the status quo nor examined its strengths and shortcomings. Most of them probably have no idea that other democratic countries operate under alternative sets of rules—including how citizens' votes are parceled out to candidates and how power is allocated among the branches of government—or that these alternative systems may offer advantages. Americans are reared to think that the United States leads the world in achieving such democratic ideals as equality of representation ("one person, one vote"), an even playing field, accountability of government to the people, and guarantees for minorities. But these ideals hold up more in the marketplace than in politics. It is worth considering whether alternative systems encourage greater competition, give citizens more options, allow citizens more nearly equal representation and equal weight, and permit greater diversity in political preferences—in other words, act more like markets.

In electoral systems, proportional representation offers an alternative to a single-member, winner-takes-all system. In government type, the parliamentary system offers an alternative to presidentialism. When the form of electoral system is combined with the form of government, the result is four basic archetypes: European-style parliamentary governments that use proportional representation to elect legislatures; British-style parliamentary governments that use first-past-the-post, single-member districts; Latin American-style presidential governments that use proportional representation; and U.S. presidential governments that use first-past-the-post.[51]

Proportional Representation Systems

Proportional representation systems for electing legislatures are designed to produce results that parallel the voting choices of the entire electorate: the number of representatives in the legislature who belong to a particular party is proportional to the number of votes received by that party. In that way, this system is more like the consumer products marketplace. Any party that receives a certain minimum number of votes (say, 5 percent of the votes cast) is entitled to a representative. Operationally, multiple members are elected from a geographic district.[52] Rather than vote for individual candidates, citizens cast their votes for a "party list."

Such systems foster a greater diversity of parties than occurs in the U.S. or British model. Because parties cater to varied political philosophies or concerns, an individual voter is more likely to find one that reflects his or her interests. As in the consumer market, the people who prefer a niche brand still have a place at the table; their vote is not wasted. Geography matters less: how individual district lines are drawn has much less impact on whether a citizen's vote "counts."

Thus, proportional representation offers greater choice, more diversity, and fairer representation. Politicians can risk forming new, innovative parties because they have less worry about being shut out of the allocation of legislative seats.

Most of Europe uses proportional representation. The United Kingdom, Canada, and the United States are the only major Western democracies that do not.[53] Voters in proportional representation countries are more likely to show up at the polls—at the rate of about 70 to 80 percent, compared with 50 percent or less in U.S. elections.[54] And newly democratizing nations transition to democracy more successfully with some form of proportional representation: "analyses provide strong evidence that single-member electoral districts and democratization do not mix . . . The winner-takes-all approach to electoral choice does not by and large appear to be conducive to establishing the power-sharing norms and the inclusive, balanced legislatures best suited to the entrenchment of democracy."[55]

Arguments against proportional representation are the mirror image of the arguments for it. Critics contend that it results in too many minority parties, none of which can muster the strength needed to run a government. A lot of political energy goes into forming and holding together coalitions rather than governing. If they are part of a coalition government, minority parties may exert influence—sometimes as spoilers—disproportionate to their electoral strength.[56]

Similarly, splinter parties that appeal to narrow interests increase divisions among the electorate, in contrast to majority parties that must find common ground. Israel and Italy are examples of the problems of having too many political parties and high turnover from one coalition government to another. On the other hand, Israel and Italy allow parties with a very small percentage of the vote to participate in the legislature; generally, countries imposing a stiffer criterion of around 5 percent avoid this situation.[57]

Presidential and Parliamentary Forms

The distinguishing feature of a presidential form of government is a president elected separately from the legislature—in most countries, by direct popular vote. (The U.S. Electoral College is unusual.) The president has a fixed term of office, and the cabinet is appointed by and serves the president.

In a typical parliamentary government, the majority party in the legislature—or a coalition of minority parties if there is no clear majority—names a prime minister and cabinet ministers from among its ranks. This executive function serves until the next scheduled election or until a no-confidence vote in parliament leads to its resignation or a new general election. (Some nations have a "semipresidential" system, in which power is constitutionally distributed between a directly elected president and a prime minister selected by parliament.)[58]

The data are clear: "Most long-established democracies have parliamentary systems. Presidentialism is poorly represented among long-established democracies."[59] The European model originated in response to the adoption of universal suffrage around 1900.[60] It has come to be viewed as particularly desirable in heterogeneous societies: rather than suppress minority representation, something that could foment national disintegration, it provides for representation of multiple political segments in parliament. The British model flourished in many former colonies; the Latin American model has a woeful record of degenerating into authoritarian rule.

In an influential essay, Juan Linz attributed the failure of presidential models to a number of inherent problems. As summarized by Mainwaring and Shugart, the central issues include the degree of accountability to the public, flexibility in adjusting to changing situations, accommodation of competing demands and interests, tolerance of democratic opposition, and restraint of power.[61] This list sounds very much like characteristics valued in the marketplace: responsiveness to public needs and wants, innovation, diversity of products and services, active competition, and checks on corporate monopolies or abuses of power. If Americans wanted to experience a government with these virtues, they would do well to consider the European or British model.

How Forms of Government Compare to Democratic Markets

Consider, for example, accountability to the public. In the U.S. and Latin American models, government powers are split between independently elected presidents and legislatures. It is not always clear to the public whom to hold accountable, particularly if the president and the legislative majority belong to different parties. In the British and European parliamentary models, the prime minister and cabinet are directly accountable to the party or coalition that controls parliament, and the party is clearly accountable to the public for the performance of the government.

Mainwaring and Shugart argue that the European model is the weaker of the two on this score, because "a deeply fragmented party system" and negotiated coalition-building makes it difficult for voters to predict who will emerge as prime minister and whom to hold accountable for government performance.[62] The aftermath of the 2005 German elections, which failed to produce a clear winner between Christian Democrats and Social Democrats, demonstrated how party positions on issues can blur as parties compromise to form a coalition government.[63]

Concerning flexibility and responsiveness, parliaments can replace a leader who has failed to adjust to changing situations or has lost the confidence of the party or a coalition partner. Although the calling of an early election may be manipulated to the advantage of the incumbent party, ultimately the election allows citizens to provide midcourse direction to the government.

In contrast, voters in a presidential system cannot easily and legitimately remove a chief executive who performs unsatisfactorily. If term limits prevent a president from running for reelection, he or she has even less reason to be accountable to the public. Bagehot argued that controversy between the executive and the legislature and lack of legislative accountability make the U.S. model slower than the British model in responding to the public's needs.[64]

In the United States, chief executives must perform quite poorly before suffering serious consequences. Over the past fifty-five years, public-opinion approval ratings that fall below 40 percent signal serious danger for presidents seeking a second term or trying to push an ambitious agenda.[65] So eventually politicians who run counter to public opinion pay a penalty.

But looked at another way, the data say that citizens have endured years of government when six or seven out of ten voters do not approve of the job their president is doing. Forced consumption of unpopular politicians promotes government stability but at the expense of being responsive to the majority of citizens. Furthermore, the rigidity of the election schedule means that election timing, or "time to next purchase," often has little to do with the timing of momentous events and decisions that could motivate voters to participate in elections.

Diversity of party choice is greatest in the European model. But in the political, as opposed to the consumer, marketplace, there is a limit to the choice and diversity that are desirable. Parties catering to ethnic, tribal, or religious divisions may generate nonnegotiable demands and an absence of democratic consensus.[66]

One possible remedy is to create government institutions that permit and encourage citizens to adopt fluid self-identifications that vary depending on the policy contexts. [67] For example, in India, instead of having individuals identify themselves by fixed ethnic category, people could classify themselves by linguistic identity in an education context, or regional identity in an employment context. Here, politicians could learn from brand marketers, which are adept at encouraging consumers to adopt multiple self-identities centered on lifestyle choices and brand affiliations.

Degeneration into authoritarianism is the curse of countries adopting the Latin American model. Possibly because this model of government incorporates a powerful executive, it is likely to be chosen by countries following a period of military dictatorship or authoritarian rule.[68]

That it offers less opportunity than other models for an effective opposition party is a weakness. On the one hand, if one party holds both the presidency and a majority of the legislature, the government is stable but has no checks on its power. As in markets, parties seizing monopolistic powers have little need to act in the public interest. Overpricing occurs in the private sector, corruption in the public sector.

On the other hand, fractionalization of parties, in which none controls more than one-third of the seats, is more common in the Latin American model than in other models.[69] The resulting deadlock can be fatal: "Combining presidentialism with a legislature where no single party has majority status is a kiss of death: such systems can expect to live only 15 years."[70] In consumer marketplaces, too, strong national brands can create efficiencies and deliver customer values that may be out of the reach of smaller, weaker players.

The possibility for a party to exert power disproportionate to the number of votes it receives is highest in the British system. In the 2005 general election, the winning Labour party received only 36 percent of the votes but took 55 percent of the seats. The Liberal Democrats came in a solid third, with 22 percent of the votes, but gained fewer than 10 percent of the seats.[71] Unlike the U.S. model, where the same situation could occur, the British model automatically gives control of the executive branch to the party winning control of the legislature. Yet the British model, despite its undemocratic aspects, has a strong track record of stable governments. Certainly, this stability is rooted in history, culture, and social institutions. Bagehot said about the British Parliament, "Its majority ought to represent the general average intelligence of that country; its various members ought to represent the various special interests, special opinions, special prejudices, to be found in that community. There ought to be an advocate for every particular sect, and a vast neutral body of no sect—homogeneous and judicial, like the nation itself."[72]

The working of a British-style parliamentary system, then, is similar to the working of mass markets for consumer goods. Citizens and consumers have diverse interests and opinions, but a party or national brand can meld these under one common denominator. It works best in comparatively homogenous countries; any cleavages are shallow enough that they can be bridged by centrist parties or centrist brands. Discipline and focus help. Political theorists believe that to function well, parliamentary systems require strict discipline among elected party members.[73] Marketing strategists believe that brands must clearly stand for something, and consistent execution by front-line employees (equivalent to members of Parliament) is essential.

If political scientists were recommending government models to countries transitioning to democracy, they likely would propose the European or British model as the optimal choice. Przeworski et al. ask why many countries transitioning to democracy adopt the U.S. or Latin American presidential models given that the British and European parliamentary democracies last longer.[74] Possible answers—including a tendency for political parties to believe that they will win the presidency, a nearly universal propensity to choose the same system used when the country was last democratic, and a preference for presidential models following military dictatorships—have little to do with benefits to citizens.

Among established democracies, it is virtually unheard of for a nation to switch from presidentialism to the parliamentary system, and rare to switch to proportional representation. If a country with the U.S. model were to switch to proportional representation—that is, the Latin American model—the result could be disastrous. Citizens must live with the status quo, flawed though it may be. But drawing on marketing to strengthen political parties and to make them more representative of citizens, more responsive to their interests, and capable of providing more value is beneficial for society. Equally important is drawing on marketing to strengthen citizens' participation in the political system.

A More Democratic Democracy

I confess that there are several parts of this Constitution which I do not
at present approve, but I am not sure I shall never approve them.
For having lived long, I have experienced many instances of
being obliged by better information, or fuller consideration,
to change opinions even on important subjects.

—Benjamin Franklin[75]

The United States ranks in the bottom fifth among democracies in participation in national elections (participation in state and local elections is lower). And that includes not only the industrialized democracies but all electoral democracies around the globe.[76] Although deep structural changes are unlikely, many other solutions have been proposed. Looking at the problem through the lens of marketing gives credence to a number of proposed reforms that aim to create a more vibrant democracy.[77]

Consider the theme of exchange, which underlies marketing concepts and practices. In politics, the transactions involved in exchange are cumbersome. Marketers try to make buying easy for anyone, anywhere, anytime. But voting procedures are designed to make participation in elections a deliberative, planned transaction open only to citizens carefully screened for eligibility.

This approach is rooted in the founding of the republic, when, in most states, a majority of adults—including women, slaves, men who could not afford poll taxes, or men who did not own land—were not eligible to vote. Although constitutional amendments and legislation have steadily expanded the right to vote, the United States has a history of repressing or denying the vote in practice; often, politicians in power have imposed barriers when they believed that the people currently excluded would vote for their opponents. In terms of equal opportunity to participate, marketers have a considerably better record than the democratic U.S. government.

To vote, U.S. citizens must register. The patchwork of state and local regulation of voting registration is not conducive to universal participation. As a result, "impulse buying" on election day is prohibited in most states; only a few allow same-day registration.

Moreover, registration often expires the moment voters move out of their current precincts, even if they move within the same city or town. This provision affects a substantial proportion of the public: between 1995 and 2000, nearly half of the population made at least one move; of these moves, at least 46 percent were to a different county or state.[78] The election reform commission headed by former president Jimmy Carter and former secretary of state James Baker proposed universal registration for a lifetime. This step would add an estimated 50 million Americans to the list of registered voters.[79] In the absence of universal registration, same-day registration helps: it increases "the likelihood that citizens will know when, where, and how to register, and it accommodates those individuals who have recently changed residence. For young adults, especially college students and recent graduates, these advantages are considerable."[80]

Rules governing eligibility to vote are more standardized than formerly but still vary from state to state. Some states allow prisoners to vote; others restore voting rights to convicted criminals who have served their time; still others permanently deny eligibility. Some state and local elections allow permanent residents to vote; others, as well as national elections, limit the vote to U.S. citizens.

Costs of Voting

Not often discussed is the cost that elections represent to voters. There are time costs, including the time required to process information on the election alternatives, to go to polls, and to wait in line. Shoppers faced with long lines at supermarkets can decide to grab something at a convenience store instead; voters have no alternative on Election Day, although they can mail in absentee ballots ahead of time.

When lines are long, the time costs impose a heavy burden on hourly workers. Twenty states have no laws requiring employers to provide time off for voting, and of the states that do, some require employees to submit advance written notification. Economists have difficulty understanding why any rational individual would bother to vote, given the costs incurred and the "odds that your vote will actually affect the outcome of a given election are very, very, very slim."[81]

There are also monetary costs to voters in the form of tax dollars spent to run an election. The decision by California governor Arnold Schwarzenegger to call an interim election, in which various policy proposals were thrown to voters to decide, was widely unpopular, in part because of the estimated $50 million cost of the election and in part because voters viewed such decision making as the job they had elected their representatives to do.[82] Turnout was low, and voters rejected all of the governor's initiatives. In consumer marketing, increasing the number of opportunities to purchase goods increases consumption; in politics, creating more elections devalues an already inconvenient exchange.

The venues where voting takes place are often unfamiliar, unappealing, and makeshift; they seem designed to alienate first-time voters. Poll workers can be uncooperative, ill informed, or even prejudiced. The mechanics of casting a vote are unfamiliar, unreliable, and highly diverse, ranging from various types of paper ballots to punch cards, lever machines, and touch screens. U.S. voters accustomed to banking at automatic teller machines scoff at the claim that it is too difficult to provide electronic voting machines with paper verification. Recent problems with the design and tabulation of ballots undermine citizens' confidence that their votes are allocated as they intended. Developing countries such as Brazil, India, and Mexico have leapfrogged the United States in the use of sophisticated electronic voting machines and counting procedures.[83]

Voting Reforms

To be sure, inconvenience and unfamiliarity are not the primary factors inhibiting people from voting. But they are likely to intimidate and discourage uninvolved voters, including young people, who are the group least likely to vote. In contrast, marketers facilitate exchange when and where it is convenient for the customer. Coca-Cola wants to bring its product within arms' reach of desire. Retailers have extended their operating hours and are open on Sundays. Sales through mail-order catalogs, the telephone, and the Internet let consumers shop from home. Voters are apt to respond to similar opportunities.

Oregon instituted voting by mail as the only voting option in 2000, following experiments, begun in 1981, with voting by mail as a supplementary option. In the Oregon system, every registered voter receives a ballot in the mail, along with an information pamphlet, and has twenty days to return a completed ballot. Comparisons among the 1992, 1996, and 2000 elections indicate that rates of *voter retention* (voting in two elections in a row) and *voter mobilization* (new voters) increased with the shift to vote by mail; the shift did not appear to change political preferences.[84] Similarly, pilot tests in which British local elections were conducted solely by mail showed that such voting increased overall turnout, primarily because it "boosted turnout among older citizens—the group who are least able to get out to polling stations and the most motivated to take advantage of this reform—by an estimated 18 per cent."[85]

Proposals to facilitate participation include allowing Internet voting, making election day a national holiday, and expanding the election period to several days. In particular, some reformers tout remote e-voting—voting by computer, telephone, text-messaging devices, digital televisions, and the like—as a means for increasing election turnout among the wired younger generation.[86] However, experiments with e-voting in the United Kingdom in 2000 through 2003 indicated that it was not effective in increasing overall turnout and increased turnout among the young only slightly.[87] These results, in concert with doubts about e-voting's ability to meet standards for security, secrecy, accuracy, and fraud protection, suggest that e-voting is not a panacea. That is not to say that it shouldn't be a voting option if the integrity of the system can be guaranteed.

Value of Voting

Making voting more convenient should produce an uptick in participation. But there remain profound barriers to citizen engagement. When it comes to marketing exchanges, success over the long run depends on creating value for both parties to a transaction. No doubt, successful candidates derive value when the electorate goes to the polls (for one thing, the more people voting for them, the more of a mandate they have). So, too, do losing candidates if citizen participation in democracy means that the candidate or the party has an opportunity to win the next time around. The value a vote delivers to members of the electorate is more elusive. What, exactly, are voters "consuming" when they go to the polls?

Some voters derive gratification from the act of participating in the democratic process, no matter who wins. The "good" citizen fulfills an obligation to participate in democratic institutions because the continuation of democracy depends on participation. But schoolbook ideals of civic virtue and democratic participation do not sufficiently motivate the nonvoting half of the eligible public. Then there are voters who care deeply about election outcomes. They hold strong political views, and they want representatives who will govern the country in accordance with their views. But even voters in this group find it difficult to assess the value they receive.

For one thing, over time, all citizens' voices have become diluted. The number of governors, senators, and congressional representatives is fixed, but the number of people they represent is steadily increasing. Following the 2000 census, the average size of a congressional district was about 647,000 people, or more than triple the size of the average district in 1900.[88] Representatives have three times as many constituents to attend to as they did a century ago.

There is no practical remedy to the district size problem: tripling the number of representatives would make Congress even more unwieldy. Although the number of staff per representative has increased to deal with constituent service, representatives could emulate marketers that use technology to supplement or substitute for person-to-person interactions.[89] Citizens may be wary of giving too much information about themselves to any politician or government official, but they should be able to opt into mailing lists and forums where they can receive and contribute information about, say, schooling, health care, or tax policies. The online Minneapolis Issues Forum is one such space, where citizens, the mayor, city council members, and city officials discuss civic issues.[90]

Voting Against One's Own Interests

Complicating the problem of measuring the value of the exchange is the complexity and shortcomings of the political "product." In product terms, any one politician bundles various positions on issues with various character traits. When consumers judge value, they implicitly consider which alternative comes closest to their *ideal point*—that is, which product characteristics matter most to them and how well they perceive the product to perform on those characteristics. The same is true in politics. But the political product bundle almost inevitably falls short of voters' ideal points. And evaluating job performance—or, for that matter, personal traits—requires knowledge that is out of reach of the average citizen.

In buying consumer goods, people aim to get the best value for their money, but U.S. citizens regularly vote at odds with their own economic interests. The same individuals who shop hard for bargains to save $20 here and there send politicians to Washington who, for example, legislate tax cuts that disproportionately benefit the wealthy few compared with the large middle class.

Bartels characterizes this unexpected behavior as citizens' "unenlightened self-interest."[91] Regarding the 2001 and 2003 tax legislation, he argues that most voters knew that income disparities had increased during the preceding two decades and considered it a bad thing. Citizens also recognized that the Bush tax cuts would increase income inequality, but "they largely failed to connect inequality and public policy."[92] It also appears that the administration successfully framed the issues and crafted the policy details so as to detach citizens from their natural preferences.[93] There is nothing to suggest that citizens would be any more prepared to evaluate the consequences of other types of economic policies, environmental regulations, foreign policies, or similarly complex governmental decisions.

In the marketplace, feedback guides purchase decisions. But dissatisfied voters appear reluctant to hold individual politicians accountable for the performance of their party, even though this is their best mechanism for obtaining policies or programs more to their liking. Data show that dissatisfaction with a party's performance does not necessarily translate into throwing out incumbents at the next opportunity. In the 1998 through 2004 elections for the House of Representatives, 98 percent of incumbents won, the majority of them Republicans.[94] In the same period, the percentage of respondents giving unfavorable ratings to the Republican Party ranged from 31 percent to 51 percent; compared with somewhat better figures for the Democratic Party of 30 percent and 41 percent.[95]

Numerous explanations are possible, including strong incumbency advantages in campaigns, the size of the party's war chest, voters torn between liking their local representatives and not liking the policies of their party, and a dearth of alternatives. Consumers make similar distinctions between a sub-brand and a corporate brand or family brand; negative attitudes toward one do not always spill over toward the other.

Part of the difficulty is that the performance of an elected representative depends on the performance of many other government actors. This is particularly the case in the legislative branch but also applies to governors and the president. The U.S. system of checks and balances ensures that government is the art of compromise. Party platforms and clear policy positions stated during campaigns give way to negotiation. Elected representatives end up repositioning themselves and not delivering on original promises.

Congressman Newt Gingrich's Contract with America movement is one of the rare exceptions. During the 1994 congressional elections, Gingrich recruited Republican candidates to sign on to a policy agenda that reflected an overarching conservative philosophy and a distinct contrast with the majority Democratic Party. In a radical shift of the electorate, Republicans gained control of the House, and with strict party discipline, strongly pushed their agenda. Still, representatives ultimately had to go back to their constituencies with an imperfect record as measured against their promises. When gaps occur between performance and promise, service marketers observe dissatisfied customers responding with apathy, acceptance, brand switching, anger, or occasionally energy to bring about change. The question is whether voters respond in these same ways.

Power of the Few

In a democracy, people want to believe that their individual voice counts, and they want to feel equal. Clearly, though, not everyone is heard equally. Wealthy, politically active individuals have a much greater say in "product design"—including selection of candidates and policy positions—than does the average citizen. Increasingly, groups who band together to exert political pressure have no influence if they have no money. The cost of running for election all but guarantees that. In the corridors of government, lobbyists' power is commensurate with the money they have to donate to election campaigns.

The founders never envisioned a United States where giant corporations, super-wealthy individuals, and heavily funded special-interest groups would have such strong voices in government. They envisioned government by an elite, but an elite based on informed opinion, reasoned debate, civic virtue, and hard work. Now, marketing is more democratic than politics. Some marketers cater to the wealthy, but many more listen to all consumers and try to design products to fill their needs. Wal-Mart makes excellent profits by serving people in the lower four-fifths of the income distribution.

To be sure, government devises programs to benefit various segments of the population. But voters have little direct say in setting policy agendas. They must trust that their influence over elected representatives is not swamped by the interests of the wealthy and politically connected. To restore democracy as envisioned by Jefferson and Madison, the public needs to press for further government reforms that limit the impact of money on election outcomes and policy decisions. In the absence of strong public pressure, the impetus for reforming voting procedures, which began after the 2000 election, has stalled.

The Long-Term Good

All in all, it appears that substantial numbers of citizens do not fully embrace what marketers would call the *value proposition* offered by elective government. At the birth of a democracy, the proposition is explicit: citizens are clearly aware that in exchange for their participation and involvement, they will receive laws and governance that, among other things, guarantee individual rights and provide public goods like education and infrastructure, clean water and safety; they accept that they may have to endure short-term disadvantages to themselves for the long-term good of society.

In the first democratic elections in Iraq, in 2005, turnout was very high despite difficult and violent conditions. In the United States, people appear to have grown complacent about the value proposition of government, and turnout is low. On representatives' side of the equation, they fail to convey the value of what government has to offer. To the contrary, a number of politicians—who should be promoting the institution—have found it expedient to focus on associated costs and shortcomings, such as taxes, waste, and corruption, rather than benefits, such as the ability to set a public agenda. On the citizens' side of the equation, they have grown frustrated or indifferent. No one has effectively marketed elective government to them.

Ultimately, the purpose of a democratic government is to serve the common good. It depends on social capital, citizen participation, and common interests. Marketing can play an integrating role. To many minds, the idea of market segmentation as a unifying mechanism is counterintuitive. To think of market segmentation typically is to think of dividing the population into separate, even mutually exclusive, groups. In fact, segmenting voters on the basis of their interests and concerns can help transcend typical ethnic and class labels.

In the 2005 New York City mayoral election, Michael Bloomberg's well-funded campaign surveyed hundreds of thousands of residents. According to Kevin Sheekey, Bloomberg's campaign manager, "We sat down in February and said we wanted to do this campaign differently, we wanted to unify the city by looking at people who had common beliefs . . . We were not going to classify them by party or race; it was thought-based."[96] The result was a classification into eight segments of voting blocs "based on people's shared everyday interests and concerns, not on their broader racial, cultural or ideological differences."[97]

Marketing can also contribute with outreach efforts to increase voter registration and turnout. A new group of citizens enters the political marketplace every year. In the United States and many other countries, younger citizens are less likely to vote, and the age gap in turnout has increased over the years.[98] Get-out-the-vote marketing efforts in the 2004 U.S. presidential election were conducted by Democrats, Republicans, and nonprofits like Rock the Vote and Pew Charitable Trusts, as well as consumer businesses like 7-Eleven stores. The initiatives targeted people under the age of thirty, reaching out to them in their preferred medium of the Internet as well as through traditional grassroots organizing. These efforts, and the heated nature of the 2004 presidential campaign, drove voter participation to its highest level since 1968. Five million more young adults voted in 2004 than did in 2000.[99]

Obviously, there are no easy cures in politics. But what if citizens demanded to be treated more democratically—to be treated more as they are in the marketplace?

CHAPTER 8

Media

Watchdog or Lapdog?

IN MODERN SOCIETIES, the media transform the nature and extent of people's experience with communication, information, entertainment, and commercial transactions, not to say their perceptions of the world. It was the advent of a new technology—the printing press, invented by Johannes Gutenberg in 1448—that marked the beginning of the media era. By the eighteenth century, books and, later, newspapers, magazines, and journals circulated widely and changed the way people received information as well as entertainment. Within a local area, news stories reached their audience within a day.

Not everyone could own a press or be a publisher, but neither could the establishment elites control the media. Paid advertising helped fund a wealth of newspapers. Access to printing businesses enabled independent authors to disseminate their work. Thanks in part to the democratic nature of the print media, dissenters such as Thomas Paine, and others with radical political, religious, or social ideas, had the opportunity to be heard.

This environment nurtured the public press—what came to be know as the fourth estate. Nineteenth-century historian Thomas Carlyle wrote, regarding the role of reporters, "Printing, which comes necessarily out of Writing, I say often, is equivalent to Democracy: invent Writing, Democracy is inevitable . . . Whoever can speak, speaking now to the whole nation, becomes a power, a branch of government, with inalienable weight in law-making, in all acts of authority. It matters not what rank he has, what revenues or garnitures, the requisite thing is, that he have a tongue which others will listen to; this and nothing more is requisite. The nation is governed by all that has tongue in the nation."[1]

Is the modern media industry living up to its role as a bulwark of democracy and guardian of the public interest? On the one hand, private-sector media democratize access to news and information via a proliferation of outlets and products, including interactive electronic media, cable television channels, specialty magazines, books, and newspapers. The industry employs professional journalists to perform the essential public services of factual reporting and analysis and scrutiny of the motives and actions of corporations and governments.

On the other hand, consumer demand for hard news is declining. Private-sector media, of course, are profit-making businesses. Many draw significant revenues from advertising, whereby consumers enjoy a "free" press in the sense of not having to pay for it or paying a low price subsidized by marketers. But financial pressures on journalism are increasing.

Consumers display rising dissatisfaction with the media's political coverage. Some people believe that journalists are overly partisan. Others think that the ongoing consolidation of media ownership into the hands of a few giant conglomerates, which control both distribution and content, means that the independence and diversity of views represented in the media will decrease. Yet the Internet and other electronic media technologies may empower individuals to create and distribute political content, thus revitalizing political discourse and democracy.

In many ways, the future media landscape promises to recapitulate the past: indications are that it will remain advertising supported, although marketers will have to work harder than ever to break through the information clutter to reach consumers with advertising that is informative, enjoyable, and persuasive. Consumers will prefer entertainment, social connections, and goal-oriented information more than national and international news. News organizations will face pressure to cut back on journalism in order to invest in new technologies, and, for publicly traded companies, to meet Wall Street's earnings demands. Ultimately, the fate of the fourth estate depends both on its status as a public good and on market forces.

Proliferating Media Choices

The media transforms the great silence of things into its opposite.
Formerly constituting a secret, the real now talks constantly.
News reports, information, statistics, and surveys are everywhere.

—Michel de Certeau[2]

The Western media industry is distinctive in several respects. One is the ideal that some segments of the media, as a vehicle for journalism, function for the public good. In service of democracy and freedom of speech, it is hoped, the press provides accurate, timely, complete, and unbiased news. To promote the free flow of ideas and information, many democratic governments reserve bandwidth for public use or try to ensure that commercial media are not exclusively controlled by a small group of major players. In the United States, Federal Communications Commission (FCC) rules allocate some channels for public use and cap national audiences for broadcast media as well as cross-media ownership of broadcast and newspapers in local markets.

The Role of Advertising Revenues

Another distinctive characteristic is the reliance of the majority of media, from small niche magazines to major television broadcasting networks, on advertising revenue. Even the public broadcasting radio and television stations turn to advertising in the form of corporate sponsorships to help cover their operating costs. This creates a push-pull dynamic with consumers. Newspapers, magazines, radio, television, and Web publishers simultaneously sell content to consumers and sell consumers—their consumer audiences—to advertisers. In effect, some media businesses have two if not three masters—consumers, advertisers, and the public good—not to mention owners, shareholders, and regulators.

Historically, advertising has always flowed to new forms of media that promise additional opportunities to connect with consumers. It thus enables media innovation and proliferation. Advertisers' stakes are significant. On average, advertising accounts for roughly 80 percent of revenues for U.S. newspapers and 60 percent for magazines, with subscriptions and newsstand sales making up the balance. Many local newspapers and business trade publications are 100 percent advertising supported.[3] Commercial radio stations and broadcast television stations in the United States also are completely reliant on advertising revenue (at their inception, the technical means did not exist to charge consumers according to what they tuned to); cable networks and cable operators receive revenue from a combination of advertisements and subscriber fees.[4] Many of the most visited Internet sites, including Yahoo!, Microsoft, and Google, depend heavily on advertising revenues.

In the advertising-driven model, media businesses must simultaneously deliver what consumers want and what marketers want. Because marketers pay more to advertise to larger and more attractive consumer audiences— for example, the highly coveted audiences of eighteen-to-forty-nine-year-olds who are the prime target customers for many consumer goods—media content providers also target these groups.

Mass Media

To their great profit, broadcast media in the twentieth century developed a mass audience. The CBS and NBC radio networks broadcast across the United States and delivered national audiences to advertisers, which in many cases controlled the programs they sponsored (for example, *Texaco Star Theater*). Soon after television took off in the early 1950s, it quickly became the most popular medium. To consumers, TV was compelling, affordable, and nearly universally accessible. By the early 1960s, more than 90 percent of homes had a television. At the same time, consumers had limited choices in television programming, with access to at most seven stations, and that only in the largest markets.[5]

Network programs aimed to appeal to mainstream tastes for entertainment. Local stations also supplied some original content, including local news reports, but filled much of their airtime with syndicated shows and reruns. A few local noncommercial television stations aired educational and higher-brow fare but had tiny audiences.

Generally, critics disdained the passive nature of the "boob tube" viewing experience, the vacuity of the programming, and the commercialism— although programs were freer from direct control by commercial sponsors than in the initial period of television and the heyday of radio. In 1961, Newton Minow, then chair of the FCC, famously challenged broadcasting executives to "sit down in front of your television set when your station goes on the air and stay there without a book, magazine, newspaper, profit-and-loss sheet or rating book to distract you—and keep your eyes glued to that set until the station signs off. I can assure you that you will observe a vast wasteland."[6]

In part in response to Minow's stinging remarks, the two leading networks expanded their news broadcasts to include a half hour of prime-time evening news and produced documentaries on social issues. The networks' news operations—including their coverage of the assassinations of John Kennedy, Robert Kennedy, and Martin Luther King, Jr. the space program, and the Vietnam war—powerfully shaped the national consciousness. Increasingly sophisticated technologies provided consumers with live, breaking news from around the world as well as stories with a visual and emotional impact that newspapers could rarely duplicate. News anchors commanded respect from the public and prestige within the networks. Television created shared national experiences.

Differentiated Media

By the 1980s, in parallel with trends in the packaged-goods market, the television market became increasingly differentiated. UHF channels and home cable connections expanded consumer choices. Choice drove consumption. Daily viewing rose from an average of six hours per household in the early 1970s to eight hours in 2004.[7] Currently, more than a hundred cable channels appeal to narrower market segments. Consumers can choose among channels specializing in news, sports, weather, children's programs, movies, comedy, travel, food, home decorating, and more. Advertising remains a prime source of revenue.[8] Although some programming is pay-per-view and consumers pay cable subscription fees, most viewing is not directly linked to consumption of particular channels or particular programs.

In market fragmentation, television is coming to resemble the magazine industry. More than seven thousand consumer-oriented magazines published in the United States—ranging from general-interest news publications to those covering fashion, sports, travel, computing, lifestyle, arts, history, science, and specialized hobbies—offer readers choices to suit every taste and every point of view. They are affordable items of consumption and conveniently delivered to the home. Some 4,500 to 4,700 titles are also sold at retail outlets.[9]

The magazine industry is inclusive, targeting consumer segments defined by region, age, income level, language, political philosophy, and more. Because marketers try to match their advertising to the content, editorial style, and audience of a publication, readers likely find the advertising relevant, interesting, and informative, or, if not, they can easily skip it. Automotive enthusiasts, for example, learn about new accessories or discover where to order hard-to-find parts. Consumers flip through fashion magazines for the ads as much as the editorial material.

Advertising revenues, along with established distribution systems and relatively low barriers to entry—much of the production can be jobbed out, and capital investment requirements are modest—permit vigorous competition. By lining up enough advertising to support an initial issue or two, an entrepreneur can test the concept. Most fail, and a few become hits, but without such financing from marketers, there would be less choice and less competitiveness. At the same time, the magazine industry is dominated by a small number of corporations, which own the top titles as measured by circulation and account for the lion's share of revenues.[10]

Economics of the News

If most magazines are niche products with a national reach, newspapers are mass-market products with a local reach. Within their geographical market area, papers seek to appeal to the broadest possible audience through articles that serve consumers' desires for news and information combined with sections and features that offer specialized information and entertainment. However, U.S. consumers have little choice among full-scale daily newspapers. During the past decade, the number has steadily declined; many markets now have only one.[11]

Although many U.S. newspapers still earn good profits, the economics of the industry are difficult. There are high fixed costs in putting out a daily paper, including newsroom staffing if a paper aspires to high-quality journalism. The bulk of the revenue comes from local advertising, which is highly sensitive to business conditions and economic trends, and new advertising media are reducing newspapers' share of the pie (e.g., free classifieds on Craigslist are cutting deeply into newspapers' paid classifieds). Circulation and readership are falling, with younger consumers, in particular, turning to online sources of news, entertainment, and classified advertising.[12] Consumers are conditioned to paying low prices; not many other consumer products cost less than a dollar. Taken together, these factors create high barriers to entry, along with pressure, if companies are public, to reduce costs to satisfy shareholders. The economics promote industry concentration.[13]

In the United States and other democracies, mass-market newspapers and mass-market television networks remain the primary source of news and information. But these media face a common quandary. They achieved their market share because of barriers to entry for smaller competitors and because they offered a low-cost or free product bundle targeted at a broad audience. They avoided alienating consumers and advertisers, perhaps at the expense of inspiring passionate commitment or deep loyalty among their consumer base. Yet that makes them vulnerable to specialized media alternatives that unbundle the all-in-one product, sparing a consumer the burden of separating out the parts of interest. Deeply entrenched consumer expectations for free or low-cost content restrain publishers' and broadcasters' ability to break free of reliance on advertisers by charging higher prices.

Because cable channels and alternative print media operate on a smaller scale than broadcast TV or major newspapers, they can be more focused and a little edgier (cable and satellite channels are also free from FCC decency regulations). For a cable channel, a series that attracts 2 million viewers may be a hit; for CBS, ABC, or NBC, it may be a flop. Premium, commercial-free cable channels, such as HBO, can take even greater risks with programming than cable channels that run advertising.

When a channel or mini-network does not try to be all things to all people, it is better able to build a strong brand identity and market itself to a particular consumer segment. Eventually, though, the marketplace may fracture to the point that no channel has enough hits to carry the rest of the programming. Then the industry may see a wave of consolidations and contractions.

Pluralism of media is democratic. But what happens to democracy in a large, heterogeneous nation like the United States if the truly mass media disappear or newspapers cannot attract a readership or the small independent media outlets vanish or are swallowed by conglomerates? One potential effect is a gradually diminishing sense of shared national identity. Another is a diminished fourth estate.

The Diminished Fourth Estate

Where the press is free, and every man able to read, all is safe.

—Thomas Jefferson[14]

Institutions like the *New York Times* and the *NBC Nightly News* aspire to objective reporting of the news, unswayed by partisan politics or vested interests. As a conduit for information, the press, more than any other business, performs fundamentally important functions in a democracy: it enables freedom of speech; it allows citizens to make well-informed choices; it watches over politicians and governments. Journalists exposed the Nixon Watergate scandal, the Iran–Contra affair, and the deficiencies at Walter Reed Hospital, to name a few instances.

But the press are marketers as well as marketplace: newspapers and magazines, television and radio broadcasters, book publishers, and cable operators are businesses that compete against one another for consumers' and advertisers' dollars. Corporate owners of news media expect profits. News divisions may receive overt or covert pressure to slant political coverage to serve corporate interests. It takes fortitude to run front-page stories criticizing a major revenue source or a politician who favors a policy beneficial to a newspaper's owners.

And if the media market, with its freedom of choice, speaks for consumer tastes, then fact-gathering, investigative journalism may become an endangered species. Of the top ten magazines, as rated by paid circulation, half are women's magazines; *Time*, the only newsmagazine to make the list, comes in at number 8.[15] Advertising and circulation figures for celebrity magazines such as *People* are growing, while those for newsmagazines are declining. In response, major publishers are cutting news staff.[16] Circulation of newspapers in the United States, Western Europe, Latin America, and Australia has been falling; their publishers, too, are spending less on journalism and shifting toward entertainment and lifestyle stories.[17]

On broadcast television, audiences for evening newscasts continued a decades-long sharp decline as of 2005; those for morning news programs declined by a half million viewers from the preceding year, prime-time newsmagazines saw cutbacks in programs and audiences, and Sunday news interview programs held on to a niche audience.[18] Meanwhile, the total audience for cable television news channels barely managed to remain stable, although MSNBC appeared to be on shaky ground financially.[19]

The Pew Research Center for the Public and the Press reports that in the past decade, Americans overall have dramatically altered their news consumption habits. The percentage of people consuming news daily shrank from 90 percent in 1994 to 82 percent in 2004; younger audiences in particular are falling off.[20] Younger people are also migrating to online sources of news. Newspapers and broadcasters have responded by diversifying into online operations.

However, the fact that more people are visiting online news sites does not mean they are consuming more news. There is evidence that online readers look at fewer pages compared with print sources and spend less time doing so. For national and international news, they are content to scan headlines. What they want to consume online, no less than offline, is short articles, coverage of local happenings, entertainment, sports, weather, and ways to enhance their lives.[21]

Major news stories—such as 9/11, the war in Iraq, the presidential election, or the destruction of New Orleans—draw large audiences. The op-ed writers on the *New York Times* appear to be popular.[22] But generic news stories, or international news not perceived as immediately relevant to Americans' daily lives even in a global economy, attracts little interest.[23]

Adapting to Consumer Tastes

Like other businesses, the news media attempt to respond to consumer preferences. If consumers find news shows dull or heavy going, producers repackage the news to make it more entertaining and easy to digest. Complicated stories are reduced to sound bites, and a narrative is imposed on real-life events that in their raw state are inconclusive or lack drama. Newspapers, magazines, and TV shows are redesigned to be snappier and more attention getting. Investigative journalism unearths novel stories that engage readers by exposing a deplorable situation or appealing to a sense of outrage.

If news consumption remains tepid, a natural step is to reduce the space or time devoted to news. The average length of a newspaper article has decreased. The major networks shortened the early evening news shows, slotted the more serious news programs like *Nightline* outside prime time, and cut the numbers of news correspondents they employ. *Time, Newsweek,* and *U.S. News and World Report* decreased reporting on national and foreign news, gave news a softer treatment, and added more entertainment and celebrity stories. (In contrast, the British *Economist* presented much more hard news, extensive world coverage, and joining of stories to create connections and contexts.)[24]

Late-night television comedy and talk shows constitute a source of political "news" for some viewers, and serious news shows strive to provide entertainment. Political comedian Jon Stewart, "the most trusted name in fake news," pointed out a lack of seriousness in some nonfake news programs when he told the hosts of *Crossfire,* "It's hurting America . . . You're doing theater, when you should be doing debate."[25]

Part of the problem for journalism is the finite amount of time and attention consumers can devote to media. So fast-growing Metro International publishes free tabloid dailies that have proved especially popular with readers under the age of forty-five. The benefit touted to consumers: "All Metro editions carry headline local, national and international news in a standardized and accessible format and design, which enables commuters to read the newspaper during a typical journey time of less than twenty minutes."[26] If lack of personal relevance is another part of the problem, then the interactivity and customizability offered by the Internet may eventually draw in more readers. Still, the general unwillingness of consumers to pay for online news (one exception is the *Wall Street Journal*) is not a sign they perceive high value in the product.

Presumably the market for news matches supply and demand. The minority of people who are deeply interested in national and international affairs can find solid investigative journalism and probing analyses of political issues. Public broadcasting, including PBS and NPR in the United States and the BBC in Britain, national newspapers of record, and thoughtful magazines of news and public affairs expose institutions and individuals to public accountability. With the Internet, activist citizens can contribute their own reporting, fact-checking, and opinions. The segments of people who prefer to consume news that displays a strong political bias and worldview consistent with their own ideology are served by talk radio, cable news, and, for the more serious, magazines of political opinion. Newspapers and network television newscasts serve a wide swath of people who want to be generally informed by reasonably objective, nonpartisan sources.

The Financial Conundrum

The trouble is that there is a growing free-rider problem in the market for top-quality journalism: the public benefits from journalism—indeed, it's indispensable for a properly functioning democracy—but fewer people are patronizing the organizations that produce it. Television has embraced journalism that consists of interviews and talking heads in part because it is relatively inexpensive to produce these types of shows.[27]

Primary newsgathering, in contrast, is expensive and labor intensive. Important stories can occur anywhere in the world at any time without warning, as did the December 2004 Asian tsunami believed to have killed more than 200,000 people, or the Hurricane Katrina flooding of New Orleans. News organizations continue to provide live, hour-by-hour coverage of such events, attracting larger than normal audiences for the duration, but do they reap sufficient benefits to directly cover these costs? It is the loyal members of their audience and the loyal advertisers that subsidize this type of coverage. When circulation or audiences fall, how can news organizations justify keeping the equipment and skilled staff needed to cover the extraordinary events—or in-depth coverage of politics and world affairs? Publicly traded companies are under pressure to make deep cuts.[28]

More fundamentally, journalism is by its nature subject to people consuming its products without paying. There are several reasons for this. First, it is often difficult to meter or restrict the use of information. Second, the objective of the press is to inform the public—to reach as much of the public as possible. In the ideals of the profession, profit considerations are necessary but secondary. Third, nearly all journalism is built on an accretion of previous reporting. Much of what appears in the daily newspapers or on radio or television news consists of retelling or adding new details to previously reported stories, many of which originate with the most deep-pocketed organizations. If you cut out the primary reporting, you undermine the entire edifice.

For all these reasons, it appears glib to assert that the salvation of journalism lies in the Internet. True, given the diffusion of the Internet to a global mass audience (enabled by marketers), even the most repressive regimes experience mounting difficulties in suppressing the fourth estate. Also, bloggers have played an important role in fact-checking and correcting errors made by the mainstream press. The democratic nature of blogs and Web sites allows ordinary people to air opinions, conjecture, and critiques of governments and corporations.

OhmyNews, based in South Korea, is an often-cited example of online citizen journalism, but lately it has come under fire for unreliable content and a partisan slant.[29] Any expectation that citizens can assume a substantial share of basic hard-news reporting to high journalistic standards is untested. Google and other news-aggregation portals direct consumers to breaking news on a huge number of stories. But these sites piggyback on the traditional news sources; they don't produce journalism.

And turning to the Internet won't remove the financial pressures on news organizations. If newspapers and magazines migrate online, they eliminate the costs of newsprint and physical distribution. Offsetting these savings, however, is the reluctance of consumers to pay for online sources of information and also any costs incurred if publishers continue to offer both traditional and online delivery systems. That would leave the fourth estate as dependent on advertisers as it is now. If tracking metrics for online journalism show that consumers prefer the softer types of news to the harder news, guess where advertising dollars and editorial content will flow.

Erosion of Trust

In newspapers, the wall separating the objective coverage of the newsroom from the client sensitivities of the advertising sales department is perpetually besieged. There is a sense that the arrangement fails to ensure trust in the news media. Nearly eight out of ten Americans polled in a recent survey thought that "a media company that receives substantial advertising revenue from a company would hesitate to report negative stories about that company."[30]

In the same survey, nearly half of the respondents said that news organizations are often inaccurate and don't get the facts straight; four out of ten thought the news media would try to cover up a serious mistake in a news story (note that the poll was taken shortly after revelations of reporting failures at the *New York Times* and *CBS News*). In contrast, in a companion survey of 673 journalists, almost 90 percent said that news organizations generally get their facts straight; three-fourths said that most news organizations quickly report mistakes. It might be expected that journalists would rate their reporting better than the general public does. But they agree with the public when it comes to corporate influence: nearly eight out of ten said that, in their experience, to some extent "media organizations either intentionally or unintentionally avoid news stories that are potentially unfavorable toward the company." Two-thirds agreed that the same was true for major advertisers.[31]

The journalism profession traditionally has seen itself as a guardian of the public interest. Some family-owned publishers feel a strong sense of public duty. However, a corporate media company is unlikely to include promotion of democracy as part of its vision statement. Media critics like David Allen argue that "media managers no longer feel the need to rely on claims of public service or aiding democracy to justify what they do."[32] Media companies are focused on getting bigger and more profitable. In an ideal democracy, policy makers could balance citizens' needs for diversity and plurality of information with large media companies' ability to leverage content across media, to innovate, and to improve services to consumers. When fourth estate issues rate low on citizens' agendas, the balance tilts toward the corporate side. That could have serious consequences for the free flow of political ideas and information necessary for democracy.

Political Discourse and the Media

"[People] may come to believe even more than they believe the very foundations of their own conduct that the ultimate good desired is better reached by free trade in ideas—that the best test of truth is the power of the thought to get itself accepted in the competition of the market.

—Oliver Wendell Holmes[33]

Justice Holmes's description of a marketplace of ideas assumes that different ideas or viewpoints compete for acceptance as truth. Collectively, the press is a forum for this marketplace of ideas. In the eighteenth century, all newspapers were partisan. The owner-editors expressed their points of view and advocated for issues they cared about, and citizens understood this to be the case. Owing to the large number of independently owned newspapers, a diversity of political opinions flourished in a true marketplace of ideas. By the twentieth century, though, diversity of opinion (not the same as diversity of media outlets) and transparency of partisanship were arguably much reduced.

One factor lessening diversity of opinion, perhaps by the law of unforeseen consequences, was the late-nineteenth-century movement to improve and professionalize journalism.[34] Within newly established journalism schools, journalistic integrity meant reporting the facts as objectively as possible—the standard who, what, where, when, and why of news stories—and reserving opinion and partisanship for the editorial page. But as major newspapers, bolstered by advertisers that liked the new, neutral environment, adopted the modern journalistic standards, they became increasingly alike.

The same was true of television. The nightly network television news programs covered the same stories, often in exactly the same order.[35]

Ironically, the stance of objectivity served to disguise any subtle biases or slants in the news. Most of the public accepted the political news they read as "the truth," or at least a piece of the truth. They trusted what television anchors Edward R. Murrow and Walter Cronkite had to say.

More Power, Fewer Voices

Consolidation of media ownership during the twentieth century raises questions of political diversity. Chains bought out independent newspapers. The book publishing industry consolidated. The big three independently owned television networks were folded into the likes of General Electric and Viacom. Only ownership rules imposed by the FCC prevented a single corporation from monopolizing all broadcast and newspaper media in a given metropolitan area or reaching more than a specified percentage of the national audience. Advocates of the public interest charge that monopolistic media companies are bound to offer a narrow range of mediocre-quality services and to accumulate enormous political power that they are tempted to use to further their own interests.[36]

Ted Turner, who founded CNN and nurtured it into a highly profitable independent news channel, maintains that his success would have been impossible under FCC ownership rules progressively loosened in response to corporate pressure starting in the 1980s: under the new rules of competition, he says, the only way for a media company to survive is to own a conglomerate of broadcast and cable networks; entertainment and news programs and the studios that produce them; and cable, satellite, and broadcast transmission systems.[37] As a result, there are fewer voices to hold government and business accountable to the public. Turner distinguishes between variety of offerings and diversity of viewpoints: "Only a few corporations decide what we can choose. That is not choice . . . Different voices do not mean different viewpoints, and these huge corporations all have the same viewpoint."[38]

Although Turner's charge may have merit, the increasing segmentation of the media seems to be spawning more distinct political viewpoints. One change is increasing polarization among politically conservative, moderate, and liberal consumers in the programs and networks they watch. Fox News, which targets political conservatives, emerges as the most partisan channel, and CNN and CNBC appeal more to moderates.[39]

In a more diverse media marketplace, citizens and consumers can choose the news coverage that appeals to them. The question, then, is what happens to the press's role in fostering informed democratic discourse. If citizens do not recognize partisan coverage for what it is, will they take opinion as fact and ideas competing for truth as the whole truth? What happens when self-selected audiences receive only reinforcement for their views and nothing to challenge their thinking? Tocqueville observed, "When an idea has taken possession of the mind of the American people, whether it is just or unreasonable, nothing is more difficult than to root it out."[40] One reason he offered is freedom of the press: "Peoples in whom this freedom exists are attached to their opinions by pride as much as by conviction . . . and also because they are their choice, and they hold to them not only as something true, but also as something that is their own."[41]

Audience members for Fox News, for example, were more likely than other viewers to prefer news consistent with their own views, to avoid news critical of the Bush administration, and to underestimate factual information about Iraq war casualties.[42] Politically conservative, moderate, and liberal consumers are also increasingly polarized in their perceptions of the press. Republicans in the Pew survey, compared with Democrats or independents, rated most of the press far lower on credibility, trustworthiness, and fairness.

The Evolution of Political Coverage

Political news coverage has evolved from more or less straightforward reporting about candidates' campaign appearances and pronouncements to "horse race" or "strategic news" coverage, such as analyses of which candidate has "momentum" and critiques of performance style and campaign strategy.[43] This coverage persists despite a lack of precision in tracking polls.[44] Results are not always statistically significant.[45] But media stories increasingly revolve around who is on top in the polls, and candidates' reactions to poll results, rather than on discussion of substantive issues.[46]

A study of presidential election coverage from 1988 through 2000 showed that "attention to the horse race increased sharply in 2000, but issue coverage did not. The tone of coverage has remained consistently negative . . . Media discourse was also less substantive and more negative than candidate discourse."[47] In the same study, voters awarded the media low marks for their performance. Although opinion among scholars is divided, a number believe that horse race coverage breeds political cynicism and lower voter turnout.[48]

But in fairness to reporters, horse race coverage began in part as an attempt to counter politicians' attempts to play to the public through news coverage of campaign events staged for that purpose. That is one reason networks radically shrank the programming hours devoted to the major party nominating conventions. Reporters who described campaign events without imposing a frame of analysis merely rehashed what politicians wanted them to say.

The game between reporters and campaign public relations consultants has now entered a new phase, *metacommunications*, defined as "the news media's self-referential reflections on the nature of the interplay between political public relations and political journalism."[49] Two types of stories are examples: navel-gazing stories about the performance of the press itself in covering politics, and stories about the performance of spin doctors in influencing the press. In other words, journalists have attempted to inform the public about the prevalence and power of modern political marketing communications. The more objective members of the media end up reporting accusations by conservatives that the press has a liberal and elitist bias, or by liberals that it is a tool of the right wing and large corporations. The partisan members of the press participate in the attacks. Few other businesses propagate self-critical messages that surely alienate their customers.

A hallmark of professional journalism is attribution of information to a "reliable source." But this criterion leads to a mutual codependence of reporters and politicians. Reporters rely on politicians and government officials as news sources, and they, in turn, channel what they want the public to hear through reporters. Media critic Mark Miller says, "American journalists, more than their European counterparts, have to get a statement from the man in charge—got to get your statement for the day from Rumsfeld; got to get your statement for the day from Karl Rove. If you don't have the statement, you don't have a story to file."[50]

At the extreme, reporters ally with their sources at the expense of informing the public. All this gives politicians a chance to present stories the way they want them to appear. And since at least the 1980s, occupants of the White House are increasingly adept at framing messages, controlling the terminology, and restricting reporters' access to information, citing executive privilege and national security concerns if they have to.

Tocqueville viewed newspapers as an instrument for political activism and cast citizens as active participants in producing the press: "Newspapers make associations, and associations make newspapers."[51] That is, the press brings people with similar ideas together into associations and helps keep them together. Associations among people create political power and form a bulwark against tyranny.[52]

Large media corporations are not likely to promote this type of political activism, but they do provide citizens and politicians cheap and accessible means to engage in political discourse. In the digital age, the media are centralized but content is decentralized. Large media companies own the new media channels and commercially produced content, but individuals disseminate their own content. Political blogs, such as the *Huffington Post* or the *Daily Kos*, fill the role played by newspapers in Tocqueville's day. Partisan radio and cable shows draw like-minded people together. Callers into talk radio shows air their political opinions. Niche media like C-Span and Court TV offer unprecedented coverage of government.

Technology also makes it easier for citizens to act on information they receive; a few seconds at the keyboard suffice to forward an article to friends, submit a petition to a congressional representative, or donate money to a political group. In one study, two-thirds of Web users sampled during the 1996 and 2000 presidential elections said their political involvement increased after turning to the Web for political information; the 2000 group said using the Web made them more likely to think they could bring about political change.[53] Still, these developments are not universal. Another study found that people who use the Web primarily for entertainment did not feel they could make a difference in the democratic process, nor did they know much about current events.[54]

A recent example illustrates the challenges for the media in fostering citizen engagement in public affairs. In the primary season leading up to the 2008 elections, CNN and Web site YouTube opened up a Democratic presidential debate by inviting citizens to pose questions via the YouTube video-sharing technology. Citizens responded by submitting nearly three thousand homemade videos. Entries selected for airing were creative, clever, and often highly emotional. Although the debate tried to break new ground in appealing to the Internet generation, it failed to attract a significant television audience. Despite a modest increase among adults aged eighteen to thirty-four, viewership was smaller than for a preceding debate in a conventional format (although many people viewed clips on the Internet). Political observers also noted that the novel approach elicited mainly stock answers from the candidates.[55]

A larger question is whether the three-pronged role of democratic media—providers of information, guardians against governmental and business abuse of power, and promoters of political discourse—can coexist in one entity. Large, corporate-owned media have inherent conflicts of interest. It appears naive to believe that large media corporations, unless led by visionary, public-spirited chief executives, would have the will to fill all three roles or that small businesses or individual consumers would have the means. For instance, to stay in the good graces of the Chinese government, Yahoo!, Microsoft, Google, and Cisco helped monitor and censor citizens' Internet use.[56]

Equally important, it appears unlikely that fulfilling these roles can be left entirely to market forces. Other democracies devote more of the broadcast spectrum and more tax dollars to public interest programming than does the United States, and they protect this programming from political interference—although European stations have increasingly undergone "tabloidization," embracing commercial-type formats that blend information and entertainment.[57] France fosters local programming by limiting the proportion of time on French television given to foreign-produced material.

A marketplace of ideas is an apt metaphor for the competition among mainstream media, niche media, and the blogosphere in the United States. But free markets do not always produce fair marketplaces. And consumers do not always access news or engage politically, and thereby they do not always act in their long-term best interests.

Just as democratic societies need to ensure that information remains in supply regardless of short-term demand, they need to ensure that the marketplace for ideas is open to participation by all citizens, regardless of their political or economic clout. For instance, that would mean adopting Internet governance policies, such as *net neutrality*—nondiscrimination in Internet traffic—versus a *tiered* strategy allowing broadband providers to award preferential treatment to information and data based on its source.[58]

Integrity in Advertising-Supported Media

Music, commercial breaks, news flashes, adverts, news broadcasts, movies, presenters—there is no alternative but to fill the screen.

—Jean Baudrillard[59]

When the World Wide Web was introduced in the early 1990s, pioneering users fiercely resisted its commercialization, preferring to reserve the medium for free publishing and communication. They condemned the first advertisers and directed "flaming" attacks against their Web sites. By mid-decade, however, Web-based commerce took hold and many sites adopted commercial sponsorship. As with periodicals and broadcast media, consumers accepted the advertising-supported media model.

To remain viable, all advertising-supported media businesses must balance the interests of advertisers, consumers, and media owners. As with news organizations, the integrity of their exchanges with consumers rests on the relationship between the editorial part (responsible for content) and the publishing part (responsible for advertising and business operations) of the business. The normal separation between the two is easily eroded by actions that cater to the advertising side.

Consider a columnist in a fashion magazine who extols a line of cosmetics. Consumers tend to accept this information as authoritative and unbiased. This assumption is violated if the columnist is touting the brand because it advertises with the magazine. That may not seem like a serious matter. But when it comes to media that choose to cover politics or business or science, the potential ramifications from biased or omitted information are graver. Consider the decades it took for scientific evidence on the dangers of smoking to be widely disseminated.

Another norm is to make transparent distinctions between what is advertising and what is editorial content. *Advertorial* sections that mimic a magazine's editorial tone and style push the limits of acceptability. Articles, or entire magazines, that are clearly identified as vehicles for sponsors or corporate owners are on the right side of the fence.

That's not to say that the line separating right and wrong is clear. Product placement—inserting products into a television show, movie, or video game, ideally showing characters interacting with the product in a positive way—has so far been deemed acceptable. But the practice violates the transparency principle, and its growing use annoys more than a few consumers.

Advertisers, of course, continually aim to get closer to their customers. They want to circumvent the stratagems that consumers use to avoid commercials—first remote controls, then videotape recorders, then digital video recorders, digital set recorders, and Internet filters. They want to break through the cluttered advertising environment and reach consumers using new media or new types of advertising in old media. And they want to use the Web's two-way communication and individual addressability capabilities to interact more effectively with consumers.

Mixed Signals

For their part, consumers send mixed signals. In a 2004 survey of U.S. consumers, 64 percent of respondents said they were concerned about the practices and motives of marketers. Some 69 percent said they were interested in products or services that would help them skip or block marketing.[60] On the other hand, consumers enjoy some commercials. For instance, Budweiser commercials airing in the 2006 Super Bowl were downloaded from the company Web site more than 700,000 times and were watched by more than 22 million visitors to other sites that posted them.[61]

If consumers are to view advertising favorably, marketers and media businesses need to ensure that this advertising informs and persuades consumers honestly without impinging on the editorial integrity of the media or creating inadvertent deception. To avoid potential missteps, some leading advertisers are reverting to the model of branded entertainment, where the advertiser produces and packages a show identified with its name. In the early 2000s, BMW hired eight noted movie directors to create a popular series of online films featuring the company's cars, which consumers viewed more than 100 million times.[62] The films were clearly attributed to the company.

In 2006, Budweiser announced plans to introduce Bud TV, an online entertainment network offering six "channels" of comedy, reality, sports, and talk programming commissioned by the company.[63] Although the project represents increasing media commercialization, the sponsorship will be entirely transparent. More likely, any misrepresentation will be on the part of consumers, who must fill out a form saying they are at least twenty-one years old. Much more problematic, if not unethical, is the practice of marketers' assuming fake onscreen identities to participate in chat rooms or blogs, where they tout the company's products.

Although all media have some capability to target selected groups of consumers—many newspapers, for example, tailor some content and advertising to neighborhoods or regions—they are crude in comparison with the Web. Google lets advertisers target ads on the basis of search terms used by consumers; among advertisers, American Express is especially adept at matching display ads for its products and services to keyword search results.

On the Web, advertisers can track an individual consumer's return visits to a site, the elements the consumer clicks on, the time spent on each Web page, and even movements from one site to another. The data allow the advertiser to select and customize online ads for that consumer. If a consumer posts a comment, fills out registration data, or makes a purchase, marketers can make well-educated guesses about which advertising the consumer perceives as relevant.

Whether or not such online targeting capabilities will help marketers build closer relationships with consumers, as marketers often claim, is debatable. After all, similar claims were made for the benefits of direct-mail marketing. In both cases, a small percentage of relevant, creative, intrinsically enjoyable ads may be favorably received by consumers and turn out to be effective for marketers. On the other hand, there are problems of privacy and of excess. Consumers may not want advertisers or Google to know about their online behavior. Consumers receiving unwanted messages, even if fewer in number, aren't apt to perceive that they have a better relationship with any of the marketers behind them.

The Prisoner's Dilemma

Unfortunately, marketers—and by extension the media and consumers—are hostage to a prisoner's dilemma: if everyone cooperated to reduce advertising clutter, they would be better off; however, if one advertiser cuts back and the others don't, it will be worse off. Unless consumers are willing to pay for advertising-free media, they will be targeted by marketers. Until then, media companies will inevitably experience pressure to be friendly to the interests of the businesses that advertise with them. Although the large majority of media publishers subscribe to the principle of insulating the editorial side from the publishing side, they don't have a perfect record in practice. Probably they never will.

In sum, a democracy must ultimately view independent media as a public good. A majority of the American public says it wants an independent press.[64] That entails rules on media ownership, as well as public support of news, independent of consumer demand, whether funded on the British BBC model of user fees or the U.S. model of a combination of audience support, philanthropy, and sponsorships. Of great value is journalism backed by nonprofit publishers, representing different sides of the political spectrum, that are freer to present controversial views and stronger critiques of corporations and governments than their commercially or publicly supported counterparts.

Technological innovations in media, rapidly disseminated through the consumer marketplace, enhance citizens' ability to participate in the political marketplace. There remains an important role for advertising-supported media, permitting citizens to consume news cheaply and on the spot. How many fewer consumers would look at the news if they had to subscribe in advance or pay a substantially higher price?

CHAPTER 9

Programs

Civic Goods, Civil Services

F AMED MANAGEMENT EXPERT PETER DRUCKER, along with leading marketing scholars, maintained that the purpose of a company is
to create satisfied customers.[1] This guiding business philosophy parallels
the guiding philosophy of democracy: the purpose of government is to serve
its citizens.

Although democratic societies frequently debate which goods and services government should provide and which belong in the private and nonprofit sectors, every well-functioning society relegates some activities to the
public sector. Governments can use marketing to inform the public, promote government programs, and improve delivery of their health, education, transportation, food, housing, and other services.

Is it possible to build citizens' confidence in government? To a citizenry
inundated with news of wrongdoing and scandals involving lobbyists like
Jack Abramoff, the notion that the public comes first may seem at odds
with reality. But public trust is vital. Business organizations that build trust
by serving their customers' interests have a better chance of survival than
companies that put customers second. Democratic governments do not face
the same kind of market competition or performance yardsticks that private enterprises do, but failure to serve citizens weakens the social bonds
that make democracy viable. Perceived failure is nearly as damaging as actual failure. A democratic government can learn from marketing how better to communicate the positive contributions it makes to citizens' lives.

In addition to the public and private sectors, nonprofit social organizations are significant providers of goods and services. Nongovernmental organizations (NGOs) address challenging problems of poverty, abuses of civil and political rights, health needs, environmental degradation, and economic development. Although they avoid the term *marketing*, a number of leading NGOs are excellent marketers. Amnesty International's letter-writing campaigns on behalf of political prisoners, UNICEF's deployment of Hollywood celebrities as roving ambassadors, and Greenpeace's political action stunts generate significant publicity that attracts donations and volunteers. Global NGO brands command high levels of consumer trust. They represent a valuable and leveragable marketing asset. Gradually, marketing is becoming both more necessary and more respected in the NGO world.

Delivering Government Programs and Services

The choice facing those who manage nonbusiness organizations is not whether to market or not to market, for no organization can avoid marketing. The choice is whether to do it well or poorly.

—Philip Kotler and Sidney J. Levy[2]

A complex mix of institutions serves society's needs. Business provides most goods and services as well as the economic benefits of employment and capital growth. Churches administer to spiritual needs and also provide charitable aid. Universities educate students and develop new knowledge. Governments handle public safety and national defense. These institutions and functions overlap. Churches run schools. Governments provide family services and significant employment opportunities. Private business contractors run jails and help fight wars.[3] The U.S. Postal Service is quasi-public, quasi-private. By virtue of history, values, and beliefs, European social democracies manage government-run national health-care systems, but the United States does not.

Measured by the quality of people's lives and setting aside ideological debates between free-market advocates and social democrats, no one alignment of public versus private services is clearly superior.[4] There are market failures and government failures. From the citizen's perspective, there is

224

ample room for improvement and innovation in services ranging from health care to snow removal, whether the government or the market is the provider.

For the foreseeable future, a blend of private, public, and nonprofit organizations will provide products and services considered to be social goods. Drucker contended that ownership is not the critical question: "The market approach can equally be 'socialist'. Whether ownership is in capitalist hands or not is no longer primary. What matters is managerial independence and accountability. What matters is whether resources are allocated to produce results and on the basis of results."[5]

Rather than start with a preconceived solution to social needs, a thoughtful consultant might ask, "What are the current and future needs of individuals, of communities, of society at large? What opportunities are there to satisfy these needs more effectively and efficiently?" An automobile company that has built its business on internal combustion engines might ask the same questions of how to provide value to customers given the dwindling supplies of fossil fuels.[6] The inventiveness of the solution may compare to the way Sears, Roebuck & Co. figured out in the early twentieth century how to serve rural families, with their distinctive needs for a huge range of products, through a new mail-order distribution channel. The strategic marketing discipline offers structured approaches for addressing these issues without presuming that leaving matters to the free market is necessarily the best or only solution.

Strategic clarity about a business comes from posing fundamental marketing questions: "Who is the customer?" "How are we going to add value to that customer?" These are building blocks for answering the question, "What business are we in?"[7] The same questions should be asked of government programs.

The questions are deceptively simple. The answers often are complex. For a school, among the many customers, constituencies, or stakeholders—each with a unique view of what a school should be or should accomplish—are students and parents, taxpayers in the community, state and federal governments (which mandate programs and contribute school funding), employers, teachers, and schools providing higher levels of education. All customer groups will value instilling numeracy and literacy in students, but perceptions of what constitutes value diverge from there. The point of asking the questions is to make sure that decisions are based on clear knowledge of and valid assumptions about the views of all stakeholder groups.

In government, the exercise almost always reveals constituencies that are at cross purposes. So if it appears obvious that the customers for a food stamp program are the poor, and the value provided is that no family goes hungry, further probing may show that other customers include city agencies, which want to verify eligibility and weed out fraud, and Congress, which wants to minimize payments.[8]

Similarly, when the U.S. Department of Agriculture thirty years ago issued a set of national dietary goals that for the first time recommended increased or decreased consumption of specific foods, strong divergences emerged among food retailers, nutritionists, consumer activists, and various government agencies on how to proceed. Splits also emerged within the food industry between "winning" and "losing" food producers. In a democratic society, for such programs to move forward, policy makers and implementers must negotiate the competing agendas.

When goals conflict, government officials often settle for the lowest common denominator. Trying not to alienate anyone, they end up pleasing no one. New York City promoted an outreach program to encourage poor families to apply for food stamps, but it left in place an inefficient system for verifying eligibility and inadequately staffed offices open only during the day. For the working poor to apply meant risking loss of pay or jobs.[9] Approaching the issue from a customer perspective and considering, as a marketer would, the entire service delivery context, might have revealed the inherent contradictions.

Embedding a customer orientation within government departments can change the focus and improve day-to-day delivery of services. In the early 1990s, the United Kingdom developed a "citizen's charter" program for government agencies, which stated that citizens and users of public services deserve fair treatment, information transparency, more choice, and accountability. Specific agency charters set service standards, performance indicators, and penalties for underperformance. Improvements in some (though not all) agencies were reported at the five-year mark.[10]

Market feedback tells businesses whether or not they are providing value. Eventually, the market weeds out the worst performers: if a company does not supply products consumers want at prices they are willing to pay, then it has failed to provide value and likely will perish. There is no such direct customer feedback loop in the government sector. Government agencies—and also many nonprofits—go on providing the services they are budgeted to deliver. In some cases feedback is almost irrelevant because the customer is captive: building permits and driver's licenses are mandated by law. In still other cases, the desired benefits from a program occur so gradually and over such a long period of time—as for example, in many health initiatives—that feedback arrives too late to have a significant effect.

On the other hand, for purposes of diagnostics and performance improvement, government can borrow customer-based measures that apply equally well in both sectors. Customer satisfaction measures that assess how well customers are served on various dimensions of service quality, for example, are an easily transferable tool. The federal Center for Medicare and Medicaid Services used it to make hospitals more accountable.[11]

Government agencies can improve. For example, satisfaction ratings for the small package shipping industry show that the U.S. Postal Service improved its ratings by nearly 12 percent during the past decade and reduced the gap with quality leader FedEx by 60 percent.[12] For information campaigns, measures of cognitive change—such as the percentage of people reading and comprehending nutrition labels on food following a label redesign or, better yet, the percentage of people following through with healthier food choices—indicate effectiveness. As government services are provided online, tracking people's behavior as they use a government Web site is valuable feedback about site design and content.

Using Social Marketing

Perhaps the most difficult challenges for government agencies arise when they are handed mandates to provide something that the primary target of the effort does not value or values very little. Many public health initiatives, such as advertising campaigns intended to prevent teenagers from using illicit drugs or driving while drinking, must overcome years of entrenched behaviors or strong resistance from targets.

Here, the field of *social marketing* contributes knowledge of consumer behavior, persuasive communications, creation of product benefits, and research design. Social marketers have aided interventions in health, school attendance, poverty alleviation, environmental protection, family planning, and other areas.[13] Consumer behavior studies of how people factor levels of risk in to prescription drug choice and consumption behavior are relevant to FDA decisions on pharmaceutical safety and labeling.[14] Fact-based consumer research can contribute to resolving debates among federal agencies and state agencies whose jurisdictions overlap.[15]

Andreasen argues that social marketing brings a businesslike discipline to programs in that it "(1) holds behavior change as its 'bottom line,' (2) therefore is fanatically customer-driven, and (3) emphasizes creating attractive exchanges that encourage behavior (the benefits are so compelling and the costs so minimal that everyone will comply)."[16]

Public service announcements and advertisements are the visible face of programs guided by social marketing principles, but underlying them is expertise in applying segmentation, targeting, and positioning; understanding usage situations; and identifying obstacles to desired behaviors. For example, marketing experts advised that product safety interventions—which had focused on cognitive changes and therefore mandated warning labels—could be more effective if agencies took into account irrational behavior and the way consumers actually use products in everyday situations.[17]

In the Rakai district of Uganda, researchers learned that programs promoting abstinence and monogamy were less effective than promotion of condom use in preventing transmission of the AIDS virus. Moreover, availability was crucial: "Condoms have to be everywhere alcohol and sex are sold."[18] Similarly, people who state they intend to recycle trash need a supportive infrastructure, such as community-provided bins and simple sorting rules, as well as reinforcement of community recycling norms in order to translate intention into behavior.[19]

Of course, such applications of marketing ideas are irrelevant to free-market proponents, who believe that government should play no role in social interventions and as small a role as possible in production and distribution of goods and services. Problems with government-provided services reinforce these views. (On the other hand, some conservatives complain that improving public services will raise demand and hence increase government spending.)[20]

The Difficulty of Resolving Conflicting Aims

Even when government embraces marketing, multiple constituencies and conflicting goals limit the ability to apply its principles freely. That is a problem for any organization but is particularly acute in government. Businesses decide to serve particular market niches where they think they have a differential advantage over competitors. As part of an integrated marketing strategy, they select the target groups they will serve, the values they will provide through their product and service design, and the ways they will price, distribute, and advertise. In contrast, governments must serve all citizens who fall under program mandates; they cannot easily offer differentiated services lest they be discriminatory or elect whom not to serve.

Public-sector service providers focus on meeting minimum standards. However, some public-sector organizations are moving from a one-size-fits-all to a more tailored approach. Giving citizens a choice of ways to interact with government agencies, including phone, mail, walk-in, and the Internet, is uncontroversial and benefits consumers through greater accessibility, convenience, and ease of finding information.

More controversial are initiatives that offer different versions of a core service. A number of urban school districts have given students and parents more choice by establishing schools specializing in different curricula or different instructional methods. Independently managed but publicly funded charter schools do the same thing. However, the tension between choice and equality is manifest in the growing movement to require all students to be educated to the same performance standards.

Furthermore, public-sector agencies can get bogged down in the simplest types of marketing decisions involving how to serve citizens. For instance, in October 2005 the New York Metropolitan Transportation Authority proposed a temporary reduction in bus and subway fares on weekends between Thanksgiving and New Year's Day in part as a way to reward customers and to reduce traffic congestion. For most businesses this type of promotion would generate little controversy. Previous discounts had increased ridership. Moreover, the authority was running a $928 million surplus, and at worst the fare reduction would cost an estimated $50 million in reduced revenues.

However, the proposal met with criticism from all sides. Some consumer advocates complained that the promotion would benefit tourists more than regular customers. Board members representing outlying counties argued that riders of commuter railroads were not receiving their fair share of the discounts. Some critics thought that the surplus should go only toward unfunded pension liabilities or service improvements.

Liberals and conservatives alike questioned the authority's prudence in reducing revenue at the same time it was urging voters to approve a $2.9 billion state bond transportation measure in November. The Democratic candidate for mayor accused the authority of handing the Republican incumbent mayor an election gift.[21] The time and effort consumed in debating the proposal—which the board wound up approving—would seem farcical were it not for the real woes facing the transportation authority, as evidenced two months later, when contract disputes led striking workers to shut down the entire system for several days.

Governments must often take on the most difficult tasks of providing goods and services, as when people are the raw material for producing a socially desired outcome. Education and health-care providers in a free-market situation would want to attract only the smartest and the healthiest consumers, because outcomes would be best and service would be cheapest. They would charge a premium for hard-to-educate students or those in poorest health, probably the very people least able to pay. The poor would not be able to participate. Because governments do not want destitute elderly people to become a social burden, they intervene in private business to regulate and guarantee company-provided retirement plans and collect social insurance taxes. If all education were private, the state would perhaps require schools to accept a certain proportion of average and slow learners, or charge tuition in proportion to family income.

Ways to Resolve Conflicts

The problems of public education and health care have proven intractable to innumerable well-intentioned reform measures. Thus, realistic expectations for the application of marketing ideas and techniques would be to achieve small-scale changes. Nevertheless, a series of modest incremental improvements could translate into meaningful differences.

One such contribution might be improving schools' outreach to various constituencies. For instance, studies of education reform link greater involvement by parents to improvements in their children's progress and the quality of their schools. Social marketers could research barriers to parental involvement, craft approaches that overcome those barriers, and effectively communicate to parents the benefits of participating.

In the realm of health care, Michael Porter has proposed a number of reforms, including some that would give more power to consumers: distributing standardized information about diseases and treatments so that patients can make informed choices about their care, and providing transparent billing and pricing mechanisms.[22] If designers of the Medicare prescription drug plan that went into effect in January 2006 had been customer oriented, they never would have come up with a plan that baffled experts, let alone elderly consumers. In the United Kingdom, the government now rates hospitals and schools against established criteria and publishes the results.

Most people who choose to work in government start out motivated by their agency's mission.[23] Unfortunately for those government employees who have worked hard to improve operations and better serve the needs of citizens, the public has little awareness of solid achievements. That lack of recognition, along with the traditional difficulties of innovating in bureaucratic organizations and the reversals of direction caused by changing political winds, dampens dedication to continued performance improvement. Low public awareness of achievements easily translates into apathy and less pressure from citizens to insist that government perform well. This leads to an additional role for marketing.

Marketing a Democratic Government to Its Citizens

I meet this American government, or its representative, the State government, directly, and face to face, once a year—no more—in the person of its tax-gatherer; this is the only mode in which a man situated as I am necessarily meets it.

—Henry David Thoreau[24]

U.S. federal, state, and local governments employed more than 21.6 million people in 2004, representing 16 percent of all employment.[25] Another 1 million or so people were employed in active-duty military service.[26] Reflecting its sizable share of the workforce, the government sector provides a wide range of services to the public. Consumer-facing activities include the judicial system, police and fire protection, public schools, public hospitals and public health programs, veterans' affairs, Social Security and welfare, housing programs, public parks and forests, sanitation, transportation infrastructure and services, public utilities, and the postal service, among others. The central banking system, licensing bureaus, and regulatory agencies oversee exchanges between consumers and businesses.

Yet consumers often take for granted the benefits provided by all these activities. The benefits recede into the background of everyday life. Or they become perceived as entitlements. The interaction with government that most stands out—and not in a positive way—is tax collection.

Give and Get

It is a fair bet that when people size up the exchange between themselves and their local, state, or national government, what they "give" dominates what they "get." People have no choice except to pay taxes. And people pay for many things they do not consume or may not want. This is a fundamental difference between business services and most government services. Home owners pay school taxes whether or not they have children. Residents subsidize hospitals whether or not they are sick. Libertarians pay for farm subsidies that they disapprove of in principle.

In democracies, people have only an indirect say about how their taxes are allocated. A leader of the British Conservative party proposed a mechanism to allow conscientious objectors to direct their tax money away from the military and to "peace-building initiatives" instead.[27] But it was mere window-dressing; it would give citizens an illusion of choice but have no effect on actual budget allocations. All in all, as a result of the loose connection between paying taxes and receiving personally relevant and desirable benefits in exchange, citizens are likely to undervalue government's contribution to the quality of life. That does not help build a cohesive society.

It also contrasts with the situation in the private sector. When consumers buy goods and services from businesses, they can connect what they receive with what they give up. They, their family, or their friends are the ones who consume the product. Direct experience informs judgments about value received. That is not to say consumers precisely quantify value. The utility of a life insurance policy or cell phone plan may not be apparent until the future, if at all, and consumers may wonder whether a different choice would have fit their needs better.

Still, cued by prices of competing products versus price paid, they can estimate values reasonably well. If anything, consumers, prodded by marketers, may overvalue commercial products' contribution to their well-being.

The marketplace is filled with persuasive advertisements designed to reinforce perceptions of product value. Ads help consumers link products with fulfillment of personal goals; ads stimulate consumers to form personal goals that can be fulfilled only by the advertiser's product.[28] In the private sector, people sometimes pay for services or product features they do not want, but often a no-frills option like Southwest Airlines emerges. Markets segment into different offerings at different price points. In the public sector, legislation does not provide for different levels of service at different tax rates. Although some user fees are tied to an immediate, specific benefit, these are a small percentage of total collections.

It is even more of a stretch for citizens to connect their taxes with what is good for the community or good for society as a whole, as opposed to what is good for them individually. Absent specific exchanges and transactions with government offices, government seems more abstract or distant compared with businesses, religious organizations, and not-for-profits that also provide social benefits and with which people have greater firsthand experience.

Knowledge about outcomes is limited. If professional economists and policy analysts dispute basic facts regarding employment statistics, income levels, and distribution of the tax burden, how are citizens to judge whether outcomes are good? How does a citizen decide which outcomes are fair, let alone which ways to reach these outcomes are the most efficient? The answer is that people extrapolate from personal experience, word of mouth, media stories, and perceived expert opinion to form general impressions and judgments.

Although consumers have more transactional experience with businesses, even so they may struggle to determine the impact of a business enterprise on the community and on society. Does a big-box store like The Home Depot create more local jobs than it displaces? Are the tax revenues generated by a local manufacturing company sufficient to offset burdensome waste products and environmental pollution? Astute companies act to shape these perceptions. Local merchants sponsor community events. Major companies fortify their reputations through philanthropic activities and corporate marketing designed to build goodwill. Corporate marketing also serves as insurance against the ill effects of an occasional negative experience— such as a bad encounter during a hotel check-in or stories of company negligence aired in the media.

Marketing Self-Audit

The idea of similarly marketing government to citizens may seem frivolous or wrong-headed. But there is a strong argument that government owes this to its citizens. If it were to do a decent job of marketing itself, a government would have to begin with a thorough marketing audit. It would have to explicate the core benefits it delivers to citizens, and the value it provides considering the costs. It would need to identify segments among its constituents and ask how well it is serving the needs of each one. Presumably, a hefty majority of the people in a democracy would need to be well served.

If a government were to market itself, it would have to eliminate outmoded features and design new features and benefits that better fit people's needs. It would have to ask which tasks it can do well and which would be done better by other providers or contractors. It would compare itself to the competition; after all, people choose among towns, cities, and states and, with increasing global mobility, among countries too. It would, as some governments have started to do, use quantitative metrics to track the performance of departments and agencies.

If a government wanted to create enduring loyalty, it would need to examine the quality of people's experiences in their interactions with government employees and systems. It would build trust through, for example, how carefully it handled personal information and how fairly it treated people in the judicial system. It would inform citizens.

In other words, marketing at its best is not only image-polishing; it is also a matter of improving substance. To be sure, thinking like a marketer will not reform governments marked by incompetence, entrenched brutality, or pervasive corruption, but it might help the citizens of governments like Chile's that are on their way to joining the list of globally competitive countries.[29]

In the case of the U.S. federal government, there appears to be no deep reservoir of positive opinion. National opinion surveys conducted by the Pew Research Center for the People and the Press between 1997 and 2005 show that, at times, half of the public, or more, have unfavorable attitudes. Further, satisfaction is volatile and driven by current events: views of the federal government gradually improved from a 38 percent favorable/59 percent unfavorable rating in October 1997 (a time of economic prosperity but a pitched battle between a Republican-controlled Congress and a Democratic White House over the role of government); bounced to a peak of 82 percent favorable/15 percent unfavorable in November 2001 (after the 9/11 terrorist attacks); and then fell down to 44 percent favorable/48 percent unfavorable by October 2005 (following the shockingly inadequate response to Hurricane Katrina).[30]

If political players—including the two major U.S. parties and individual politicians—were marketers, they would collectively worry about building the public's faith in their institution. They would want to convey value in what government delivers to citizens, just as Pfizer or Merck bolsters not only its own reputation but that of the entire pharmaceutical industry. That might also restore faith in public servants. But politicians, for whatever reason, have done very little to market government. They are as likely to campaign against the idea of government as to campaign for it.

Says one former State Department official who is now working in the private sector, "When people who run against government arrive here [Washington], they undermine preparedness and professionalism by underfunding government operations and by making the wrong appointments. If you don't value the job, you don't think talent and experience are necessary. The Katrina aftermath is a perfect example of that."[31]

Many Democrats subscribe to the idea that government programs are, or can be, beneficial in addressing social needs but are too afraid of being labeled as supporters of "big government"—a pejorative in U.S. politics—to talk much about the institution itself. Libertarians and conservatives are in the somewhat odd position of wanting to run for government so that they can dismantle many of its functions. The distinction between Republicans who believe "government needs to be trimmed and made more efficient" and "government is bad" easily escapes the public. The well-bankrolled conservative Club for Growth targets Republicans as well as Democrats deemed insufficiently anti-government.[32] Nor does politicians' behavior help; corruption scandals involving politicians and government officials taint the entire institution. Ultimately, if citizens lose faith in the possibility of good government, they are not likely to demand good government and not likely to get it.

Signs of Improvement

The good-and-bad news for the federal government is that the public respects certain "product lines" more than others: for instance, in fall 2005, the public regarded the military and the Supreme Court much more highly than Congress or the Department of Defense.[33] These and other numbers suggest that citizens reserve satisfaction for the less partisan institutions within government.

Also, efforts over the years to make civil-service branches of government more responsive are beginning to show results. The information technology revolution allowed government agencies to put massive amounts of information online and implement "e-government" for routine transactions. Ideas about service quality improvement and efficiency have diffused from the private sector to the public sector. Civil-service agencies within the federal government started scoring reasonably well in the American Customer Satisfaction Index (ACSI): in 2004, the aggregate score across business industries was in the neighborhood of 74, and the aggregate score for federal agencies was 72.1; if the Internal Revenue Service were excluded, the government did quite well.[34] Claes Fornell, head of the ACSI, notes, "In general, people who actually interact with the government are reasonably satisfied. There are some striking contrasts when you get citizens to assess their actual experience with government as opposed to just general attitudes. And there is evidence that interaction improves trust, which is good for our democracy."[35]

The city of Cambridge, Massachusetts, was prompted to do a better job of marketing itself to residents following an outcry over a sharp jump in real estate taxes for fiscal year 2005. Taxpayers knew precisely what they were contributing but less about what they were getting back. Concerning its value to citizens, the city had a reasonably good story to tell: sound fiscal management marked by a AAA rating from all three major credit rating agencies; tax rates that, despite the increase, were low in comparison with neighboring cities; major infrastructure improvements; and signs of progress in the public schools. It was not that the information was unavailable; by law the city government must operate transparently. Extensive data about the city's operations are on its Web site, and citizens are invited to attend public hearings and council meetings. But residents had to seize the initiative.

Taking a more customer-oriented approach, city management mailed citizens a series of newsletters that acknowledged the impact of the tax hike on residents, documented tax facts and program results, answered typical questions, and invited citizen involvement. Other steps included starting an e-mail subscription service to residents who wanted immediate updates on city operations.

Marketing is sometimes equated with civic boosterism, but that is not what this effort was about. It was about making local government more responsive and thereby increasing its perceived legitimacy to act on behalf of voters.

Marketing to Attract Qualified Workers

If government agencies are to do their job, they need qualified employees. To meet quotas in a difficult recruitment situation during the Iraq war, the U.S. military services needed to step up their marketing efforts. In addition to person-to-person recruiting, the military services relied heavily on mass-media advertising; the Army and Army Reserve expected to spend $1.53 billion on advertising campaigns between 2006 and 2010.[36]

Emulating product marketers, the military increased recruiting efficiency by adopting targeted approaches to connect with likely prospects. The Army National Guard, for instance, identified four segments of recruits, ranked them in likelihood of joining, and developed promotions for each segment, such as free iTunes downloads in exchange for viewing material and filling out personal information on the Guard's Web site.[37]

In 2005 Britain's Secret Intelligence Service, "once so secret that it denied its own existence," unveiled a public Web site intended to recruit potential employees from a wide range of backgrounds. Following the marketing principle of tailoring communications to customer segments, versions of the site appeared in Spanish, French, Arabic, Chinese, and Russian.[38]

Playing by the Rules

For good reason, democracies demarcate the circumstances and the ways in which government can market itself. At the federal level in the United States, laws prevent government departments from spending money to influence Congress or government policies. Intense partisanship goes into fashioning legislation, but execution of policies and programs, once passed, should not promote the White House's particular policy interests. Regarding communications, departments are prohibited from engaging in "covert propaganda."

Occasionally, Congress has authorized government agencies to pay public-relations and marketing experts to promote specific programs; most of these communications present straightforward information, such as eligibility criteria for assistance programs or public health warnings, although emotional appeals may aid in efforts like military recruitment or campaigns to promote seat-belt use. However, the Government Accountability Office concluded that the Bush administration violated the propaganda rule when it produced and distributed television "news" segments about the effects of drug use by teenagers and other segments that touted the benefits of the new Medicare drug law without identifying the source of the spots.[39]

Rules on unauthorized spending and propaganda were violated when government departments paid syndicated columnists to promote marriage counseling programs and educational policies favored by the administration, again without disclosing the government connection.[40] Federal payments to public-relations firms grew from $37 million in 2001 to $88 million in 2004.[41] These payments are likely to undergo tougher scrutiny. Such incidents also demonstrate that marketing by government is a special case, with special ethical rules.

Marketing by Nongovernmental Organizations

The United Nations once dealt only with Governments. By now we know that peace and prosperity cannot be achieved without partnerships involving Governments, international organizations, the business community and civil society. In today's world we depend on each other.

—Kofi Annan[42]

Although marketing fulfills many of societies' needs for goods and services—for consumers who can afford them—and governments supply additional public goods and services deemed crucial for social welfare, that still leaves significant gaps. Traditionally, charity from well-off individuals and family members, religious organizations, and civic organizations filled some of these gaps.

Currently a large class of nonprofit organizations (commonly labeled nongovernmental organizations, or NGOs) provide vital humanitarian and social services. Many operate nationally and also internationally. One of the best known and oldest is the International Red Cross relief organization.

In addition to disaster relief, *operational* NGOs address problems such as inadequate nutrition, shelter, sanitation, access to potable water, disease prevention and treatment, education, and job training. *Advocacy* breeds of NGO, such as Amnesty International, focus on pressing governments and corporations to address social, economic, and political problems. Others combine humanitarian service and advocacy roles.

By and large, these organizations don't think of themselves as marketers; to many people in the nonprofit sector, *marketing* is a word to be avoided. But under the labels of "outreach" or "institutional development" or "client education," they are, in effect, marketing to bring about exchanges with key stakeholder groups, including funding sources, program recipients, and government authorities.

Ironically, many NGOs enjoy an enviable brand position. Edelman Public Relations, which tracks consumer trust in global brands, has found that in Europe the four most trusted brands are global NGOs: Amnesty International and the World Wildlife Fund lead the list, outscoring Microsoft and Coca-Cola. In the United States, the NGO brands are further down the list but have gained ground in the past several years.[43]

These NGOs achieved their brand stature by earning consumers' respect and admiration for effort and performance. Consumers trust their motives and dedication to a worthy cause, in contrast to growing distrust of the motives of private-sector businesses in the wake of egregious corporate scandals and an era of sky-high executive compensation or the increasing disenchantment with government aid that ends up in the pockets of corrupt third world officials. The successful NGOs also benefit from concentrating on their chosen niche; they stay focused, and they do not diminish the meaning of the brand by overextending it. The best-known NGO brands communicate clearly and consistently to consumers and other stakeholders what their organizations are about, and descriptive names such as World Wildlife Fund help. It also helps that their names appear before the public in contexts, such as natural disasters and wars, that receive extensive news coverage and that the nature of their missions evokes a strong emotional response.

According to the World Bank, NGOs have dramatically expanded in number, scope, and capacity over the past decade: for example, the number of international NGOs increased from about six thousand in 1990 to twenty-six thousand in 1999. NGOs play a significant role on their own and as channels for developmental efforts by intergovernmental organizations such as the United Nations, the World Bank, and the Organisation for Economic Co-operation and Development.[44]

The Importance of Branding for NGOs

But this success means that NGOs increasingly compete against one another for the same government, foundation, and private funding. To maintain their momentum, it may be time for NGOs to do more active marketing. They are also competing for a supporter base of committed volunteers and staffers. That, too, requires marketing skills. Advocacy NGOs, in particular, need to persuade corporate and government officials, as well as the general public, of the merits of their causes.

Internally, growing NGOs are apt to experience *mission creep*. Different units or divisions may want to pursue new or variant objectives. One of the challenges for nonprofit staff is to juggle various important stakeholders. In particular, the priority given to donors may compete with the priority given to the recipients. And what makes donors happy may diverge from the organization's traditional way of doing things.

Increasingly, corporations are interested in partnering with NGOs. With Habitat for Humanity, for example, corporate partnerships originally took the form of cash donations or in-kind gifts of building materials. Corporations liked partnering with Habitat because of the concrete results—a house—and the concept that recipients participate in the building process. For Habitat, and others, success brought more-complicated partnering opportunities: some companies became interested in using Habitat's volunteer opportunities as a way to train managers; corporate partners looked to link their brand with the Habitat brand. Consequently, Habitat needed to sort out the potential benefits and risks of various types of partnerships and of specific potential partner corporations. It also had to recognize the potential risks to corporate partners if a sponsored project didn't turn out as planned.[45]

In all these situations, a nonprofit's mission statement (as well as the vision of founders if they're still around) provides guidance. So does marketing. Segmenting and targeting a market and positioning offerings based on market research bring discipline and long-term thinking to an organization. Management must think hard about what the organization excels at, whom it can best serve, and how it can convince people.

For instance, to develop a positioning statement for a brand, marketers must articulate three components: the target audience; a superiority claim (what the brand can do better than others); and a reason the target audience should believe the superiority claim. An example from the corporate sector is: "For businesspeople who rent cars, Avis is the company that will give you the best service because the employees own the company." Developing a strong positioning statement is not easy but is invaluable. For NGOs, the process is bound to uncover conflicting external and internal stakeholder views, but achieving consensus on a single positioning statement can deepen mutual understanding and reenergize an organization. Mainly, it curbs the temptation to be all things to all people.

In particular, a positioning exercise may underscore the tension between being a relief organization and being an advocacy organization. The move toward advocacy is driven by two main forces: a desire to see that all people enjoy the human rights experienced in democratic societies and the desire, along with the belief that it is possible, to address the root causes of the world's problems. The belief that people have the right not to be hungry, for example, leads to advocating for political change, access to markets, and the right to decent wages. As a result, even strictly humanitarian organizations are now calling for changes in the underlying structures of the societies in which they operate.

Advocacy complicates matters for nonprofit organizations because achieving structural changes usually means working with governments, but an NGO's credibility depends on remaining financially independent of governments. Also, being an effective advocate requires different skills from hands-on relief work.

Protecting an NGO Brand

It is important for any organization, for-profit or not-for-profit, to know the value of its brand so that it can allocate adequate resources to nurturing, building, and protecting it. For many nonprofit organizations and consumer goods companies, their brand, along with their people, is the most important asset they have. In some cases, such as Médecins Sans Frontières (Doctors without Borders), the organization is so decentralized that the brand is a main source of organizational cohesion.

Often, potential donors or collaborators cannot directly evaluate the quality of the services and programs delivered by a nonprofit. Instead, they rely on its brand reputation and their belief that the organization is doing good work and will continue to do so. The keys to managing that asset are to track its value and understand which activities increase or decrease it. Furthermore, as traditional sources of funding erode, nonprofits are turning to private-sector businesses for funding and partnership opportunities. If nonprofits are not aware of the value of their brand, they run the risk of not extracting the full financial value from these partnerships and cobranding opportunities.[46]

For an NGO, program recipients are the ultimate constituency—the organization's reason for being. As with government social programs, good marketing skills allow NGOs to serve their constituencies more effectively. For example, Médecins Sans Frontières is involved in AIDS treatment and prevention. In many countries, this requires providing information to the public to dispel local myths, pride, and fears and persuade people to use preventive measures that may be at odds with deep-seated practices. That calls for consumer research skills, such as identifying impediments to changing behavior, as well as skills in designing communications. Branding is important with recipient groups, too: the odds that people will believe in and avail themselves of services should increase when a client trusts an NGO's local staff because the client is familiar with and trusts the NGO brand.

The importance of trust for NGOs cuts two ways. On the downside, it takes only one or two mistakes to cast doubt on a nonprofit organization but many years and much hard work to reestablish credibility and rebuild consumer trust. The corrosive impact of the American Red Cross's diversion of funds designated for 9/11 victims to other missions decreased donations to allied European Red Cross organizations, even though they were not implicated.

Similarly, it is good for NGOs to be seen working in the field, actively and effectively helping in a humanitarian crisis. However, crises may hamper coordination between NGOs, resulting in duplication and inefficiencies, which, if highlighted by the media, may create a backlash. In a crisis aid also may be misdirected or miss its target. During the post-genocide period in Rwanda, many NGOs found themselves providing humanitarian relief to individuals who had perpetrated the genocide and were intending to renew the violence. Following this revelation, some NGOs chose to withdraw.

Despite inevitable mishaps, NGOs as a group deserve their deep reservoir of public esteem. In addition to their commitment to such lofty goals as eliminating poverty, enforcing human rights, and conserving natural resources, many have developed exceptional operational capacities for serving hard-to-reach populations. They are usually responsive to local needs, ecumenical in whom they serve, adaptive to local conditions (including poor or nonexistent infrastructure), and inclined to empower local communities. They have proven to be entrepreneurial in adapting to changing conditions, such as vacuums left by the withdrawal of government social welfare programs, or in taking on new issues, such as globalization. They have shown resourcefulness in shaping public opinion to their views. In short, many possess marketing capabilities that some companies might do well to emulate.

Yet there are limits to what NGOs can accomplish on their own. That reality, and not only the need for funding, prompts some NGOs to enter into strategic alliances with business (although this step would not be appropriate for those positioned as anti-corporate or anti-capitalist). James Austin, who has documented a number of such alliances, sees corporations using alliances with NGOs to benefit themselves—say, to improve company reputation or aid in marketing specific products. Nevertheless, if the nature of the relationship progresses along a continuum from philanthropy to resource exchange to collaboration, the social value created surpasses what either partner could do alone.[47]

Some observers believe that a convergence, or at least a partnership, between the NGOs and corporations offers the best hope for democratizing social and economic opportunities worldwide.[48] The quotation earlier from UN Secretary General Kofi Annan encapsulates a growing view that the greatest progress will happen when the public, private, and social sectors work together to improve public welfare. In this endeavor, a role for marketing may not be the first thing that comes to mind. But marketing skills and capacities are clearly transferable to the public and social sectors and are demonstrably valuable in achieving social welfare goals.

CHAPTER 10

Nations

No Quick Fix

NATION-STATES COMPETE with one another in the global economy for foreign investors, highly skilled workers, visitors, and consumers of their exports. In the political realm, they compete for influence and favorable global attention. Success on both fronts requires countries to know their strengths and the benefits they offer, to recognize how the outside world views them, and to promote their advantages to the entities and people they wish to attract. In other words, nation-states need to market themselves in much the same way as do the best companies.

Applying marketing to countries might seem a superficial way to tackle development challenges. Skeptics are correct in arguing that marketing in the form of branding, advertising, and public relations can go only so far. Advertising and word of mouth may have drawn European workers to the United States and Australia in previous centuries, but now economic development is more complicated than attracting immigrants. If countries want to stand out from the crowd, they must gather and structure information about markets and the needs of various "buyers," whether other nations, organizations, or individuals. They require a complete marketing strategy.

Furthermore, nation-states competing in the economic realm frequently want to convince potential buyers that the country supports human rights and anti-corruption measures. To be credible such promises must be backed up with genuine reforms. Thus, to the extent that a nation markets itself as a trustworthy partner, marketing spurs democratization.

Democratic nations believe that a world in which most governments are democratic is in their best interests. In what is called *public diplomacy*, the U.S. government has tried to market democracy to the Middle East—and, as a corollary, to market its foreign policies to its own citizens. This effort has met with failure or questionable success abroad, demonstrating the truism that it is nearly impossible to market a product that is flawed in the eyes of the beholder, especially when strategy, execution, and source credibility are faulty.

Political economists have long investigated the question of whether democracy leads to economic development or vice versa. Although a causal relationship cannot be proved, the two are closely associated. In addition, sustainable development appears to benefit from an active civil society marked by high levels of citizen participation and engagement. In this respect, participation in marketing systems fosters traits that are valuable for countries' economic and political development.

The Marketing of Nation-States

Great nations write their autobiographies in three manuscripts—
the book of their deeds, the book of their words, and the book of their arts.

—John Ruskin[1]

Thanks to decolonization and breakups, the number of nation-states is growing. As of 2006, the United Nations had 192 members, compared with 51 in 1946. Nearly all are competing for mobile capital—about $1 trillion moves every day—and jobs. Nations compete to sell their exports and to attract tourists, workers, students, or retirees. They compete for power, prestige, and the ability to influence world events.

Like it or not, nations are ranked on all sorts of measures, including basic statistics such as GDP, population trends, and balance of trade. They are also ranked on metrics such as freedom, transparency, world competitiveness, environmental sustainability, innovativeness, or simply "best country."[2] Depending on how they measure up, nations are invited to join important international organizations, such as the United Nations, Organisation for Economic Co-operation and Development (OECD), and European Union.

To increase their international standing and economic competitiveness, many nation-states engage in rudimentary marketing, although they may not call it that. Government ministries of trade, tourism bureaus, and foreign ministries work at promoting business and projecting a favorable national image. However, these efforts often fall short of full-fledged marketing in that they are not coordinated and integrated but rather are done piecemeal. Often they are not adequately funded and not considered a high priority. Quite likely, these agencies have not completed the necessary groundwork to develop a compelling image.

Nations also market themselves internally to their own people. They try to instill a common understanding of national purpose and signal the nation's aspirations. At its worst, this type of marketing degenerates into flag-waving and jingoistic slogans unleashed for cynical political purposes. At its best, it bridges sectarian and religious divides as well as gaps between town and country, rich and poor.

Managing a nation's overall image is similar in principle to managing a corporate brand. Just as a corporate brand is a summary perception of what people believe and feel about an organization and its products and services, a national image is a summary perception about a nation, its citizens, its culture, and its business enterprises. A strong national image differentiates the country from its peers based on positive substance rather than prejudice or ignorance.

Positive Traits

To stand out, a country must stand for something. Consider how the following countries have differentiated themselves from their neighbors: Singapore, best entry point to Asia for Western multinationals; Dubai, Western gateway to the Middle East; Switzerland, neutrality and confidential financial services; Costa Rica, pacifistic democracy; Finland, home of Nokia phones; Germany, outstanding engineering and cars. Each of these positions rests on a solid foundation. Singapore's, for instance, is backed up by the reality that its laws and institutions and educated English-speaking workforce make it safe and easy to do business there.

When marketing to foreign investors, a developing country with a clear positioning can avoid competing on price in a "race to the bottom" dynamic. Heavy reliance on extra tax credits and discounts to attract new factories and jobs usually ends up being counterproductive.[3] Moreover, these incentives are not the most important factor in corporations' location decisions. Although corporations are interested in low costs of doing business, what they also look for in developing countries is high-quality physical infrastructure; a reliable labor force; macroeconomic and political stability; even-handed enforcement of laws, taxes, and regulation; and competitive markets.[4]

Until a nation can identify a strong positive element, there is no point in marketing itself. Fortunately, there are many potential sources of competitive advantage. Complementing those mentioned are economic factors such as natural resources, technology capabilities, and membership in regional trade alliances, along with political factors such as human rights and competent administration. A number of small Northern European countries outscore the United States and Japan on measures of innovation and also do very well on environmental sustainability and poverty measures.[5]

"Soft" characteristics of a nation can contribute powerfully to its appeal. Consider a country's aesthetic and cultural attractions, such as Bali's natural environment, arts, architecture, dress, language, religion, and customs. Or a country's accomplishments, such as Italy's Renaissance and Roman history, sports, and brands. Or a country's lifestyle and panache, such as France's cuisine, fashions, and visual icons like the Eiffel Tower. All these soft factors directly and indirectly influence buying decisions. In addition to influencing individual consumers, they help market the country to investors, exporters, or other business interests. And compared with "hard" characteristics, they are not easily duplicated and are more likely to foster loyalty.

The power of emotional connections means that symbols, ceremonies, or pride in artistic and sports achievements—if not carried to an ultranationalist extreme—can all be effective in building the national image. Greece's hosting of the Olympics in 2004 drew more of the world's attention to it as an attractive place to do business than its joining the European Union.

Moreover, first impressions and firsthand experience are key. A business or leisure traveler passing through an international airport forms a nearly indelible impression of the nation. Accordingly, one goal of internal marketing to citizens is to motivate them to deliver on the promises implicit in a nation's marketing to foreigners. It's the equivalent of motivating employees in consumer marketing to create an excellent customer experience resulting in satisfaction and repeat business.

The Basics of Place Branding

Marketing a nation is not identical to marketing a product or service. Place-branding expert Simon Anholt says, "In an ideal world, countries would not and should not be branded like products," but "the tendency to sum up countries and their governments in a simple and convenient formula is a habit of the marketplace, faithfully reflected in the media," so nation branding is necessary in self-defense.[6]

Furthermore, the marketing challenges facing nation-states and corporations differ in important respects. First is the problem of setting strategy. In corporations, the chief executive is ultimately responsible for developing and retaining the customer relationships on which the cash flow of the corporation depends. The CEO sets a marketing strategy that targets the likeliest customer prospects and ignores the rest. In contrast, a nation's political leader cannot so easily pursue a clearcut strategy. A democratically elected leader negotiates policies with legislatures and key constituencies and must make compromises among competing interests in order to be reelected.

Then there are problems of implementing strategy. It is easier for the corporate CEO to enlist the support of employees than for national leaders who are not dictators to enlist the support of the public, civil servants, and other stakeholder groups. The CEO pays employees to follow the strategy; if they cannot in conscience do so, they are invited to leave. But the national political leader in a democracy has only the power of persuasion to motivate a broad coalition of citizenry and stakeholder groups to follow the marketing program. If most citizens do not buy in to or are cynical about the marketing proposition, it simply will not work.

Also, power is typically more diffuse in a nation than a corporation. Local governors and mayors, along with their bureaucracies, do not necessarily pull in the same direction as the national leadership. Officials naturally want to promote their own regions and cities more than the nation as a whole, especially when the nation, as in the case of the United Kingdom, is identified overseas with a single world-class city like London. In this case, it is difficult for the central government to rally resources behind a single, integrated national campaign. Even within smaller governments, or governmental units, coordination across agencies is difficult. An analysis of Wales's marketing communications concluded that it may be impossible to achieve true integration in promoting Wales as a brand.[7]

Particularly in the nations that could most profit from a better-known positive image, financial resources may be lacking to follow through on raised expectations. India, with its outstanding cultural attractions, is trying to increase tourism. But under India's federal system, the funds to maintain historical monuments and improve tourist amenities come from the twenty-eight state governments, most of which are mired in debt.[8] Some of India's marketing promises can be fulfilled only if the private sector agrees to invest in tourist hotels and restaurants.

Corporations can eliminate unpopular brands or introduce new ones. Although some nations change name or redraw boundaries, countries cannot easily escape their history. Larger or historically important countries already have an image. It is often harder to unfreeze an existing, perhaps outdated, image and build a new one than to start with a clean slate. Particularly challenging is image building for small countries that have become, rightly or wrongly, tarnished with a negative image. Colombia's association with drug production, for example, makes image-building almost impossible until the drug trade vanishes.

Successful and Unsuccessful Nation Marketing

Two examples illustrate successes and disappointments in meeting these marketing challenges for nation-states. During the Franco period, Spain was economically, politically, and culturally isolated from Western Europe. In the 1970s, the country was ready for change. It embarked on political and economic reform, but its image was largely associated with cheap package tours and backwardness. So business and political leaders jointly worked to restore national pride and economic performance.

By the 1980s, Spain was reborn as a vibrant emerging democracy and was accepted into the European Union the same year the EU implemented the single-market program to reduce nontariff barriers and boost intra-European trade. Marketing programs adopted Joan Miro's sun image as a symbol of Spain's rebirth. The 1992 Barcelona Olympics successfully showcased the new Spain to the world. Spain backed up its new image with public-sector reforms and improved infrastructure, and Spanish GDP accelerated throughout the 1990s.[9]

Less successful was the Blair government's "Cool Britannia" marketing program (as it was dubbed by the press) launched in the United Kingdom in the late 1990s. Britain was widely known for traditional things (the monarchy, the museums, the stately homes and gardens), which brought in substantial tourism dollars each year. But policy makers wanted the world to erase this stereotype and learn about British creativity, adventurousness, and entrepreneurship in science, technology, and business—a positioning presumably intended to jibe with the emergence of a new knowledge economy, where the United Kingdom had competitive advantages.

The resulting campaign was widely derided in the media, particularly outside London. Most Britons did not want to be "cool," and no amount of persuasion could budge them. Cynical media commentators also poked fun at the idea of rebranding a country like a packaged consumer product.[10] Any expectations that the campaign would produce quick results were dispelled by a survey published by the British Council two years into the effort.[11] Not surprisingly, the research showed that foreigners continued to see Britain as very traditional (but favorably so). The campaign was dropped after about three years.[12]

Elements of Success

Effective nation-state marketing depends on stakeholders having a common cause. In this respect, smaller nations may have an advantage. They often have greater cultural, ethnic, religious, and linguistic homogeneity and consequently greater convergence of citizens' views. The political and business elites are used to dealing with each other and can more easily coalesce around a common policy. In newly independent states, such as a Slovenia or a Croatia, a sense of national purpose can underpin a global marketing effort, particularly when a country is, in economic development terms, ahead of others in the same region and therefore eager to develop a distinct identity.

Marketing is not a quick fix for nations' problems. Leaders need to have realistic expectations. Although marketing can act as an accelerator, the product must speak for itself. Persuading audiences that a country offers significant benefits will not succeed in the long run if the nation cannot deliver the promised advantages. Updating or changing a country's image usually takes years. As in Spain's case, sustained commitment is a key factor.

Here, too, a political leader of a smaller country—more so, a city-state like Singapore or Dubai—who understands the potential power of global marketing can make significant strides, particularly if the leader is not subject to periodic elections and can pursue a ten- or twenty-year vision. In

Singapore, Lee Kuan Yew, who held the top job for thirty-one years, passed the leadership to his son, who shares the same vision.[13] This is not to endorse benign authoritarianism; even in countries that are democratic in more than name, it is possible to build long-term commitment. Securing membership in clubs such as the World Trade Organization, European Union, or NATO ratifies a country's newfound status and promotes adherence to club norms.

Successful initiatives to promote exports, attract foreign investment, and secure image-enhancing events such as international sports competitions often involve public–private partnerships. ProChile, the Chilean Trade Commission agency within the Chilean Ministry of Foreign Affairs, has been jointly funded for thirty years by the public and private sectors. In rebuilding the reputation of Chile in the post-Pinochet era, ProChile has sought to leverage the quality reputation developed by its own exporters—among them Chilean vintners and fruit-growers—in much the same way that the national images of France and Germany are buttressed by the worldwide reputations of their manufacturers for superb fashion and engineering excellence, respectively. (In contrast, during the seventeen years of the Pinochet regime, many of Chile's exporters did not want to identify their products with Chile, for fear of putting off consumers in Europe and North America.)[14] And, as with word of mouth in the consumer marketplace, endorsements from foreign companies already invested in Chile help immeasurably in marketing to new foreign direct investors.

Measuring Success

Governments, especially democratic governments, owe their constituents measures of progress. Not all dollars spent on marketing have equal returns. During the 1990s, the United Kingdom, for example, found that promoting foreign direct investment had much greater economic impact than promoting British exports.[15] Like corporate marketers, nations should track the economic results of marketing investments and adjust the allocations against different target groups accordingly.

If Greece runs a marketing campaign aimed at increasing tourism, then tracking the number of tourist visits and tourism dollars is a straightforward measure. If Ireland is marketing itself as a desirable location for high-tech companies, it can count the number of jobs created, the number of companies locating facilities there, and the amount of foreign direct investment.

If a campaign is designed for general image-building, researchers can benchmark awareness, knowledge, and perceptions of what a nation stands for among key stakeholder groups as well as measure the gaps between perception and reality and progress over time against comparable nations. If a campaign is targeting prospective foreign tourists or prospective foreign direct investors, then achieving top-of-mind awareness and getting on the short list of alternatives are relevant measures.

Clearly, though, tracking gains from intangibles, such as favorable global awareness or high standing on one of the international scorecards, will be imprecise. Chile's promotional material to support reaching a Chile–U.S. free-trade agreement cited its good marks on rankings of economic freedom, global competitiveness, market access, transparent government, corruption, e-business readiness, and human development. The material also promoted the country's democratic institutions and human rights protection, economic and social progress, and history of participation in bilateral and multilateral trade agreements.[16] But without seeing into the minds of U.S. negotiators, Chile cannot precisely pinpoint which factors led to the trade agreement or the extent to which marketing played a decisive role.

Image Matters

Clearly, countries are sensitive to the disadvantages they may encounter if they are perceived as undemocratic or hostile to human rights or exploitive of labor or the environment. With the Internet, twenty-four-hour news, and mass international travel, it is impossible for a government totally to suppress or control information about such issues. Consumers in industrialized countries may not, at the moment, factor such unfavorable national images in to the bulk of their buying decisions, but national images rub off onto corporate brands, a segment of tourists favors eco-friendly destinations, and corporations prefer to deal with countries that prevent child labor. In the presence of such trends, the desired image may stimulate genuine reform.

The face a nation presents to the world is increasingly important in an era of globalization and multinational partnerships. But the face it presents to its citizens is equally important. In its bid to join the European Union, Turkey, for example, must balance a secular identity, a traditionalist Islamic heritage, and an EU requirement for more democracy—including human rights, especially women's rights—and a market-based economy.[17] To the extent that Turkey can construct and market a "democratic, secular, free-market, Islamic" identity to these two audiences, there is hope for resolving some of the global conflicts between traditionalism and modernism.

A nation can also "demarket" itself. The Dutch government recently positioned the Netherlands to potential immigrants as a country that is free, permissive, and protective of women's rights. A two-hour DVD prepared to help immigrants pass an exam for entrance into the country depicts topless beaches and two men kissing in a meadow. Prepared in the context of rising tensions between native Dutch and a growing Muslim immigrant population, the controversial film also demarkets the country by depicting unfriendly people, traffic jams, and unemployment.[18]

Marketing may be relevant to small nations trying to build awareness and break through the clutter on the world stage, but is it relevant to a dominant commercial and military power like the United States? In the world of commerce, no brand, however long established and well known, can afford to take its image for granted. A brand that is widely recognized but not liked is poised for a downward slide, because esteem drives consumer preference.[19]

When U.S. government policy is unpopular, there is an effect on the national image. Normally, repercussions are not seen immediately, because most of the world's citizens do not let opposition to current U.S. government policy diminish their respect for individual Americans or U.S. brands. The cumulative goodwill built up by the United States over generations—and the values it historically stands for—helps inoculate against an immediate backlash. In addition, U.S. multinational corporations, from McDonald's to IBM, have worked over the past decade to build goodwill through localizing their brands by adapting product offerings to national cultural preferences, promoting local managers to senior positions in overseas subsidiaries, and contributing to local community development in host countries.[20]

Nevertheless, Pew Research Center surveys measure a decline in positive attitudes toward the United States.[21] Although some people argue that foreign policy should not be concerned with matters of image, others contend that a sustained decline will eventually spill over to affect every U.S. citizen traveling and every brand selling itself overseas. Attitudes toward the United States certainly affect its public diplomacy campaign to market democracy abroad.

The Marketing of Democracy

Our government rests in public opinion. Whoever can change public opinion,
can change the government, practically just so much.

—Abraham Lincoln[22]

In his last letter, written in the fortnight before he died and fifty years after the American colonies declared their independence, Thomas Jefferson expressed the hope that rational thinking and "general spread of the light of science" would lead people in all parts of the world to adopt democracy, that "all eyes are opened, or opening, to the rights of man."[23] Jefferson did not estimate how long it might take for democracy to become universal. Probably he would be surprised and disappointed that one-third or more of the world's nations are undemocratic some two hundred years later (although there are many more democratic nations than in 1950).[24] He might or might not have been surprised that the U.S. government has been trying to accelerate the pace of democratization by promoting the ideal of democracy (the Declaration of Independence itself is a brilliant piece of persuasive communication).

Promoting democracy internationally was an early key objective of the George W. Bush administration. Along with military invasions of foreign countries in the name of democracy, the administration engaged in public diplomacy designed both to spread democracy and to improve the image of the United States overseas. Among citizens of Western democracies, the desirability of more countries becoming democratic is not seriously in question. But how active a country should be in spreading democracy abroad is contentious. On one side, the United States has intervened on many occasions, and idealists like Natan Sharansky argue for activism on moral and pragmatic grounds.[25] On the other side, Western European nations have been reluctant to intervene, and realists like Amy Chua and Fareed Zakaria argue that rapid switches to democratic forms of government frequently go awry, because practicing the art of democracy is a learned skill.[26]

Four years after the 9/11 attacks that provided justification for the Bush administration's position, a majority of the U.S. public doubted the premises underlying international interventions. According to a U.S. poll conducted by the University of Maryland and the University of Chicago, a little over one-fourth of respondents, 28 percent, agreed with the statement, "The world is safer when there are more democracies," whereas many more, 68 percent, agreed with the statement, "Democracy may make life better within a country but does not make the world safer." Only four in ten agreed that "countries that become more democratic are more likely to agree with the United States."[27]

Shortcomings of U.S. Marketing of Democracy

Aside from great uncertainty about the nation's ability to attain peaceful democracies that support U.S. interests, the administration's marketing of democracy is open to criticism on functional grounds. Viewed from a marketing perspective, the effort has serious flaws. Among these are problems with the credibility of the marketer; a lack of understanding or a misunderstanding of the customer market; lack of access to local media; a product that appears flawed to the target customers; inconsistency between the message and its delivery; and insufficient resources to execute well.

All these problems are seen in the campaign to market democracy to the Middle East. Consider credibility. Following the 9/11 attacks (and before the invasion of Iraq on March 20, 2003), the U.S. State Department tried to boost the image of the United States among Muslims. The task was entrusted to Under Secretary for Public Diplomacy and Public Affairs Charlotte Beers, a former Madison Avenue advertising executive.

The centerpiece was a series of five TV advertisements intended for airing in countries from Egypt to Indonesia. Each ad depicted an American Muslim going about his or her daily business and enjoying the tolerance and freedom of the American way of life. The point of the ads was to emphasize U.S. respect for Muslims and values held in common: freedom and democracy.[28] However, several Arab countries refused to air the commercials, which they considered condescending, and the ads were pulled after less than two months.[29]

Among several weaknesses, the campaign failed to address the concerns of the target audience. For one thing, a lack of Arabists in the State Department plus post–cold war cutbacks in public diplomacy meant that few staffers spoke Arabic or ever communicated directly with Arabs and Muslims.[30] Perhaps for that reason, the ad campaign was myopic: the experience of Muslims living in the United States was not highly relevant to Arabs or Muslims living in their home countries. The examples were especially irrelevant to the Arab street. And people in the target audience said the problem with the U.S image was not values; rather, it was current U.S. policies and actions.[31] Arabs and Muslims perceived a United States that backed repressive regimes and their supporters.[32] They saw a United States prepared to invade Iraq unilaterally.

Not surprisingly, the State Department's public-relations efforts failed to boost the U.S. image. In opinion polls taken in the month before the Iraq invasion, very few people in Arab countries had a favorable view of the United States.[33] Moreover, other opinion polls from the same period show that, in the preceding six months, attitudes toward the United States had declined steeply even among its allies; in the United Kingdom, one of its strongest supporters, only 48 percent of the people surveyed held a favorable view.[34]

The invasion of Iraq did nothing to improve the picture. A year later, in March 2004, people in Muslim countries exhibited "pervasive" anger toward the United States, and Europeans remained critical.[35] Later, news stories and media images depicting abuse of U.S.-held prisoners at Abu Ghraib and Guantanamo reinforced negative perceptions.

When it began to market democracy, the United States started with a modest store of respect. Being disconnected from the views and concerns of the target audience eroded credibility and trust. For example, few Americans appreciated the depth of the antipathy of the Arab world toward policies it regards as consistently pro-Israel.[36]

Closer to home, the United States cast Latin American nations and politicians who disagreed with the "Washington consensus"—the policy that couples promotion of free markets with promotion of democracy—as being insufficiently democratic.[37] If marketing messages are not based on a more nuanced recognition—which is not the same as acceptance—of the target audience's perspectives, then the reaction likely will be dismissal or derision. Some commentators believe that his opposition to the United States increased the appeal of Venezuela's Hugo Chavez.[38]

It was a step in the right direction when Karen Hughes, who assumed the State Department public diplomacy post in August 2005, emphasized the importance of understanding the audience. In her words, "I am mindful that before we seek to be understood, we must first work to understand ... I am eager to listen. I want to learn more about you and your lives, what you believe, what you fear, what you dream, what you value most."[39] Hughes followed up these words by traveling on a listening trip to the Middle East, accompanied by an Arabic-speaking deputy.[40] But Hughes's "efforts to speak with Muslim women as fellow 'moms' and religious believers received poor reviews."[41]

What About the Product?

A great product virtually markets itself, but good marketing cannot compensate for a bad product. On the continuum from great to poor, democracy generally appears to be a good "product" with wide popular acceptance. According to a survey of sixty-five countries conducted by the Gallup organization for the World Economic Forum (WEF)—the sample statistically represented the views of more than 1.3 billion people—"eight out of ten global citizens (79%) believe that in spite of its limitations, democracy is the best system of government . . . More than six (65%) out of ten surveyed say they are satisfied with democracy."[42]

At the same time there appears to be an unmet need for democracy, or a better version of democracy: "More than six out of ten (65%) do not feel that their country is ruled by the will of the people"; almost half (48 percent) of citizens do not believe "elections are free and fair in their countries."[43]

To put it in marketing terms, democracy appears to be a desirable product with the potential to gain market share. However, a segmentation analysis of the same data points to lurking problems in a number of countries that are currently democratic.[44] What Gallup/WEF calls the "malcontent" segment—people who believe that their country is not governed by the will of the people and who believe that elections are not free and fair—constitutes 38 percent of citizens in North America, 61 percent in Eastern and Central Europe, and 55 percent in Latin America.

In contrast, the "pillars of democracy" segment—people who believe that their country is governed by the will of the people and who believe elections are free and fair—ranges from highs of only 32 percent of citizens in North America and 29 percent in Western Europe, down to lows of 20 percent in Eastern and Central Europe and 19 percent in Latin America. Worldwide, the malcontent segment grew from 38 percent of the population in 1999 to 45 percent in 2005.[45] That raises the question of whether the best product version is being marketed. It also raises the question of how democracies compare with competing forms of government.

When members of the U.S. administration talk about promoting democracy, they usually cast democracy in the abstract or as an ideal. Essentially, they are referring to what marketers call the *core product* or *core benefit* offered to consumers. In actuality, most products are augmented products, with multiple attributes that offer additional psychological or functional benefits (or possibly disadvantages). For Pepsi and Coca-Cola, the cola beverage is the core product; the branded cola beverage, entertainingly advertised, attractively packaged, and widely distributed, is the augmented product. For Ford and GM, a basic sedan is the core product; the brand, the cup holders, the heated seats, and all the other bells and whistles make up the augmented product.

Consumers' product attitudes and preferences depend on the importance and perceived performance of the many characteristics of the augmented product. In the same way, citizens' views of democracy cannot readily be separated from their experience with augmented versions of democracy, each of which comes with particular constitutional frameworks, electoral systems, legal systems, economic policies, country brands, and so on.

Comparing various augmented versions of democracy, as well as substitute forms of government, offers clues about the strengths and weaknesses of the offering. U.S. democracy is associated with free-market policies and economic growth but also with a growing gap between rich and poor, with human rights but also with capital punishment, with religious freedom but also (in the minds of theocratic and other states) with moral decadence. Latin American democracy is associated with a moderate degree of civil rights but also with economic and political instability and a huge gap between rich and poor. The former authoritarian states of Eastern and Central Europe were associated with repression of rights and stagnant economies but also with political and social stability. Uganda and Ethiopia are only partially free in political and civic rights but hold together competing ethnic and tribal groups.[46] Singapore and China repress individual rights but are associated with rapid economic growth and national unity.

The point is that marketers of democracy need to consider a variety of citizens' needs and assess how the whole package serves them. In that respect, it is worth noting that a global survey representing more than 2 billion citizens found that, in descending order, the following tasks were nominated by citizens as the top priority for political leaders: closing the gap between rich and poor, economic growth, protecting the environment, and eliminating poverty.[47] These priorities represent a closer fit with the social democracies of Western Europe than with the free-market democracy of the United States.

Consistency in Word and Deed

Marketing efforts suffer when there are inconsistencies between the core values of a product, the message, and the delivery of the message. The marketing of democracy is inherently problematic because message and messenger are held to democracy's high standards for transparency, principled actions, equal treatment, and tolerance of dissent. It hurt the efforts of the United States to market democracy in the Middle East when its motives for bringing democracy to Iraq were widely perceived as a pretext for controlling oil supplies, when the stated reason for going to war was based on flimsy or nonexistent evidence, when the United States brushed off the United Nations (the closest institution the world has to a democratic government of nations), and when it said it could not countenance parties like Hamas, Hezbollah, or the Muslim Brotherhood winning in a free election.

Selective marketing of democracy looks self-serving and undemocratic. In the Middle East, the promotion of democracy seemed opportunistic, popping up overnight, rather than representing a sustained effort over decades. A United Nations report on the state of freedom in the Arab world criticized double standards held by world powers like the United States—accepting undemocratic government in countries like Saudi Arabia and Egypt in exchange for oil and political stability—and warned that it impeded the transition to democracy in all Arab nations.[48] The report also noted the contradiction between the United States' calls for freedom and democracy and its curtailing of civil rights for Arabs and Muslims in the so-called fight against terrorism and said that this inconsistency weakened the position of Arab reformers.[49]

U.S. efforts to promote democracy in the Middle East also were compromised by revelations about stealth operations to deliver the message. Shadowing the overt State Department programs were separately managed, covert Defense Department programs. One multimillion-dollar campaign attempted to shape opinions abroad by planting unattributed news stories and misleading information in the media.[50] Combat information units used psychological warfare techniques and sought to deceive the enemy by spreading deliberate falsehoods.

The danger, as critics inside and outside the Defense Department pointed out, is that the government cannot confine information to its intended audiences; any false or misleading information that comes to light damages the credibility of the United States as a country that stands for truth and freedom.[51] When he was director of the U.S. Information Agency, Edward R. Murrow said, "To be persuasive, we must be believable. To be believable, we must be truthful."[52]

Sustained Commitment

In any case, marketing democracy requires a substantial commitment of resources. The United States was in search of urgent fixes after 9/11, but in certain parts of the world, resentment of U.S. policy had been building for years. Convincing citizens in those areas to embrace democracy will be much tougher than it was in the conquered nations of Germany and Japan following World War II. Then, the fighting was over at the time of the Marshall Plan, and no organized opposition was in a position to resist U.S. wishes. In the case of Germany, there was a closer connection to and understanding of the culture. Imposition of democracy went hand in hand with rapid economic development, and communication of the democratic message faced little competition from alternative views widely carried in the media.

That is quite different from the situation at the beginning of the twenty-first century, when a democracy proposed or imposed by the United States must vie with established regimes and opposition groups, must overcome deeply entrenched economic troubles, must compete with religious and cultural values inhospitable to democracy as the United States sees it, and must combat resentment toward uses of U.S. power. In recent presidential elections in Venezuela, Brazil, Ecuador, Argentina, and Uruguay, the victors were the candidates most opposed to U.S.-supported free-market policies.

Communications alone, not to mention other forms of promotion, are expensive, and government funding for them is inconsistent. In part to reduce expenses, the U.S. government downsized, in the post–cold war period, the Voice of America, which had exemplified the values of U.S. democracy through objective journalism broadcast in as many as sixty languages. Then, in 2004, the government spent $62 million to launch an Arabic language television station, Alhurra (the Free One), which airs popular music and a small amount of news.[53] A State Department program called the Middle East Partnership Initiative spent $219 million from late 2002 through early 2005 on grants largely intended to finance independent Arab groups working on economic reform, democratic institutions, education, and women's empowerment.[54] However, for 2004, Congress approved a budget of about one-third of the $145 million requested by the administration.[55] Of course, these numbers pale next to the $5.5 billion in U.S. aid to governments in the region.[56]

If the United States, on the one hand, sends massive aid to prop up repressive governments and, on the other hand, hesitates to attach democracy as a condition of support, it is difficult to see how it can expect minor initiatives like the Middle East Partnership to reform or unseat these governments by changing popular opinion any time soon. Indeed, the United States partially backed off when about $1 million in grants to five local Egyptian groups promoting democratic reform triggered strenuous objections from the Egyptian government.[57] Also, in a backlash against U.S. interventionism, a growing number of governments around the world, including Russia's, are expelling, shutting down, or punishing foreign and local nongovernmental organizations that promote democracy.[58]

Successful private-sector marketing campaigns depend on a consistent and mutually reinforcing combination of product, brand image, advertising, and other forms of promotion. That requires coordination and control, something that is much more easily achieved in a corporate setting than in government. Under Secretary Hughes set out to embed public diplomacy in "every aspect of the State Department" and to integrate her agency's communications strategy with a governmentwide communications strategy.[59] Still, with the infighting in Washington over resources and influence, it will be an extremely difficult task.

A Better Approach

All these issues argue for a different approach toward marketing democracy: instead of the U.S. government promoting its notions of democracy *to* citizens in the Middle East, Asia, Africa, or South America, it could work in a viral marketing or word-of-mouth fashion *with* citizens to exemplify the values of democracy, leaving them to promote their homegrown versions.

Such efforts might include open engagement with important media outlets like Al Jazeera in the Arab world. Following 9/11, an Arabic speaker from the U.S. State Department who was assigned to respond to a taped statement by Osama bin Laden was "reduced to reading a statement attacking bin Laden that had been so carefully vetted that it seemed to lack sincerity and spontaneity."[60] Participating in honest debates would more effectively convey democratic values like freedom of expression. If government officials do not want to be put on the spot, perhaps American academics or journalists could take their place.

Demonstrating a desire for international cooperation by endorsing the Kyoto agreement and the World Court would show that the United States respects other nations. Demonstrably improving the lot of people in the lower nine-tenths of the socioeconomic strata through policies and programs that increase prosperity and security would promote democratic ideals more effectively than any words. For example, the United States could lower agricultural subsidies and trade barriers and contribute substantially to debt relief and prevention of infectious disease. Supporting education that widens horizons, perhaps through exchange programs, could open minds to democracy.

All this would require patience, but the Eastern European, as well as the Turkish, experience has shown that these are paths to democracy.[61] Moreover, the current U.S. message based on war and terror would give way to a more positive appeal based on economic prosperity and human potential.

A country's private and social sectors model its values to other nations. In the case of the United States, the generosity of the Bill & Melinda Gates Foundation will do more to promote positive U.S. values, and, indirectly, democracy, than all the government campaigns. The behavior of U.S. multinational corporations and their employees leaves a powerful impression abroad.

Keith Reinhard, chair of advertising agency DDB Worldwide, commissioned a seventeen-country survey in October 2001 to examine anti-American perceptions. The beliefs were, in Reinhard's words, "One, American companies are exploiters and they take more than they give back. Two, American companies promote values that are in conflict with local cultures, mores and religion. Three, Americans are viewed as insensitive and arrogant—Americans assume everyone wants to be like them. Four, American companies only want to sell."[62]

Spurred by these findings, Reinhard founded Business for Democratic Action, which aims to reshape these perceptions through small steps such as publishing etiquette guidelines for Americans traveling abroad and teaching executives how to listen to local concerns; tellingly, the group avoids advertising the virtues of the United States. Of course, a more powerful force for change lies in the everyday actions of U.S. marketers and their willingness to reform practices that cause them to be regarded as takers rather than givers.

Prosperity, Poverty, and Democracy

*In the terrible history of famines in the world, no substantial famine has
ever occurred in any independent and democratic country with a
relatively free press. We cannot find exceptions to this rule.*

—Amartya Sen[63]

Is there any role for marketing in improving human welfare on a broad
scale? First, consider the broader relationships among welfare, democracy,
and economic development. Overall, human welfare is on the rise. In the
past century, the world's population nearly quadrupled, growing from 1.6
billion people in 1900 to 6.1 billion people in 2000.[64] For 20 percent or so
of the population, ingenuity and economic development have raised the
standard of living far beyond what could have been imagined five hundred
or even one hundred years ago. But conditions are uneven: a large gulf sep-
arates the rich and the remaining 80 percent. In large part, this division follows national boundaries.

A person can expect a vastly different quality of life depending on which
of the world's two hundred or so countries he or she lives in.[65] Consider life
expectancy: a child born today in Sierra Leone can expect to live on average
to the age of thirty-nine; a child born in Japan, Australia, or Italy can expect
to live more than twice as long, to at least eighty years of age.[66] Income level
varies dramatically. For those fortunate to live in the United States, annual
GDP per capita is $39,618. For the less favored who live in Sierra Leone, the
corresponding GDP is $815.[67]

The extent to which people exercise individual rights and freedoms is
strictly determined by citizenship. In an authoritarian regime like North
Korea, individuals have virtually no freedom; political, economic, and social
aspects of life are subject to government control. Citizens of Sweden, on the
other hand, can pursue the education and career they want, freely express their
political and religious views, and participate fully in the political process.

Patterns of Well-Being

Taking a geopolitical map of the world and overlaying these three indicators
of human welfare—life expectancy, income level, and freedom—shows that
for the most part, life expectancy and income level are closely associated:
people in wealthier countries live longer than people in poor countries.

The pattern for freedom is slightly more complex. Citizens in the great majority of high-income countries have high levels of freedom. But a few oil-rich, high-income, authoritarian states in the Middle East and Asia repress individual freedoms. Countries at the middle levels of income range from free to authoritarian. At the low end of the income scale, only one of every six or seven countries allows its citizens free political rights and civil liberties.[68] Overall, though, the three indicators of human welfare are consistent.

What explains the differences in welfare from one country to another? It is not geographical size. Well-off countries range from the very small to the quite large, and so do worse-off countries. Population size confers no advantage: of the twenty most populous countries, four are high income; six are low income, and the remaining ten are developing economies.[69] A country's natural resources also fail to explain differences in welfare. But there is a strong regional pattern. On all three measures, North America, Europe, and the Pacific Rim rank the highest. Sub-Saharan Africa ranks lowest.

Nearly all the wealthy countries of North America, Europe, and the Pacific Rim have in common a democratic government and a free-market economy; nearly all have a European-derived culture and legal system. Aside from increasing human welfare by guaranteeing basic individual rights, democracy appears close to being a necessary condition for prosperity: the only high-income countries (or dependent territories) that are not democracies are the former European dependencies of Singapore, Hong Kong, and Macau, along with a handful of oil-rich countries in the Middle East.

That is not to say that democratic, free-enterprise systems invariably produce optimal results. Within the successful Western democracies, environmental problems—some resulting from private ownership or control of natural resources like water and minerals—are a growing concern. Another concern is the degree to which income inequalities resulting from the market economy are a good incentive for people to work hard or are instead a spur to political unrest or a source of excessive influence over the democratic process.[70] Within many democracies, inequalities of opportunity, such as those resulting from unequal access to education, health, housing, or public safety, remain a problem, both from a social justice point of view and in light of empirical research demonstrating the lasting impact of education, nutrition, and public safety on human development.[71]

Countries that are democracies but do not possess good governance—including the will and the ability to apply public resources to advance the public welfare—have not done a good job of eliminating poverty.[72] Experts would probably agree that both strong governments and strong economies depend on societies' having values, norms, and institutions that promote "consensus, community, legitimacy, organization, effectiveness, [and] stability."[73]

The Complex Relationship of Democracy and Economic Development

For poor countries, Western policy makers and political economists dispute whether one or the other should come first—democracy or economic development. If democracy requires educated middle classes that have something to gain by sharing power and that can mobilize against entrenched rulers, then, so one argument goes, economic development must come first. A number of economic development proponents further argue that authoritarian regimes may be better than democracies during early phases of development, because they can plan for the long term, maintain stability, hold down wages, limit consumption, and force savings; in the end, economic growth eventually leads to rising incomes, an emerging middle class, and democracy.[74] China's, Singapore's, and Malaysia's rapid economic expansions in recent decades are offered as examples of the authoritarian advantage; South Korea and Taiwan are held out as examples of eventual democratization.

During and after the cold war, this viewpoint was influential in U.S. foreign policy circles and among international development organizations, including the World Bank and the International Monetary Fund.[75] Often, the economic results were disappointing. The dismal experience with economic reforms intended to spur Russia and other former communist states to make the transition to a market economy and eventual full democracy speaks to problems in states where social institutions are fragile and citizens' welfare comes second. Without a fully functioning government and legitimate legal system, privatization enriched a privileged few and further corrupted already weak social institutions.[76]

A recent study published by the Council on Foreign Relations comes out squarely in favor of policies that promote democratization ahead of achieving a certain level of economic development. The authors' interpretation of an extensive body of literature and economic data builds a strong case that, on the whole, poor democratic states outperform poor nondemocratic states on a wide array of measures of social well-being, including life expectancy and child mortality, secondary education and female literacy, access to clean drinking water, agricultural productivity, and HIV/AIDS rates.[77] Sen's observation that so far, no democracy with a reasonably free press has ever had a famine fits this pattern.[78] And poor democracies' record of economic growth is equivalent to or slightly better than that of poor autocracies.[79]

These favorable results imply that low-income countries should pursue democracy. According to the authors of the Council on Foreign Relations study, the reasons for the superior developmental performance of democracies "boil down to three core characteristics of representative government: shared power, openness, and adaptability."[80] In other words, democracies disperse power and foster a broad range of interests. They create a climate in which innovation can flourish and people can improve their lot in life.[81]

Nevertheless, the path toward economic growth is perilous. About 120 countries are considered functioning electoral democracies, but half of these have gross national income (GNI) per capita of less than $3,000.[82] And in poorer countries, new democracies are very susceptible to failure. On the positive side, democratic countries that reach a per capita income greater than $6,000 are highly likely to remain democracies.[83] Democracy and economic development appear to work best hand in hand.

By the end of the 1990s, prominent World Bank officials and economists, including Joseph Stiglitz and Amartya Sen, concluded that political freedoms and democracy were necessary for sustainable development. The following were recurrent themes at a 1999 World Bank conference: "Democracy and markets are 'two wheels of a cart'... both ... are needed to improve the lives of citizens"; "Participation is fundamental to democracy and development."[84] Meanwhile, there is compelling evidence that "women are critical to economic development, active civil society, and good governance, especially in developing countries" and that "allowing women to participate in politics also benefits democracy."[85]

Sen proposed that democracy has three important benefits in terms of economic development: "First, it enriches individual lives through more freedom (involving political and civil rights). Second, it provides political incentives to the rulers to respond positively to the needs and demands of the people. Third, the process of open dialogues and debates that democracy allows helps in the formation of values and priorities."[86] Further, "political rights, including freedom of expression and discussion, are . . . central to the conceptualization of economic needs."[87] Importantly, democracy is a matter not only of institutions but also of citizen actions and values.

Sen's observations imply that macroeconomic policies imposed from the top down need to be connected with economic and political choices formed from the bottom up. Differing directions for economic and political reforms need to be resolved through a participatory and inclusive process.

In the end, progress among developing countries depends on paying more attention to the role of citizens and to processes that help build democratic institutions. Stiglitz calls for strengthening participatory processes in local and regional government, the workplace, and capital markets; he notes that if people believe they have had a meaningful part in decisions that affect them, they are more willing to accept change.[88] Throughout U.S. history, according to some historians, the values and beliefs of the middle class have provided the impetus for populist democracy.[89]

A straightforward approach to building democratic institutions is to support and encourage nascent citizen participation in politics—expressing opinions, voting, party organizing, running for office. This is not always feasible. A second approach is to encourage participation in social institutions that foster the same norms and behaviors that support democracy. The consumer marketplace is one such institution.

In particular, people who have the opportunity to participate as buyers or as sellers in well-functioning consumer marketplaces discover that consumers' preferences and choices shape what the market offers. They learn that information empowers consumers and that accountability improves quality. They share the experience that exchanges based on fair and impartial rules lead to efficient outcomes and that organizations and institutions can be trustworthy. They hone the capacity to make self-directed, discerning choices in the marketplace—virtually the same capacity required to make discerning political choices. In effect, marketing institutions and transactions breed social capital, which in turn breeds a culture of responsible citizenship.[90] And to the extent that the marketing system delivers products that improve consumers' welfare or generates work that improves economic livelihoods, people are better placed to exercise political power.

CONCLUSION

Toward a Greater Good

"THE CONSUMER IS BOSS." Those are the words of A. G. Lafley, chairman and chief executive of Procter & Gamble, perhaps the world's most reputed marketing-led organization. Economists, too, acknowledge consumer sovereignty in a market economy: "Consumers, by registering their dollar votes, determine which goods and services shall be provided and in what quantities."[1]

Economists, however, tend to see consumer sovereignty as an automatic mechanism, occurring in an environment of perfect competition and information. This concept overlooks or underestimates the role of marketing in shaping the market, changing consumer behavior, and seeking insights into latent as well as explicit consumer needs.

Good marketers listen closely to consumers to develop new insights into how to help them. They identify, even anticipate, consumers' wants and the problems that they need to solve. Marketers then design products and services that add value by fulfilling these wants and needs. Good marketers know that consumers don't buy products, they buy solutions; they don't buy quarter-inch drill bits, they buy products that will deliver quarter-inch holes.[2]

Good marketers listen to consumers not only to glean information and ideas but also to show respect. Lafley visits a number of consumers' homes each year, observing and discussing their household needs.[3] Leonard Marsh, one of the three founders of Snapple, explained the brand's success: "We never thought of ourselves as being any better than our customers."[4] Good marketers don't just listen to their consumers. They invite them to engage in a conversation, to join online communities, to help shape marketing decisions,

269

to co-create brand meaning. These practices reinforce brand loyalty, boost repeat sales, and stimulate positive word of mouth.

Some Common Criticisms of Marketing

Not all marketing is good. The demise of Arthur Andersen in the wake of the Enron scandal proved that not all accounting is good, and the elections of Mahmoud Ahmadinejad in Iran and Hamas in Palestine showed that not all democracy is good. In the same way, the unscrupulous can hijack marketing tactics for selfish and evil purposes. Bad marketers have, for example, sold products known to cause harm, purposefully deceived or withheld information from consumers, and charged excessive prices for shoddy goods.

The community of good marketers censures such practices and strives to prevent them. What might be termed the NRA (National Rifle Association) defense, which asserts that marketing does not deceive people, people deceive people, is inadequate. So is the defense that marketing is not very effective. Similarly, the statement—applicable to both the commercial and the political marketplaces—that you can fool some of the people some of the time but you cannot fool all of the people all of the time provides little comfort. However, we believe that critics of marketing often overestimate both the level of intentional deception and, more important, the vulnerability of the public. As advertising icon David Ogilvy famously said in an earlier era, "The consumer isn't a moron. She is your wife."[5]

In addition to deception and misrepresentation, a common complaint about marketing is its intrusiveness, the blizzard of marketing messages directed at consumers every day. The good news here is that marketing efficiency and effectiveness are improving. Marketers are growing better at targeting their messages at those consumers likely to be interested. Marketers have no interest in wasting money on reaching consumers who are uninterested in or, worse, are offended by their messages.

Marketing is also accused of promoting materialism, homogenizing culture, and magnifying inequalities. On occasion, all of us buy something we later realize we do not need. We learn from such experiences and become savvier consumers. We embrace a diversity of products, including borrowing from many cultures, but we do not abandon all that is traditional. On occasion, all of us dream of a lifestyle that is beyond our reach; we either look on the bright side of life and work harder to achieve the goal, or we become mired in envy. It's true that the poor cannot exercise as much freedom of choice as the rich. But interestingly, the political marketplace of one-person-one-vote does not offer a more level playing field. Like consumers, not all voters are created equal. The wealthy cannot vote twice, but they can exert disproportionate influence on politicians by donating the legal maximum contribution and by giving to political action committees and party organizations.

Unlike accountants or lawyers, marketers are not licensed. Absent licensing, good marketers know that their reputations and those of the brands they represent depend on their good behavior and their willingness to disavow improper as well as illegal practices. Industry associations, backed by leading firms, promulgate marketing standards. However, they cannot always keep pace with the inventiveness of marketers who constantly explore new technologies and develop new competitive tactics. Neither can regulators, but government regulations are essential in the case of genuine market failures or health and safety issues or deceptive advertising claims. There exist certain products and services for which the principle of caveat emptor is simply not sufficient.

Important Benefits of Marketing

For all the negatives, the vast majority of marketing is good for individual consumers, good for firms, and good for society. Marketplace exchanges are based on mutual trust between buyers and sellers; they create value for both parties; the billions of daily marketplace transactions are a large part of the glue that holds societies together. Good marketers offer consumers choices. Choice stimulates consumption and economic growth and enables personal expression. Good marketers provide consumers with information about new products and services.

Additionally, good marketers engage consumers and make them partners in the production and consumption of brands. Good marketers also reach beyond the wealthy elites and imagine how to bring expensive innovations to the mass market. Wal-Mart and Google are much maligned, but their missions are inclusive: to "lower the cost of living of everyone everywhere" and "to organize the world's information and make it accessible to everyone."

A powerful force for democracy is the mission adopted by many good marketers: to enable poor consumers around the world to enjoy the advantages of the developed world's innovations at lower-than-ever prices. Efforts to mass-produce a standard $20 mobile phone by consolidating orders from mobile operators around the world and to mass-produce a $100 personal computer to deliver one laptop per child are reminiscent of Henry Ford's one-size-fits-all black Model T. The objective is to bridge the digital divide and open new opportunities and life choices to poor consumers in the same way that the marketing of refrigerators saved on shopping trips, expanded food choices, and improved food safety for middle-class European and U.S. households in the twentieth century. Such initiatives require not only creative product design but often new distribution and service support models.

We believe that marketing itself is marketed poorly and that the social value created by the 17 million Americans who are employed in marketing deserves more credit. The fault is largely with marketers themselves. They should be more conscious of the social importance of their work and of the moral principles that underpin their daily decisions. Marketers are most comfortable judging marketing as a business practice, where the issue is how well a particular marketing tool, technique, or process helps a business meet its objectives. But marketers also need to consider the impact of marketing on individual consumers, the marketplace, and society.

Among the important questions are, How does a business's use of marketing tools and practices affect a consumer's purchase and consumption experience and quality of life? How does a particular marketing practice affect marketplace competition? Some practices may help individual companies and individual consumers but create monopolistic conditions, while others may undermine consumer trust. Finally, what is the impact of marketing on society? How does a marketing practice or the totality of marketing practices affect the kind of society or the kind of world that citizens want to live in? Does a seemingly innocuous tool like humorous advertising increase sales and add value by amusing consumers, or, as critic Benjamin Barber says in a recent book, does it infantilize people, create "artificial needs," and undermine responsible citizenship?[6] These are all relevant questions.

272

Improving the Political Marketplace

Linking marketing with democracy, Franklin D. Roosevelt reportedly said that if he could place one American book in the hands of every Russian, that volume would be a Sears Roebuck catalog.[7] We have argued that the same six benefits—exchange, consumption, choice, information, engagement, and inclusion—that characterize good democracy characterize good marketing. But turning the argument around, we have also asked how well modern democracies live up to the standards set by good marketing. We conclude that they fall short in many ways and could improve by borrowing from marketing's best practices.

Of course, the representative democracy of the political marketplace differs in key respects from the more direct democracy of the consumer marketplace. For one thing, in the political marketplace, citizens delegate authority to representatives, who make choices for them. There is forced rather than discretionary "consumption" of winning candidates, legislation, and government programs. There are limited opportunities to vote for an alternative. Rather than satisfy the narrow interests of various segments of the population, representative democracy is a collective process of compromise and bargaining that attempts to achieve a common good.

Even so, current political practices and the structure of the political marketplace diminish citizen sovereignty. In political exchanges, some citizens' votes have more impact than those of others, the counting of votes is marred, the returns that citizens receive for voting are nebulous, and the process is inconvenient. In the United States, choice is all but confined to two options, and winner takes all. When partisanship prevails, slim political majorities compel citizens to consume policies many of them find unpalatable. A surfeit of attack ads and a paucity of factual information lower citizens' trust in politicians. Too many politicians solicit citizens' support but have little interest in learning about their needs. Market share dominates market size, so rather than try to bring more people into the process, they focus on swing voters in a few swing districts. It is no surprise that voter cynicism has risen and voter participation has fallen.

Citizens' power diminishes as the power of special-interest groups, big money, and big business increases. In mature democracies, too few elected officials and public servants comprehend that they are the beneficiaries of an exchange, of a social contract, in which the citizen is the boss. What is required is a new generation of politicians who treat citizens with respect rather than view them merely for what they can give as voters, donors, and taxpayers. Commercial marketers view even consumers who complain as an asset; their insights can help companies improve their performance. Too many politicians view dialogue with citizens as an annoyance, a cost of doing business to get elected.

Politicians constantly sell themselves to raise money to fund campaigns, and their marketing efforts diminish rather than enhance marketing's reputation. This is especially true of politicians who harness marketing tactics such as negative advertising to achieve short-term results at the polls. In contrast, commercial marketers must earn the consumer's vote at the cash register every day. With decades of experience, they therefore view marketing as a long-term investment to boost their brands' reputations. They rarely indulge in negative comparison advertising with their direct competitors, knowing that consumers respect brands that offer positive reasons to buy them. What is needed in the political marketplace is not less marketing but better marketing. Politicians need to understand that marketing, practiced properly, is grounded in the concept of a fair exchange that builds trust.

Marketing in the Public Sector

Good marketing can assist public policy objectives that involve changing citizens' attitudes and behaviors regarding, for example, energy conservation, seat-belt use, and healthy diets. However, politicians recoil at the word *marketing* (despite marketing themselves) and habitually underfund marketing programs that come up for budgetary approval. Often the solution to society's needs is a matter not only of inventing programs or products but also of delivering them and educating people on their use. Public-sector agencies that aim to be financially self-supporting, such as the U.S. Postal Service and Amtrak, clearly need professional marketing to deliver good service and compete against private-sector alternatives. Good marketing can improve the taxpayers' return on investment in these agencies.

Private-sector marketing in conjunction with public policy initiatives and nongovernmental organizations shows promise in improving the welfare of the world's poor and in enabling them to become self-sufficient. Campaigns to promote a nation's image and attract foreign direct investment or tourism can also benefit from a disciplined marketing approach. When marketing fails to deliver in the public arena, typically it is because programs are under-funded or are not sustained long enough to make a difference.

In emerging democracies and non-democracies, increased economic free-dom and consumer choice in the commercial marketplace raise citizens' expectations for comparable choices among elected representatives, poli-cies, and programs in the political marketplace. The spread of television and cell phones and the development of lower-cost business models by lead-ing multinationals are introducing people worldwide to Western democratic values as well as to better standards of living. Many people around the world who violently disagree with U.S. foreign policy say that there are things about the United States they admire, things they learn about from movies, televi-sion, and radio. This pattern of events occurred in the former communist countries of Eastern and Central Europe and may eventually play out in China and Vietnam.

Marketing Needs Democracy, Democracy Needs Marketing

Does marketing undermine democracy? By virtue of marketing's very success, the answer may be yes, but unwittingly. Barber, for one, says that marketing is "sucking up the air from every other domain to sustain the sector devoted to consumption."[8] When Alexis de Tocqueville studied U.S. democracy, he observed that voluntary civic, political, religious, and other associations bound people together to pursue common ends. But memberships in churches, trade unions, and political parties are in decline as these institutions, so important to a healthy democracy, fail to market themselves successfully to citizens.

The consumer marketplace—which includes favorite sports teams—has a near monopoly on good marketing. As a result, individuals increasingly focus their loyalties on trusted brands. With families fragmenting and life-time employment with a single employer or long-term residence in a single community ever more unlikely, brands compete successfully for an even big-ger share of the finite level of loyalty that each of us can bestow. Starbucks, for example, wants to be the third place in consumers' lives, after home and the workplace. As television commentator Lou Dobbs points out, we are increasingly consumers first and citizens second, rather than vice versa.[9]

The practice of marketing is far from perfect. But its value to consumers has grown and is growing. Good marketers respect and respond to consumer differences. Technological advances that lower the costs of storing and analyzing customer databases enable marketers to segment markets more finely and profitably than ever before, to customize solutions, and ultimately to design products for "a segment of one." Few marketers can survive without repeat sales or recommendations, so they focus on giving consumers a reason to sustain a long-term relationship with them.

However, marketing can flourish only in a healthy democracy. Democracy is "a meta-institution for building good institutions."[10] To eliminate bad marketing and ensure a fair consumer marketplace, we need effective regulatory frameworks (not hijacked by special interests and industry lobbyists). Without citizen sovereignty over societal institutions, including marketing, consumers—and many businesses—will be less well off.

In turn, democracy needs marketing. Marketing improves standards of living and contributes to economic growth. It offers consumers diverse choices that reflect pluralistic needs and values. It sustains institutions of civil society through legal, fair, transparent, and trustworthy exchanges with consumers. It extends systems for providing goods and services to all consumers. Marketers are partnering with NGOs and policy makers to find market and nonmarket solutions for recognized and emerging public needs. A world without marketing would be a world that would not respect consumer differences, would not listen to consumer aspirations, and would not solve consumer problems. It would be a wasteland of sameness, commoditization, and inertia.

Good democracy depends on freedom of expression and the timely availability of accurate information. Former vice president Al Gore indicts politicians, the media, marketers, and citizens for diminishing and debasing the marketplace of ideas in the public sphere; at the same time, he sees a remedy in the Internet as a "platform for pursuing the truth, and the decentralized creation and distribution of ideas, in the same way that markets are a decentralized mechanism for the distribution of goods and services."[11] Marketing plays a key role in providing citizens with such a platform. It aids democracy by making the Internet, other media, and media content widely available and affordable.

A good democracy strives to engage as many citizens as possible in the political discourse and to have as many as possible act in the political process by voting. It depends on the existence of a level playing field in which citizens are offered distinct choices. Consumption of politics and government services should be satisfying and enriching, and not something to be scorned or avoided. To achieve these ends, we need to improve the quality of marketing in the political marketplace.

Further, we believe that both a better democracy and a better marketplace are possible if people aspire to combine the strengths they have as citizens with the strengths they have as consumers. A citizen is called on to subordinate narrow self-interest to the goal of the common good. A citizen joins political coalitions that span multiple constituencies and diverse sets of interests within a society. A citizen understands that achieving some public goals may require sustained effort over time and a degree of self-sacrifice. A citizen committed to democracy is motivated by values of freedom and equal opportunity (if not equal outcomes) for all.

A consumer expects value in exchange and holds providers accountable. A consumer embraces change and innovation. A consumer expresses fluid, multiple, cosmopolitan social affiliations through personal choices. A consumer sees himself or herself as an autonomous actor who is skillful in making decisions and accepts responsibility for choice.

The consumer in each of us can learn from the citizen, and the citizen can learn from the consumer. Marketers must learn from both. Rather than view marketing as a threat to democracy, let us explore how the benefits common to both give us opportunities to build bridges between the two. To recognize the commonalities between marketing and democracy is to grant people the power to create a greater good.

Notes

INTRODUCTION

1. A Factiva keyword search on *democracy* for articles published in major U.S. news and business sources revealed a substantial increase in 2005 mentions compared with 1995 mentions; a keyword search on Library of Congress acquisitions for 1995, 2000, and 2005 showed that the number published was highest in 2000, followed by 1995 and 2005.

2. For instance, influential interior designer Elsie de Wolfe was characterized in this way: "Her style may have been reactionary, but her convictions were democratic." Ruth Franklin, "A Life in Good Taste: The Fashions and Follies of Elsie De Wolfe," *New Yorker*, September 27, 2004, 142–146.

3. Michael Kimmelman, "In a Saffron Ribbon, a Billowy Gift to the City," *New York Times*, February 13, 2005, 1.

4. Johnson & Johnson, "Our Credo," Our Company Page, 2006, <http://www.jnj.com/our _company/our_credo/index.htm>.

5. Johnson & Johnson recalled Tylenol again in 1986, after another tampering incident, and withdrew all capsule products from over-the-counter sales. The second recall cost about $150 million.

6. American Marketing Association, "Dictionary of Marketing Terms," <www.marketing power.com>.

7. Bureau of Labor Statistics, *Occupational Employment and Wages, May 2005* (Washington, DC: U.S. Department of Labor, 2005), <http://www.bls.gov/oes/current/oes410000.htm>.

8. Fernand Braudel, *Civilization and Capitalism 15th–18th Century*, vol. II, *The Wheels of Commerce*, translated by Sian Reynolds (New York: Harper & Row, 1979).

9. Paul D. Converse and Harvey W. Huegy, *The Elements of Marketing*, 5th ed. (Englewood Cliffs, NJ: Prentice-Hall, Inc., 1952), 1.

10. Marshall I. Goldman, "The Marketing Structure in the Soviet Union," *Journal of Marketing* 25, no. 5 (July 1961): 7–14.

11. Richard S. Tedlow, *New and Improved: The Story of Mass Marketing in America* (Boston: Harvard Business School Press, 1996), 5.

12. Ibid.

13. Peter F. Drucker, *The Practice of Management* (New York: Harper & Row, 1954), 39.

14. Robert J. Keith, "The Marketing Revolution," *Journal of Marketing* 24, no. 1 (January 1960): 35–38.

15. See Glen L. Urban, *Don't Just Relate—Advocate! A Blueprint for Profit in the Era of Consumer Power* (Upper Saddle River, NJ: Wharton School Publishing, 2005).

16. In one representative textbook definition, marketing is "the performance of business activities that direct the flow of goods and services from producer to consumer or user in order to best satisfy consumers and accomplish the firm's objectives." E. Jerome McCarthy, *Basic Marketing: A Managerial Approach* (Homewood, IL: Richard D. Irwin, Inc., 1960), 33.

17. Ralph F. Breyer, *The Marketing Institution* (New York: McGraw-Hill Book Company, Inc., 1934).

18. The Roman deity Mercury was known as the god of commerce; the name shares an

etymology with the words *market* and *merchant*, from the Latin *merc-* or *merx*, "commodity." *Oxford English Dictionary Online*, <http://www.dictionary.oed.com>. Mercury personifies a variety of marketing functions: he was "the patron god of circulation, the movement of goods, people, and words and their roles," Simon Hornblower and Antony Spawforth, eds., *The Oxford Classical Dictionary* (Oxford: Oxford University Press, 1996). His cult had "close links with shopkeepers and transporters of goods, notably of grain." But there were negative as well as positive aspects: "his function was not simply the protection of businessmen . . . Mercury is also a deceiver, since he moves on the boundaries and in the intervening spaces; he is patron of the shopkeeper as much as the trader, the traveller as well as the brigand."

19. Aristotle, *Politics* [350 BC], translated by Benjamin Jowett (Oxford: Oxford University Press, 1885), <www.classics.mit.edu>.

20. "Ethical Shopping: Feeding Your Conscience," *Marketing Week*, January 25, 2007, 42.

21. For reviews, see Robert A. Dahl, *On Democracy* (New Haven, CT: Yale University Press, 1998). John Dunn, *Setting the People Free: The Story of Democracy* (London: Atlantic, 2005).

22. Dahl, *On Democracy*, chapter 4.

23. Ibid., chapter 6.

24. Partha Dasgupta, "Well-Being and the Extent of Its Realisation in Poor Countries," *Economic Journal* 100, no. 400 (Conference Papers) (1990): 1–32.

25. This type of distinction is made by, for example, J. Roland Pennock, *Democratic Political Theory* (Princeton, NJ: Princeton University Press, 1979). Dahl, *On Democracy*. Dunn, *Setting the People Free*.

26. Pennock, *Democratic Political Theory*, 5.

27. For example, the U. S. Bill of Rights appended to the Constitution; or United Nations General Assembly, *Universal Declaration of Human Rights, Resolution 217 a (Iii)* (New York: United Nations, 1948).

28. Dunn, *Setting the People Free*.

29. John Rawls, *A Theory of Justice*, revised ed. (Cambridge, MA: Belknap Press/ Harvard University Press, 1999).

30. Dunn, *Setting the People Free*, 143.

31. Pennock, *Democratic Political Theory*.

32. For some comparisons, see Joseph A. Schumpeter, *Capitalism, Socialism, and Democracy* [1942], 5th ed. (New York: HarperCollins, 1976). Joshua Cohen, "Maximizing Social Welfare or Institutionalizing Democratic Ideals? Commentary on Adam Przeworski's Article," *Politics and Society* 19, no. 1 (1991): 39–58. Adam Przeworski, "Could We Feed Everyone? The Irrationality of Capitalism and the Infeasibility of Socialism," *Politics and Society* 19, no. 1 (1991): 1–38.

33. Laza Kekic, "The Economist Intelligence Unit's Index of Democracy," in *The World in 2007* (London: The Economist, 2007), <http://www.economist.com/media/pdf/DEMOCRACY_INDEX_2007_v3.pdf>.

34. Ibid.

35. Schumpeter, *Capitalism, Socialism, and Democracy*, chapter XXI.

36. In addition to the difficulties of measuring and computing citizens' wants, demands, and preferences, Pennock notes that government itself creates and shapes citizens' wants. Pennock, *Democratic Political Theory*, chapter VII.

37. Schumpeter, *Capitalism, Socialism, and Democracy*, chapter XXII.

38. See Dunn, *Setting the People Free*.

39. Raymond A. Bauer and Stephen A. Greyser, *Advertising in America: The Consumer View* (Boston: Graduate School of Business Administration, Harvard University, 1968).

CHAPTER 1

1. Adam Smith, *An Inquiry into the Nature and Causes of the Wealth of Nations* [1776], edited by Edwin Cannan, 5th ed. vol. 1, bk. 1, ch. 2 (London: Methuen & Co., 1904) <http://www.econlib.org/LIBRARY/Smith/smWN.html>.

2. Christopher Dyer, *Standards of Living in the Later Middle Ages: Social Change in England C. 1200–1520* (Cambridge, UK: Cambridge University Press, 1989).

3. Kathryn H. Anderson and Richard Pomfret, *Consequences of Creating a Market Economy: Evidence from Household Surveys in Central Asia* (Cheltenham, UK: Edward Elgar, 2003), 145.

4. See Robert E. Lucas Jr., "The Industrial Revolution: Past and Future," *2003 Annual Report*, Federal Reserve Bank of Minneapolis, Minneapolis, 2003, <http://www.minneapolisfed.org/pubs/region/04-05/essay.cfm>. Robert C. Allen, Tommy Bengtsson, and Martin Dribe, eds., *Living Standards in the Past: New Perspectives on Well-Being in Asia and Europe* (Oxford: Oxford University Press, 2005).

5. Ramsay MacMullen, "Market-Days in the Roman Empire," *Phoenix* 24, no. 4 (Winter 1970): 333–341.

6. Two leading exponents are Karl Polanyi and Moses Finley. Karl Polanyi, *The Great Transformation* (New York: Rinehart & Company, 1944). Moses I. Finley, *The Ancient Economy* (Berkeley: University of California Press, 1973).

7. See Karl Polanyi and R. F. G. Sweet, "Review: Foreign Trade in the Old Babylonian Period as Revealed by Texts from Southern Mesopotamia," *Journal of Economic History* 22, no. 1 (March 1962): 116–117. Morris Silver, "Karl Polanyi and Markets in the Ancient Near East: The Challenge of the Evidence," *Journal of Economic History* 43, no. 4 (December 1983): 795–829. Anne Mayhew, Walter C. Neale, and David W. Tandy, "Markets in the Ancient Near East: A Challenge to Silver's Argument and Use of Evidence," *Journal of Economic History* 45, no. 1 (March 1985): 127–134. Thomas Barfield, "Review: Economic Structures of the Ancient Near East," *American Anthropologist* 89, no. 1 (March 1987): 194–195. Kirsty M. W. Shipton, "The Private Banks in Fourth-Century B.C. Athens: A Reappraisal," *Classical Quarterly* 47, no. 2 (1997): 396–422. Peter Temin, "A Market Economy in the Early Roman Empire," *Journal of Roman Studies* 91 (2001): 169–181. Norman Yoffee, "Review: Privatization in the Ancient Near East and Classical World," *Journal of the American Oriental Society* 121, no. 2 (April–June 2001): 303–305.

8. Richard P. Bagozzi, "Marketing as Exchange," *Journal of Marketing* 39 (October 1975): 32–39.

9. Marcel Mauss, *The Gift: The Form and Reason for Exchange in Archaic Societies*, translated by W. D. Halls (London: Routledge, 1990).

10. See, for example, Al Ries and Jack Trout, *Marketing Warfare* (New York: McGraw-Hill, 1986).

11. See, for example, Jagdish Sheth and Atul Parvatiyar, eds., *Handbook of Relationship Marketing* (Thousand Oaks, CA: Sage Publications, 2000).

12. "Brands: Who's Wearing the Trousers?" *Economist*, September 8, 2001, 27.

13. See ibid. "Crowned at Last: A Survey of Consumer Power," *Economist*, April 2, 2005, 1–15.

14. "The Global Brand Scorecard: The 100 Top Brands," *BusinessWeek*, August 2, 2004, 68–71. Chad Terhune, "Market Shares Drop at Coca-Cola, Pepsico," *Wall Street Journal*, March 7, 2005, B10.

15. Ron Chernow, *Titan: The Life of John D. Rockefeller, Sr.* (New York: Random House, 1998).

16. Naomi Klein, *No Logo: Taking Aim at the Brand Bullies* (New York: Picador, 2000).

17. Quoted in Clayton M. Christensen, Scott Cook, and Taddy Hall, "Marketing Malpractice," *Harvard Business Review* (December 2005).

18. Mya Frazier, "Star-Stuck Gap Follows Celebs Off a Sales Cliff," *Advertising Age*, November 28, 2005, 3–4.

19. Max H. Bazerman, "Consumer Research for Consumers," *Journal of Consumer Research* 27 (March 2001): 499–504.

20. Kathy Peiss, *Hope in a Jar: The Making of America's Beauty Culture* (New York: Henry Holt and Company, 1998).

21. Ibid.

22. Jose Antonio Rosa et al., "Sociocognitive Dynamics in a Product Market," *Journal of Marketing* 63, Special Issue (1999): 64–77.

23. R. Craig Endicott, "50th Annual 100 Leading National Advertisers," *Advertising Age*, June

27, 2005, S1. Maria Fredriksson, "U.K. Advertising Spending Rose 2.6% in 2005, Helped by TV," *Bloomberg.com*, June 25, 2006.

24. Jeremy Rifkin, *The European Dream: How Europe's Vision of the Future Is Quietly Eclipsing the American Dream* (New York: Jeremy P. Tarcher/Penguin, 2004).

25. "Crowned at Last: A Survey of Consumer Power."

26. Costco Wholesale, "Code of Ethics," Investor Relations, Costco, Issaquah, WA, 2007, <http://www.phx.corporate-ir.net/phoenix.zhtml?c=83830&p=irol-govhighlights>.

27. Marcus Tullius Cicero [44 B.C.], in *Columbia World of Quotations*, edited by Robert Andrews, Mary Biggs, and Michael Seidel (New York: Columbia University Press, 1996).

28. Daniel Kahneman, Jack L. Knetsch, and Richard H. Thaler, "Fairness as a Constraint on Profit Seeking: Entitlements in the Market," *American Economic Review* 76, no. 4 (September 1986): 728–741.

29. Marielza Martins and Kent B. Monroe, "Perceived Price Fairness: A New Look at an Old Construct," in *Advances in Consumer Research*, edited by Frank Kardes and Mita Sujan vol. 21, (Provo, UT: Association for Consumer Research, 1994), 75–78.

30. Kahneman, Knetsch, and Thaler, "Fairness as a Constraint on Profit Seeking."

31. Ibid.

32. Lauren Keller Johnson, "Dueling Pricing Strategies: Everyday Low Prices Vie with Aggressive Promotional Pricing in an Increasingly Competitive Retail Environment," *MIT Sloan Management Review* 44, no. 3 (Spring 2003): 10.

33. See, for example, Daniel Kahneman, Jack L. Knetsch, and Richard H. Thaler, "Fairness and the Assumptions of Economics," *Journal of Business* 59, no. 4, pt. 2 (October 1986): S285–S300.

34. Sarah McBride, "Film Industry Vows Crackdown on Online Movie Thieves," *Wall Street Journal*, November 5, 2004, B1.

35. Gary McWilliams, "Minding the Store: Analyzing Customers, Best Buy Decides Not All Are Welcome: Retailer Aims to Outsmart Dogged Bargain-Hunters, and Coddle Big Spenders: Looking for 'Barrys' and 'Jills,'" *Wall Street Journal*, November 8, 2004, A1.

36. Lisa E. Bolton, Luk Warlop, and Joseph W. Alba, "Explorations in Price (Un) Fairness," *Journal of Consumer Research* 29 (March 2003): 474–491.

37. Claes Fornell, "Q1 2004: Transportation/Communications/Utilities and Services: Industry and Company Results," Commentary, American Customer Satisfaction Index, Ann Arbor, MI, June 3, 2004.

38. Ralph W. Emerson, *Essays: First Series* (Boston: J. Munroe, 1841), reprinted at <http://www .gutenberg.org/etext/2944>.

39. Daniel J. Boorstin, *Americans: The Democratic Experience* (New York: Random House, 1973).

40. Ibid.

41. Charles R. Hickson and Earl A. Thompson, "A New Theory of Guilds and European Economic Development," *Explorations in Economic History* 28, no. 2 (April 1991): 127–168.

42. Avner Greif, Paul Milgrom, and Barry Weingast, "Coordination, Commitment, and Enforcement: The Case of the Merchant Guild," *Journal of Political Economy* 102, no. 4 (August 1994): 745–776.

43. For arguments in favor of making management a profession, see Rakesh Khurana, Nitin Nohria, and Daniel Penrice, "Management as a Profession," in *Restoring Trust in American Business*, edited by Jay W. Lorsch, Andy Zelleke, and Leslie Berlowitz (Cambridge, MA: American Academy of Arts and Sciences, 2005).

44. See Anderson and Pomfret, *Consequences of Creating a Market Economy*.

45. Frank Trentmann, "Bread, Milk and Democracy: Consumption and Citizenship in Twentieth-Century Britain," in *The Politics of Consumption: Material Culture and Citizenship in Europe and America*, edited by Martin Daunton and Matthew Hilton (New York: Oxford, 2001), 129–161.

46. Craig N. Smith and John Quelch, *Ethics in Marketing* (Homewood, IL: Richard D. Irwin, Inc., 1993).

47. Thomas W. Dunfee, N. Craig Smith, and William T. Ross Jr., "Social Contracts and Marketing Ethics," *Journal of Marketing* 63, no. 3 (July 1999): 14.

48. Robert B. Reich, "Don't Blame Wal-Mart," *New York Times*, February 28, 2005, A25.

49. "Survey: Profit and the Public Good," *Economist*, January 22, 2005, 15.

50. Peter Capella, "Global Elite at Davos Gives Thumbs Down to Economic Focus," *Agence France Presse*, January 26, 2005.

51. Aristotle, *Nicomachean Ethics* [350 B.C.], translated by David Ross (Oxford: Oxford University Press, 1980), Book 3, Part VII.

52. For example, Frances Moore Lappé, *Democracy's Edge: Choosing to Save Our Country by Bringing Democracy to Life* (San Francisco: Jossey-Bass, 2006).

CHAPTER 2

1. Paul Solman, "Attention Shoppers: Paul Solman Reports on Consumer Activity in the Wake of the September 11th Attacks," *NewsHour with Jim Lehrer*, PBS, October 19, 2001, <http://www.pbs.org/hewshour/bb/business/july-dec01/shop_10-19.html>.

2. U.S. Census Bureau and Bureau of Labor Statistics, *Consumer Expenditures in 2004* (Washington, DC: U.S. Department of Labor, 2006). Note that there are differences in how GDP and household expenditures are calculated; for example, the former includes the rental value of owner-occupied housing.

3. For other examples, see William L. Wilkie and Elizabeth S. Moore, "Marketing's Contribution to Society," *Journal of Marketing* 63, Special Issue (1999): 198–218.

4. Louis Uchitelle, "We Pledge Allegiance to the Mall," *New York Times*, December 6, 2004, 12.

5. National Association of Home Builders, *Housing Facts, Figures and Trends 2004* (Washington, DC: National Association of Home Builders, 2004).

6. Bureau of Labor Statistics, *Consumer Expenditures in 2003* (Washington, DC: U.S. Department of Labor, 2004).

7. David Welch, "Sorry, Detroit, the Garage Is Full: Demand May Slow as Rates Rise and Incentives Fall," *BusinessWeek*, December 6, 2004, 40.

8. John Quelch, "Too Much Stuff," in *The World in 2002* (London: The Economist, 2001), 32.

9. Diana Fong, "A Rental Nation: Germans Looking to Buy Those Four Walls," *Deutsche Welle*, September 5, 2006, <http://www.dw-world.de>.

10. Paul Taylor, Cary Funk, and Peyton Craighill, "Once Again, the Future Ain't What It Used to Be," Social Trends, Pew Research Center, Washington, DC, May 2, 2006.

11. Martin Fackler, "Japan Looks to Its Savers to Consume," *New York Times*, July 11, 2006, 1.

12. Uchitelle, "We Pledge Allegiance to the Mall."

13. Ted Conover, "Capitalist Roaders," *New York Times*, July 2, 2006, 6.30.

14. Susan Sontag, "AIDS and Its Metaphors," [1989] in *The Columbia World of Quotations*, edited by Robert Andrew, Mary Biggs, and Michael Seidel (New York: Columbia University Press, 1996).

15. B. Wansink, "Can Package Size Accelerate Usage Volume?" *Journal of Marketing* 60, no. 3 (July 1996): 1–14. B. Wansink, R. J. Kent, and S. J. Hoch, "An Anchoring and Adjustment Model of Purchase Quantity Decisions," *Journal of Marketing Research* 35, no. 1 (February 1998): 71–81. B. Wansink and J. M. Gilmore, "New Uses That Revitalize Old Brands," *Journal of Advertising Research* 39, no. 2 (March–April 1999): 90–98. B. Wansink and S. B. Park, "Sensory Suggestiveness and Labeling: Do Soy Labels Bias Taste?" *Journal of Sensory Studies* 17, no. 5 (November 2002): 483–491. B. Wansink and K. Van Ittersum, "Bottoms Up! The Influence of Elongation on Pouring and Consumption Volume," *Journal of Consumer Research* 30, no. 3 (December 2003): 455–463.

16. V. R. Nijs et al., "The Category-Demand Effects of Price Promotions," *Marketing Science* 20, no. 1 (Winter 2001): 1–22.

17. Marnik G. Dekimpe and Dominique M. Hanssens, "Sustained Spending and Persistent Response: A New Look at Long-Term Marketing Profitability," *Journal of Marketing Research* 36, no. 4 (November 1999): 397–412.

18. Enforcing Statutes of Apparel (1574), Book of Proclamations, 154, 16 Elizabeth I, 15 June <http://www.elizabethan.org/sumptuary/who-wears-what.html>.

19. Sumptuary Laws (1651), Colonial Laws of Massachusetts, <http://www.personal.pitnet .net/primarysources/sumptuary.html>.

20. Franklin D. Roosevelt, "Second Acceptance Speech 'Rendez Vous with Destiny,'" [1936] in *FDR Speaks: Authorized Edition of Speeches, 1933–1945*, edited by Henry S. Commager (Washington Records, Inc, 1960), in *Columbia World of Quotations*, edited by Robert Andrews, Mary Biggs, and Michael Seidel (New York: Columbia University Press, 1996).

21. Robert B. Avery, Paul S. Calem, and Glenn B. Canner, "Credit Report Accuracy and Access to Credit," *Federal Reserve Bulletin* (Summer 2004): 297–322.

22. Ana M. Aizcorbe, Arthur B. Kennickell, and Kevin B. Moore, "Recent Changes in U.S. Family Finances: Evidence from the 1998 and 2001 Survey of Consumer Finances," *Federal Reserve Bulletin* (January 2003): 32.

23. Brian K. Bucks, Arthur B. Kennickell, and Kevin B. Moore, "Recent Changes in U.S. Family Finances: Evidence from the 2001 and 2004 Surveys of Consumer Finances," *Federal Reserve Bulletin* 92 (February 2006): A1–A38.

24. Malcolm Gladwell, "The Coolhunt," *New Yorker*, March 17, 1997.

25. See Susan M. Gianinno, "Is Populism Death for Luxury? There Is Opportunity for High-End, Value Brands That Embrace Democratic Trend," *Advertising Age*, October 4, 2004, 36. Michael J. Silverstein and Neil Fiske, "Luxury for the Masses," *Harvard Business Review* 81, no. 4 (April 2003). After several years of courting younger, less affluent customers via inexpensive products, Tiffany reversed direction to maintain its brand cachet. See Ellen Byron, "Fashion Victim: To Refurbish Its Image, Tiffany Risks Profits: After Silver Took Off, Jeweler Raises Prices to Discourage Teens," *Wall Street Journal*, January 10, 2007, A1.

26. See Bradley Hitchings, "Before You Buy, Learn the ABC's of Hi-Fi Equipment," *Business-Week*, February 13, 1978, 101. Jerry Tortorella, "Hi-Fi's Latest Lure," *BusinessWeek*, March 16, 1981, 40.

27. "The Future of Fast Fashion," *Economist*, June 16, 2005.

28. Michael Booth, "Imixing Your Music: Apple Pushes Synergy with Idea of iTunes Playlists," *Denver Post*, 2004, F.01. Gideon D'Archangelo, "Profile: Personal Playlists Online," *Marketplace Morning Report*, Minnesota Public Radio, January 6, 2005.

29. Daniel J. Boorstin, *Americans: The Democratic Experience* (New York: Random House, 1973), 90.

30. Ibid., 90.

31. Russell W. Belk, "Possessions and the Extended Self," *Journal of Consumer Research* 15, no. 2 (September 1988): 139–168.

32. Ibid., 139.

33. William Shakespeare, *As You Like It* [1600], Act 4, Scene 1, <http://www.shakespeare.mit .edu/asyoulikeit/index.html>.

34. Donald E. Frey, "The Puritan Roots of Daniel Raymond's Economics," *History of Political Economy* 32, no. 3 (Fall 2000): 607–629.

35. John Blake, "Cashing In on the Faithful: Some Pastors Adopt Strong-Arm Tactics to Shame Parishioners into Selling Out," *Atlanta Journal-Constitution*, April 27, 2002, B.1.

36. Juliet B. Schor, *Born to Buy: The Commercialized Child and the New Consumer Culture* (New York: Scribner, 2004).

37. Ibid., 11.

38. See Jason Hoffe, Kevin Lane, and Victoria Miller Nam, "Branding Cars in China," *McKinsey Quarterly*, Special Edition (2003): 14. "China Forum Stirs Debate on Sustainable Growth: Retailers Are Checking Out Chinese Consumers' New Eagerness to Spend," *Knowledge@Wharton*, May 18–21, 2005, <http://www.knowledge.wharton.upenn.edu/weblink/130.cfm>.

39. Robert Biswas, Ed Diener, and Maya Tamir, "The Psychology of Subjective Well-Being," *Daedalus* 133, no. 2 (Spring 2004): 18–25. Ed Diener and Martin E. P. Seligman, "Beyond Money: Toward an Economy of Well-Being," *Psychological Science in the Public Interest* 5, no. 1 (2004): 1–31. Schor, *Born to Buy*.

40. See, for example, Diener and Seligman, "Beyond Money: Toward an Economy of Well-Being." Richard Easterlin, "The Economics of Happiness," *Daedalus* 133, no. 2 (Spring 2004): 26–33. Robert H. Frank, "How Not to Buy Happiness," *Daedalus* 133, no. 2 (Spring 2004): 69–79. Carol Graham and Sandip Sukhtankar, "Is Economic Crisis Reducing Support for Markets and Democracy in Latin America? Some Evidence from the Economics of Happiness," working paper no. 30, Center on Social and Economic Dynamics, Brookings Institution, Washington, DC, November 2002. Andrew Eggers, Clifford Gaddy, and Carol Graham, "Well Being and Unemployment in Russia in the 1990's: Can Society's Suffering Be Individuals' Solace?" Center on Social and Economic Dynamics, Brookings Institution, Washington, DC, April 2004.

41. For a review of this research, see Diener and Seligman, "Beyond Money: Toward an Economy of Well-Being." Daniel Kahneman et al., "Toward National Well-Being Accounts," *American Economic Review* 94, no. 2 (May 2004): 429–434.

42. Diener and Seligman, "Beyond Money: Toward an Economy of Well-Being."

43. Ibid.

44. Biswas, Diener, and Tamir, "The Psychology of Subjective Well-Being."

45. Diener and Seligman, "Beyond Money: Toward an Economy of Well-Being." Easterlin, "The Economics of Happiness."

46. Frank, "How Not to Buy Happiness."

47. Paul R. Lawrence and Nitin Nohria, *Driven: How Human Nature Shapes Our Choices* (San Francisco: Jossey-Bass, 2002).

48. Thorstein Veblen, *The Theory of the Leisure Class, with the Addition of a Review by William Dean Howells* [1899] (New York: Augustus M. Kelley, 1975).

49. Alan B. Krueger, "Economic Scene: It Turns Out Thorstein Veblen Was Right: A Princeton Doctoral Thesis Says Rich People Spend More on Conspicuous Things," *New York Times*, January 6, 2005, C2.

50. Frank, "How Not to Buy Happiness," 69.

51. Jeremy Rifkin, *The European Dream: How Europe's Vision of the Future Is Quietly Eclipsing the American Dream* (New York: Jeremy P. Tarcher/Penguin, 2004).

52. Po Bronson, "Just Sit Back and Relax!" *Time*, June 26, 2006, 78.

53. Biswas, Diener, and Tamir, "The Psychology of Subjective Well-Being."

54. Brady E. Hamilton et al., "Final Births for 2004," Health E-stats, National Center for Health Statistics, Hyattsville, MD, July 6, 2006, <http://www.cdc.gov/nchs/products/pubs/pubd/hestats/finalbirths04/finalbirths04.htm>.

55. Caitlin Flanagan, "Bringing Up Baby: Parents Spend Billions to Keep Their Children Safe and Happy," *New Yorker*, November 15, 2004, 46–52.

56. Daniel Kahneman et al., "A Survey Method for Characterizing Daily Life Experience: The Day Reconstruction Method," *Science* 306, no. 5702 (December 3, 2004): 1776–1780. Note that intimate relations and socializing with friends were rated as the most enjoyable activities.

57. Adam Smith, "The Wealth of Nations," [1776] in *The Essential Adam Smith*, edited by Robert L. Heilbroner (New York: W.W. Norton & Company, 1986), 241.

58. Albert Ando and Franco Modigliani, "The 'Life Cycle' Hypothesis of Saving: Aggregate Implication and Tests," *American Economic Review* 53, no. 1 (March 1963): 55–84.

59. On average, U.S. consumers in the lowest income quintile spend more than they earn in a year. Although some cases may reflect unreported income or other reasons, some of these consumers are students using loans and others are retirees cashing in on assets, according to Abby Duly, "Consumer Spending for Necessities," *Consumer Expenditure Survey Anthology* (Washington, DC: Bureau of Labor Statistics, 2003), 35–38, <www.bls.gov/cex/csxanthol03.htm>.

60. See Martin Browning and Thomas F. Crossley, "The Life-Cycle Model of Consumption and Saving," *Journal of Economic Perspectives* 15, no. 3 (Summer 2001): 3–22.

61. Gary Burtless, "Social Norms, Rules of Thumb, and Retirement: Evidence for Rationality in Retirement Planning," CSED working paper, CSED #37, Brookings Institution, Washington, DC, October 2004. F. Thomas Juster et al., "The Decline in Household Saving and the Wealth Effect," Finance and Economics Discussion Series papers, no. 2004-32, Federal Reserve Board, Washington, DC, June 2004.

62. Burtless, "Social Norms, Rules of Thumb, and Retirement."

63. Michael D. Hurd and Susann Rohwedder, "Some Answers to the Retirement-Consumption Puzzle," NBER working paper no. 12057, National Bureau of Economic Research, Cambridge, MA, February 2006.

64. See Michael J. Mandel, "Our Hidden Savings: Americans Don't Set Much Aside, but Include R&D and Education and the Picture Changes," *BusinessWeek*, January 17, 2005, 34–36.

65. Ross Harvey, "Comparison of Household Saving Ratios—Euro Area/United States/Japan," Statistics Brief, Organisation for Economic Co-operation and Development, Paris, June 2004. These are standardized ratios.

66. Bureau of Economic Analysis, "Personal Incomes and Outlays: December 2006," news release, U.S. Department of Commerce, Washington, DC, February 1, 2007, <http://www.bea.gov/newsreleases/national/pi/pinewsrelease.htm>.

67. Harvey, "Comparison of Household Saving Ratios—Euro Area/United States/Japan."

68. Ibid.

69. Aizcorbe, Kennickell, and Moore, "Recent Changes in U.S. Family Finances."

70. Alan Greenspan, "Understanding Household Debt Obligations" (paper presented at Credit Union National Association conference, 2004 Governmental Affairs Conference, Washington, DC, 2004).

71. Aizcorbe, Kennickell, and Moore, "Recent Changes in U.S. Family Finances."

72. Juster et al., "The Decline in Household Saving and the Wealth Effect."

73. Ibid.

74. Greenspan, "Understanding Household Debt Obligations."

75. Joint Center for Housing Studies of Harvard University, "Remodeling Spending Hits New High," press release, January 13, 2005.

76. Administrative Office of the U.S. Courts, "Number of Bankruptcy Cases Filed in Federal Courts Down Less Than One Percent," news release, Washington, DC, August 27, 2004.

77. Industry Canada, "Canadian Bankruptcy Statistics (1980–2004)," <www.bankruptcycanada.com>. U.S. ratio is adjusted for percentage of joint filings by husband and wife.

78. Elizabeth Warren, "Financial Collapse and Class Status: Who Goes Bankrupt?" *Osgoode Hall Law Review* 41, no. 1 (Spring 2003): 114.

79. Elizabeth Warren, "A Growing Army of Bankrupts: Is There Any Way to Stop the Rising Filings?" *Credit World* 79, no. 1 (September/October 1990): 18–20.

80. David B. Gross and Nicholas S. Souleles, "An Empirical Analysis of Personal Bankruptcy and Delinquency," Wharton FIC working paper no. 98-28-B, University of Pennsylvania, Wharton School, Philadelphia, PA, November 1999. Todd J. Zywicki, "An Economic Analysis of the Consumer Bankruptcy Crisis," Law and Economics working paper series, No. 04-35, George Mason University School of Law, Arlington, VA, 2004.

81. Igor Livshits, James MacGee, and Michele Tertilt, "Consumer Bankruptcy: A Fresh Start," working paper no. 617, Federal Reserve Bank of Minneapolis, Minneapolis, MN, January 2003.

82. Avery, Calem, and Canner, "Credit Report Accuracy and Access to Credit."

83. John Price and Guillaume Corpart-Muller, "Mexico's Economic Performance: Boring Is Beautiful," *InfoAmericas Tendencias*, no. 50 (November 17, 2004).

84. Henry D. Thoreau, *Walden* [1845], <http:www.//thoreau.eserver.org>, Economy chapter.

85. See Duane Elgin, "Voluntary Simplicity and the New Global Challenge," in *The Consumer Society Reader*, edited by Juliet B. Schor and Douglas B. Holt (New York: The New Press, 2000), 397–413.

86. John Tagliabue, "Sometimes Slowing Down Can Really Get Hectic," *New York Times*, June 7, 2002, 4. "Endangered Species: Slow Food," *New York Times*, July 26, 2003, 9.

87. Tagliabue, "Sometimes Slowing Down Can Really Get Hectic."

88. Meg Jacobs, "The Politics of Plenty in the Twentieth-Century United States," in *The Politics of Consumption: Material Culture and Citizenship in Europe and America*, edited by Martin Daunton and Matthew Hilton (New York: Oxford, 2001), 223–239. Frank Trentmann, "Bread, Milk and Democracy: Consumption and Citizenship in Twentieth-Century Britain," in *The Politics of Consumption*, ibid., 129–161.

89. Hartmut Berghoff, "Enticement and Deprivation: The Regulation of Consumption in Pre-War Nazi Germany," in *The Politics of Consumption*, ibid., 165–184.

90. British Petroleum, *Statistical Review of World Energy* (London: BP, 2004), <http://www.bp.com>. World Bank, "Population 2003," World Development Indicators, World Bank, September 2004, <http://www.web.worldbank.org>.

91. Nat Ives, "Kraft Foods to Stop Some Children's Ads," *New York Times*, January 13, 2005, 9.

CHAPTER 3

1. Barry Schwartz, *The Paradox of Choice: Why More Is Less* (New York: HarperCollins, 2004).

2. Aristotle, *Nicomachean Ethics* [350 B.C.], translated by David Ross (Oxford: Oxford University Press, 1980), Book 6.

3. Paul R. Lawrence and Nitin Nohria, *Driven: How Human Nature Shapes Our Choices* (San Francisco: Jossey-Bass, 2002). Abraham H. Maslow, *Motivation and Personality* (New York: Harper, 1954).

4. William G. Huitt, "Maslow's Hierarchy of Needs," Educational Psychology Interactive, Valdosta State University, Valdosta, GA, 2004, <http://www.chiron.valdosta.edu/whuitt/col/regsys/maslow.html>.

5. Ibid.

6. See Jerry Z. Muller, *The Mind and the Market: Capitalism in Modern European Thought* (New York: Alfred A. Knopf, 2002), 156–159.

7. Edward L. Deci, *The Psychology of Self-Determination* (Lexington, MA: Lexington Books, 1980). Edward L. Deci and Richard M. Ryan, *Intrinsic Motivation and Self-Determination in Human Behavior* (New York: Plenum, 1985).

8. Samuel Johnson, 1783 entry, in James Boswell, *Boswell's Life of Johnson, Abridged and Edited* [1791], edited by Charles Grosvenor Osgood (New York: Scribner's Sons, 1917), reprinted as *The Project Gutenberg EBook Life of Johnson*, <http://www.gutenberg.org/etext/1564>.

9. Sheena S. Iyengar and Mark R. Lepper, "Rethinking the Value of Choice: A Cultural Perspective on Intrinsic Motivation," *Journal of Personality and Social Psychology* 76, no. 3 (March 1999): 349–366.

10. Elke U. Weber and Christopher K. Hsee, "Models and Mosaics: Investigating Cross-Cultural Differences in Risk Perception and Risk Preference," *Psychonomic Bulletin & Review* 6, no. 4 (December 1999): 611–617.

11. Ibid.

12. Jamie Harper, "The Coca-Cola Company: The Global Teenager Project," Case 1-595-065 (Boston: Harvard Business School, 1996).

13. Pierre Bourdieu, *Distinction: A Social Critique of the Judgement of Taste* [1979], translated by Richard Nice (London: Routledge and Kegan Paul, 1986). Jeremy F. Lane, *Pierre Bourdieu: A Critical Introduction*, series ed. Keith Reader (London: Pluto Press, 2000).

14. Alexis de Tocqueville, *Democracy in America* [1835], translated by Harvey C. Mansfield and Delba Winthrop (Chicago: University of Chicago Press, 2000).

15. Naomi Klein, "Interview," *Frontline: The Persuaders*, PBS, January 22, 2004, <http://www.pbs.org/wgbh/pages/frontline/shows/persuaders/interviews>.

16. See David Barboza, "China: A Big Supplier Becomes a Big Consumer, Too," *New York Times*, December 6, 2004, 6.

17. Wroe Alderson, "The Analytical Framework for Marketing," [1958] in *Marketing Classics: A Selection of Influential Articles*, edited by Ben M. Enis, Keith K. Cox, and Michael P. Mokwa (Upper Saddle River, NJ: Prentice Hall, 1990), 15–28, 23.

18. Clotaire Rapaille, "Interview," *Frontline: The Persuaders*, PBS, December 15, 2003, <http://www.pbs.org/wgbh/pages/frontline/shows/persuaders/interviews>. Sandra Blakeslee, "If Your Brain Has a 'Buy Button,' What Pushes It?" *New York Times*, October 19, 2004.

19. Patrick Barwise and Sean Meehan, *Simply Better* (Boston: Harvard Business School Press, 2004).

20. Clayton M. Christensen and Michael Overdorf, "Meeting the Challenge of Disruptive Change," *Harvard Business Review* (March 2000).

21. Aristotle, *Nicomachean Ethics*, Book 6.

22. Peter R. Dickson and Alan G. Sawyer, "The Price Knowledge and Search of Supermarket Shoppers," *Journal of Marketing* 54, no. 3 (July 1990): 42.

23. Eric Lapersonne, Gilles Laurent, and Jean-Jacques Le Goff, "Consideration Sets of Size One: An Empirical Investigation of Automobile Purchases," *International Journal of Research in Marketing* 12, no. 1 (May 1995): 55–66.

24. J. Jeffrey Inman and Russell S. Winer, "Where the Rubber Meets the Road: A Model of In-Store Consumer Decision Making," working paper no. 98-122, Marketing Science Institute, Cambridge, MA, 1998.

25. Malcolm Gladwell, *Blink: The Power of Thinking without Thinking* (New York: Little, Brown and Co., 2005).

26. A. C. Nielsen, "Half of How Consumers Differentiate between Brands Is Based on 'Habit' with Only 50% Based on Specific Brand Knowledge," press release, May 20, 2004, <http://www2.acnielsen.com/news/20040520_ap.shtml>.

27. Schwartz, *The Paradox of Choice: Why More Is Less.*

28. Ibid.

29. For examples of common "decision traps," see J. Edward Russo and Paul J. H. Shoemaker, *Decision Traps: Ten Barriers to Brilliant Decision-Making and How to Overcome Them* (New York: Simon & Schuster, 1990).

30. Seminal work in this area is Amos Tversky and Daniel Kahneman, "Judgment under Uncertainty: Heuristics and Biases," *Science* 185, no. 4157 (September 27, 1974): 1124–1131. Daniel Kahneman and Amos Tversky, "Prospect Theory: An Analysis of Decision under Risk," *Econometrica* 47, no. 2 (March 1979): 263–292. Daniel Kahneman and Amos Tversky, "Choices, Values, and Frames," *American Psychologist* 39, no. 4 (April 1984): 341–350.

31. Jacob Jacoby, George J. Szybillo, and Jacqueline Busato-Schach, "Information Acquisition in Brand Choice Situations," *Journal of Consumer Research* 3, no. 4 (March 1977): 209–216.

32. There is extensive literature on such choice effects and whether or not they are the result of rational decisions. For example, see Joel Huber and Christopher Puto, "Market Boundaries and Product Choice: Illustrating Attraction and Substitution Effects," *Journal of Consumer Research* 10, no. 1 (June 1983): 31–44. Srinivasan Ratneshwar, Allan D. Shocker, and David W. Stewart, "Toward Understanding the Attraction Effect: The Implications of Product Stimulus Meaningfulness and Familiarity," *Journal of Consumer Research* 13, no. 4 (March 1987): 520–533. Itamar Simonson, "Choice Based on Reasons: The Case of Attraction and Compromise Effects," *Journal of Marketing Research* 16, no. 2 (September 1989): 158–174. Birger Wernerfelt, "A Rational Reconstruction of the Compromise Effect: Using Market Data to Infer Utilities," *Journal of Consumer Research* 31, no. 4 (March 1995): 627–633. A. V. Muthukrishnan and Luc Wathieu, "Superfluous Choices and Persistent Brand Preferences," working paper no. 05-032, Division of Research, Harvard Business School, Boston, 2004. Itamar Simonson, "In Defense of Consciousness: The Role of Conscious and Unconscious Inputs in Consumer Choice," *Journal of Consumer Psychology* 15, no. 3 (2005): 211–217.

33. Schwartz, *The Paradox of Choice: Why More Is Less.*

34. George Moore, *The Bending of the Bough*, Act iv, quoted in *Familiar Quotations*, 10th ed., revised and enlarged by Nathan Haskell Dole (Boston: Little, Brown, 1919), <www.bartleby.com /100/>.

35. D. J. Reibstein, S. A. Youngblood, and H. L. Fromkin, "Number of Choices and Perceived Decision Freedom as a Determinant of Satisfaction and Consumer-Behavior," *Journal of Applied Psychology* 60, no. 4 (August 1975): 434–437.

36. Sheena S. Iyengar and Mark R. Lepper, "When Choice Is Demotivating: Can One Desire Too Much of a Good Thing?" *Journal of Personality and Social Psychology* 79, no. 6 (December 2000): 995–1006.

37. Ibid.

38. Jonathan Clements, "What Privatizing Social Security Would Mean for Your Retirement Plans," *Wall Street Journal*, November 24, 2004, D1.

39. "Crowned at Last: A Survey of Consumer Power," *Economist*, April 2, 2005, 1–15.

40. Peter Boatwright and Joseph C. Nunes, "Reducing Assortment: An Attribute-Based Approach," *Journal of Marketing* 65, no. 3 (July 2001): 50–63.

41. Dell, <www.dell.com>.

42. Cynthia Huffman and Barbara Kahn, "Variety for Sale: Mass Customization or Mass Confusion?" *Journal of Retailing* 74, no. 4 (Fall 1998): 491–513.

43. For a discussion of these techniques, see Luc Wathieu et al., "Consumer Control and Empowerment: A Primer," *Marketing Letters* 13, no. 3 (August 2002): 297–305.

44. Monica Langley, Ian McDonald, and Theo Francis, "Marsh Faces $500 Million in Penalties: Settlement over Bid-Rigging Is Likely to Include Disgorgement of 'Contingent Commissions,'" *Wall Street Journal*, October 28, 2004, C1.

45. John Stuart Mill, *Considerations on Representative Government* (New York: Harper & Brothers, 1862), <http://www.mtholyoke.edu/acad/polit/damy/articles/jsmill.htm>, chapter 7.

46. Surowiecki argues that in many circumstances, group decisions are best: James Surowiecki, *The Wisdom of Crowds* (New York: Doubleday, 2004).

47. Adam Przeworski, "Freedom to Choose and Democracy," *Economics and Philosophy* 19, no. 2 (October 2003): 265–279.

CHAPTER 4

1. David Warsh, *Knowledge and the Wealth of Nations: A Story of Economic Discovery* (New York: W.W. Norton and Company, 2006).

2. Adam Smith, "Lectures on Jurisprudence," [1766] in *The Essential Adam Smith*, edited by Robert L. Heilbroner (New York: W.W. Norton & Company, 1986), 50.

3. Matthew P. McAllister, *The Commercialization of American Culture: New Advertising, Control and Democracy* (Thousand Oaks, CA: Sage Publications, 1996).

4. David Buchan, "Something to Sell Now: Hungarian Advertising," *Financial Times*, June 6, 1985, 34. Clay Harris, "No Rate Cards in E Europe," *Financial Times*, March 1, 1990, 24. Alice Rawsthorn, "Beware the Eastern Promise," *Financial Times*, November 15, 1990, 16.

5. McAllister, *The Commercialization of American Culture*.

6. T. H. Breen, *The Marketplace of Revolution: How Consumer Politics Shaped American Independence* (New York: Oxford University Press, 2004), 53.

7. Rosser Reeves, *Reality in Advertising* (New York: Knopf, 1961), 47.

8. See Gerald Zaltman, "Thinking Market Research: Putting People Back In," *Journal of Marketing Research* 34, no. 4 (November 1997): 424–437.

9. Vance Packard, *The Hidden Persuaders* (New York: McKay, 1957).

10. Leonard M. Lodish et al., "How T.V. Advertising Works: A Meta-Analysis of 389 Real World Split Cable T.V. Advertising Experiments," *Journal of Marketing Research* 32, no. 2 (May 1995): 125–139.

11. Marketing Science Institute, "Measuring and Allocating Marcom Budgets: Seven Expert Points of View," Joint Report, Marketing Science Institute and the University of Michigan Yaffe Center for Persuasive Communication, Cambridge, MA, January 2003.

12. Marcia Angell, *The Truth About the Drug Companies: How They Deceive Us and What to Do About It* (New York: Random House, 2004). Malcolm Gladwell, "High Prices: How to Think About Prescription Drugs," *New Yorker*, October 25, 2004, 86–92.

13. Kevin Roberts, "Interview," *Frontline: The Persuaders*, PBS, December 15, 2003, <http://www.pbs.org/wgbh/pages/frontline/shows/persuaders/interviews>.

14. For a summary of the debate, see Mark S. Albion and Paul W. Farris, *The Advertising Controversy: Evidence on the Economic Effects of Advertising* (Boston: Auburn House Publishing Company, 1981).

15. Antitrust cases tend to focus not on advertising but rather on other industry practices, such as exclusive arrangements with suppliers and distributors. New brands and new firms typically need to advertise heavily when they enter the market, and established firms often counter by boosting their own advertising in an attempt to drown them out; nevertheless, many new entrants succeed.

16. In the consumer mass market, heavily advertised, branded products cost more than unadvertised second-tier or private-label products, even though quality differences may be minimal. On the other hand, without informational efficiencies created by advertising, all prices might go up. It is difficult to say what would happen to consumer prices in heavily advertised product categories if leading firms cut back across the board on advertising. First, few firms have dared to experiment in this way for a sustained period. Second, decreases in advertising tend to go hand in hand with other events, such as general economic slowdowns, making it difficult to untangle the effects.

17. George A. Akerlof, "The Market for 'Lemons': Quality Uncertainty and the Market Mechanism," *Quarterly Journal of Economics* 84, no. 3 (1970): 488–500. In the used-car market, suspicious buyers offer low prices for fear of getting a lemon or go to the new-car market instead. Low selling prices are not attractive to suppliers of good used cars, so dealers end up with a disproportionate number of lemons.

18. Phillip Nelson, "Advertising as Information," *Journal of Political Economy* 82, no. 4 (July/August 1974): 729–754.

19. Jason Hoffe, Kevin Lane, and Victoria Miller Nam, "Branding Cars in China," *McKinsey Quarterly*, Special Edition (2003): 14.

20. Adam Nagourney and Janet Elder, "Americans Show Clear Concerns on Bush Agenda," *New York Times*, November 23, 2004.

21. Quoted in Kate MacArthur, "Drucker—Author, Scholar and Prophet—Dead at 95: Father of Management Theory Has Profound Impact," *Advertising Age*, November 21, 2005, 11.

22. Craig N. Smith and John Quelch, *Ethics in Marketing* (Homewood, IL: Richard D. Irwin, Inc., 1993), 145.

23. CASRO, "U.S. Government Supports Survey Research," *Research & Regulation* 1, no. 2 (November 2004): 2.

24. Sarah Nassauer, "Personal Is Political in France: Marketer's Queries on Minorities' Habits Test Nation's Self Image," *Wall Street Journal*, May 18, 2005, A12.

25. CASRO, "'Fruggers' Join 'Suggers' in FTC Regulations," *Research & Regulation* 1, no. 1 (September 2004): 1.

26. Smith and Quelch, *Ethics in Marketing*, 171.

27. Pew/Internet, "86% of Internet Users Want to Prohibit Online Companies from Disclosing Their Personal Information without Permission," press release, Pew Internet & American Life Project, Washington, DC, August 21, 2000. Harris Interactive, "Consumer Privacy Attitudes and Behavior Survey, Wave 1," The Privacy Leadership Initiative, 2001.

28. Bob Chatham, "Online Privacy Concerns: More Than Hype," Trends, Forrester, Cambridge, MA, March 30, 2004.

29. Attributed to Italo Calvino, <http://www.brainyquote.com/quotes/quotes/i/italocalvi156560 .html>.

30. Alan F. Westin, "Social and Political Dimensions of Privacy," *Journal of Social Issues* 59, no. 2 (2003): 431–453.

31. Ibid., 434.

32. Ibid.

33. Rajiv Lal and Patricia Martone Carrolo, "Harrah's Entertainment Inc.," case 9-502-011 (Boston: Harvard Business School, 2004),12.

34. "Radioshack Ends Asking for Customer Info," *Dallas Business Journal*, November 25, 2002.

35. Stephanie Kirchgaessner and Bob Sherwood, "Companies Selling Personal Information Have Been Allowed to Operate Relatively Free of Regulation: Public Concern at Identity Theft Means That May Change," *Financial Times*, May 20, 2005, 17.

36. Kevin J. Delaney, "Identity Theft Made Easier: Hackers Use Simple Tricks with Google, Yahoo Searches to Tap Personal Information," *Wall Street Journal*, March 29, 2005, B1.

37. Associated Press, "A List of AIDS Names Is Mailed in Error," *New York Times*, February 21, 2005, 16.

38. Heather Timmons, "Security Breach at LexisNexis Now Appears Larger," *New York Times*, April 13, 2005. Also, Tom Zeller Jr., "Westlaw to Curtail Access to Personal Data," *New York Times*, March 18, 2005, C4.

39. Tom Zeller Jr., "U.P.S. Loses a Shipment of Citigroup Client Data," *New York Times*, June 7, 2005, C1.

40. Chatham, "Online Privacy Concerns: More Than Hype."

41. Mary J. Culnan and Robert J. Bies, "Consumer Privacy: Balancing Economic and Justice Considerations," *Journal of Social Issues* 59, no. 2 (2003): 323–342.

42. Franklin D. Roosevelt, "Second Acceptance Speech 'Rendez Vous with Destiny,'" [1936] in *FDR Speaks: Authorized Edition of Speeches, 1933-1945*, edited by Henry S. Commager (Washington Records, Inc, 1960), in *Columbia World of Quotations*, edited by Robert Andrews, Mary Biggs, and Michael Seidel (New York: Columbia University Press, 1996).

43. Dorothy Cohen, "Advertising and the First Amendment," *Journal of Marketing* 42, no. 3 (July 1978): 59–68.

44. Karl A. Boedecker, Fred W. Morgan, and Linda Berns Wright, "The Evolution of First Amendment Protection for Commercial Speech," *Journal of Marketing* 59, no. 1 (January 1995): 38–47.

45. Ibid. In any particular case, the Court might consider such issues as the message sender's right to communicate with target markets or the general public; the message receiver's right to receive information about products and choices, to ignore information, or not to be aggressively exposed to information; the content of the message (information versus persuasion, product information versus corporate image versus general information); and the medium used by the marketer, including its intrusiveness, pervasiveness, and substitutability with alternative media.

46. ANA Government Relations, *The Role of Advertising in America* (Washington, DC: Association of National Advertisers, 2005), <http://www.ana.net/gov/what/role_of_advertising.cfm>.

47. Monle Lee and Fred Naffziger, "When Deceptive Advertising Is the Ill, Is Corrective Advertising the Cure?" *PanPacific Management Review* 4, no. 1 (February 2001): 111–126. On rare occasions the FTC has mandated corrective remedies to counter deceptive commercial information. In the 1970s, Warner-Lambert, for example, was ordered to spend $10 million on advertisements to correct previous deceptive advertising claims that gargling with Listerine mouthwash would prevent colds and sore throats; however, the corrective advertising accomplished little in overturning fifty years' use of the claim.

48. Susan Hansen, *The USA Patriot Act: A Century Foundation Guide to the Issues* (New York: The Century Foundation, 2004).

49. Westin, "Social and Political Dimensions of Privacy."

50. Federal Trade Commission, "A Summary of Your Rights under the Fair Credit Reporting Act," For the Consumer Page, Washington, DC, 2005, <http://www.ftc.gov/bcp/conline/pubs/credit/fcrasummary.pdf>.

51. An individual's file can include data on where the consumer has lived and worked, bill payment history, credit balances, check writing history, medical records, legal history, and a numerical score computed by the agency to indicate creditworthiness. The FCRA gives consumers the rights to know what is in their file, to ask for a credit score, to dispute incomplete or inaccurate information, and to give permission before a report is provided to employers. The consumer reporting agency must correct or delete inaccurate, incomplete, or unverifiable information and may give the file only to those with a valid need for access. Any business that uses information in a consumer report to deny a consumer's application for credit, employment, insurance, and the like must inform the consumer.

52. Eve M. Caudill and Patrick E. Murphy, "Consumer Online Privacy: Legal and Ethical Issues," *Journal of Public Policy and Marketing* 19, no. 1 (2000): 7–20.

53. Kirchgaessner and Sherwood, "Companies Selling Personal Information Have Been Allowed to Operate Relatively Free of Regulation."

54. John F. Kennedy, "Special Message to the Congress on Protecting the Consumer Interest," *The Public Papers of President John F. Kennedy 1962* (Washington, DC: U.S. Government Printing Office, 1962).

55. Federal Reserve Bank of Philadelphia, *Applying for Credit and Charge Cards* (Philadelphia, PA: Federal Reserve, 2005), <http://www.phil.frb.org/consumers/apply.html>.

56. Caudill and Murphy, "Consumer Online Privacy: Legal and Ethical Issues."

57. George J. Stigler, "The Process and Progress of Economics" (paper presented at Nobel Foundation conference, Nobel Prize Memorial Lecture, Stockholm, Sweden, December 8, 1982), <http://www.nobelprize.org/economics/laureates/1982/stigler-lecture.pdf>.

58. Alex Berenson, "Despite Vow, Drug Makers Still Withhold Data," *New York Times*, May 31, 2005, 1.

59. Ibid.

60. ICC Commission on Marketing Advertising and Distribution, *ICC International Code of Advertising Practice* (Paris: International Chamber of Commerce, 1997), <http://www.iccwbo.org/home/statements_rules/1997/advercod.asp>.

61. The National Advertising Review Board (NARB) and the National Advertising Division (NAD) of the Better Business Bureau.

62. Rita Marie Cain, "Federal Do Not Call Registry Is Here to Stay: What's Next for Direct Marketing Regulation?" *Journal of Interactive Marketing* 19, no. 1 (Winter 2005): 54–61.

63. Federal Trade Commission, "Annual Report to Congress for 2003 and 2004, Pursuant to the Do Not Call Implementation Act on Implementation of the National Do Not Call Registry," FTC Office of Public Affairs, Washington, DC, September 2005. Cain, "Federal Do Not Call Registry Is Here to Stay."

64. Federal Trade Commission, "Privacy Online: Fair Information Practices in the Electronic Marketplace," Report to Congress, FTC Office of Public Affairs, Washington, DC, May 2000. Notice means that individuals are told what information is being collected and how it will be used. Choice means that individuals can object when data is collected for one purpose and used for another or shared with a third party. Access means that individuals can see and correct their information. Security means that organizations should ensure data integrity and protect data from unauthorized access. Redress means that the industry has a mechanism to impose sanctions.

65. Kirchgaessner and Sherwood, "Companies Selling Personal Information Have Been Allowed to Operate Relatively Free of Regulation."

66. Asaf Buchner, "Do Customers Ever Stop Banking Online? In Other Words, Is Attrition a Real Issue?" Clients Have Asked, JupiterResearch, 2005, <www.jupiterresearch.com/bin/item.pl/interact:commentary/jup/id=96297>.

67. Alvin Toffler, *Powershift: Knowledge, Wealth, and Violence at the Edge of the 21st Century* (New York: Bantam Books, 1990), 20.

68. Food and Drug Administration, "Claims That Can Be Made for Conventional Foods and Dietary Supplements," Center for Food Safety and Applied Nutrition, Office of Nutritional Products, Labeling, and Dietary Supplements, Washington, DC, September 2003, <http://www.cfsan.fda.gov/~dms/hclaims.html>.

69. David Leonhardt, "Why That Doggie in the Window Costs a Lot More Than You Think," *New York Times*, May 16, 2005, C5.

70. Reineke Reitsma, "The European Online Consumer: Consumer Technographics Europe," Data Overview, Forrester Research, Cambridge, MA, March 16, 2005.

71. Christopher M. Kelley and John E. McCarthy, "The Chinese and Australians Soak up Broadband: Executive Summary," Trends, Forrester Research, Cambridge, MA, May 2, 2006.

72. Reitsma, "The European Online Consumer: Consumer Technographics Europe."

73. "Crowned at Last: A Survey of Consumer Power," *Economist*, April 2, 2005, 12.

74. Ted Schadler, "Benchmark 2004 Data Overview: Consumer Technographics North America," Data Overview, Forrester Research, Cambridge, MA, June 29, 2004.

75. "The Wi-Fi Debate: Should Cities Be in the Business of Broadband?" *Knowledge@Wharton*, May 18–31, 2005, <http://www.knowledge.wharton.upenn.edu/article/1204.cfm>.

76. Rohit Saran, "To Boldly Go Where . . ." *India Today International*, December 13, 2004, 16–21.

77. Frances Moore Lappé, *Democracy's Edge: Choosing to Save Our Country by Bringing Democracy to Life* (San Francisco: Jossey-Bass, 2006).

CHAPTER 5

1. 1775 entry in James Boswell, *Boswell's Life of Johnson, Abridged and Edited* [1791], edited by Charles Grosvenor Osgood (New York: Scribner's Sons, 1917), The Project Gutenberg EBook Life of Johnson, <http://www.gutenberg.org/etext/1564>.

2. Susan Fournier, "Consumers and Their Brands: Developing Relationship Theory in Consumer Research," *Journal of Consumer Research* 24, no. 4 (March 1998): 343–373.

3. Ibid., 365.

4. Fred Reichheld, "The Microeconomics of Customer Relationships," *MIT Sloan Management Review* 47, no. 2 (Winter 2006): 73–78.

5. Ibid.

6. See Paul Lazarsfeld, Bernard Berelson, and Hazel Gaudet, *The People's Choice*, 2nd ed. (New York: Columbia University Press, 1948). Lawrence F. Feick and Linda L. Price, "The Market Maven: A Diffuser of Marketplace Information," *Journal of Marketing* 51, no. 1 (January 1987): 83–97.

7. Feick and Price, "The Market Maven: A Diffuser of Marketplace Information."

8. Peter N. Golder and Gerard J. Tellis, "Growing, Growing, Gone: Cascades, Diffusion, and Turning Points in the Product Life Cycle," *Marketing Science* 23, no. 2 (Spring 2004): 207–218.

9. Ibid.

10. Keith Crain, "At CBS, Shades of Audi Debacle," *Automotive News*, September 20, 2004, 12.

11. Data from John Goodman, vice chair of TARP Worldwide, Arlington, VA, 2006.

12. Jim Nail, "The Consumer Advertising Backlash," Trends, Forrester Research, Cambridge, MA, May 28, 2004.

13. Nielsen BuzzMetrics, "Consumer-Generated Media Exceeds Traditional Advertising for Influencing Consumer Behavior, Finds Intelliseek Survey," press release, BuzzMetrics, Cincinnati, OH, September 26, 2005, <http://www.nielsenbuzzmetrics.com/release.asp?id=141>.

14. Nancy Koehn, *Brand New: How Entrepreneurs Earned Consumers' Trust from Wedgwood to Dell* (Boston: Harvard Business School Press, 2001), 331. Starbucks, "Company Timeline," Starbucks Coffee Company, Seattle, WA, February 2006, <http://www.starbucks.com/aboutus /Company_Timeline_Feb06.pdf>.

15. "Bedeviling P&G," *BusinessWeek*, July 19, 1982, 64. Zachary Schiller, "P&G Is Still Having a Devil of a Time," *BusinessWeek*, September 11, 1995, 46.

16. David Kesmodel, "Doctors Sue to Shush Online Complaints," *Wall Street Journal*, September 22, 2005, B9A.

17. Gunjan Bagla, "Interactive, Inside Innovator: New Line's Paddison One of the First to See Potential of Web's Global Reach," *Variety*, June 28, 2005.

18. Wendy Kaufman, "Word-of-Mouth Marketing Creates a Buzz," *NPR: Morning Edition*, NPR, April 18, 2006.

19. Robert Berner, "I Sold It through the Grapevine," *BusinessWeek*, May 29, 2006, 32–34.

20. Ibid.

21. For skills marketers need in managing online brand communities, see Gil McWilliam, "Building Stronger Brands through Online Communities," *MIT Sloan Management Review* 41, no. 3 (Spring 2000): 43–54.

22. William Shakespeare, *As You Like It* [1600], Act 2, Scene 7, <http://www.shakespeare.mit .edu/asyoulikeit/index.html>.

23. Organisation for Economic Co-operation and Development, *OECD in Figures: Statistics on the Member Countries*, 2005 ed. (Paris, 2005). Sectoral contributions to gross value added.

24. John Deighton, "The Consumption of Performance," *Journal of Consumer Research* 19, no. 3 (December 1992): 362–372.

25. Spike Feresten, "The Soup Nazi, Episode 116," *Seinfeld*, NBC, November 2, 1995.

26. Michael R. Solomon et al., "A Role Theory Perspective on Dyadic Interactions: The Service Encounter," *Journal of Marketing* 49, no. 1 (Winter 1985): 99–111.

27. Ibid.

28. Procter & Gamble, "Lemon Ice 'Squeezes' out a Victory! America Has Spoken and Lemon

Ice Is the New Flavor of Crest Whitening Expressions Toothpaste," press release, Procter & Gamble, Cincinnati, OH, September 7, 2005.

29. Jim Yardley, "The Chinese Get the Vote, If Only for 'Super Girl,'" *New York Times*, September 4, 2005, 4.3.

30. See Julie Bosman, "An Agency's Worst Nightmare: Ads Created by Users," *New York Times*, May 11, 2006, C2. Rob Walker, "Free Advertising: What Does It Mean When Consumers Become Producers—of Commercials?" *New York Times*, May 28, 2006, 20.

31. Eric von Hippel, *Democratizing Innovation* (Cambridge, MA: MIT Press, 2005), chapter 10.

32. Richard Donkin, "If the Customer Is King, He Deserves a Few More Servants," *Financial Times*, July 12, 2005, 12.

33. Duff McDonald, "Customer, Support Thyself," *Business 2.0*, April 2004, 56.

34. Ibid.

35. Quoted in Robert D. Hof, "The Web for the People," *BusinessWeek*, December 6, 2004, 18.

36. Greg Keizer, "Linux to Ring Up $35 Billion by 2008," *TechWeb*, December 16, 2004, <http://www.techweb.com/wire/55800522>.

37. Quoted in "Getting the Most Value Out of Open Source Software," *Knowledge@Wharton*, March 25, 2004, <http://www.knowledge.wharton.upenn.edu/index.dfm?fa=printArticle&ID=946>.

38. *Wikipedia*, <http://www.wikipedia.org>.

39. *Wikipedia*, <http://www.en.wikipedia.org/wiki/Wikipedia:Overview_FAQ>.

40. Stephen Baker and Heather Green, "Blogs Will Change Your Business," *BusinessWeek*, May 2, 2005, 57–67.

41. Podcasts are radio-type shows that can be created by anyone with audio-editing software and pushed out (much like news feeds) to subscribers' iPods or other music devices.

42. Baker and Green, "Blogs Will Change Your Business."

43. YouTube, "YouTube Fact Sheet," 2007, <http://www.youtube.com/t/fact_sheet>.

44. See Newgrounds, "Numa Numa Dance Page," <http://www.newgrounds.com/portal/view/206373>.

45. Hoover's Inc., *Hoover's Company Profiles* (Austin, TX: Hoover's, 2005), <www.hoovers.com>.

46. Ibid.

47. Quoted in Alex Hutchinson, "The Craigslist We Deserve: Ten Million People Use Craigslist, a Celebrated Bulletin Board, in 175 Cities Worldwide: Why Then, after Nearly a Year, Has Adoption by Plugged-in Ottawans Been, Well, Listless?" *Ottawa Citizen*, September 29, 2005, F1.

48. von Hippel, *Democratizing Innovation*.

49. Lawrence Lessig, *The Future of Ideas: The Fate of the Commons in a Connected World* (New York: Random House, 2001).

50. See interview with Steven Weber in Edward Baker, "Open Source, Open Market for Ideas," *CIO Insight*, July 5, 2005.

51. See G. S. Day, "Continuous Learning About Markets," *California Management Review* 36, no. 4 (Summer 1994): 9–31.

52. Sam Jaffe, "Online Extra: eBay: From Pez to Profits," *BusinessWeek Online*, May 14, 2001, <http://www.businessweek.com/magazine/content/01_20/b3732616.htm>.

53. Ibid. In 2004, gross sales reached $3.3 billion and operating profit exceeded $1 billion. Source: eBay, *2004 Annual Report, Letter to Shareholders*, San Jose, CA, 2004, <http://www.investor.ebay.com>.

54. eBay, *2004 Annual Report, Letter to Shareholders*.

55. Yochai Benkler, "Sharing Nicely: On Shareable Goods and the Emergence of Sharing as a Modality of Economic Production," *Yale Law Journal* 114, no. 2 (November 2004): 273–358.

56. Mark S. Granovetter, "The Strength of Weak Ties," *American Journal of Sociology* 78, no. 6 (May 1978): 1360–1380.

57. Insurance has existed from ancient times but did not become a nearly universal institution until government regulation—first imposed in Massachusetts in 1858—raised public confidence

by driving out swindlers and disreputable companies and instituting fair and honest actuarial tables, policy amounts, and premiums: Daniel J. Boorstin, *Americans: The Democratic Experience* (New York: Random House, 1973), 174–180.

58. This is in addition to identity verification, borrowers' credit histories, and Zopa's practice of reducing risk by spreading loans among a minimum number of borrowers and capping a lender's exposure to any one borrower: Iain S. Bruce, "You Wouldn't Lend Your Money to a Complete Stranger You Met in the Street, So Why Do It on the Internet?" *Sunday Herald*, March 20, 2005, 5.

59. Ibid.

60. Robert D. Hof, "The Power of Us," *BusinessWeek*, June 20, 2005, 75–82.

61. Hutchinson, "The Craigslist We Deserve."

62. Patrick Barwise and Sean Meehan, *Simply Better* (Boston: Harvard Business School Press, 2004).

63. Marc Lacey, "Neglected Poor in Africa Make Their Own Safety Nets," *New York Times*, August 28, 2005, 3.

64. James Madison, "Speech at the Virginia Convention, 1829," in *The Mind of the Founder: Sources of the Political Thought of James Madison*, edited by Marvin Meyers (Indianapolis: Bobbs-Merrill, 1973), 513.

65. Flickr Blog, <http://www.blog.flickr.com/flicrblog/2005/03/yahoo_actually_.html>.

66. Benkler, "Sharing Nicely: On Shareable Goods."

67. For a review of altruism in the economics literature, see Elias L. Khalil, "What Is Altruism?" *Journal of Economic Psychology* 25, no. 1 (February 2004): 97–123. See also Gary S. Becker, "Altruism, Egoism and Genetic Fitness," *Journal of Economic Literature* 14, no. 3 (September 1976): 817–826. Herbert A. Simon, "Altruism and Economics," *American Economic Review* 83, no. 2 (May 1993): 151–161.

68. Robert L. Trivers, "The Evolution of Reciprocal Altruism," *Quarterly Review of Biology* 46, no. 1 (March 1971): 35–57.

69. Flickr Blog, <http://www.blog.flickr.com/flicrblog/2005/03/yahoo_actually_.html>.

70. Larry Sanger, "The Early History of Nupedia and Wikipedia, Part II," From the Recent Past Department, Slashdot, April 19, 2005, <http://www.features.slashdot.org/article.pl?sid=05/04/19/1746205&tid=95>.

71. MSDN, <http://www.msdn.microsoft.com/office>.

72. InnoCentive, <www.innocentive.com>.

73. Forrester Research, "Downloads Did Not Cause the Music Slump, but They Can Cure It," press release, Forrester Research, Cambridge, MA, August 13, 2002.

74. Karen Richardson, "Tracking the Numbers: Street Sleuth: Bankers Hope for a Reprise of 'Bowie Bonds,'" *Wall Street Journal*, August 23, 2005, C1.

75. Jeff Leeds, "Apple, Digital Music's Angel, Earns Record Industry's Scorn," *New York Times*, August 27, 2005, A1.

76. Tip O'Neill, *All Politics Is Local and Other Rules of the Game* (New York: Times Books, 1994).

77. Joshua Cohen, "Secondary Associations and Democratic Governance," *Politics and Society* 20, no. 4 (December 1992): 393–472.

78. All this money came from single donors, who legally could contribute at most $2,000 to any one candidate. From January 2003 through July 2004, the Bush–Cheney campaign and the Republican National Committee raised more than $487 million; the Kerry–Edwards campaign and the Democratic National Committee raised about $387 million. See Glen Justice, "Money: No Object," *New York Times*, September 5, 2004, 4.5.

79. Pew Research Center for the People and the Press, "The Dean Activists: Their Profile and Prospects: An In-Depth Look," Survey Reports, Pew Research Center, Washington, DC, April 6, 2005, <http://www.people-press.org/reports/pdf/240.pdf>.

80. Michael Cornfield et al., "Buzz, Blogs and Beyond: The Internet and the National Discourse in the Fall of 2004," Preliminary Report, Pew Internet & American Life Project/BuzzMetrics, Washington, DC, May 16, 2005, 33.

CHAPTER 6

1. C. K. Prahalad and Allen L. Hammond, "Serving the World's Poor, Profitably," *Harvard Business Review* 80, no. 9 (September 2002): 48–57, 6.

2. George Peterson and Dana Sunblad, "Corporations as Partners in Strengthening Urban Communities," Conference Board, New York, 1995, reprinted in Jaan Elias, ed., "Supermarkets in Inner Cities," Case 9-796-145 (Boston: Harvard Business School, 1998).

3. "Retailing in Eastern Europe: A Shortage of Shopkeepers," *Economist*, April 7, 1990, 82.

4. C. K. Prahalad, *The Fortune at the Bottom of the Pyramid* (Upper Saddle River, NJ: Wharton School Publishing, 2005), 1.

5. Booz-Allen Hamilton, "Creating Value for Emerging Consumers in Retailing: Breaking the Myths About Emerging Consumers, Learning from Small Scale Retailers," study conducted for the Coca-Cola Retailing Research Council in Latin America, Booz-Allen Hamilton, McLean, VA, May 1, 2003.

6. Prahalad and Hammond, "Serving the World's Poor, Profitably."

7. Sharon LaFraniere, "Cellphones Catapult Rural Africa to 21st Century," *New York Times*, August 25, 2005, A1. Nic Fildes, "Mobile-Phone Service Benefits Africa," *Wall Street Journal*, February 16, 2006, B4.

8. Eric Sylvers, "Connecting Developing Nations: Cellphone Firms Turn to the Last Big Market," *International Herald Tribune*, February 17, 2006, 1.

9. David J. Arnold and John A. Quelch, "New Strategies in Emerging Markets," *Sloan Management Review* 40, no. 1 (Fall 1998): 7–20, 9.

10. LaFraniere, "Cellphones Catapult Rural Africa to 21st Century."

11. Anne Trafton, "$100 Laptop Idea Taking Off," MIT News Office, Massachusetts Institute of Technology, Cambridge, MA, October 5, 2005.

12. Sylvers, "Connecting Developing Nations: Cellphone Firms Turn to the Last Big Market."

13. Allen L. Hammond and C. K. Prahalad, "Selling to the Poor," *Foreign Policy*, no. 142 (May/June 2004): 30–37.

14. "Wholesale Supermarket Opens in Delta," *Vietnam Investment Review*, September 20, 2004, 19. Ngoc Mai, "Wholesale Giant Boosts Local Operation," *Vietnam Investment Review*, October 18, 2004, 6.

15. Booz-Allen Hamilton, "Creating Value for Emerging Consumers in Retailing."

16. Ibid., 2.

17. Carl Mortished, "Unilever Cleans Up by Learning How to Sell to the Poorest of the World," *Times*, December 10, 2005, 64.

18. Booz-Allen Hamilton, "Creating Value for Emerging Consumers in Retailing."

19. Wilson A. Jacome, Luis E. Loria, and Luis Reyes, "Multiahorro: Successful Business Model Innovations to Better Serve BOP Customer Needs for Goods and Services, Profitably" (paper presented at Harvard Business School conference, Global Poverty: Business Solutions & Approaches, Boston, December 1–3, 2005).

20. Frances X. Frei and Ricardo Reisen de Pinho, "Magazine Luiza: Building a Retail Model of 'Courting the Poor,'" Case 606048 (Boston: Harvard Business School, 2005).

21. Arthur Segel and Nadeem Meghji, "Patrimonio Hoy: A Groundbreaking Corporate Program to Alleviate Mexico's Housing Crisis" (paper presented at Harvard Business School conference, Global Poverty: Business Solutions & Approaches, Boston, December 1–3, 2005).

22. John Goodman et al., "Marketing Programs to Reach India's Underserved" (paper presented at Harvard Business School conference, Global Poverty: Business Solutions & Approaches, Boston, December 1–3, 2005).

23. Arnold and Quelch, "New Strategies in Emerging Markets." Mortished, "Unilever Cleans Up by Learning How to Sell to the Poorest of the World."

24. Gary Silverman, "How Can I Help You?" *Financial Times*, February 4–5, 2006, 16–21.

25. Jaime Augusto Zobel De Ayala II et al., "Developing Viable Business Models to Serve Low-Income Consumers: Lessons from the Philippines" (paper presented at Harvard Business School conference, Global Poverty: Business Solutions & Approaches, Boston, December 1–3, 2005).

26. Karen Richardson, "Tracking the Numbers: Street Sleuth: Bankers Hope for a Reprise of 'Bowie Bonds,'" *Wall Street Journal*, August 23, 2005, C1.

27. Arnold and Quelch, "New Strategies in Emerging Markets," 9.

28. Prahalad, *The Fortune at the Bottom of the Pyramid.*

29. World Resources Institute, "Tomorrow's Markets: Global Trends and Their Implications for Business," World Resources Institute, United Nations Environment Programme, and World Business Council for Sustainable Development, Washington, DC, 2002, 41.

30. Ibid. Six of the ten fastest-growing cities are in developing countries.

31. Arnold and Quelch, "New Strategies in Emerging Markets."

32. "Watch out, Coke and Pepsi—Here Comes Wahaha," *Knowledge@Wharton*, July 13, 2005, <http://www.knowledge.wharton.upenn.edu/article/1235.cfm>.

33. Kwame Anthony Appiah, "The Case for Contamination: No to Purity, No to Tribalism, No to Cultural Protectionism: Toward a New Cosmopolitanism," *New York Times*, January 1, 2006, 34.

34. Benjamin R. Barber, *Jihad vs. McWorld*, Ballantine 2001 ed. (New York: Random House, 1995), xxi.

35. Naomi Klein, *No Logo: Taking Aim at the Brand Bullies* (New York: Picador, 2000), 5.

36. Tyler Cowen, *Creative Destruction: How Globalization Is Changing the World's Cultures* (Princeton, NJ: Princeton University Press, 2002), 6.

37. Robert Berner and David Kiley, "Global Brands: Businessweek/Interbrand Rank the Companies That Best Built Their Images—and Made Them Stick," *BusinessWeek*, August 1, 2005, 86–94.

38. "Protests Continue in Muslim Cartoon Row," *Financial Times*, February 11, 2006, 12. "'Better a Boycott Than a Fatwa': Issue of the Week: Cartoon Protests Hit Companies," *Financial Times*, February 6, 2006, 18. Farhan Bokhari, "Pakistan Cartoon Protests Mount," *Financial Times*, February 15, 2006, 7.

39. Cowen, *Creative Destruction: How Globalization Is Changing the World's Cultures.* Kwame Anthony Appiah, *Cosmopolitanism: Ethics in a World of Strangers*, series ed. Henry Louis Gates (New York: W.W. Norton, 2006).

40. Appiah, "The Case for Contamination," 34.

41. Guliz Ger and Russell W. Belk, "I'd Like to Buy the World a Coke: Consumptionscapes of the 'Less Affluent World,'" *Journal of Consumer Policy* 19, no. 3 (September 1996): 271–304.

42. Ibid.

43. Giana M. Eckhardt and Humaira Mahi, "The Role of Consumer Agency in the Globalization Process in Emerging Markets," *Journal of Macromarketing* 24, no. 21 (December 2004): 136–146.

44. John A. Quelch and Edward J. Hoff, "Customizing Global Marketing," *Harvard Business Review* (May 1986): 60–64.

45. Sharon LaFraniere, "Africa, and Its Artists, Belatedly Get Their MTV," *New York Times*, February 24, 2005, E1.

46. Jack Welch, "Discussion at Leaders and Values Forum," videotape, Harvard Business School, Boston, April 12, 2005, <http://www.video.hbs.edu/videotools/portal/showcase>.

47. Prahalad and Hammond, "Serving the World's Poor, Profitably," 51.

48. Hammond and Prahalad, "Selling to the Poor."

49. Ian McDonald, Liam Pleven, and Eric Bellman, "Agents of Change: Insurers Seek Growth in Developing Markets," *Wall Street Journal*, February 12, 2007, A1.

50. Prahalad and Hammond, "Serving the World's Poor, Profitably."

51. Herman B. Leonard, "When Is Doing Business with the Poor Good—for the Poor?" (paper presented at Harvard Business School conference, Global Poverty: Business Solutions & Approaches, Boston, December 1–3, 2005).

52. Op. cit., *Vietnam Investment Review*, 20 September 2004; Mai, "Wholesale Giant Boosts Local Operation."

53. Leonard, "When Is Doing Business with the Poor Good—for the Poor?"

54. "Microcredit Is Becoming Popular, Which Means New Players and New Problems," *Knowledge@Wharton*, April 6, 2005, <http://www.knowledge.wharton.upenn.edu/article/1177.cfm>.

55. For example, loan sharks in Mexico City charge interest as high as 10 percent a day: Mitchell Pacelle and John Lyons, "Branching Out: Citigroup Courts a New Clientele, Mexican Workers: Once Focused on the Ultra Rich, It Now Eyes the 'Unbanked,'" *Wall Street Journal*, July 27, 2004, A1. Also, "Muhammad Yunus, Banker to the World's Poorest Citizens, Makes His Case," *Knowledge@Wharton*, March 9, 2005, <http://www.knowledge.wharton.upenn.edu/article/1147.cfm>.

56. "Microcredit Is Becoming Popular, Which Means New Players and New Problems." Betsy Cummings, "Small Business: Tiny Loans Stimulate the Appetite for More," *New York Times*, January 27, 2005, 20.

57. "Muhammad Yunus, Banker to the World's Poorest Citizens, Makes His Case."

58. Donald G. McNeil Jr., "India Alters Law on Drug Patents," *New York Times*, March 24, 2005, A1.

59. Donald G. McNeil Jr., "Bristol-Myers Allows Powerful AIDS Drug to Be Sold Cheaply," *New York Times*, February 15, 2006, 8.

60. David Rose, Daniel Schneider, and Peter Tufano, "H&R Block's Refund Anticipation Loan: A Paradox of Profitability?" (paper presented at Harvard Business School conference, Global Poverty: Business Solutions & Approaches, Boston, December 1–3, 2005).

61. Sarah Ellison and Eric Bellman, "Clean Water, No Profit," *Wall Street Journal*, February 23, 2005, B1.

62. Pacelle and Lyons, "Branching Out: Citigroup Courts a New Clientele."

63. Tobacco Free Initiative, *The Tobacco Industry Documents: What They Are, What They Tell Us, and How to Search Them* (Geneva, Switzerland: World Health Organization, undated), <http://www.who.int/tobacco/communications/TI_manual_content.pdf>, 14.

64. Katharine M. Esson and Stephen R. Leeder, "The Millennium Development Goals and Tobacco Control: An Opportunity for Global Partnership," World Health Organization, Geneva, Switzerland, 2004, x.

65. Ibid., xiii.

66. Tobacco Free Initiative, "Tobacco Industry and Corporate Responsibility: An Inherent Contradiction," World Health Organization, Geneva, Switzerland, 2004, <http://www.who.int/tobacco/communications/CSR_report.pdf>.

67. Marcela Valente, "South America: Private Water Companies Leave, Now What?" *Inter Press Service*, July 24, 2006. Juan Forero, "Latin America Fails to Deliver on Basic Needs," *New York Times*, February 22, 2005, A1.

68. Sheila M. Bonini, Lenny T. Mendonca, and Jeremy M. Oppenheim, "When Social Issues Become Strategic," *McKinsey Quarterly*, no. 2 (2006): 20–32, 23.

69. Ibid.

70. Peter F. Drucker, "Marketing and Economic Development," *Journal of Marketing* 22, no. 3 (January 1958): 252–259, 255-256.

71. A study by Leonard Waverman, Meloria Meschi, and Melvyn Fuss, reported in "Economics Focus: Calling across the Divide: New Research Examines the Link between Mobile Phones and Growth in the Developing World," *Economist*, March 12, 2005, 74.

72. Marc Lacey, "Illinois Democrat Wins Kenyan Hearts, in a Landslide," *New York Times*, October 25, 2004, A4.

73. "Investing in Africa Can Be a Challenge—but Good Deals Are on the Horizon," *Knowledge@Wharton*, March 9, 2005, <http://www.knowledge.wharton.upenn.edu/article/1146.cfm>.

74. Transparency International, *Global Corruption Report 2006* (London: Pluto Press, 2006), <www.transparency.org/publications/gcr>.

75. Jeffrey D. Sachs, *The End of Poverty: Economic Possibilities for Our Time* (New York: Penguin Press, 2005).

76. Jeffrey Sachs, "The Development Challenge," *Foreign Affairs* 84, no. 2 (March/April 2005): 78.

77. Ibid. Sachs writes that such lack of follow-through and apparent lack of interest will widen the divide between the United States and impoverished countries—and also between the United States and the rest of the international community.

78. Sarah Murray, "An Opportunity Rather Than a Problem," *Financial Times*, July 6, 2005, 16.
79. Ibid.
80. Andrew England, "Drought Ends for Africa's 'Unbankable,'" *Financial Times*, March 2, 2005, 10.
81. Sarah Murray, "Partnerships That Profit the Poor," *Financial Times*, March 31, 2005, 10.

CHAPTER 7

1. See Fritz Plasser, "Parties' Diminishing Relevance for Campaign Professionals," *Harvard International Journal of Press/Politics* 6, no. 4 (October 2001): 44–59. David M. Farrell, "Review: Global Political Campaigning: A Worldwide Analysis of Campaign Professionals and Their Practices," *Political Science Quarterly* 118, no. 2 (Summer 2003): 344–346. Holli A. Semetko, "Review: Global Political Campaigning: A Worldwide Analysis of Campaign Professionals and Their Practices," *Perspectives on Politics* 1, no. 3 (September 2003): 628–629.

2. Winfried Schulz, Reimar Zeh, and Oliver Quiring, "Voters in a Changing Media Environment: A Data-Based Retrospective on Consequences of Media Change in Germany," *European Journal of Communication* 20, no. 1 (March 2005): 55–88.

3. Mark Twain, "Municipal Corruption: January 4 Speech" [1901], in *Mark Twain's Speeches*, edited by Albert Bigelow Paine (New York: Harper and Brothers, 1923), cited in Robert Andrew, Mary Biggs, and Michael Seidel, eds., *The Columbia World of Quotations* (New York: Columbia University Press, 1996).

4. Michael Barbaro, "A New Weapon for Wal-Mart: A War Room," *New York Times*, November 1, 2005, 1.

5. Sean Wilentz, "Bush's Ancestors: What Contemporary Conservatism's Ties to the American Past Tell Us About Its Future," *New York Times*, October 16, 2005, 6.18.

6. Federal Election Commission, "2004 Presidential Campaign Financial Activity Summarized," press release, Washington, DC, February 3, 2005, <http://www.fec.gov/press/press2005/20050203 pressum/20050203pressum.html>.

7. "US Pres Campaign Ad Spending Hit $600m, 3 Times 2000 Sum," *Dow Jones International News*, October 31, 2004.

8. David M. Halbfinger and Jim Rutenberg, "Frantic Presidential Race Ends with a Flood of Ads: Still Even, Candidates Crisscross Nation from Rallies to Churches to TV," *New York Times*, November 1, 2004, 1.

9. Ibid.

10. Bradley Johnson, "The Cost of Democracy," *Advertising Age*, November 20, 2006, 3.

11. Plasser, "Parties' Diminishing Relevance for Campaign Professionals." James Stanyer, "Political Communication in Transition: Conceptualizing Change and Understanding Its Consequences," *European Journal of Communication* 18, no. 3 (September 2003): 385–394.

12. Daniel J. Boorstin, *The Image or, What Happened to the American Dream* (New York: Atheneum, 1962).

13. Ibid., 42–43.

14. David J. Jackson and Thomas I. A. Darrow, "The Influence of Celebrity Endorsements on Young Adults' Political Opinions," *Harvard International Journal of Press/Politics* 10, no. 3 (July 2005): 80–98.

15. Steven Edwards, "The Boss Doing Kerry No Favours: Poll Shows Rock Star Bruce Springsteen Turning Voters Away," *National Post*, October 30, 2004, A14.

16. Matthew Hindman, "The Real Lessons of Howard Dean: Reflections on the First Digital Campaign," *Perspectives on Politics* 3, no. 1 (March 2005): 121–128.

17. Data from University of Wisconsin Advertising Project, based on data from Nielsen Monitor-Plus; cited in Halbfinger and Rutenberg, "Frantic Presidential Race Ends with a Flood of Ads."

18. More important factors were party affiliation, liberal versus conservative ideology, and attitudes toward the economy, the Iraq war, and terrorism. Further, the moral values issue did not appear to increase turnout among religious voters over the previous election: D. Sunshine Hillygus

and Todd G. Shields, "Moral Issues and Voter Decision Making in the 2004 Presidential Election," *Political Science and Politics* 38, no. 2 (April 2005): 201–209.

19. See Thomas E. Patterson, *The Vanishing Voter: Civic Involvement in an Age of Uncertainty* (New York: Alfred A. Knopf, 2002).

20. Ibid.

21. Ibid.

22. Ibid.

23. Andre Blais, "How Many Voters Change Their Minds in the Month Preceding an Election?" *Political Science and Politics* 37, no. 4 (October 2004): 801–803.

24. Paul Freedman, Michael Franz, and Kenneth Goldstein, "Campaign Advertising and Democratic Citizenship," *American Journal of Political Science* 48, no. 4 (October 2004): 723–741, 723.

25. Ibid.

26. Andrew W. Barrett and Lowell W. Barrington, "Is a Picture Worth a Thousand Words? Newspaper Photographs and Voter Evaluations of Political Candidates," *Harvard International Journal of Press/Politics* 10, no. 4 (October 2005): 98–113, 98.

27. Barry C. Burden, "When Bad Press Is Good News: The Surprising Benefits of Negative Campaign Coverage," *Harvard International Journal of Press/Politics* 7, no. 3 (July 2002): 76–89, 76.

28. Stephen Earl Bennett, Staci L. Rhine, and Richard S. Flickinger, "The Things They Cared About: Change and Continuity in Americans' Attention to Different News Stories, 1989–2002," *Harvard International Journal of Press/Politics* 9, no. 1 (January 2004): 75–99.

29. Robin Lustig, "Ad War 2004," *The Connection*, WBUR Boston and NPR, August 11, 2004, <http://www.theconnection.org/shows/2004/08/20040811_a_main.asp>.

30. Louis Menand, "The Unpolitical Animal," *New Yorker*, August 30, 2004, 92–96.

31. Angus Campbell et al., *The American Voter* (New York: Wiley, 1960).

32. Stephen Earl Bennett, "Review: The Unchanging American Voter," *Public Opinion Quarterly* 55, no. 3 (Autumn 1991): 463–470.

33. Joe Klein, "Barnyard Platitudes," *New Yorker*, January 24, 2000, 30.

34. Joe Klein, "Fireworks?" *New Yorker*, September 25, 2000, 36.

35. Newt Gingrich, "Quote from International Herald Tribune," [1988] in *The Columbia World of Quotations*, edited by Robert Andrew, Mary Biggs, and Michael Seidel (New York: Columbia University Press, 1996).

36. See "Red Vs. Blue: The Few Decide for the Many," *BusinessWeek*, June 14, 2004, 62.

37. Thomas E. Patterson, "Young Voters and the 2004 Election," Shorenstein Center, Kennedy School of Government, Harvard University, Cambridge, MA, 2005.

38. John F. Bibby and L. Sandy Maisel, *Two Parties—or More? The American Party System*, 2nd ed. (Boulder, CO: Westview Press, 2003).

39. See John F. Bibby, *Politics, Parties, and Elections in America*, 5th ed. (Belmont, CA: Wadsworth, 2002).

40. See Bibby and Maisel, *Two Parties—or More? The American Party System*.

41. See Bibby, *Politics, Parties, and Elections in America*.

42. David L. Weakliem, "A New Populism? The Case of Patrick Buchanan," *Electoral Studies* 20, no. 3 (September 2001): 447–461.

43. Patterson, *The Vanishing Voter: Civic Involvement in an Age of Uncertainty*.

44. Ibid.

45. Ibid.

46. Patterson, "Young Voters and the 2004 Election."

47. See Jacob S. Hacker and Paul Pierson, "The Center No Longer Holds: Why Bad Times for the Republicans Do Not Mean Good Times for the Democrats," *New York Times*, November 20, 2005, 32–36.

48. Fairvote, "Monopoly Politics," Center for Voting and Democracy, Takoma, MD, 2004, <http://www.fairvote.org/?page=198>.

49. Rick Lyman, "In Exurbs, Life Framed by Hours Spent in the Car," *New York Times*, December 18, 2005, 41.

50. James Madison, "Majority Governments," [1833] in *The Mind of the Founder: Sources of the Political Thought of James Madison*, edited by Marvin Meyers (Indianapolis: Bobbs-Merrill, 1973), 525.

51. Since World War II, the United States and the countries of Latin America have been strongly presidential. Elsewhere, democracies likely employ a parliamentary or semipresidential form of government. Matt Golder, "Democratic Electoral Systems around the World, 1946–2000," *Electoral Studies* 24, no. 1 (March 2005): 103–121.

52. Often, there is a pool of national at-large seats distributed so as to correct any imbalances carrying over from the district level.

53. Great Britain uses proportional representation to elect its representatives to the European parliament.

54. Douglas J. Amy, "What Is Proportional Representation and Why Do We Need This Reform?" April 8, 2005, <http://www.mtholyoke.edu/acadpolit/damy/BeginningReading/whatispr .htm>.

55. Sarah Birch, "Single-Member District Electoral Systems and Democratic Transition," *Electoral Studies* 24, no. 2 (June 2005): 281–301, 295.

56. Jack Straw, "Those Who Demand PR Must Face the Truth," *Independent*, June 24, 2005, 35.

57. Amy, "What Is Proportional Representation and Why Do We Need This Reform?"

58. See Robert Elgie, "Variations on a Theme: A Fresh Look at Semipresidentialism," *Journal of Democracy* 16, no. 3 (July 2005): 98–112. Matthew S. Shugart, "Semi-Presidential Systems: Dual Executive and Mixed Authority Patterns," *French Politics* 3 (2005): 323–351.

59. Scott Mainwaring and Matthew S. Shugart, "Juan Linz, Presidentialism, and Democracy: A Critical Appraisal," *Comparative Politics* 29, no. 4 (July 1997): 449–471, 456.

60. In countries with newly strong socialist worker parties and established elite parties that had previously shared a roughly equal balance of power, the establishment calculated that it could either adopt proportional representation rules or risk losing political power entirely. Carles Boix, "Setting the Rules of the Game: The Choice of Electoral Systems in Advanced Democracies," *American Political Science Review* 93, no. 3 (September 1999): 609–624.

61. Mainwaring and Shugart, "Juan Linz, Presidentialism, and Democracy."

62. Ibid.

63. Bertrand Benoit and Ralph Atkins, "German Grand Coalition Opts for Dose of Fiscal Probity," *Financial Times*, November 14, 2005, 2.

64. Walter Bagehot, *The English Constitution* [1867], edited by Paul Smith (West Nyack, NY: Cambridge University Press, 2001), 12.

65. Richard Benedetto, "History Shows Bush Has a Challenge Ahead of Him: Re-Election Not Issue, but Low Job Approval Can Hold Back Agenda," *USA Today*, November 25, 2005, A2.

66. Kanchan Chandra, "Ethnic Parties and Democratic Stability," *Perspectives on Politics* 3, no. 2 (June 2005): 235–252.

67. Ibid.

68. Adam Przeworski et al., "What Makes Democracies Endure?" *Journal of Democracy* 7, no. 1 (January 1996): 39–55.

69. Ibid.

70. Ibid., 46.

71. Samuel Brittan, "Democracy Alone Is Simply Not Enough," *Financial Times*, May 13, 2005, 19.

72. Bagehot, *The English Constitution*, 17.

73. Mainwaring and Shugart, "Juan Linz, Presidentialism, and Democracy."

74. Przeworski et al., "What Makes Democracies Endure?"

75. Benjamin Franklin, "Speech in the Constitutional Convention, Philadelphia, Pennsylvania, September 17, 1787," in *Notes of Debates in the Federal Convention of 1787, Reported by James Madison*, edited by E. H. Scott (Chicago: Scott Foresman and Co., 1893), 741.

76. "Red vs. Blue: The Few Decide for the Many."

77. Steven Hill, *10 Steps to Repair American Democracy* (Sausalito, CA: PoliPointPress, 2006). Spencer Overton, *Stealing Democracy: The New Politics of Voter Suppression* (New York: W.W. Norton & Company, 2006).

78. Jason P. Schachter, Rachel S. Franklin, and Mark J. Perry, "Migration and Geographic Mobility in Metropolitan and Nonmetropolitan America: 1995 to 2000," Census 2000 Special Reports, U.S. Census Bureau, Washington, DC, August 2003.

79. Rob Richie and Steven Hill, "What Baker-Carter Got Right," republished from TomPaine .com, Fairvote, the Center for Voting and Democracy, Takoma, MD, September 27, 2005, <http:// www.fairvote.org/?page=200&articlemode=showspecific&showarticle=803>.

80. Patterson, "Young Voters and the 2004 Election,"7.

81. Stephen J. Dubner and Steven D. Levitt, "Why Vote? There's No Good Economic Rationale for Going to the Polls: So What Is It That Drives the Democratic Instinct?" *New York Times*, November 6, 2005, 6.30–6.32.

82. John M. Broder, "This Time, Schwarzenegger May Not Get a Hollywood Ending," *New York Times*, November 7, 2005, A14.

83. Tim Bittiger, "Innovative Technology and Its Impact on Electoral Processes," in *Voter Turnout in Western Europe since 1945: A Regional Report*, edited by Rafael Lopez Pintor and Maria Gratschew (Stockholm: International Institute for Democracy and Electoral Assistance, 2004), 37–40.

84. Michael J. Hanmer and Michael W. Traugott, "The Impact of Voting by Mail on Voter Behavior," *American Politics Research* 32, no. 4 (July 2004): 375–405.

85. Pippa Norris, "Will New Technology Boost Turnout? Experiments in E-Voting and All-Postal Voting in British Local Elections," in *Voter Turnout in Western Europe since 1945: A Regional Report*, 37–40.

86. Bittiger, "Innovative Technology and Its Impact on Electoral Processes."

87. Norris, "Will New Technology Boost Turnout?"

88. National Atlas of the United States, "Congressional Apportionment," United States Department of the Interior, Washington, DC, December 13, 2005, <http://www.nationalatlas.gov /articles/boundaries/a_conApport.html>.

89. See, for example, Jeffrey F. Rayport and Bernard J. Jaworski, *Best Face Forward: Why Companies Must Improve Their Service Interfaces with Customers* (Boston: Harvard Business School Press, 2005).

90. The forum is at <www.e-democracy.org/mpls/>.

91. Larry M. Bartels, "Homer Gets a Tax Cut: Inequality and Public Policy in the American Mind," *Perspectives on Politics* 3, no. 1 (March 2005): 15–31.

92. Ibid., 15.

93. Hacker et al. say that the "growing sophistication of political message-control," the "deliberate crafting of policy to distort public perceptions," and increasing incentives for politicians to cater to an ideological base, along with politicians' ability to escape retribution for abandoning the middle, all contributed to passage of the tax cuts: Jacob S. Hacker and Paul Pierson, "Abandoning the Middle: The Bush Tax Cuts and the Limits of Democratic Control," *Perspectives on Politics* 3, no. 1 (March 2005): 33–53.

94. Fairvote, "Dubious Democracy 2005," Center for Voting and Democracy, Takoma Park, MD, 2005, <www.fairvote.org/?page=111>.

95. Pew Research Center for the People and the Press, "Public Sours on Government and Business: Delay, Rove Viewed Unfavorably," Pew Research Center, Washington, DC, October 25, 2005.

96. Quoted in Jim Rutenberg, "Bloomberg Voter Profiles Stressed Common Concerns, Not Race or Ethnic Labels," *New York Times*, November 15, 2005, A25.

97. Ibid.

98. Alan D. Monroe, "Review: Where Have All the Voters Gone?" *Perspectives on Politics* 1, no. 3 (September 2003): 614.

99. Patterson, "Young Voters and the 2004 Election."

CHAPTER 8

1. Thomas Carlyle, *The Hero as Man of Letters: Johnson, Rousseau, Burns [Lecture V, May 19, 1840], Sterling Edition of Carlyle's Complete Works, in 20 volumes*, (1840), Project Gutenberg, September 4, 2003, <http://www.victorianweb.org/authors/carlyle/heroes/hero5.html>.

2. Michel de Certeau, *The Practice of Everyday Life* (Berkeley: University of California Press, 1984), cited in Robert Andrew, Mary Biggs, and Michael Seidel, eds., *The Columbia World of Quotations* (New York: Columbia University Press, 1996).

3. James Peters and William H. Donald, "Publishing," Industry Surveys, Standard & Poor's, March 9, 2006, <http://www.netadvantage.standardandpoor.com>.

4. Tuna N. Amobi, "Broadcasting, Cable & Satellite," Industry Surveys, Standard & Poor's, June 15, 2006.

5. The limited options were due to a combination of technology, marketing decisions (equipping TV sets to receive only VHF stations), and government regulation. Not until the mid-1970s were there enough local stations to support three national networks.

6. Quoted in Michael Curtin, "Minow, Newton," in *The Encyclopedia of Television*, edited by Horace Newcomb (Chicago: The Museum of Broadcast Communications, 1997).

7. Television Bureau of Advertising, "Media Trends Track," TVB Online, New York, 2006, <http://www.tvb.org>.

8. From 427 companies advertising 2,348 brands on network TV in 1970, advertising grew to 1,198 companies advertising 5,360 brands in 2005. Ibid.

9. Peters and Donald, "Publishing."

10. Magazine Publishers of America, quoted in ibid.

11. Steve Lacy et al., "The State of the News Media 2006: An Annual Report on American Journalism," Project for Excellence in Journalism, Washington, DC, 2006, <www.stateofthenewsmedia.org>. Mark Cooper, "Analysis Shows Media Markets Are Already Highly Concentrated: Consumer Groups Question Wisdom of Further Consolidation," news release, Consumers Union /Consumer Federation of America, Washington, DC, May 12, 2003.

12. See Lacy et al., "The State of the News Media 2006." Peters and Donald, "Publishing." Katharine Q. Seelye, "What-Ifs of a Media Empire," *New York Times*, August 27, 2006, 3.1.

13. Although there are almost 1,500 daily newspapers in the United States, "the top 10 newspaper companies own more than 270 newspapers, whose combined daily circulation accounts for roughly 40% of the industry total," and "the 20 largest US newspapers accounted for 24% of average weekday circulation in 2004." Peters and Donald, "Publishing."

14. Thomas Jefferson, "Letter to Colonel Thomas Yancey, 6 January," [1816] Electronic Text Center, University of Virginia Library, University of Virginia, Charlottesville, VA, <http://www.etext.virginia.edu/toc/modeng/public/JefLett.html>.

15. ABC, "Consumer Magazines: Circulation Averages for the Six Months Ended 6/30/2006," Audit Bureau of Circulations, Schaumburg, IL, 2006.

16. Lacy et al., "The State of the News Media 2006," Magazine chapter.

17. "Leaders: Who Killed the Newspaper?—Who Killed the Newspaper; The Future of Newspapers," *Economist*, August 26, 2006, 10.

18. Lacy et al., "The State of the News Media 2006," Network TV chapter.

19. Ibid., Cable TV chapter.

20. Pew Research Center for the People and the Press, "Media: More Voices, Less Credibility," in *Trends 2005* (Washington, DC: Pew Research Center, 2005), 41.

21. "More Media, Less News," *Economist*, August 26, 2006, 58.

22. The publishers bet that placing op-ed columnists in the subscribers-only portion of the online version of the paper would lure people to ante up for a subscription.

23. Pew Research Center for the People and the Press, "Media: More Voices, Less Credibility," 48.

24. Lacy et al., "The State of the News Media 2006."

25. Tucker Carlson, Paul Begala, and Wolf Blitzer, "Jon Stewart's America," *Crossfire*, CNN, October 15, 2004.

26. Metro International,<http:www.metro.lu/overview/indexmain.php>.

27. Philip Kierstead, "News: Networks," in *The Encyclopedia of Television*, edited by Horace Newcomb (Chicago: The Museum of Broadcast Communications, 1997).

28. Seelye, "What-Ifs of a Media Empire."

29. Jennifer Veale, "Seoul Searching," *Foreign Policy* (January/February 2007).

30. Annenberg Public Policy Center, "Public and Press Differ About Partisan Bias, Accuracy and Press Freedom," press release and Topline report, University of Pennsylvania, Philadelphia, May 24, 2005.

31. Ibid.

32. David S. Allen, *Democracy, Inc.: The Press and the Law in the Corporate Rationalization of the Public Sphere*, series edited by Robert W. McChesney and John C. Nerone (Chicago: University of Illinois Press, 2005), 151.

33. *Abrams v. United States*, 250 U.S. 616 (1919). Cited in Allen, *Democracy, Inc.: The Press and the Law*.

34. See Allen, *Democracy, Inc.: The Press and the Law*, 55–62.

35. Ibid., 55.

36. Lord Falconer, "Media and Democracy," personal communication, 2004.

37. Ted Turner, "Break Up This Band! How Government Protects Big Media—and Shuts Out Upstarts Like Me," *Washington Monthly* 36, no. 7/8 (July/August 2004): 30–36.

38. Ibid., 34.

39. Pew Research Center for the People and the Press, "Media: More Voices, Less Credibility."

40. Alexis de Tocqueville, *Democracy in America* [1835], translated by Harvey C. Mansfield and Delba Winthrop (Chicago: University of Chicago Press, 2000), 178.

41. Ibid., 179.

42. Jonathan S. Morris, "The Fox News Factor," *Harvard International Journal of Press/Politics* 10, no. 3 (July 2005): 56–79.

43. See Claes H. de Vreese, "The Spiral of Cynicism Reconsidered," *European Journal of Communication* 20, no. 3 (September 2005): 283–301.

44. Generally the polls' lack of consensus results from a combination of differences in sample size, criteria for picking people to be interviewed, weights applied to the data to account for factors such as likelihood of voting, and the wording of questions.

45. For example, after the first Gore–Bush debate, three polling organizations showed the race nudging from a dead heat to about 2 points in favor of Bush; however, Gallup reported that "an 11-point Gore lead became a 7-point Bush lead within 48 hours—a swing of 18 percentage points." Meanwhile, all four "instant polls" based on probability samples of voters interviewed immediately after the debate indicated that Gore had "won" the debate. Three instant polls based on people volunteering their views on open Web sites estimated that Bush had done better. Although the entire race was extremely close—the margin in the final popular vote was within one-half of 1 percent—and pollsters knew it was going to be close, "journalists often reported statistically insignificant leads or changes in the lead." In the end, the majority of polls predicted, wrongly, that Bush would win the popular vote. Michael W. Traugott, "Assessing Poll Performance in the 2000 Campaign," *Public Opinion Quarterly* 65, no. 3 (Fall 2001): 389–419.

46. Bill Kovach, "The Impact of Public Opinion Polls," *Nieman Reports* 44, no. 3 (Autumn 1990). Reprinted in Double Issue, vol. 53, no. 4 (Winter 1999) and vol. 54, no. 1 (Spring 2000).

47. S. Robert Lichter, "A Plague on Both Parties: Substance and Fairness in TV Election News," *Harvard International Journal of Press/Politics* 6, no. 3 (July 2001): 8–30, 8.

48. For a review, see de Vreese, "The Spiral of Cynicism Reconsidered."

49. Frank Esser, Carsten Reinemann, and David Fan, "Spin Doctors in the United States, Great Britain, and Germany: Metacommunication About Media Manipulation," *Harvard International Journal of Press/Politics* 6, no. 1 (February 2001): 16–45, 16.

50. Mark Crispin Miller, "Interview," *Frontline: The Persuaders*, PBS, May 26, 2004, <http://www.pbs.org/wgbh/pages/frontline/shows/persuaders/interviews>.

51. Tocqueville, *Democracy in America*, 494.

52. Ibid.

53. Thomas J. Johnson and Barbara K. Kaye, "A Boost or Bust for Democracy? How the Web Influenced Political Attitudes and Behaviors in the 1996 and 2000 Presidential Elections," *Harvard International Journal of Press/Politics* 8, no. 3 (July 2003): 9–34.

54. Dietram A. Scheufele and Matthew C. Nisbet, "Being a Citizen Online: New Opportunities and Dead Ends," *Harvard International Journal of Press/Politics* 7, no. 3 (July 2002): 55–75.

55. See Adam Cohen, "YouDebate: If Only the Candidates Were as Interesting as the Questioners," *New York Times*, July 25, 2007, A20; Amy Schatz, "Snowman Video in YouTube Debate Chills Some Politicos—Brothers Who Created Are All the Rage, but GOP Doesn't Entirely Get It," *Wall Street Journal*, July 31, 2007, A1; Benjamin Toff, "Debate Ratings Lag," *New York Times*, July 27, 2007, E3.

56. Joseph Kahn and Saul Hansell, "Yahoo Role Documented in Chinese Trial," *New York Times*, September 8, 2005, C11.

57. Winfried Schulz, Reimar Zeh, and Oliver Quiring, "Voters in a Changing Media Environment: A Data-Based Retrospective on Consequences of Media Change in Germany," *European Journal of Communication* 20, no. 1 (March 2005): 55–88.

58. Michael Copps, "Media Mergers Are Damaging American Democracy," *Financial Times*, June 21, 2006, 15. Jennifer Rooney, "There at the Start, and Divining the Web's Future: Vint Cerf," *Advertising Age* 77, no. 14 (April 3, 2006): 19, Special Section. Patti Waldmeir, Stephanie Kirchgaessner, and Richard Waters, "Google Campaign Tests Power of Cash Versus Votes in Washington," *Financial Times*, July 18, 2006, 10.

59. Jean Baudrillard, *Cool Memories* [1987], translated by Chris Turner (London and New York: Verso, 1990), chapter 4.

60. Yankelovich Partners Inc., "Consumer Resistance to Marketing Reaches an All-Time High: Marketing Productivity Plummets," press release, Miami, April 15, 2004.

61. Stuart Elliott, "This Web TV Is for You, Especially If You're a Male Aged 21 to 34," *New York Times*, September 6, 2006, C4.

62. BMW North America, "The Hire—the Acclaimed Film Series by BMW—Will End a Four and a Half Year Internet Run October 21st," press release, BMW North America, Woodcliff Lake, NJ, October 11, 2005, <http://www.bmwusa.com/bmwexperience/filmspr.htm>.

63. Elliott, "This Web TV Is for You, Especially If You're a Male Aged 21 to 34."

64. Pew Research Center for the People and the Press, "Media: More Voices, Less Credibility."

CHAPTER 9

1. Peter F. Drucker, *The Practice of Management* (New York: Harper & Row, 1954), 39. Frederick E. Webster Jr., "The Role of Marketing and the Firm," in *Handbook of Marketing*, edited by Barton Weitz and Robin Wensley (London: Sage Publications, 2002), 66–82.

2. Philip Kotler and Sidney J. Levy, "Broadening the Concept of Marketing," *Journal of Marketing* 33, no. 1 (January 1969): 10–15, 15.

3. P. W. Singer, "Outsourcing War," *Foreign Affairs* 84, no. 2 (March/April 2005): 119.

4. Rifkin compares European and U.S. approaches: Jeremy Rifkin, *The European Dream: How Europe's Vision of the Future Is Quietly Eclipsing the American Dream* (New York: Jeremy P. Tarcher/Penguin, 2004).

5. Peter F. Drucker, *Management: Tasks, Responsibilities, Practices*, abridged and revised ed. (Oxford: Butterworth Heinemann, 1999), 146.

6. The classic formulation of this issue is Theodore Levitt, "Marketing Myopia," *Harvard Business Review* 61, no. 3 (July–August 1960): 45–56.

7. From Drucker, *Management: Tasks, Responsibilities, Practices*, 72–83.

8. Errol Louis, "New Yorkers Hunger for Food Stamps," *New York Daily News*, January 17, 2006, 33.

9. Ibid.

10. James Blitz, "Citizen's Charter Cheered Despite Failures," *Financial Times*, September 20,

1996, 10. David Davis, "Accountancy: Made-to-Measure Outcomes," *Financial Times*, July 30, 1998, 12. Alvin Powell, "Governments Are 'for the People,' Too," *Harvard University Gazette*, April 21, 2005, 5.

11. Laura Landro, "The Informed Patient: How Did You Find Our Jell-O? Government Prods Hospitals to Survey Patients on Quality: Gauging the Bathroom Factor," *Wall Street Journal*, April 20, 2005, D1.

12. Claes Fornell, "Q1 2004: Transportation/Communications/Utilities and Services: Industry and Company Results," Commentary, American Customer Satisfaction Index, Ann Arbor, MI, June 3, 2004.

13. Alan R. Andreasen, *Social Marketing in the 21st Century* (Thousand Oaks, CA: Sage Publications, 2006).

14. Seven D. Galson, "Statement of Acting Director, Center for Drug Evaluation and Research, before the Committee on Government Reform, United States House of Representatives," U.S. Food and Drug Administration, Washington, DC, May 5, 2005. Nat Ives, "Survey Says Consumers Are Looking Past Commercials to Study the News About Prescription Drugs," *New York Times*, March 25, 2005, C6.

15. John A. Quelch, "The Resource Allocation Process in Nutrition Policy Planning," *American Journal of Clinical Nutrition* 32, no. 5 (May 1979): 1058–1065.

16. Alan R. Andreasen, "Marketing Social Marketing in the Social Change Marketplace," *Journal of Public Policy and Marketing* 21, no. 1 (Spring 2002): 3–13, 7.

17. Alan R. Andreasen, "Review: Marketing and Consumer Research in the Public Interest," *Journal of Public Policy and Marketing* 16, no. 1 (Spring 1997): 191–193.

18. Lawrence K. Altman, "Study Challenges Abstinence as Crucial to AIDS Strategy," *New York Times*, February 24, 2005, A19.

19. Debra J. Dahab, James W. Gentry, and Su Wanru, "New Ways to Reach Non-Recyclers: An Extension of the Model of Reasoned Action to Recycling Behaviors," in *Advances in Consumer Research* (Vancouver, WA: Washington State University, 1995), vol. 22, 251–256.

20. See Andrew Adonis, "Success of Spending Reforms 'an Illusion,'" *Financial Times*, November 20, 1995, 7.

21. Sewell Chan, "M.T.A. To Offer Fare Discount over Holidays," *New York Times*, October 19, 2005, A1. Sewell Chan, "Fare Cuts for Holidays Are Called into Question," *New York Times*, October 20, 2005, B1. Sewell Chan, "M.T.A. Board Approves Holiday Fares, but Only after Disagreement and Debate," *New York Times*, October 28, 2005, B5.

22. Michael E. Porter and Elizabeth Olmsted Teisberg, "Redefining Competition in Health Care," *Harvard Business Review* 82, no. 6 (June 2004): 65–76.

23. Frank Ostroff, "Change Management in Government," *Harvard Business Review* (May 2006): 141–147.

24. Henry D. Thoreau, "Civil Disobedience," [1849], *The Thoreau Reader: Annotated Works of Henry D. Thoreau, 1817–1862*, <http://www.thoreau.eserver.org>.

25. Bureau of Labor Statistics, "Industry at a Glance: Government," U.S. Department of Labor, Washington, DC, 2006, <http://www.bls.gov/iag/government.htm>.

26. Some 1.1 million as of September 2005.

27. "The You-Choose Tax," *Wall Street Journal Europe*, February 8, 2005, A8.

28. Richard P. Bagozzi and Utpal Dholakia, "Goal Setting and Goal Striving in Consumer Behavior," *Journal of Marketing* 63, Special Issue (1999): 33–44.

29. Augusto Lopez-Claros, "Executive Summary," in *Global Competitiveness Report 2004–2005* (Geneva, Switzerland: World Economic Forum, 2004), ix–xxiii.

30. Pew Research Center for the People and the Press, "Public Sours on Government and Business: Delay, Rove Viewed Unfavorably," Survey Report, Pew Research Center, Washington, DC, October 25, 2005.

31. Garry Emmons, "A Capital Asset," *HBS Alumni Bulletin*, June 2006, 32–34.

32. Jacob S. Hacker and Paul Pierson, "Abandoning the Middle: The Bush Tax Cuts and the Limits of Democratic Control," *Perspectives on Politics* 3, no. 1 (March 2005): 33–53.

33. Pew Research Center for the People and the Press, "Public Sours on Government and Business."

34. American Customer Satisfaction Index, "ACSI Overall Federal Government Scores with Historic Scores of Agencies Measured 1999–2004," Ann Arbor, MI, December 2004, <http://www.theacsi.org/government/govt-all-04.html>.

35. American Society for Quality and American Customer Satisfaction Index, "Index Says Citizens Have Low Expectations of Government, but Find a Lot to Like," press release, Milwaukee, WI, December 15, 2004.

36. Will Dunham, "US Army Achieves Minimal December Recruiting Goal," *Reuters News*, January 10, 2006.

37. Mitch Lipka, "Guard Turns to Pizza, iTunes for Recruiting," *Philadelphia Inquirer*, December 26, 2005.

38. Alan Cowell, "Britain's Secret Service Indeed! Spy on It on Its Web Site," *New York Times*, October 14, 2005, 4.

39. John Files, "Bush's Drug Videos Broke Law, Accountability Office Decides," *New York Times*, January 7, 2005, A16. Anne Marie Squeo, "FCC Issues Rebuke in Political Flap over Video Spots," *Wall Street Journal*, April 14, 2005, B8.

40. "Fourth Estate or Fifth Column? Journalists, Politicians and Ethics," *Economist*, February 5, 2005, 44.

41. Ibid.

42. Kofi Annan, "The United Nations and Civil Society," 2006, <http://www.un.org/issues /civilsociety/>.

43. John A. Quelch and Nathalie Laidler-Kylander, *The New Global Brands: Managing Non-Government Organizations in the 21st Century* (Belmont, CA: Thomson South-Western, 2006), 9–11.

44. World Bank, "The World Bank and Civil Society," Washington, DC, 2006, <www.world bank.org>.

45. Quelch and Laidler-Kylander, *The New Global Brands: Managing Non-Government Organizations in the 21st Century*, Case 10, Habitat for Humanity International: Brand Valuation.

46. Manda Salls, "The Tricky Business of Nonprofit Brands: Q&A with John Quelch," *Harvard Business School Working Knowledge*, March 14, 2005.

47. James E. Austin, *The Collaboration Challenge: How Nonprofits and Businesses Succeed through Strategic Alliances* (San Francisco: Jossey-Bass, 2000).

48. For instance, Jeb Brugmann and C. K. Prahalad, "MNC.Org Meets NGO Inc.: The Democratization of Commerce," working draft, The Next Practice, San Diego, CA, 2005.

CHAPTER 10

1. John Ruskin, *St. Mark's Rest: The History of Venice Written for the Few Travellers Who Care for Her Monuments* (New York: Alden, 1885), preface, p. 1.

2. Ratings are conducted by Freedom House, Transparency International, World Economic Forum with IMD, World Economic Forum, European Union, and *Newsweek*, respectively.

3. Diana Farrell, "The Case for Globalization: The Results of McKinsey's Latest Study of the Pros and Cons of Emerging Market Foreign Investment," *International Economy* 18, no. 1 (January 1, 2004): 52.

4. Ibid.

5. Clive Cookson, "Smaller Nations Shine in Key Areas," *Financial Times*, September 27, 2001, 23.

6. Simon Anholt, "Editorial: Nation Brand as Context and Reputation," *Place Branding* 1, no. 3 (July 2005): 224–228, 224.

7. Heather Skinner, "Wish You Were Here? Some Problems Associated with Integrating Marketing Communications When Promoting Place Brands," *Place Branding* 1, no. 3 (July 2005): 299–315.

8. Ray Marcelo, "Not Just an Eastern Promise: The Indian Government Is Working Out How to Meet Expectations Created by the Incredible India Advertising Campaign," *Financial Times*, November 4, 2004, 13.

9. Wally Olins, "Trading Identities: Why Countries and Companies Are Taking on Each Others' Roles," The Foreign Policy Centre, London, 1999. Fiona Gilmore, "A Country: Can It Be Repositioned? Spain: The Success Story of Country Branding," *Journal of Brand Management* 9, no. 4/5 (April 2002): 281–293.

10. Bagehot, "Cognitive Dissonance," *Economist*, April 4, 1998, 66. Carol Midgley, "Getting to Grips with Branding Britain: The Ad Agency That Helped to Bring Labour to Power Is Now Intent on Making Britain a Winner," *Times*, November 19, 1999, 46.

11. British Council, "Through Other Eyes: How the World Sees the United Kingdom," London, October 1999.

12. A. A. Gill, "It's Official: Cool Britannia Has Finally Been Canned," *Sunday Times*, March 25, 2001. "Selling Britain: The Shock of the Old: At Last, Britain Seems to Have Given Up Trying to Be Hip," *Economist*, July 13, 2002, 49.

13. "From Father to Son," *Economist Global Agenda*, August 12, 2004.

14. Hugo Lavados, "Interview: Creating the Right 'Image' for Chile," *Santiago Times/ El Mercurio*, March 8, 2004.

15. HM Treasury, *Comprehensive Spending Review*, 1998, <http://www.hm-treasury.gov.uk/spending_review/spend_csr98/spend_csr98_index.cfm>.

16. Embassy of Chile in the United States, "Chile-U.S. Free Trade Agreement Backgrounder," Washington, DC, 2004, <http://www.chileusafta.com>.

17. Alfred Von Liechtenstein, Mansoor Ijaz, and James Abrahamson, "Turkey's Route to Empowerment," *Financial Times*, October 6, 2004, 17.

18. Gregory Crouch, "A Candid Dutch Film May Be Too Scary for Immigrants," *New York Times*, March 16, 2006.

19. Landor Associates, "Measuring a Brand's Impact on the Bottom Line Now Possible," press release, Archive 2002, San Francisco, February 26, 2002.

20. John Quelch, "How Soft Power Is Winning Hearts, Minds and Influence," *Financial Times*, October 10, 2005, 17.

21. Pew Research Center for the People and the Press, "America's Image Erodes Further, Europeans Want Weaker Ties," Washington, DC, March 18, 2003. Ibid., "A Year after Iraq War: Mistrust of America in Europe Ever Higher, Muslim Anger Persists," Washington, DC, March 16, 2004.

22. Abraham Lincoln, *Collected Works of Abraham Lincoln* [1856], vol. 2 (Piscataway, NJ: Rutgers University Press, 1953), cited in Robert Andrew, Mary Biggs, and Michael Seidel, eds., *The Columbia World of Quotations* (New York: Columbia University Press, 1996).

23. Thomas Jefferson, "Letter to Roger C. Weightman, 24 June," [1826] Electronic Text Center, University of Virginia Library, University of Virginia, Charlottesville, <http://www.etext.virginia.edu/toc/modeng/public/JefLett.html>.

24. By Golder's count, only since 1992 has the number of democracies exceeded the number of dictatorships; "a regime is classified as a dictatorship if either (i) the chief executive is not elected; (ii) the legislature is not elected; (iii) there is no more than one party; or (iv) there has been no alternation in power." Matt Golder, "Democratic Electoral Systems around the World, 1946–2000," *Electoral Studies* 24, no. 1 (March 2005): 103–121.

25. Vitali Silitski, "The Quintessential Dissident," *Journal of Democracy* 16, no. 3 (July 2005): 170–174.

26. Fareed Zakaria, "How to Wage the Peace," *Newsweek*, April 21, 2003. Michelle Goldberg, "Review: 'World on Fire' by Amy Chua," *Salon.com*, January 13, 2003. Geoff Mulgan, "Power to the People—of a Kind," *Financial Times*, April 30 / May 1, 2005, W4.

27. Will Lester, "Poll: Americans Have Doubts About Whether More Democracy Makes the World Safer," Associated Press, September 29, 2005.

28. John Quelch, "Against the Grain: Why Uncle Sam's Touch of the Uncle Ben's Left the Arab Street Cold," *Independent.co.uk*, July 27, 2003.

29. Michael Dobbs, "Envoy to 'Arab Street' Stays Hopeful," *Washington Post*, June 10, 2003, A19.

30. Ibid.

31. George S. Hishmeh, "'Queen of Madison Avenue' Leaves Hole in State Department," *Daily Star, Beirut* (March 21, 2003).

32. Dobbs, "Envoy to 'Arab Street' Stays Hopeful." Richard Tomkins, "Why Nobody Believes Uncle Sam's Nice," *Financial Times*, March 6, 2003, 19.

33. Hishmeh, "'Queen of Madison Avenue' Leaves Hole in State Department."

34. Pew Research Center for the People and the Press, "America's Image Erodes Further, Europeans Want Weaker Ties."

35. Pew Research Center for the People and the Press, "A Year after Iraq War."

36. Christopher Marquis, "Efforts to Promote U.S. Fall Short, Critics Say," *New York Times*, December 29, 2003.

37. See Francis Fukuyama, "Cracks in the Consensus: Debating the Democracy Agenda in U.S. Foreign Policy," *Foreign Affairs* 77, no. 2 (March/April 1998): 140–141.

38. Juan Forero, "Opposition to U.S. Makes Chavez a Hero to Many," *New York Times*, June 1, 2005, A1.

39. Karen Hughes, "The Mission of Public Diplomacy: Testimony at Confirmation Hearing before the Senate Foreign Relations Committee," U.S. Department of State, Washington, DC, July 22, 2005, <http://www.state.gov/r/us/2005/49967.htm>.

40. Karen Hughes, "Keynote Address: Remarks to the 2005 Forum on the Future of Public Diplomacy," U.S. Department of State, Washington, DC, October 14, 2005, <http://www.state.gov/r/us/2005/55165.htm>.

41. George Packer, "Knowing the Enemy: Can Social Scientists Redefine the 'War on Terror'?" *New Yorker*, December 18, 2006, 60–69, 67.

42. Gallup International, "Voice of the People 2005: Trends in Democracy: Global Summary," Gallup International Association, Zurich, Switzerland, September 19, 2005.

43. Ibid.

44. Compare with Freedom House, "Freedom in the World 2003," 2003, <www.freedomhouse.org/research/freeworld/2003>.

45. Gallup International, "Voice of the People 2005: Trends in Democracy: Global Summary."

46. Marc Lacey, "By Fits and Starts, Africa's Brand of Democracy Emerges," *New York Times*, November 23, 2005, A4.

47. Gallup International, "'Voice of the People' Worldwide Survey Shows Optimism About Security and Prosperity Despite Lack of Faith in Leaders," press release, World Economic Forum, Geneva, Switzerland, January 17, 2006.

48. United Nations Development Programme, "Arab Human Development Report 2004," E.04.III.B.5, United Nations, New York, 2004, 12.

49. Ibid.

50. Jeff Gerth and Scott Shane, "U.S. Is Said to Pay to Plant Articles in Iraq Papers," *New York Times*, December 1, 2005.

51. Thom Shanker and Eric Schmitt, "Hearts and Minds: Pentagon Weighs Use of Deception in a Broad Arena," *New York Times*, December 13, 2004.

52. Quotation appears in Sanford J. Ungar, "Pitch Imperfect: The Trouble at the Voice of America," *Foreign Affairs* 84, no. 3 (May/June 2005): 7–13.

53. Ibid.

54. Neil King Jr., "Democracy Drive by America Meets Reality in Egypt: U.S. Funds Mideast Activists, but in Cairo, Strong Ties to Regime Limit the Effort: For Grant Recipients, a Stigma," *Wall Street Journal*, April 11, 2005, A1.

55. Thomas Oliphant, "Promoting Democracy," *Boston Globe*, June 14, 2005, A19.

56. Ibid.

57. King, "Democracy Drive by America Meets Reality in Egypt."

58. Thomas Carothers, "The Backlash against Democracy Promotion," *Foreign Affairs* 85, no. 2 (March/April 2006): 55–68.

59. Hughes, "Keynote Address: Remarks to the 2005 Forum on the Future of Public Diplomacy."

60. Dobbs, "Envoy to 'Arab Street' Stays Hopeful."

61. Some foreign policy figures consider this to be the European approach: Guillaume Parmentier, "A Transatlantic Taskforce to Fight for Freedom," *Financial Times*, March 10, 2005, 19. Javier Solana, "Europe's Leading Role in the Spread of Democracy," *Financial Times*, March 14, 2005, 19.

62. Suzanne Vranica, "The Advertising Report: Nonprofit-Group Founder Aims to Combat Anti-Americanism," *Wall Street Journal*, June 9, 2004, B6E. Also, "Face Value: Selling the Flag: Can Keith Reinhard Persuade the World to Love American Business?" *Economist*, February 28, 2004, 64.

63. Amartya Sen, "Democracy and Social Justice," in *Democracy, Market Economics and Development: An Asian Perspective*, edited by Farrukh Iqbal and Jong-Il You (Washington, DC: The World Bank, 2001), 7–24.

64. Population Reference Bureau, "Human Population: Fundamentals of Growth: Population Growth and Distribution," 2004, <www.prb.org>.

65. The exact number fluctuates along with disputes over nationhood, territorial status, secessions, and annexations.

66. World Health Organization, "WHO Issues New Healthy Life Expectancy Rankings: Japan Number One in New 'Healthy Life System,'" press release, Washington, DC, June 4, 2000, <www.who.int/inf-pr-2000/en/pr2000-life.html>.

67. World Bank, "GDP Per Capita, PPP (Current International $), 2004," World Development Indicators, World Bank, Washington, DC, 2006, <http://www.worldbank.org>.

68. Freedom ratings are from Freedom House, "Freedom in the World 2003."

69. World Bank, "Population 2003," World Development Indicators, World Bank, Washington, DC, September 2004, <http://web.worldbank.org>. World Bank, "List of Economies, July 2004," World Development Indicators, World Bank, Washington, DC, 2004, <http://www.worldbank.org>.

70. An influential postwar school of thought suggested that income inequalities can eventually lead to greater future prosperity by increasing savings and investment; subsequently, "persuasive microeconomic evidence suggests that inequalities in wealth, power, and status have efficiency costs": Francisco H. G. Ferreira and Michael Walton, "Inequality of Opportunity and Economic Development," Policy Research working paper, WPS 3816, World Bank, Washington, DC, January 2006.

71. Ibid.

72. Larry Diamond, "Moving Up out of Poverty: What Does Democracy Have to Do with It?" Center on Democracy, Development, and the Rule of Law, CDDRL working paper no. 4, Stanford University, Palo Alto, CA, August 11, 2004.

73. Samuel P. Huntington, *Political Order in Changing Societies* (New Haven, CT: Yale University Press, 1968), 1.

74. Lipset was an important influence on this line of reasoning: Seymour Martin Lipset, "Some Social Requisites of Democracy: Economic Development and Political Legitimacy," *American Political Science Review* 53, no. 1 (March 1959): 69–105.

75. See Huntington, *Political Order in Changing Societies*. Robert J. Barro, *Getting It Right: Markets and Choices in a Free Society* (Cambridge, MA: The MIT Press, 1996). The World Bank revisited earlier assumptions about the authoritarian advantage: Shahid Yusuf, "The East Asian Miracle at the Millenium," in *Rethinking the East Asia Miracle*, edited by Joseph E. Stiglitz and Shahid Yusuf (New York: Oxford University Press, 2001), 1–54.

76. Joseph E. Stiglitz, "Whither Reform? Ten Years of the Transition," in *Annual World Bank Conference on Development Economics 1999*, edited by Boris Pleskovic and Joseph E. Stiglitz (Washington, DC: World Bank Group, 1999), Report No. 21837, 27-50.

77. Morton H. Halperin, Joseph Siegle, and Michael M. Weinstein, *The Democracy Advantage: How Democracies Promote Prosperity and Peace* (New York: Routledge, 2005), chapter 2.

78. Sen, "Democracy and Social Justice."

79. Halperin, Siegle, and Weinstein, *The Democracy Advantage*, chapter 2.

80. Ibid., 12.

81. Ibid., chapter 2.

82. Freedom House, "Freedom in the World 2003."

83. Adam Przeworski et al., "What Makes Democracies Endure?" *Journal of Democracy* 7, no. 1 (January 1996): 39–55.

84. Farrukh Iqbal and Jong-Il You, eds., *Democracy, Market Economics and Development: An Asian Perspective* (Washington, DC: The World Bank, 2001), ix–x.

85. Isobel Coleman, "The Payoff from Women's Rights," *Foreign Affairs* 83, no. 3 (May/June 2004): 80.

86. Sen, "Democracy and Social Justice," 8.

87. Ibid.

88. Joseph Stiglitz, "Participation and Development: Perspectives from the Comprehensive Development Paradigm," in *Democracy, Market Economics and Development: An Asian Perspective*, 49–68.

89. Nancy Cohen, "Review: The Radical Middle Class: Populist Democracy and the Question of Capitalism in Progressive Era Portland, Oregon," *Business History Review* 78, no. 1 (Spring 2004): 131–134.

90. Diamond spells out a parallel argument for a virtuous cycle linking good governance, social capital, and commerce: Diamond, "Moving Up out of Poverty: What Does Democracy Have to Do with It?"

CONCLUSION

1. William J. Baumol and Alan S. Blinder, *Economics: Principles and Policy*, 2nd ed. (New York: Harcourt Brace Jovanovich, 1982), 786.

2. Clayton M. Christensen, Scott Cook, and Taddy Hall, "Marketing Malpractice," *Harvard Business Review* (December 2005).

3. Jeremy Grant, "Procter Doctor: How Lafley's Prescription Is Revitalizing a Tired Consumer Titan," *Financial Times*, December 22, 2005, 11. Jack Neff, "Well-Balanced Plan Allows P&G to Soar," *Advertising Age*, December 12, 2005, S2–S3. Carol Hymowitz, "CEOs Are Spending More Quality Time with Their Customers," *Wall Street Journal*, May 14, 2007, B1.

4. Gerry Khermouch, "All Snapple Needs Is Love—and a Dash of Cleverness," *Brandweek*, May 17, 1993, 44–46.

5. Cited in Brainy Quote, <http://www.brainyquote.com/quotes/authors/d/david_ogilvy.html>.

6. Benjamin R. Barber, *Consumed: How Markets Corrupt Children, Infantilize Adults, and Swallow Citizens Whole* (New York: W.W. Norton, 2007).

7. David M. Potter, *People of Plenty: Economic Abundance and the American Character* (Chicago: University of Chicago Press, 1954), 80.

8. Barber, *Consumed*, 212.

9. Lou Dobbs, *War on the Middle Class: How the Government, Big Business, and Special Interest Groups Are Waging War on the American Dream and How to Fight Back* (New York: Viking Adult, 2006).

10. Dani Rodrik, "Institutions for High-Quality Growth: What They Are and How to Acquire Them," working paper No. 7540, National Bureau of Economic Research, Cambridge, MA, February 2000.

11. Al Gore, *Assault on Reason: How the Politics of Fear, Secrecy, and Blind Faith Subvert Wise Decision Making, Degrade Our Democracy, and Put Our Country and Our World in Peril* (New York: The Penguin Press, 2007), Introduction.

Index

About the Authors

JOHN A. QUELCH is the Lincoln Filene Professor of Business Administration and Senior Associate Dean at Harvard Business School, where he teaches marketing to senior executives in the flagship Advanced Management Program. Formerly Dean of London Business School, he is a nonexecutive director of Pepsi Bottling Group and WPP Group plc, the second-largest marketing services company in the world. He also serves pro bono as Chairman of the Massachusetts Port Authority. He holds degrees from Oxford University, the University of Pennsylvania, and Harvard University.

KATHERINE E. JOCZ is a research associate at Harvard Business School. Previously, she was Senior Director of Networks and Relationships and Thought Leader at Marketspace, a Monitor Group company, and before that, Vice President of Research Operations at the Marketing Science Institute. She has served on the editorial review board of the *Journal of Marketing*, the board of directors of the Association for Consumer Research, committees for the annual Marketing and Public Policy conference, and the U.S. Census Bureau Advisory Committee.